CULTURE WARS IN AMERICA

A Documentary and Reference Guide

GLENN H. UTTER

GREENWOOD PRESS
An Imprint of ABC-CLIO, LLC

A B C ⬥ C L I O

Santa Barbara, California • Denver, Colorado • Oxford, England

Library of Congress Cataloging-in-Publication Data

Utter, Glenn H.
Culture wars in America : a documentary and reference guide / Glenn H. Utter.
   p. cm.
 Includes bibliographical references and index.
 ISBN 978–0–313–35038–2 (hard copy : alk. paper) — ISBN 978–0–313–35039–9 (ebook)
1. Social values—United States. 2. Social problems—United States. 3. Politics and culture—United States. 4. Religion and culture—
United States. 5. United States—Social conditions—21st century. 6. United States—Moral conditions. I. Title.
HN90.M6U85 2010
306.0973—dc22   2009034072

ISBN: 978–0–313–35038–2
EISBN: 978–0–313–35039–9

14 13 12 11 10   1 2 3 4 5

This book is also available on the World Wide Web as an eBook.
Visit www.abc-clio.com for details.

Greenwood Press
An Imprint of ABC-CLIO, LLC

ABC-CLIO, LLC
130 Cremona Drive, P.O. Box 1911
Santa Barbara, California 93116-1911

This book is printed on acid-free paper ∞

Manufactured in the United States of America

CONTENTS

LIST OF DOCUMENTS
AND SIDEBARS

Chapter 4: Gun Control and Gun Rights

Chapter 5: Immigration

Chapter 6: Sex Education, Homosexuality, and Gay Marriage

READER'S GUIDE TO RELATED DOCUMENTS AND SIDEBARS

Reader's Guide to Related Documents and Sidebars

PREFACE

When Patrick J. Buchanan spoke before the Republican National Convention in 1992, he represented members of the conservative faction of the Republican Party that was dissatisfied with President George H. W. Bush but nonetheless supported him for reelection, because they certainly did not want a Democrat elected president. Therefore, Buchanan, after challenging Bush for the Republican presidential nomination, mended fences and delivered a speech that presented a list of issues about which conservatives differed strongly with liberals. Buchanan used a term that had not yet entered the political lexicon: culture war. According to Buchanan, the United States had entered a domestic war, with defenders of traditional values on one side and progressives who threatened those values on the other. Ever since, the United States has been characterized by commentators as engaged in a culture war over fundamental social and religious values. This book includes various documents that express the differences between a more conservative and a more liberal perception of American society on several issues commonly considered important constituents of the culture wars.

The U.S. culture wars can be divided into a conflict *about* the culture wars and a conflict *within* the culture wars. The first involves disagreement over whether in fact there is, or recently has been, social conflict sufficiently profound to merit the label "culture war." The Introduction deals briefly with this debate before moving on to the primary subject of the book, which is the expression of strong disagreement over basic issues involving conflicting social, moral, and religious values. Whether or not these disagreements merit the label culture war, political activists, news analysts, and organization leaders have announced positions that patently collide on social and religious issues.

This book offers an objective approach to the subject, balancing conservative and liberal positions without declaring that one side or the other has won the argument. The ultimate purpose of this volume is to provide good examples of what are called the culture wars in order to enlighten the reader about this important phenomenon within the study of U.S. politics. Undoubtedly no one will approach these documents without settled positions on at least some of the topics. If so, the documents can provide an appreciation for alternative viewpoints and perhaps grounds for resolving some of the conflicts, or at least for understanding alternative positions and hence gaining a clearer perspective about the nature of the disagreement. The authors of the selected documents are skilled at argumentation and therefore present clearly the positions they support as well as reasons for rejecting the stands they reject.

Although not all issues considered a part of the culture wars have been addressed, a good representation of key issues are included. The documents include U.S. Supreme Court rulings on issues commonly understood as central to the culture wars, such as abortion and sexual relations. Other documents were written by advocates of various positions on the conservative and liberal sides of the conflict.

In addition to the documents, each chapter contains several shorter side bars that either deal with an interesting event or that provide additional information relevant to the topic. Following the 2008 election, in which a Democrat was elected to the presidency and Democrats gained larger majorities in both houses of Congress, questions arose about the continuation of the culture wars. An examination of these documents will provide the reader with a basis for making a judgment about the outlook for differing interests on the subjects that have divided at least the more politically active of Americans during the past four decades of political conflict and competition.

Many people assisted in the preparation of this volume. I would especially like to express my appreciation to the following people who made the project easier than it otherwise would have been: Jim Ball, president and chief executive officer, Evangelical Environmental Network; Robert Frey, editor of the interdisciplinary journal *Bridges*; Don B. Kates Jr., an attorney associated with the Pacific Research Institute, San Francisco; James G. Molina, legislative correspondent for U.S. Representative Michael R. Turner; Michael Parenti, political scientist, historian, and lecturer; and Rev. Gerald Haglund, chaplain of Heritage Park Health Care Center in Jamestown, New York, with whom I have had many fruitful conversations about the topics covered in this book. Of course I accept full responsibility for any errors of fact or judgment.

INTRODUCTION

The term "culture war," which has become a much-used expression in describing contemporary U.S. politics, suggests that political conflict on certain issues, usually having to do with deeply held social, moral, and religious values, has reached a stage at which significant numbers of individuals hold starkly differing positions, and thus find it extremely difficult to reach compromises and perhaps no longer are able to communicate effectively with one another. Different groups of individuals not only advocate opposing policy positions, but those different positions reflect conflicting world views.

Rogene A. Buchholz (2007, ix) identifies the culture wars as essentially conflicts over views about what role religion should play in the public realm, and certainly in many of the documents selected for this volume, religious understandings play a significant part. A crucial element in the culture war defined internationally is the insistence on the distinction between Christianity and Islam (and all other religions) versus the desire to find common ground for beliefs among varying religious cultures.

The term culture war can be analyzed into its two parts—"culture" and "war"—in order to understand what those who use the term in fact are claiming. Michael Thompson, Richard Ellis, and Aaron Wildavsky (1990) have noted a distinction between two "families of definitions" for culture. The first "views culture as composed of values, beliefs, norms, rationalizations, symbols, ideologies, i.e., mental products" (1). The second "sees culture as referring to the total way of life of a people, their interpersonal relations as well as their attitudes." Instead of placing weight on the distinction between the two definitions, Thompson, Ellis, and Wildavsky distinguish among three terms: cultural biases, which they use to refer to "shared values and beliefs"; social relations, which they define as "patterns of interpersonal relations"; and way of life, which the authors use to refer to "a viable combination of social relations and cultural bias." Roger Scruton (2007a, 159) suggests that the term culture involves "habits, customs and attitudes that are specific to leisure" and distinguishes "high" and "common" culture. Scruton includes in high culture the pursuit of aesthetic values and assigns to common culture such activities as entertainment and sport that involve relaxation and social interaction. Elsewhere (*Culture Counts* 2007b, ix), Scruton specifies high culture as including the literary, artistic, and philosophical traditions of Western civilization that are conveyed to new generations by humanities departments in the United States and Europe.

Sam Francis (2006, 2) has defined culture as involving "the whole set of norms by which a people live, by which they define and govern themselves." Where Scruton uses the term "common," others—including Martha Bayles (2008)—refer to "popular" culture, which involves what is "appealing to ordinary people," whereas "high" refers to those cultural elements that are "cherished by elites."

In sum, culture includes knowledge and understanding of, and attitudes toward, such things as religious belief, authority, the value of the artifacts of human activity, sexual identity and relations, social and political interaction, political participation, national identity, and the beginning and ending of life.

"War" typically refers to the use of military force by states against each other in the pursuit of political or economic ends. War in this sense can be extended to armed conflicts termed "civil," as in the American Civil War, or insurgent conflicts referred to as guerrilla wars. In each of the above uses, a key element is the resort to armed force. In contrast, the use of "war" in "culture war" is largely symbolic of extreme disagreement on public policy issues in which moral values or religious beliefs play a major role.

The possibility of a culture war perhaps can be glimpsed in the notion of the presence of subcultures within a society. Daniel Elazar (1966) suggested that three identifiable political subcultures could be detected in differing geographical areas in the United States: the moralistic, the individualistic, and the traditionalistic. The moralistic political subculture involves beliefs that government plays a positive role in people's lives, regulating society to help the disadvantaged, and that government officials are public servants who provide positive benefits for the population. Citizens in turn have the responsibility to become informed about political issues and to participate in the political realm in order to maintain government accountability to the society. The individualistic subculture involves the belief that government action should be limited as much as possible, that the average citizen's main concern should be for prospering in private life, and that public officials are well-paid experts who should run the government like a business within a highly circumscribed area. Finally, the traditionalistic subculture includes the tenet that the government has the duty to maintain the existing social order, including an established class system. An upper class tends to dominate the political order and those lower in the social and economic structure are discouraged from participating. Different political subcultures are claimed to dominate in differing parts of the country. For instance, those who study Texas politics contend that, as a result of the historical development of the state, the individualistic and traditionalistic subcultures tend to predominate among the state's residents. These differing understandings of politics can result in strong disagreements about the nature and scope of politics.

Morris P. Fiorina, Samuel J. Abrams, and Jeremy C. Pope (2006, 8) attack the very idea that anything approaching a culture war has recently characterized American politics, claiming that "The simple truth is that there is no culture war in the United States—no battle for the soul of America rages, at least none that

Americans are aware of." They distinguish "normal" individuals (meaning typical or representative persons) from those who are more politically active. In contrast to the normal population, the politically active are more well-informed about political issues, have more intensely held opinions, are ideological, and hold more extreme views (19). Fiorina, Abrams, and Pope attribute what they consider the mistaken view that there is a culture war to four factors: confusing closely divided views with those that are deeply divided; assuming that the extreme views of the politically active reflect the positions of the general population; allowing the mass media to define issues in terms of the politically active; and confusing policy positions with personal choices (12–25). The authors marshal extensive public opinion survey data in support of their position that on such issues as abortion, homosexuality, and religious belief, the general population is not nearly as divided as is often assumed. Contrary to the claim that social issues and religiosity have acquired greater significance, the authors conclude that economic issues remain highly salient for Americans. Issues such as the right to die, abortion, gun control, the constitutionality of the Pledge of Allegiance, and the medical use of marijuana gain prominence among the politically active even though most Americans do not regard these issues of crucial importance.

Robert Booth Fowler, in his examination of liberalism in American political thought (1999), presents a similar evaluation of the divisions within American society and politics: "I maintain that there has not been a collapse of consensus among the general public since the 1960s" (ix). Fowler claims that liberal values have remained triumphant among the vast majority of Americans. However, a liberal consensus has disintegrated among the "public intellectuals," represented by the proliferation of ideological positions, including feminism, postmodernism, and conservatism, among the elite, and the proponents of these alternative ideologies attempt to compete with the tenets of liberalism.

Theda Skocpol's discussion (2002) of historical trends in group membership in the United States provides some confirmation for this position regarding an elite-mass division in the so-called culture war. Although post-World War II associations tended to be characterized by local membership groups that held regular meetings and cultivated interaction between the leaders and the rank-and-file members as well as among local, regional, and national adherents, such groups have declined in membership. Taking a prominent place in more recent years are advocacy groups, often with a small active membership, that are led by professionals. Such groups depend on monetary support from citizens who otherwise play a small role in the group's operation (132). The leaders are undoubtedly the sorts of people that both Fiorina et al. and Fowler have in mind when they refer to a relatively small group of activists conducting the culture war.

Among the possible responses to Fiorina's argument, one comes from the left of American politics. Michael Parenti (2007, 192) claims that the general belief prevails that "the moderate centrists can do no evil" (192). However, Parenti claims instead that "those who occupy the mainstream center are capable of immoderate, brutal actions" and labels those people "the extremists of the center," or the "moderate extremists." Parenti notes that "These same moderates supported the overthrow of popular governments in Guatemala, Indonesia, Iran, and Chile, and helped install fascist military regimes in their stead." According to Parenti, those in the center of American politics who claim to represent the majority of citizens in fact may support the more extreme policy alternatives, particularly in international relations.

James Davison Hunter (1991), who initiated much of the debate over whether deep cultural differences now divide the American political landscape, continues to affirm the existence of such division. He argues more recently (2006) that beneath many of the current conflicts in American politics lie deeper struggles over "the very meaning and purpose of the core institutions of American civilization." For instance, according to Hunter, underlying the question of abortion is the "debate over the meaning of motherhood, of individual liberty, and our obligations to one another" (13), and basic to arguments about the legal rights of gays and lesbians is "the more serious debate over the fundamental nature of the family and appropriate sexuality" (14).

Hunter de-emphasizes the importance of the results of public opinion surveys that attempt to determine the attitudes of individual persons, focusing instead on the social institutions and the discourse that emanates from them. He views culture as involving "systems of symbols and other cultural artifacts, institutions that produce and promulgate those symbols, discourses that articulate and legitimate particular interests, and competing fields where culture is contested" (20). The culture war hypothesis has to do with a "realignment in American public culture" that finds expression not primarily in the measurement of public opinion, but "through special interest organizations, religious denominations, political parties, foundations, competing media outlets, professional associations," and the leadership of these organizations who provide direction.

Alan Wolfe (2006), a critic of the culture war hypothesis, agrees with Hunter that issues identified with cultural conflict have more to do with advocacy groups than with the political views of average citizens. He identifies a "central paradox of the American culture war": the country has become more conservative politically while at the same time becoming more liberal culturally (55). This paradox, Wolfe argues, has frustrated conservatives who have become more influential politically, but find that their cultural goals are impeded by a greater acceptance of more liberal viewpoints in the general population.

Recognizing the disagreement among scholars over the meaning and significance of the culture war idea, this volume will focus on those issues that often inspire expressions of disagreement among at least the politically active within organized interests and the mass media, which play a key role in structuring public opinion.

U.S. CULTURE WARS: HISTORICAL AND CONTEMPORARY (CHAPTER 1)

The first chapter introduces the notion of "culture war" as the term can be used to refer to political and social conflict throughout U.S. history. Documents illustrating two past cultural conflicts are first introduced. The first document, excerpts from

U.S. Supreme Court Chief Justice Roger B. Taney's majority opinion in the 1857 *Dred Scott v. Sandford* case, fomented strong reactions in both the North and the South, as expressed in newspaper editorials. The decision and the public response to it illustrate the deep cultural divisions between northern and southern states over the issue of slavery that led ultimately to the Civil War. The group of documents that follows includes excerpts from the national Prohibition (Volstead) Act, H. L. Mencken's public statement of opposition to Prohibition, and the portion of President Herbert Hoover's 1932 presidential nomination acceptance speech in which he expressed concern over the failure of Prohibition. The nation was deeply divided over the issue of prohibiting the sale of alcoholic beverages, thus representing a cultural conflict that only subsided with the Great Depression and repeal of the Prohibition Amendment. More recently, Patrick Buchanan's speech to the 1992 Republican National Convention expounds a conservative perspective on the idea of a culture war and the issues over which the "war" is being fought. Next, Howard P. Kainz's analysis of the divisions between liberals and conservatives presents an interpretation of the culture wars as fundamentally a matter of religious divisions. Finally, Michael Parenti presents an alternative approach to the notion of culture war, emphasizing the importance of a self-interested, economically privileged elite, in structuring a society's culture.

DIFFERING RELIGIOUS UNDERSTANDINGS (CHAPTER 2)

As Howard P. Kainz's document in the first chapter claims, many of the issues said to constitute the culture wars emanate from differing religious understandings. The contemporary conflicts within mainline Christian denominations, such as the Episcopalians, the Presbyterians, and the Methodists, over questions of doctrine, biblical authority and interpretation, and their church's relationship to the larger society and culture exhibit the major questions involved in the culture war. The first document, Douglas LeBlanc's discussion of the Episcopal Church's 75th General Convention, held in 2006, focuses on the deepening divide between liberals and conservatives in that denomination. Solange De Santis's report on Episcopal Bishop Gene Robinson's attendance (though uninvited due to the church-wide controversy over his open homosexuality) at the Anglican Communion's Lambeth Conference highlights a major controversy within mainline denominations that centers around human sexuality. Among Evangelicals, a controversy has arisen over the question of human responsibility for global warming. Two documents indicate the nature of the disagreement: one, from the Evangelical Environmental Network expressing concern for global warming, and the other issued by Cornwall Alliance for the Stewardship of Creation criticizing the claim that human activity is primarily responsible for environmental change. Two additional documents—David A. Noebel's discussion of publications that criticize recently published books written by atheists, and Ronald Aronson's advice to nonreligious Americans to organize and engage more actively in politics—conclude the chapter.

ABORTION, EMBRYONIC STEM CELL RESEARCH, AND THE RIGHT TO DIE (CHAPTER 3)

This chapter deals with crucial issues within the culture wars, setting against one another what religious conservatives term the "culture of life" and the "culture of death," but what liberals refer to as concerns for individual liberty versus the desire to place limitations on individuals' right to choose for themselves. The first document, the U.S. Supreme Court decision in *Roe v. Wade* (1973) establishing extensive abortion rights, initiated the key issue in the culture wars. The second document, excerpts from *Gonzales v. Carhart et al.* (2007), presents the most recent Supreme Court ruling on the issue of abortion, in which the Court upheld a legal restriction on so-called "partial birth" abortions, medically termed "in-tact dilation and extraction." The third document, the National Women's Law Center's response to the Supreme Court decision, demonstrates the strong views of those who defend the right of abortion. Shifting to the question of embryonic stem cell research, the fourth document is President George W. Bush's 2001 statement establishing federal government policy limiting the public funding of such research, and the fifth document is President Barack Obama's remarks at the public signing of an executive order removing limitations on federal funding, thus reversing Bush's executive order. In the sixth document, the U.S. Conference of Catholic Bishops reiterates that organization's strong opposition to embryonic stem cell research. In the seventh document, the U.S. Conference of Catholic Bishops presents the Catholic Church's position on euthanasia. Finally, the eighth document, excerpts from Oregon's Death with Dignity Act, deals with the issue of the right to die.

GUN CONTROL AND GUN RIGHTS (CHAPTER 4)

For several decades differing interpretations of the meaning of the Second Amendment to the U.S. Constitution have reflected distinct cultural understandings of the role of firearms in American society. The first document—excerpts from David Hemenway's *Private Guns, Public Health*—presents the basic arguments in favor of greater controls on the sale and use of firearms. Although Hemenway argues against the position that the Second Amendment guarantees an individual right to keep and bear arms, the second document, excerpts from U.S. Supreme Court Justice Antonin Scalia's majority opinion in *District of Columbia v. Heller* (2008), declares that the Second Amendment in fact does establish such an individual right. The third and fourth documents—responses to the *Heller* decision from the National Rifle Association and the Legal Action Project of the Brady Center to Prevent Gun Violence—present views from each side of the gun control/gun rights debate. In the fifth document, Don B. Kates, a civil liberties attorney and gun rights supporter, questions the effectiveness of gun laws to prevent criminals from gaining firearms.

IMMIGRATION (CHAPTER 5)

Although conservatives on economic issues tend to support immigration, cultural conservatives express concern about immigration, both legal and illegal, claiming that such immigration, especially from non-Western parts of the world, threaten the cultural traditions of the country. In the first document, the National Immigration Forum calls for reform of immigration laws that will allow for the streamlining of legal immigration and provide more lenient treatment for illegal aliens. In the second document, David Hartman expresses the basic arguments of the cultural conservative perspective, while in the third document, Heidi Ernst presents the viewpoint often associated with mainline Christian churches to illegal immigration, expressing the biblical directive to assist those in need. In the fourth document, Gregory McNamee raises questions about the potentially harmful effects of immigration, while the fifth document, issued by the Lynde and Harry Bradley Foundation, calls for the continued integration of immigrants into American society. Finally, Thomas Fleming presents, from a social conservative perspective, a less optimistic view of the possible consequences of continued immigration.

SEX EDUCATION, HOMOSEXUALITY, AND GAY MARRIAGE (CHAPTER 6)

With the exception of abortion, no issue has mobilized the participants in the culture wars more thoroughly than those related to sexuality. The first document, Margaret Talbot's analysis of sex education and teen pregnancy, raises questions about the effectiveness of abstinence education, the preferred policy alternative of cultural and religious conservatives. The second document, the 1996 Federal Defense of Marriage Act, gained the approval of large majorities in Congress. It asserts that no state can be required to recognize a same-gender marriage performed in another state. The third and fourth documents are excerpts from the majority opinion and a dissenting opinion in the U.S. Supreme Court *Lawrence et al. v. Texas* decision that overturned a Texas sodomy law. In the fifth document, Gerard V. Bradley and William L. Saunders Jr. argue for an amendment to the U.S. Constitution to restrict marriage in the United States to a union between one man and one woman. The conservative argument for such an amendment gained further impetus with the California state supreme court's ruling *In re Marriage Cases* which declared unconstitutional the state's prohibition on homosexual marriages. However, in November 2008 California voters approved a state constitutional amendment defining marriage as a union between one man and one woman. One of the arguments marshaled against gay marriage involves arguing reductio ad absurdum: if gay marriage is allowed, logically many other objectionable practices, such as plural marriages, would have to be permitted. In the final document, Wendy Kaminer argues that no valid reasons can in fact be marshaled against polygamy.

SCIENCE AND EDUCATION (CHAPTER 7)

When science becomes involved in public policy decisions and the question of science education is raised, what generally is considered a neutral and objective enterprise can become embroiled in the culture war. In the first document, federal district judge John E. Jones's decision in *Kitzmiller v. Dover Area School District et al.* involves the attempt to introduce into the local public school system a reference to Intelligent Design as an alternative to the Darwinian theory of evolution. Next, William Dembski and Sean McDowell, supporters of Intelligent Design, respond to 10 objections to their preferred theory. In the following document, John G. West notes disapprovingly that several conservatives have accepted evolution theory. In the fourth document, Matthew C. Nisbet reviews the documentary on evolution and Intelligent Design, *No Intelligence Allowed*, narrated by Ben Stein. The final document is an excerpt from a National Academy of Sciences Institute of Medicine publication that presents a detailed case against Intelligent Design.

THE GLOBAL CULTURE WAR (CHAPTER 8)

Ever since the terrorist attacks of September 11, 2001, political commentators have debated a larger worldwide cross-cultural conflict as a crucial aspect of the culture wars. In the first document, Robert de Mattei argues that Christianity and Islam are engaged in a centuries-long conflict in which Muslims regard Christian nations to be a major enemy. In the second document, Juan Cole presents a more moderate view of Muslim extremism, arguing for U.S. policies toward Muslim nations that focus on peaceful diplomatic overtures. In the third document, Roger Scruton presents background information about the characteristics of Islam that have tended to bring that religion into conflict with Western nations. Finally, President Barack Obama, in a speech delivered at Cairo University in Egypt, explores the common values and the possibilities for understanding and cooperation among Christians, Muslims, and Jews.

THE FUTURE OF THE CULTURE WARS (CHAPTER 9)

The authors of the documents in this chapter speculate about the continuance and possible demise of the culture wars. First, George Packer contends that the Republican Party's alliance with cultural conservatives has lost its effectiveness in electoral politics, largely because Republicans failed to govern effectively when they controlled Congress and the presidency. In the second document, Gertrude Himmelfarb, a conservative thinker, notes that although conservatives have been effective in the political realm, the larger culture has continued to become more liberal. In the third document, Richard Kim, focusing on the California supreme court decision regarding same-gender marriage, claims that the culture war has come to an end. Finally, President Barack Obama, in his inaugural address, in addition to concentrating on the economic troubles the nation faces, expresses his desire to dispense with "childish things," which involve many of the intense disagreements of the culture wars.

SOURCES

Bayles, Martha. "Popular Culture." In *Understanding America: The Anatomy of an Exceptional Nation*, edited by Peter H. Schuck and James Q. Wilson. New York: Public Affairs, 2008.

Buchholz, Rogene A. *America in Conflict: The Deepening Values Divide*. Lanham, MD: Hamilton Books, 2007.

Elazar, Daniel. *American Federalism: A View from the States*. New York: Thomas Y. Crowell, 1966.

Fiorina, Morris P., Samuel J. Abrams, and Jeremy C. Pope. *Culture War? The Myth of a Polarized America*. New York: Pearson Longman, 2006.

Fowler, Robert Booth. *Enduring Liberalism: American Political Thought since the 1960s*. Lawrence, KS: University Press of Kansas, 1999.

Francis, Sam. Peter B. Gemma, editor. *Shots Fired: Sam Francis on America's Culture War*. Vienna, VA: Fitzgerald Griffin Foundation, 2006.

Hunter, James Davison. *Culture Wars: The Struggle to Define America*. Jackson, TN: Perseus Books, 1991.

Hunter, James Davison. "The Enduring Culture War." In *Is There a Culture War? A Dialogue on Values and American Public Life*, edited by James Davison Hunter and Alan Wolfe. Washington, DC: Brookings Institution Press, 2006.

Parenti, Michael. *Contrary Notions: The Michael Parenti Reader*. San Francisco: City Lights Books, 2007.

Scruton, Roger. *Dictionary of Political Thought*. New York: Palgrave Macmillan, 2007a.

Scruton, Roger. *Culture Counts: Faith and Feeling in a World Besieged*. New York: Encounter Books, 2007b.

Skocpol, Theda. "United States: From Membership to Advocacy." In *Democracies in Flux: The Evolution of Social Capital in Contemporary Society*, edited by Robert D. Putnam. New York: Oxford University Press, 2002.

Thompson, Michael, Richard Ellis, and Aaron Wildavsky. *Cultural Theory*. Boulder, CO: Westview Press, 1990.

Wolfe, Alan. "The Culture War That Never Came." In *Is There a Culture War? A Dialogue on Values and American Public Life*, edited by James Davison Hunter and Alan Wolfe. Washington, DC: Brookings Institution Press, 2006.

1

THE U.S. CULTURE WARS: HISTORICAL AND CONTEMPORARY

Dred Scott v. Sandford (1857)

- **Document:** Excerpts from Roger B. Taney's majority opinion.
- **Date:** March 6, 1857.
- **Where:** Supreme Court building, Washington, DC
- **Significance:** In the 1850s opinion in the United States had become increasingly polarized over the issue of slavery and the extent to which that institution would be extended into the territories. Dred Scott's long legal struggle, beginning in 1847, to gain his freedom from slavery ultimately led to a controversial U.S. Supreme Court decision. The justices agreed to hear Scott's case, expecting to resolve the "culture war" issue through legal means. However, the Court's decision against Scott's claim to freedom contributed to the descent of the nation into disintegration and civil war. (Note: Litigant John Sanford's name was misspelled in the official record.)

DOCUMENT

The question is simply this: Can a negro, whose ancestors were imported into this country, and sold as slaves, become a member of the political community formed and brought into existence by the Constitution of the United States, and as such become entitled to all the rights, and privileges, and immunities, guarantied by the instrument to the citizen? One of which rights is the privilege of suing in a court of the United States in the cases specified in the Constitution. . . .

The words "people of the United States" and "citizens" are synonymous terms, and mean the same thing. They both describe the political body who . . . form the sovereignty, and who hold the power and conduct the Government through their representatives. . . . The question before us is, whether the class of persons described in the plea in abatement [African Americans] compose a portion of this people, and are constituent members of this sovereignty? We think they are not, and that they are not included, and were not intended to be included, under the word "citizens" in the Constitution, and can therefore claim none of the rights and privileges which that instrument provides for and secures to citizens of the United States. On the contrary, they were at that time considered as a subordinate and inferior class of beings, who had been subjugated by the dominant race, and, whether emancipated or not, yet remained subject to their authority, and had no rights or privileges but such as those who held the power and the Government might choose to grant them.

It is not the province of the court to decide upon the justice or injustice, the policy or impolicy, of these laws. The decision of that question belonged . . . to those who formed the sovereignty and framed the Constitution. The duty of the court is, to interpret the instrument they have framed, with the best lights we can obtain on the subject, and to administer it as we find it, according to its true intent and meaning when it was adopted.

In discussing this question, we must not confound the rights of citizenship which a State may confer within its own limits, and the rights of citizenship as a member of the Union. It does not by any means follow, because he has all the rights and privileges of a citizen of a State, that he must be a citizen of the United States. He may have all of the rights and privileges of the citizen of a State, and yet not be entitled to the rights and privileges of a citizen in any other State. For, previous to the adoption of the Constitution of the United States, every State had the undoubted right to confer on whomsoever it pleased the character of citizen, and to endow him with all its rights. But this character of course was confined to the boundaries of the State, and gave him no rights or privileges in other States beyond those secured to him by the laws of nations and the comity of States. Nor have the several States surrendered the power of conferring these rights and privileges by adopting the Constitution of the United States. Each State may still confer them upon an alien, or any one it thinks proper, or upon any class or description of person; yet he would not be a citizen in the sense in which that word is used in the Constitution of the United States, nor entitled to sue as such in one of its courts, nor to the privileges and immunities of a citizen in the other States. The rights which he would acquire would be restricted to the State which gave them. The Constitution has conferred on Congress the right to establish an uniform rule of naturalization, and this right is evidently exclusive, and has always been held by this court to be so. Consequently, no State, since the adoption of the Constitution, can by naturalizing an alien invest him with the rights and privileges secured to a citizen of a State under the Federal Government, although, so far as the State alone was concerned, he would undoubtedly be entitled to the rights of a citizen, and clothed with all the rights and immunities which the Constitution and laws of the State attached to that character.

It is very clear, therefore, that no State can, by any act or law of its own . . . introduce a new member into the political community created by the Constitution of the United States. It cannot make him a member of this community by making him a member of its own. . . .

The front page of *Frank Leslie's Illustrated*, June 27, 1857, depicts Dred Scott; his wife, Harriet; and their daughters Eliza and Lizzie. Wood engravings after photoprints by Fitzgibbon. (Library of Congress, Prints & Photographs Division, LC-USZ62-79305)

The question then arises, whether the provisions of the Constitution, in relation to the personal rights and privileges to which the citizen of a State should be entitled, embraced the negro African race ... made free in any State; and to put it in power of a single State to make him a citizen of the United States, and endue him with the full rights of citizenship in every other State without their consent? Does the Constitution of the United States act upon him whenever he shall be made free under the laws of a State, and raised there to the rank of a citizen, and immediately clothe him with all the privileges of a citizen in every other State, and in its own courts?

The court think the affirmative of these propositions cannot be maintained. And if it cannot, [Dred Scott] could not be a citizen of the State of Missouri, within the meaning of the Constitution of the United States, and, consequently, was not entitled to sue in its courts.

It is true, every person, and every class and description of persons, who were at the time of the adoption of the Constitution recognized as citizens in the several States, became also citizens of this new political body; but none other; it was formed by them, and for them and their posterity, but for no one else. And the personal rights and privileges guarantied to citizens of this new sovereignty were intended to embrace those only who were then members of the several State communities, or who should afterwards by birthright or otherwise become members, according to the provisions of the Constitution and the principles on which it was founded. ...

It becomes necessary, therefore, to determine who were citizens of the several States when the Constitution was adopted. ...

... [T]he legislation and histories of the times, and the language used in the Declaration of Independence, show, that neither the class of persons who had been imported as slaves, nor their descendants, whether they had become free or not, were then acknowledged as a part of the people, nor intended to be included in the general words used in that memorable instrument. ...

[African Americans] had for more than a century before [the writing of the Declaration of Independence and the adoption of the Constitution] been regarded as beings of an inferior order, and altogether unfit to associate with the white race, either in social or political relations; and so far inferior, that they had no rights which the white man was bound to respect; and that the negro might justly and lawfully be reduced to slavery.... He was bought and sold, and treated as an ordinary article of merchandise and traffic, whenever a profit could be made by it. This opinion was at that time fixed and universal in the civilized portion of the white race. It was regarded as an axiom in morals as well as in politics, which no one thought of disputing, or supposed to be open to dispute; and men in every grade and position in society daily and habitually acted upon it in their private pursuits, as well as in matters of public concern, without doubting for a moment the correctness of this opinion. ...

... [Colonial] laws ... show, too plainly to be misunderstood, the degraded condition of this unhappy race.... They show that a perpetual and impassable barrier was intended to be erected between the white race and the one which they had reduced to slavery, and governed as subjects with absolute and despotic power, and which they then looked upon as so far below them in the scale of created beings, that intermarriages between white persons and negroes or mulattoes were regarded as unnatural and immoral, and punished as crimes, not only in the parties, but in the person who joined them in marriage. And no distinction in this respect was made between the free negro or mulatto and the slave, but this stigma, of the deepest degradation, was fixed upon the whole race. . . .

. . . [T]he men who framed [the Declaration of Independence] were great men—high in literary acquirements—high in their sense of honor, and incapable of asserting principles incoherent with those on which they were acting. They perfectly understood the meaning of the language they used, and how it would be understood by others; and they knew that it would not in any part of the civilized world be supposed to embrace the negro race, which, by common consent, had been excluded from civilized Governments and the family of nations, and doomed to slavery. . . .

[There] are two clauses in the Constitution which point directly and specifically to the negro race as a separate class of persons, and show clearly that they were not regarded as a portion of the people or citizens of the Government then formed.

One of these clauses reserves to each of the thirteen States the right to import slaves until the year 1808. . . . And by the other provision the States pledge themselves to each other to maintain the right of property of the master, by delivering up to him any slave who may have escaped from his service, and be found within their respective territories. . . . And these two provisions show, conclusively, that neither the description of persons therein referred to, nor their descendants, were embraced in any of the other provisions of the Constitution; for certainly these two clauses were not intended to confer on them or their posterity the blessings of liberty, or any of the personal rights so carefully provided for the citizen. . . .

And upon a full and careful consideration of the subject, the court is of opinion, that, . . . Dred Scott was not a citizen of Missouri within the meaning of the Constitution of the United States, and not entitled as such to sue in its courts; and, consequently, that the Circuit Court had no jurisdiction of the case, and that the judgment on the plea in abatement is erroneous. . . .

. . . [I]t appears affirmatively on the record that he is not a citizen, and consequently his suit against Sandford was not a suit between citizens of different States, and the court had no authority to pass any judgment between the parties. The suit ought, in this view of it, to have been dismissed by the Circuit Court, and its judgment in favor of Sandford is erroneous, and must be reversed. . . .

. . . [I]f the Constitution recognizes the right of property of the master in a slave, and makes no distinction between that description of property and other property owned by a citizen, no tribunal, acting under the authority of the United States, whether it be legislative, executive, or judicial, has a right to draw such a distinction, or deny to it the benefit of the provisions and guarantees which have been provided for the protection of private property against the encroachments of the Government.

Now, as we have already said . . . the right of property in a slave is distinctly and expressly affirmed in the Constitution. The right of traffic in it, like an ordinary article of merchandise and property, was guarantied to the citizens of the United States, in every State that might desire it, for twenty years. And the Government in express terms is pledged to protect it in all future time, if the slave escapes from his owner. This is done in plain words—too plain to be misunderstood. And no word can be found in the Constitution which gives Congress a greater power over slave property, or which entitles property of that kind to less protection than property of any other description. The only power conferred is the power coupled with the duty of guarding and protecting the owner in his rights.

Upon these considerations, it is the opinion of the court that the act of Congress which prohibited a citizen from holding and owning property of this kind in the territory ... is not warranted by the Constitution, and is therefore void; and that neither Dred Scott himself, nor any of his family, were made free by being carried into this territory; even if they had been carried there by the owner, with the intention of becoming a permanent resident. . . .

Upon the whole, therefore, it is the judgment of this court, that it appears by the record before us that the plaintiff in error is not a citizen of Missouri, in the sense which that word is used in the Constitution; and that the Circuit Court of the United States, for that reason, had no jurisdiction in the case, and could give no judgment in it. Its judgment for the defendant must, consequently, be reversed, and a mandate issued, directing the suit to be dismissed for want of jurisdiction.

SOURCE: *Dred Scott v. Sandford* 19 Howard (60 U.S.) 393; 15 L.Ed. 691 (1857).

ANALYSIS

Since the writing of the U.S. Constitution and before, slavery stood out as an issue over which there were deep divisions between northern and southern states. The Constitution contained provisions that reflected the need to compromise on this sensitive question and that reflected cultural disagreement over the understanding of human nature and equality. Article I, section 2 of the Constitution contained the so-called three-fifths compromise, which mandated that representation in the House of Representatives, as well as taxes, would be apportioned among the states according to population and that total population included "the whole Number of free persons" plus "three fifths of all other Persons"—in other words, slaves. Southern states thereby gained assurance that northern states would not overwhelm them in congressional representation and thus their sectional interests would gain added protection in the federal government. In addition, the Constitution (Article I, section 9) declared that Congress could not prohibit the importation of slaves until 1808, thus guaranteeing that southern states would be assured of a large slave population. Finally, fugitive slaves were to be returned to their owners (Article IV, section 2). Although, as Benjamin Fletcher Wright (1984) argued, the original Constitution reflected a great deal of fundamental agreement over governing principles, the attempts to reach compromises on the question of slavery in order to gain support for adoption of the new Constitution in effect only placed a thin veneer over a structural fault within the nation's foundation. Nonetheless, Taney, in his *Dred Scott* decision, referred to these constitutional provisions as important elements in what he hoped would be a final settlement of the slavery matter.

The Dred Scott case did not begin a culture war between northern and southern states, but certainly affirmed its existence. A long series of events in this culture war preceded the Supreme Court decision. For instance, in 1836 Southerners in the House of Representatives were successful in passing a "gag" resolution that required the tabling of any petitions involving the issue of slavery. The House of Representatives approved such a gag rule in each congressional session until 1844. Although the U.S. Supreme Court in the 1842 decision *Prigg v. Commonwealth of Pennsylvania* declared unconstitutional a Pennsylvania law prohibiting the seizure of fugitive slaves, the Court declared that enforcement of fugitive slaves laws was solely a federal responsibility. Subsequently, various northern states took advantage of this proviso to enact personal liberty laws.

In 1848, the Treaty of Guadalupe Hidalgo ending the war with Mexico added 500,000 square miles to the United States, leading to further conflict between pro- and anti-slavery groups over whether slavery would be permitted in the new territories. In 1852 Harriet Beecher Stowe published the anti-slavery novel *Uncle Tom's Cabin*, which had been serialized in the *National Era* magazine the year before. The novel generated increasing controversy over the slavery question in both the North and the South. Passage of the 1854 Kansas-Nebraska Act establishing two new territories initiated a bitter conflict in Kansas over whether the territory would allow slavery. As tempers rose over the issue of slavery, the level of invective in Congress increased. In 1856 South Carolina Representative Preston Brooks, resenting Senator Charles Sumner's speech against slavery, entered the Senate chamber, found the senator seated at his desk, and beat him with a cane. Sumner, who was severely injured, became a martyr for northern abolitionists.

The U.S. Supreme Court added to the divisions between the North and the South in 1857. Dred Scott, a slave, sued for his freedom, claiming that his owner, John Emerson, had taken Scott with him from Missouri to the free state of Illinois and then on to Fort Snelling in what would become St. Paul, Minnesota. In January 1850 Scott, his wife, and two daughters gained their freedom from a St. Louis, Missouri, court, but in 1852 the Missouri Supreme Court reversed the verdict. Two years later the U.S. Circuit Court in Missouri ruled that Scott

DID YOU KNOW?

Evaluating President Abraham Lincoln

The consensus opinion among contemporary Americans and historians is that the U.S. Supreme Court seriously erred in its *Dred Scott v. Sandford* decision in 1857 and that Abraham Lincoln subsequently saved the union by using military force to compel southern states to return to the union. Historians and political scientists generally rank Lincoln as one of the top two presidents. However, some conservative commentators present a starkly different interpretation of Lincoln. For instance, conservative spokesman Sam Francis, addressing the Claremont Institute's Colloquium on Lincoln, Reagan, and National Greatness, held in Washington, DC, in February 1998, presented an alternative image of the Civil War president. According to Francis, Lincoln's decision to re-provision Fort Sumter was "the greatest single blunder in American history" because it led to the Confederacy firing on the fort, in response to which Lincoln called up 75,000 troops. Francis emphasized Lincoln's lack of experience and incompetence, which contributed to mistakes that led to war rather than negotiation with the South. Francis further claims that states had the right to secede from the union. Referring to Lincoln's suspension of the right of habeas corpus, Francis asserted that "Lincoln 'saved the union' like Adolf Hitler 'saved Germany.'" Francis's unorthodox interpretation of a crucial period in American history reflects an aspect of the current culture war concerned with the position of states within the federal system, how conflicts between the federal and state governments are to be resolved, and which level of government has the ultimate authority to decide major issues.

Francis, Sam. "Looking Into Lincoln's Legacy." In *Shots Fired: Sam Francis on America's Culture War*, edited by Peter B. Gemma. Vienna, VA: Fitzgerald Griffin Foundation, 2006.

had a right to sue in federal court, but ultimately decided against Scott's argument for freedom.

The U.S. Supreme Court justices agreed to hear Scott's appeal, and when the Court finally issued an opinion on March 6, 1857, a 7–2 majority ruled against Scott's claim to emancipation. Although all nine justices issued concurring or dissenting opinions of varying length, Chief Justice Taney's majority opinion became the major focus of reaction, both North and South. For half a century public officials had attempted to structure renewed compromises over the issue of slavery that would be acceptable to both sections of the country. Taney's opinion made clear to the general population, as Paul Finkelman observes, "that no black person could ever be a citizen of the United States and thus blacks could not sue in federal courts, and . . . that Congress did not have the power to prohibit slavery in the federal territories and thus the Missouri Compromise of 1820 was unconstitutional, as were all other restrictions on slavery in the territories" (1997, 4).

Many historians and legal scholars agree that the *Dred Scott* decision is among the worst, if not the worst, in Supreme Court history, first because of the claimed consequences of the decision, and second, because of the alleged weaknesses in Taney's argumentation. The Court certainly defined the political question in stark terms for both the North and the South, and thereby contributed to strident political conflict that ultimately led to the Civil War. At the time no public opinion polls could have been taken that would have provided a measure of the differing political attitudes in the North and the South in reaction to the Court's ruling. However, newspaper editorials offer some indication of the deep division between the two sections of the country.

Although Chief Justice Taney expected, or at least hoped, that the *Dred Scott* decision would end controversy over the issue of slavery, the reaction within the nation's newspapers presaged a very different result. While Southern editorials generally applauded the decision, some, such as the Charleston, South Carolina, *Mercury* of April 2, 1857, were far less optimistic about the outcome. The *Mercury* editorial claimed that the decision would "precipitate rather than retard" the "final conflict between Slavery and Abolition" (Finkelman 1997, 131). Abolitionists would be further emboldened and the ruling could be overturned by "the vote of the popular majority."

The Richmond, Virginia, *Enquirer* editorial of March 10, 1857, more optimistically praised the Supreme Court as the "proper umpire," in achieving a victory for the nation against purely sectional interests, and as a result "abolitionism has been staggered and stunned." Various controversies over the question of slavery were now resolved favorably for the South against the "enemies of the institutions of the South."

The *Mercury* editorial subsequently proved more prescient, for national politics became engulfed in the slavery issue, which predominated in the 1858 congressional elections and the 1860 presidential election. The newly established Republican Party was dedicated to preventing the extension of slavery into the territories (Finkelman 1997, 44). Undoubtedly the *Dred Scott* decision contributed to the fortunes of the nascent party, given that its presidential candidate, Abraham Lincoln, won the presidency in 1860. That election represented a major shift of fortunes away from the Democratic Party's victory in 1856, which at the time perhaps signaled an incorrect message to Taney that the nation had granted a mandate for deregulating slavery in the territories (Finkelman 1997, 44). The sectional differences, based in part on contrasting cultural understandings, could not be resolved by the pronouncements of the Supreme Court.

Many in the North supported the *Dred Scott* decision, due to partisan politics (many Democrats, in alliance with their fellow party members in the southern states, were in agreement), racism, and a concern for maintaining business relations with the South (Finkelman 1997, 136) and hoped that the decision would end the conflict over slavery. Opposition was varied, expressing concern for the nationalizing of the slave question, disillusionment with the Supreme Court, and revulsion from the immorality of slavery (Finkelman 1997, 144).

The New York *Tribune* editorial of March 7, 1857, identified three major consequences of the decision: an African American had no rights as a citizen; a slave taken to a free state still remained a slave; and Congress had no authority under the Constitution to prohibit slavery in the territories. The Chicago *Tribune*, in the derisive editorial "Who Are Negroes?" of March 12, 1857, raised probing questions about Taney's definition of a Negro. Are persons who are only part white to be granted the status of citizens? "How much white blood is necessary to make a native born American a citizen?" (Finkelman 1997, 155). "Will Chief Justice Taney settle the question?" The editorial raised serious issues regarding race relations in a nation that officially sanctioned slavery, and where African Americans were related by blood to some of the "First Families of Virginia."

The cultural clash between the North and the South had become a national issue as never before. Whether average persons in the North and their counterparts in the South essentially opposed or supported the institution of slavery, national politics for the next 15 years would be largely defined by the issue. Unfortunately, aspects of Taney's decision, and the questions raised in the Chicago *Tribune* editorial, remained salient especially in the southern states following the Civil War, with segregation policies being instituted that placed primary emphasis on a person's racial background despite ratification of the Thirteenth (prohibiting slavery), Fourteenth (guaranteeing rights of citizenship), and Fifteenth (guaranteeing the right to vote to those formerly enslaved) Amendments to the U.S. Constitution. Arguably, Taney's majority opinion outlasted the Civil War and Reconstruction by nearly 90 years. In the late nineteenth century southern state governments, in the hands of whites, instituted policies, called Jim Crow laws, to deny African Americans basic

DID YOU KNOW?

U.S. House of Representatives Apologizes for Slavery

In July 2008 the U.S. House of Representatives passed a resolution by voice vote that apologized "on behalf of the people of the United States" for the wrongs committed against the ancestors of African Americans and the suffering they endured during slavery and the long period of segregation enforced by Jim Crow laws enacted in southern states in the late nineteenth century. Representative Steve Cohen (D-TN), the sole white representative from a majority black district, proposed the resolution, which states that Africans brought to the United States were "brutalized, humiliated, dehumanized and subjected to the indignity of being stripped of their names and heritage" and that African Americans continue to experience the consequences of discrimination and segregation. The resolution is an indication that the effects of the pre-Civil War cultural conflict over slavery continued far beyond the conclusion of the military struggle between the North and the South.

political and social rights. The U.S. Supreme Court, in *Plessy v. Ferguson* (1896), accepted the "separate but equal" doctrine, thus legitimizing segregation, a precedent that the Court did not overturn until the 1954 decision in *Brown v. Board of Education*. Hence, Taney's argument regarding the place of the African American in U.S. society gained dominance in American social, economic, and political life, the consequences of which still have not been undone.

Orlando Patterson (2008) presents abundant data indicating that contemporary African Americans still suffer from the vestiges of discrimination. For instance, although blacks have made inroads into various aspects of American affluence, and there is now a "substantial black middle class," in 2003, 34 percent of blacks earned an income of $50,000 or more, but 59 percent of whites achieved that income (390). Regarding net worth, Patterson notes that in 2000 "the median net worth of non-Hispanic whites was $79,400, which was 10.5 times that of black householders, estimated at $7,500" (392). The unemployment rate among young black men in 2006 was 37 percent. Patterson states that in 2005 "approximately 25 percent of the 2.2 million persons incarcerated in U.S. prisons and jails were black men between twenty and thirty-nine years of age" (398). Patterson also notes that blacks marry at significantly lower rates than do other ethnic groups. In 2004, 54 percent of white women over 15 were married and living with their husband and 21.5 percent had never married, but the comparable figures for black women were 28.4 percent and 42 percent (401). While 82 percent of white families are headed by a married couple, 44.7 percent of black families are headed by a single female (402). Such data indicate a continuing divide between blacks and whites in American society more than 50 years after the *Brown v. Board of Education* decision. Affirmative action—an ambiguous policy of at least guaranteeing fairness in the allocation of positions in education or employment, or taking positive steps to give preference to minorities in that allocation (Citrin 2008)—has created a conflict over the fundamental understanding of the value of equality and how that concept is to be defined in contrast to the commitment to individual liberty (164). Hence the consequences of a cultural conflict that began at the nation's birth continue to the present.

National Prohibition (Volstead) Act

- *Document:* Excerpts from Title II of the Volstead Act: Prohibition of Intoxicating Beverages.
- *Date:* October 28, 1919.
- *Where:* Washington, DC
- *Significance:* The National Prohibition Act, more popularly know as the Volstead Act, contained provisions to enforce the Eighteenth Amendment to the U.S. Constitution instituting prohibition of the manufacture, sale, and transportation of intoxicating liquors. Ratification of the amendment and passage of the act (over President Woodrow Wilson's veto) demonstrates the keen influence that culturally distinct groups, when allied with public officials, can have on public policy.

DOCUMENT

SECTION 3. No person shall on or after the date when the Eighteenth Amendment to the Constitution of the United States goes into effect, manufacture, sell, barter, transport, import, export, deliver, furnish or possess any intoxicating liquor except as authorized in this Act, and all the provisions of this act shall be liberally construed to the end that—the use of intoxicating liquor as a beverage may be prevented.

Liquor . . . for nonbeverage purposes and wine for sacramental purposes may be manufactured, purchased, sold, bartered, transported, imported, exported, delivered, furnished and possessed, but only as herein provided, and the commissioner may, upon application, issue permits therefore. . . . Provided, that nothing in this Act shall prohibit the purchase and sale of warehouse receipts covering distilled spirits on deposit in Government bonded warehouses, and no special tax liability shall attach to the business of purchasing and selling such warehouse receipts. . . .

SECTION 6. No one shall manufacture, sell, purchase, transport, or prescribe any liquor without first obtaining a permit from the commissioner so to do, except that a person may, without a permit, purchase and use liquor for medicinal purposes when prescribed by a physician as herein provided, and except that any person who in the opinion of the commissioner is conducting a bona fide hospital or sanatorium engaged in the treatment of persons suffering from alcoholism, may, under such rules, regulations, and conditions as the commissioner shall prescribe, purchase and use, in accordance with the methods in use in such institution, liquor, to be administered to the patients of such institution under the direction of a duly qualified physician employed by such institution.

All permits to manufacture, prescribe, sell, or transport liquor, may be issued for one year, and shall expire on the 31st day of December next succeeding the issuance thereof. . . . Permits to purchase liquor shall specify the quantity and kind to be purchased and the purpose for which it is to be used. No permit shall be issued to any person who within one year prior to the application therefor or issuance thereof shall have violated the terms of any permit issued under this Title or any law of the United States or of any State regulating traffic in liquor. No permit shall be issued to anyone to sell liquor at retail, unless the sale is to be made through a pharmacist designated in the permit and duly licensed under the laws of his State to compound and dispense medicine prescribed by a duly licensed physician. No one shall be given a permit to prescribe liquor unless he is a physician duly licensed to practice medicine and actively engaged in the practice of such profession. . . .

Nothing in this title shall be held to apply to the manufacture, sale, transportation, importation, possession, or distribution of wine for sacramental purposes, or like religious rites, except section 6 (save as the same requires a permit to purchase) and section 10 hereof, and the provisions of this Act prescribing penalties for the violation of either of said sections. No person to whom a permit may be issued to manufacture, transport, import, or sell wines for sacramental purposes or like religious rites shall sell, barter, exchange, or furnish any such to any person not a rabbi, minister of the gospel, priest, or an officer duly authorized for the purpose by any church or congregation, nor to any such except upon an application duly subscribed by him, which application, authenticated as regulations may prescribe, shall be filed and preserved by the seller. The head of any conference or diocese or other ecclesiastical jurisdiction may designate any rabbi, minister, or priest to supervise the manufacture of wine to be used for the purposes and rites in this section mentioned, and the person so designated may, in the discretion of the commissioner, be granted a permit to supervise such manufacture.

SECTION 7. No one but a physician holding a permit to prescribe liquor shall issue any prescription for liquor. And no physician shall prescribe liquor unless after careful physical examination of the person for whose use such prescription is sought, or if such examination is found impracticable, then upon the best information obtainable, he in good faith believes that the use of such liquor as a medicine by such person is necessary and will afford relief to him from some known ailment. Not more than a pint of spiritous liquor to be taken internally shall be prescribed for use by the same person within any period of ten days and no prescription shall be filled more than once. Any pharmacist filling a prescription shall at the time indorse upon it over his own signature the word "canceled," together with the date when the liquor was delivered, and then make the same a part of the record that he is required to keep as herein provided. . . .

SECTION 18. It shall be unlawful to advertise, manufacture, sell, or possess for sale any utensil, contrivance, machine, preparation, compound, tablet, substance, formula direction, recipe advertised, designed, or intended for use in the unlawful manufacture of intoxicating liquor. . . .

SECTION 21. Any room, house, building, boat, vehicle, structure, or place where intoxicating liquor is manufactured, sold, kept, or bartered in violation of this title, and all intoxicating liquor and property kept and used in maintaining the same, is hereby declared to be a common nuisance, and any person who maintains such a common nuisance shall be guilty of misdemeanor and upon conviction thereof shall be fined not more than $1,000 or be imprisoned for not more than one year, or both. . . .

SECTION 25. It shall be unlawful to have or possess any liquor or property designed for the manufacture of liquor intended for use in violating this title or which has been so used, and no property rights shall exist in any such liquor or property. . . . No search warrant shall issue to search any private dwelling occupied as such unless it is being used for the unlawful sale of intoxicating liquor, or unless it is in part used for some business purposes such as a store, shop, saloon, restaurant, hotel, or boarding house. . . .

SECTION 29. Any person who manufactures or sells liquor in violation of this title shall for a first offense be fined not more than $1,000, or imprisoned not exceeding six months, and for a second or subsequent offense shall be fined not less than $200 nor more than $2,000 and be imprisoned not less than one month nor more than five years.

Any person violating the provisions of any permit, or who makes any false record, report, or affidavit required by this title, or violates any of the provisions of this title, for which offense a special penalty is not prescribed, shall be fined for a first offense not more than $500; for a second offense not less than $100 nor more than $1,000, or be imprisoned not more than ninety days; for any subsequent offense he shall be fined not less than $500 and be imprisoned not less than three months nor more than two years. . . .

SECTION 33. After February 1, 1920, the possession of liquors by any person not legally permitted under this title to possess liquor shall be prima facie evidence that such liquor is kept for the purpose of being sold, bartered, exchanged, given away, furnished, or otherwise disposed of in violation of the Provisions of this title . . . . But it shall not be unlawful to possess liquors in one's private dwelling while the same is occupied and used by him as his dwelling only and such liquor need not be reported, provided such liquors are for use only for the personal consumption of the owner thereof and his family residing in such dwelling and of his bona fide guests when entertained by him therein; and the burden of proof shall be upon the possessor in any action concerning the same to prove that such liquor was lawfully acquired, possessed, and used. . . .

SOURCE: National Prohibition (Volstead) Act, October 28, 1919. U.S. Statutes at Large, volume 41, pp. 3-5-323 (41 Stat. 305).

ANALYSIS

The prohibition of the manufacture, sale, or transportation of alcoholic beverages by the ratification of the Eighteenth Amendment and the subsequent passage of the Volstead Act represented the victory of reform and religious interests in the battle against the perceived evils of alcoholic beverages. Section 1 of the amendment stated: "After one year from the ratification of this article the manufacture, sale, or transportation of intoxicating liquors within, the transportation thereof into, or the exportation thereof from the United States and all territory subject to the jurisdiction thereof for beverage purposes is hereby prohibited." The amendment granted to Congress and the states the authority to pass legislation to enforce its provisions.

Various social, economic, and cultural forces combined to push for a prohibition on the sale of alcohol. In 1851 Maine became the first state to pass a temperance law, and by 1917, 27 states, as well as many counties and municipalities, had instituted such laws. Evangelical Christians were major supporters of temperance and considered it a major social reform. Many women, concerned that husbands spent a large percentage of income in taverns, also supported prohibition. The Woman's Christian Temperance Union was established in 1874 and the Anti-Saloon League followed in 1893. Both organizations lobbied Congress for legislation and a constitutional amendment to enforce temperance. The Prohibition Party, formed in 1869, ran presidential candidates during the late nineteenth century, garnering nearly 265,000 votes in 1892. One reason for the creation of the party was to counter the formation of the United States Brewers' Association.

Temperance activist Carry Nation drew attention to the temperance cause with her widely publicized denunciations of alcohol and raids on saloons, wielding a hatchet with destructive force. Her activities were labeled "hatchetation." Attitudes toward alcohol and its social uses tended to vary according to cultural differences of individuals and groups. For instance, those of German descent regarded alcoholic beverages an important part of their ethnic heritage

The campaign for prohibition began in earnest with the strengthening of the Anti-Saloon League of America that resulted from the merger of state and local organizations. Howard Hyde Russell, a Congregational minister, played a major role in establishing the group, and he recruited Wayne Bidwell Wheeler to the cause. Wheeler proved to be an extremely effective organizer, lobbyist, and money raiser. Wealthy industrialists such as Henry Ford, Andrew Carnegie, and John D. Rockefeller, concerned about the ill effects of alcohol consumption on the productivity of workers, supported the cause with generous donations (Burns 2004, 159).

U.S. entry into World War I contributed to the campaign for prohibition for two reasons: First, the need to conserve food products denied to breweries the raw materials for producing alcoholic products, and second, with most brewers of German ancestry, they came under suspicion, as did many things of German origin. In contrast to the well-managed campaign that the Anti-Saloon League conducted, the liquor industry's actions were in many circumstances counterproductive, involving bribery, physical violence, and embarrassing revelations about brewers' intentions and tactics that came to light from private communications.

The battle over prohibition divided the country along various lines, but a major split was between rural and urban residents; in 1910 each composed approximately half of the population. The ultimate victory of the "drys" over the "wets" can to a large extent be attributed to the disproportionate representation that rural areas possessed in Congress and state legislatures due to lack of legislative reapportionment to reflect population shifts. Congress proposed the Prohibition amendment in 1918, and less than a year later, on January 16, 1919, with the Nebraska legislature approving it, the necessary three-fourths of state legislatures had ratified the amendment. Ultimately 46 of the 48 states ratified, with just two—Connecticut and Rhode Island—failing to do so.

Although cultural divisions led to the adoption of the Prohibition amendment, which President Herbert Hoover called a "noble experiment" intended to eliminate undesirable influences on American society, ironically for the Prohibition movement, the approximately 14 years of prohibition (Prohibition opponent H. L. Mencken expressed the exact time period: "twelve years, ten months, and nineteen days" [Mencken 1980]) contributed to widespread lawbreaking by average Americans, gangsterism, and other changes in American life. So extensive was the dissatisfaction with "the noble experiment" that Congress proposed the Twenty-First Amendment repealing Prohibition, which popularly elected state conventions ratified in December 1933.

Daniel J. Boorstin (1973, 77) quotes Walter Lippman as commenting in 1931 that "The high level of lawlessness is maintained by the fact that Americans desire to do so many things which they also desire to prohibit." Lippman's comment fails to reflect the deep-seated cultural divisions that led some Americans to favor prohibiting things that other Americans desired to do. Prohibition, beginning with a small group of individuals, perceiving the personal and social evils of alcohol, and dedicated to their cause, was able to bring about a major change in American society, with results they could not have anticipated. The bootleggers, classic American entrepreneurs who gave many Americans what they wanted, even if legally prohibited, moved on to other illegal pursuits, including gambling and prostitution, once Prohibition came to an end. A culture war need not, at least initially, engulf a large proportion of the population. Relatively small minorities, given a quiescent population, have the capacity to bring public officials to enact policies that ultimately can influence in various ways, expected as well as unexpected, the entire society.

"The Perihelion of Prohibition"

- *Document:* Excerpts from a commentary by Henry Louis (H. L.) Mencken on Prohibition.
- *Date:* July 20, 1922.
- *Where:* The Sydney, Australia, *Bulletin.* Reprinted in H. L. Mencken, *A Mencken Chrestomathy.* New York: Alfred A. Knopf, 1962.
- *Significance:* H. L. Mencken, a noted editor and critic of the first half of the twentieth century, expressed his strong opposition to Prohibition before, during, and after its reign in American society. In this piece, originally published three years into the Prohibition era, Mencken asserts the failure of the "noble experiment." Mencken tended to attribute the introduction of Prohibition to the continuing Puritan heritage of the country.

DOCUMENT

From the Sydney (Australia) *Bulletin,* July 20, 1922. This piece, of course, is now of only antiquarian interest, but I am printing it to recall to America what went on during the glaring noonday of Prohibition, when its agents controlled all branches of the government at Washington and in most of the States, and its end seemed far away. There is yet no adequate history of those years. Americans always tend to forget things so disagreeable. They have put the memory of Prohibition out of their minds just as they have put the memory of the great influenza epidemic of 1918–1919.

Prohibition by constitutional amendment has been in force in the United States for three years, everywhere with the full power of the Federal Government behind it, and in most of the 48 States with stringent State laws to help. The results of that colossal effort to enforce it may be briefly summarized as follows:

1. The State and Federal Governments, taken together, have lost the $500,000,000 annual revenue that was formerly derived from excises and licenses, and general taxation has had to be increased to make it up.

2. There has been created, at a cost of $50,000,000 a year, a great army of Prohibition detectives, spies and *agents provocateurs*, four-fifths of whom are already corrupt.

3. There has been created another army of so-called bootleggers, dealing partly in wines and liquors smuggled from Canada and the West Indies, and partly in beers, wines and liquors manufactured illicitly at home, and its members take a joint profit that is certainly not less than $750,000,000 a year, and probably runs to $1,500,000,000.

4. Brewing and distilling and wine-making have been reestablished as home industries, and the business of supplying the necessary materials—malt syrup, bottles, corks, etc.—has taken on gigantic proportions.

5. In every American city, and in nine-tenths of the American towns, every known alcoholic beverage is still obtainable—at prices ranging from 100% to 500% above those of pre-Prohibition days—and even in the most remote districts there is absolutely no place in which any man who desires to drink alcohol cannot get it.

In brief, Prohibition is a failure, and it grows a worse failure every day. There was a time, shortly after the Eighteenth Amendment went into effect, when it showed some promise of being a success, especially in the farming regions, and on the strength of that promise very optimistic reports were sent broadcast by the extremely diligent press-agents of the Anti-Saloon League, and a number of confiding foreigners—for example, Sir Arthur Newholme, the Englishman—were made to believe that the New Jerusalem was actually at hand. But that was simply because the great majority of Americans had not been taking the thing seriously—because they had been caught unawares by the extraordinarily drastic provisions of the Volstead Enforcement Act. The instant they realized what was upon them they applied the national ingenuity and the national talent for corruption to the problem, and in six months it was solved. On the one hand they devised a great multitude of schemes for circumventing the law; on the other hand they proceeded gallantly to the business of debauching the officers sworn to enforce it. Since then there has been a continuous struggle between guns and armament, with guns gradually drawing into the lead. No man, not even the most romantic Prohibitionist, argues that there is anything remotely resembling a general enforcement of Prohibition today. And no unbiased and reflective man, so far as I know, sees the slightest sign that it will ever be enforced hereafter.

The business of evading it and making a mock of it, in fact, has ceased to wear any of the customary aspects of crime, and has become a sort of national sport. The criminal, in the public eye, is not the bootlegger and certainly not his customer, but the enforcement officer. This new-fangled agent of justice has begun to take on an almost legendary character. He is looked upon by the plain people as corruption incarnate—a villainous snooper and blackmailer whose sole public function is to increase the price of drinks. When he comes into court for attacking an illicit distiller with firearms, as happens often, juries handle him roughly. Not infrequently he is mobbed while he is at his work. The effects of this public sentiment are obviously very damaging to the *morale* of the service. In the

H. L. Mencken, photographed by Carl Van Vechten in July 1932. (Library of Congress, E13 Prints & Photographs Division, Carl Van Vechten Photograph Collection, LC-USZ62-42489)

Federal branch there is a constant changing of personnel, and the average agent now lasts no more than six months. In that time, if he is honest, he has become disgusted by the work he is called upon to do, and alarmed by the general view of it. And if, as is probably more usual, he has gone into it simply to get as much as he can while the getting is good, he has made enough to retire. I have heard of one Federal agent in New York who, on a salary of $2000 a year, paid $4000 rent for his apartment, and kept two automobiles.

Most of the strong liquors sold in the large cities of the East come either from Canada or from the Bahamas. Those from Canada are brought across the international border in large motor-lorries, and the business is so extensive and so well organized that the bribes paid to the officers employed to oppose it, both on the Canadian side and on the American side, are standardized, and so, barring accident, a bootlegger can estimate the cost of his goods to within a few dollars a case, and prepare for financing his operations accordingly. The supplies that come from the Bahamas are transported in small schooners. Some put in by night at lonely places along the immense American coast, where motor transportation awaits their cargoes. Others boldly enter the ports, and the Customs officers are either deceived with false manifests or boldly bribed.

Most of the stuff thus brought in is Scotch whiskey. In pre-Prohibition days it sold in New York at from $30 to $40 a case. Now it brings from $80 to $110, according to the supply. In the main, it is honest goods. But some of the lesser bootleggers—those who sell it, not by the case, but by the bottle—sophisticate it with home-made imitations, chiefly compounded of cologne spirits, prune-juice, pepper and creosote. Very little gin is imported, for it is too easily made at home. As for wines, the bootleggers chiefly confine their attentions to champagne, which brings $120 a case in New York. Under the Volstead Act it is perfectly lawful to import wines for "medicinal and sacramental" purposes. The bootleggers import champagne as "medicine" and then trust to the venality of the Prohibition enforcement officers to get it released for the general trade. The business of bringing in still wines is now almost entirely in the hands of Jewish rabbis in the ghettos of the coast towns. The law allows a Jew in good standing to buy 15 gallons of wine a year for ritualistic use. These gentlemen of God, in return for a profit of from $10 to $15 a case, inscribe all solvent comers on their books as orthodox Ashkenazim—and if the customer has money enough, he may go upon the books of a dozen different rabbis, and under a dozen different safely Jewish names.

As I have said, very little gin is imported, though the widespread popularity of the cocktail makes a steady and immense demand for it. It is manufactured at illicit distilleries, or by the simple process of diluting grain alcohol to 50% strength and adding a few drops of juniper oil and glycerine to the quart. It sells at from $40 to $65 a case, according to quality. All the known liqueurs are made by the same bootleggers, even absinthe. The necessary oils and herbs are imported from France, Italy and Germany, and added to a mixture of alcohol, water and syrup. Some of the liqueurs thus concocted are of surprisingly good quality. In fact, the absinthe now on tap in New York is quite as good as the Swiss absinthe formerly sold in the bars. It costs $15 a quart. Everywhere south of New York so-called corn whiskey, made of maize, is manufactured in stupendous quantities; in one southern State there are said to be no less than 10,000 stills in operation. It is an extremely bad drink, but the native palate, particularly in the country, favors it—and in the cities it is often transformed by devious arts into a very fair rye whiskey. It sells for from $10 to $30 a gallon.

I have left beers and light native wines to the last. The extent to which brewing has been revived in the home in the United States is almost incredible. In some States every second housewife has become a brewer, and some of the beers and ales thus produced are extremely agreeable. A batch of wort may be cooked in an hour, the fermentation is over in four or five days, and two weeks after bottling the brew is fit to drink. In one American city of 750,000 inhabitants there are now 100 shops devoted exclusively to the sale of beer-making supplies, and lately the proprietor of one of them, by no means the largest, told me that he sold 2000 pounds of malt-syrup a day. Two thousand pounds of malt-syrup will make 4000 gallons of prime ale. It costs 2 cents a pint-bottle to make. When the breweries were still running the cheapest beer cost about 4 cents.

Before Prohibition the American people drank very little wine. They were, in fact, just beginning to appreciate their excellent California wines when the Eighteenth Amendment was passed. Some of the California grape-growers, in despair, plowed up their vineyards and planted oranges and olives. Now they wish that they had been less hasty. Last Autumn wine was made in hundreds of thousands of American households, and the price of grapes rose to $125 a ton. I know of no American home, indeed, in which some sort of brewing, wine-making or distilling is not going on. Even in the country, where belief in Prohibition still persists, practically every housewife at least makes a jug or two of blackberry cordial. Every known fruit is expectantly fermented; in the cities raisins and currants are in enormous demand. Even the common dandelion, by some process unknown to me, is converted into a beverage that gently caresses.

Well, if the American people are thus so diligently alcoholic—in the city folk patronize the bootleggers and make beer, and the far-flung yokels experiment with wines and set up stills—why does Prohibition remain the law of the land? In the large cities the majority against it is now at least 4 to 1; in the country it loses public confidence steadily. Then, why isn't it abandoned, and the vast losses that go with it saved, and the inconceivable corruption abated? The answer is too complex to be made in the space that I have remaining. Part of it lies in the fact that the process of amending the Constitution in the United States is very deliberate and vexatious; it took fully 75 years of persistent agitation to get Prohibition adopted, and it will take years of attack to get it formally rejected. But another part of the answer lies in the curious power that fanatical minorities have in American politics—a power that enables them, by playing upon the weaknesses of the two great parties, to overcome their lack of votes.

SOURCE: From *A Mencken Chrestomathy* by H. L. Mencken, copyright 1916, 1918, 1919, 1920, 1921, 1922, 1924, 1926, 1927, 1929, 1932, 1934, 1942, 1949 by Alfred A. Knopf, a division of Random House, Inc. Used with permission of Alfred A. Knopf, a division of Random House, Inc.

ANALYSIS

As Wayne Bidwell Wheeler expertly led the forces for Prohibition, H. L. Mencken stirred the opposition to the Eighteenth Amendment with his newspaper opinion pieces, expressing his anger toward the "bluenoses" and "boobs," the alliance of middle-class businessmen, Protestant denominations, and rural interests who wished to legislate morality by making alcoholic beverages illegal—as well as restricting freedom of the press and sexual conduct—and ridiculed the very idea of prohibiting what so many people enjoyed doing—including himself. As Prohibition approached, Mencken announced that he had stored away enough alcoholic beverages to last for at least two years (Bode 1969, 172). After three years of Prohibition, Mencken readily pronounced the "noble experiment" a failure. Obviously he had become a connoisseur of illegal beverages, both of his own making and of those purchased from others. Mencken undoubtedly reflected the attitudes of many Americans who saw nothing wrong with partaking in an activity that had been made illegal, and he remained throughout the 1920s a popular spokesman for those who regarded the Eighteenth Amendment and the Volstead Act, along with various state laws, absurd public policy. Even as the end of Prohibition approached, Mencken, perhaps overestimating the influence of conservative groups (as he undoubtedly exaggerated the extent of brewing in private households) and the slowness of the amending process, did not express optimism that repeal of the Eighteenth Amendment was possible in the near future. However, the failure of Prohibition, obvious to anyone willing to observe the behavior of American citizens, led to a movement to repeal the Eighteenth Amendment. Because many state legislatures remained under the control of conservative, pro-Prohibition, forces, the repeal amendment (the twenty-first) specified that ratification would be by conventions called in the several states. As Prohibition finally ended, Mencken was one of the first to be photographed drinking a legal glass of beer.

President Herbert Hoover's Address Accepting the Republican Presidential Nomination

- *Document:* Excerpt from Herbert Hoover's speech accepting the Republican Party's presidential nomination for a second term.
- *Date:* August 11, 1932.
- *Where:* Constitution Hall, Washington, DC
- *Significance:* Although he supported Prohibition, President Herbert Hoover, in accepting the Republican presidential nomination, admitted that the Eighteenth Amendment and the Volstead Act, along with numerous state laws, had failed to stem the tide of alcohol consumption, indicating that many Americans were willing to violate the law in order to engage in an activity that others had decided they should not participate. Despite the grave economic situation the nation was facing, the president nonetheless considered it necessary to confront the issue of Prohibition in his acceptance address. Hoover hesitantly recommended that some modifications be made in the Prohibition regulations.

DOCUMENT

Across the path of the Nation's consideration of these various problems of economic and social order there has arisen a bitter controversy over the control of the liquor traffic. I have always sympathized with the high purpose of the 18th amendment, and I have used every power at my command to make it effective over this entire country. I have hoped that it was the final solution of the evils of the liquor traffic against which our people have striven for generations. It has succeeded in great measure in those many communities where the majority sentiment is favorable to it. But in other and increasing numbers of communities there is a majority sentiment unfavorable to it. Laws which are opposed by the majority sentiment create resentments which undermine enforcement and in the end produce degeneration and crime.

Our opponents pledge the members of their party to destroy every vestige of constitutional and effective Federal control of the traffic. That means that over large areas the return of the saloon system with its corruption, its moral and social abuse which debauched the home, its deliberate interference with the States endeavoring to find honest solution, its permeation of political parties, its perversion of legislatures, which reached even to the Capital of the Nation. The 18th amendment smashed that regime as by a stroke of lightning. I cannot consent to the return of that system again.

We must recognize the difficulties which have developed in making the 18th amendment effective and that grave abuses have grown up. In order to secure the enforcement of the amendment under our dual form of government, the constitutional provision called for concurrent action on one hand by the State and local authorities and on the other by the Federal Government. Its enforcement requires, therefore, independent but coincident action of both agencies. An increasing number of States and municipalities are proving themselves unwilling to engage in that enforcement. Due to these forces there is in large sections increasing illegal traffic in liquor. But worse than this there has been in those areas a spread of disrespect not only for this law but for all laws, grave dangers of practical nullification of the Constitution, an increase in subsidized crime and violence. I cannot consent to a continuation of that regime.

I refuse to accept either of these destinies, on the one hand to return to the old saloon with its political and social corruption, or on the other to endure the bootlegger and the speakeasy with their abuses and crime. Either of them are intolerable, and they are not the only ways out.

Now, our objective must be a sane solution, not blind leap back to old evils. Moreover, a step backwards would result in a chaos of new evils not yet experienced, because the local systems of prohibition and controls which were developed over generations have been in a large degree abandoned under this amendment.

The Republican platform recommends submission of the question to the States and that the people themselves may determine whether they desire a change, but insists that this submission shall propose a constructive and not a destructive change. It does not dictate to the conscience of any member of the party.

The first duty of the President of the United States is to enforce the laws as they exist. That I shall continue to do to the best of my ability. Any other course would be the abrogation of the very guarantees of liberty itself.

Now, the Constitution gives the President no power or authority with respect to changes in the Constitution itself; nevertheless, my countrymen have a right to know my conclusions upon this question. They are based upon the broad facts that I have stated, upon my experience in this high office, and upon my deep conviction that our purpose must by the elimination of the evils of this traffic from this civilization by practical measures.

President Herbert Hoover accepts the Republican Party's presidential nomination at Constitution Hall in Washington, DC, on August 11, 1932; Underwood & Underwood Photograph. (Library of Congress, E13 Prints & Photographs Division, LC-DIG-ppmsca-19178)

It is my belief that in order to remedy present evils a change is necessary by which we resummon a proper share of initiative and responsibility which the very essence of our Government demands shall rest upon the States and the local authorities. That change must avoid the return of the saloon.

It is my conviction that the nature of this change, and one upon which all reasonable people can find common ground, is that each State shall be given the right to deal with the problem as it may determine, but subject to the absolute guarantees in the Constitution of the United States to protect each State from interference and invasion by its neighbors, and that in no part of the United States shall there be a return of the saloon system with its inevitable political and social corruption and its organized interference with other States and other communities.

American statesmanship is capable of working out such a solution and making it effective.

SOURCE: Herbert Hoover Address Accepting the Republican Presidential Nomination. http://americanhistory.about.com/library/docs/blhooverspeech1932.htm.

ANALYSIS

President Herbert Hoover faced an extremely difficult situation upon his nomination in 1932 by the Republican Party to run for reelection. Besides the devastating circumstances of economic depression, Hoover had to contend with a Prohibition policy that had obviously failed. The president recognized that he stood between two undesirable stools: the previous "saloon system" to which he vowed the country would not return, and the current situation of widespread lawbreaking. Apparently Hoover wished to allow the state and local governments to decide on their own the level of enforcement of Prohibition, but at the same time to require the federal government to regulate interstate trade in alcoholic beverages and to prevent the return of the "saloon system" and its perceived evils. The 1932 election was undoubtedly decided on economic issues rather than Prohibition, but with the election of Democrat Franklin Delano Roosevelt to the presidency and with a large Democratic majority in the new Congress, an amendment simply to repeal Prohibition won the day. Congress stipulated that popularly elected conventions rather than state legislatures would consider the amendment in each state so that the still-strong Prohibition forces in state legislatures would not be able to govern the outcome. With ratification of the Twenty-First Amendment, Prohibition became an issue to be decided by state and local governments, thus defusing a major cultural conflict.

1992 Republican National Convention Speech

- **Document:** Patrick J. Buchanan's speech to the Republican National Convention.
- **Date:** August 12, 1992
- **Where:** Houston, Texas
- **Significance:** Patrick Buchanan's speech expressed many of the key issues that were, and continued to be, major focuses for the so-called culture war in American politics.

DOCUMENT

Well, we took the long way home, but we finally got here.

And I want to congratulate President [George H. W.] Bush, and remove any doubt about where we stand: The primaries are over, the heart is strong again, and the Buchanan brigades are enlisted—all the way to a great comeback victory in November.

Like many of you last month, I watched that giant masquerade ball at Madison Square Garden [site of the Democratic National Convention]—where 20,000 radicals and liberals came dressed up as moderates and centrists—in the greatest single exhibition of cross-dressing in American political history.

One by one, the prophets of doom appeared at the podium. The Reagan decade, they moaned, was a terrible time in America; and the only way to prevent even worse times, they said, is to entrust our nation's fate and future to the party that gave us [George] McGovern, [Walter] Mondale, [Jimmy] Carter, and Michael Dukakis.

No way, my friends. The American people are not going to buy back into the failed liberalism of the 1960s and '70s—no matter how slick the package in 1992.

The malcontents of Madison Square Garden notwithstanding, the 1980s were not terrible years. They were great years. You know it. I know it. And the only people who don't know it are the carping critics who sat on the sidelines of history, jeering at one of the great statesmen [President Ronald Reagan] of modern time.

Out of [President] Jimmy Carter's days of malaise, Ronald Reagan crafted the longest peacetime recovery in US history—3 million new businesses created, and 20 million jobs.

Under the Reagan Doctrine, one by one, the communist dominoes began to fall. First, Grenada was liberated, by US troops. Then, the Red Army was run out of Afghanistan, by US weapons. In Nicaragua, the Marxist regime was forced to hold free elections—by Ronald Reagan's contra army—and the communists were thrown out of power.

Have they forgotten? It was under our party that the Berlin Wall came down, and Europe was reunited. It was under our party that the Soviet Empire collapsed, and the captive nations broke free.

It is said that each president will be recalled by posterity—with but a single sentence. George Washington was the father of our country. Abraham Lincoln preserved the Union. And Ronald Reagan won the Cold War. And it is time my old colleagues, the columnists and commentators, looking down on us tonight from their anchor booths and sky boxes, gave Ronald Reagan the credit he deserves—for leading America to victory in the Cold War.

Most of all, Ronald Reagan made us proud to be Americans again. We never felt better about our country; and we never stood taller in the eyes of the world.

But we are here, not only to celebrate, but to nominate. And an American president has many, many roles.

He is our first diplomat, the architect of American foreign policy. And which of these two men is more qualified for that role? George Bush has been UN ambassador, CIA director, envoy to China. As vice president, he co-authored the policies that won the Cold War. As president, George Bush presided over the liberation of Eastern Europe and the termination of the Warsaw Pact. And Mr. Clinton? Well, [Democratic presidential candidate] Bill Clinton couldn't find 150 words to discuss foreign policy in an acceptance speech that lasted an hour. As was said of an earlier Democratic candidate, Bill Clinton's foreign policy experience is pretty much confined to having had breakfast once at the International House of Pancakes.

The presidency is also America's bully pulpit, what Mr. Truman called, "preeminently a place of moral leadership." George Bush is a defender of right-to-life, and lifelong champion of the Judeo-Christian values and beliefs upon which this nation was built.

Mr. Clinton, however, has a different agenda.

At its top is unrestricted abortion on demand. When the Irish-Catholic governor of Pennsylvania, Robert Casey, asked to say a few words on behalf of the 25 million unborn children destroyed since *Row v. Wade*, he was told there was no place for him at the podium of Bill Clinton's convention, no room at the inn.

Yet a militant leader of the homosexual rights movement could rise at that convention and exult: "Bill Clinton and Al Gore represent the most pro-lesbian and pro-gay ticket in history." And so they do.

Bill Clinton supports school choice—but only for state-run schools. Parents who send their children to Christian schools, or Catholic schools, need not apply.

Elect me, and you get two for the price of one, Mr. Clinton says of his lawyer-spouse. And what does Hillary believe? Well, Hillary believes that 12-year-olds should have a right to sue their parents, and she has compared marriage as an institution to slavery—and life on an Indian reservation.

Well, speak for yourself, Hillary.

Friends, this is radical feminism. The agenda Clinton & Clinton would impose on America—abortion on demand, a litmus test for the Supreme Court, homosexual rights, discrimination against religious schools, women in combat—that's change, all right. But it is not the kind of change America wants. It is not the kind of change America needs. And it is not the kind of change we can tolerate in a nation that we still call God's country.

A president is also commander in chief, the man we empower to send sons and brothers, fathers and friends, to war.

George [H. W.] Bush was 17 when they bombed Pearl Harbor. He left his high school class, walked down to the recruiting office, and signed up to become the youngest fighter pilot in the Pacific war. And Mr. Clinton? When Bill Clinton's turn came in Vietnam, he sat up in a dormitory in Oxford, England, and figured out how to dodge the draft.

Which of these two men has won the moral authority to call on Americans to put their lives at risk? I suggest, respectfully, it is the patriot and war hero, Navy Lieutenant J. G. George Herbert Walker Bush.

My friends, this campaign is about philosophy, and it is about character; and George Bush wins on both counts—going away; and it is time all of us came home and stood beside him.

As running mate, Mr. Clinton chose Albert Gore. And just how moderate is Prince Albert? Well, according to the Taxpayers Union, Al Gore beat out Teddy Kennedy, two straight years, for the title of biggest spender in the Senate.

And Teddy Kennedy isn't moderate about anything.

In New York, Mr. Gore made a startling declaration. Henceforth, he said, the "central organizing principle" of all governments must be: the environment.

Wrong, Albert!

The central organizing principle of this republic is freedom. And from the ancient forests of Oregon, to the Inland Empire of California, America's great middle class has got to start standing up to the environmental extremists who put insects, rats and birds ahead of families, workers and jobs.

One year ago, my friends, I could not have dreamt I would be here. I was then still just one of many panelists on what President Bush calls "those crazy Sunday talk shows."

But I disagreed with the president; and so we challenged the president in the Republican primaries and fought as best we could. From February to June, he won 33 primaries. I can't recall how many we won.

But tonight I want to talk to the 3 million Americans who voted for me. I will never forget you, nor the great honor you have done me. But I do believe, deep in my heart, that the right place for us to be now—in this presidential campaign—is right beside George Bush. The party is our home; this party is where we belong. And don't let anyone tell you any different.

Yes, we disagreed with President Bush, but we stand with him for freedom to [choose] religious schools, and we stand with him against the amoral idea that gay and lesbian couples should have the same standing in law as married men and women.

We stand with President Bush for right-to-life, and for voluntary prayer in the public schools, and against putting American women in combat. And we stand with President Bush in favor of the right of small towns and communities to control the raw sewage of pornography that pollutes our popular culture.

We stand with President Bush in favor of federal judges who interpret the law as written, and against Supreme Court justices who think they have a mandate to rewrite our Constitution.

My friends, this election is about much more than who gets what. It is about who we are. It is about what we believe. It is about what we stand for as Americans. There is a religious war going on in our country for the soul of America. It is a cultural war, as critical to the kind of nation we will one day be as was the Cold War itself. And in that struggle for the soul of America, Clinton & Clinton are on the other side, and George Bush is on our side. And so, we have to come home, and stand beside him.

My friends, in those 6 months, from Concord to California, I came to know our country better than ever before in my life, and I collected memories that will be with me always.

There was that day-long ride through the great state of Georgia in a bus Vice President Bush himself had used in 1988—a bus they called Asphalt One. The ride ended with a 9:00 PM speech in front of a magnificent southern mansion, in a town called Fitzgerald.

There were the workers at the James River Paper Mill, in the frozen North Country of New Hampshire—hard, tough men, one of whom was silent, until I shook his hand. Then he looked up in my eyes and said, "Save our jobs!" There was the legal secretary at the Manchester airport on Christmas Day who told me she was going to vote for me, then broke down crying, saying, "I've lost my job, I don't have any money; they're going to take away my daughter. What am I going to do?"

My friends, even in tough times, these people are with us. They don't read Adam Smith or Edmund Burke, but they came from the same schoolyards and playgrounds and towns as we did. They share our beliefs and convictions, our hopes and our dreams. They are the conservatives of the heart.

They are our people. And we need to reconnect with them. We need to let them know we know they're hurting. They don't expect miracles, but they need to know we care.

There were the people of Hayfork, the tiny town high up in California's Trinity Alps, a town that is now under a sentence of death because a federal judge has set aside 9 million acres for the habitat of the spotted owl—forgetting about the habitat of the men and women who live and work in Hay Fork. And there were the brave people of Koreatown who took the worst of the LA riots, but still live the family values we treasure, and who still believe deeply in the American dream.

Friends, in those wonderful 25 weeks [of the primary campaign], the saddest days were the days of the bloody riot in LA, the worst in our history. But even out of that awful tragedy can come a message of hope.

Hours after the violence ended I visited the Army compound in south LA, where an officer of the 18th Cavalry, that had come to rescue the city, introduced me to two of his troopers. They could not have been 20 years old. He told them to recount their story.

They had come into LA late on the 2nd day, and they walked up a dark street, there the mob had looted and burned every building but one, a convalescent home for the aged. The mob was heading in, to ransack and loot the apartments of the terrified old men and women. When the troopers arrived, M-16s at the ready, the mob threatened and cursed, but the mob retreated. It had met the one thing that could stop it: force, rooted in justice, backed by courage.

Greater love than this hath no man than that he lay down his life for his friend. Here were 19-year-old boys ready to lay down their lives to stop a mob from molesting old people they did not even know. And as they took back the streets of LA, block by block, so we must take back our cities, and take back our culture, and take back our country.

God bless you, and God bless America.

SOURCE: Patrick J. Buchanan, 1992 Republican National Convention Speech, August 17, 1992. http://buchanan.org/blog/1992-republican-national-convention-speech-148. Reprinted courtesy of the Republic National Committee.

ANALYSIS

Patrick Buchanan had challenged President George H. W. Bush for the Republican presidential nomination in 1992. Buchanan's attack on the president from the right wing of the Republican Party led Bush to focus on maintaining support among the social conservatives within his party—those who opposed abortion and gay rights and supported school prayer and strict limitations on immigration (Baker 1993, 46). Buchanan ultimately won 37 percent of the Republican primary vote in New Hampshire, compared to Bush's 53 percent. However, Buchanan's respectable showing against a sitting president evidently resulted not so much from the support of social conservatives than from those disillusioned with Bush's economic policies. For instance, the Buchanan campaign ran televised attack ads against the president in which Bush states "Read my lips: no new taxes," a promise he was widely understood to have broken. One poll indicated that among those stating that they were financially worse off in 1992 than in 1988, Buchanan was preferred to Bush 57 to 39 percent. Buchanan never attracted a higher percentage in the subsequent primaries than he did in New Hampshire, and Bush went on to win the nomination once more, although a fatal weakness on economic issues had been revealed in Buchanan's challenge.

In his speech at the Republican National Convention in summer 1992, Buchanan emphasized the importance of social issues, providing a litany of subjects that define the fundamental nature of the culture war, and announcing that indeed such a war was in full swing. Although Buchanan did not coin the term culture war—sociologist James Davison Hunter is often given credit for doing that a year earlier in his book *Culture Wars: The Struggle to Define America*—Buchanan's speech presented to millions of Americans the terms of the conflict.

Speaking at the national nominating convention, Buchanan understandably argued for the superiority of the Republican Party's accomplishments, especially during Ronald Reagan's presidency. He contrasted Bush's right-to-life stance with what he called Bill Clinton's agenda of "unrestricted abortion on demand." Buchanan chided Clinton for allowing a leader of the homosexual rights movement to speak at the Democratic Convention while at the same time prohibiting an anti-abortion governor from doing the same. According to Buchanan, Clinton's wife Hillary had disparaged the institution of marriage—a bedrock notion for social conservatives—and he called such a position "radical feminism." Criticizing the Democratic vice presidential candidate for his advocacy of environmentalism, Buchanan encouraged opposition to "environmental extremists" who allegedly preferred protection of lower animals instead of creating jobs and maintaining a strong economy. Also, local communities should have the right to control those elements of the popular culture deemed to be pornographic. In all these social conservative stances, Buchanan expressed support for President Bush, but he in fact was expressing his own views and those of people on the right of American politics with whom he claimed a close kinship.

In 1996 Buchanan again entered the race for the Republican presidential nomination. William G. Mayer (1997), in his analysis of the 1996 primaries, noted that Buchanan certainly had a loyal constituency, but it was a limited one, composed of considerably less than a majority of the Republican primary voters (53) and a much smaller proportion of the general electorate. Mayer stated that nearly half of Republican voters considered Buchanan an "extremist." The 15 to 25 percent of the vote that Buchanan consistently received in the 1996 primaries repeated his 1992 performance and tended to mirror the estimates of the support for more conservative positions in the culture war.

DID YOU KNOW?

Grover Norquist and Economic Conservatism

The culture wars are generally associated with such social issues as abortion, gay marriage, sex education, and embryonic stem cell research. These issues tend to relate to individuals' moral concerns. However, social issues tend to overlap more economically and politically oriented questions such as taxation and free enterprise. For more than 25 years Grover Norquist, president of Americans for Tax Reform (ATR), has lobbied for lower taxes and more limited government regulation. He has stated that his goal is not to eliminate government, but to "reduce it to the size where I can drag it into the bathroom and drown it in the bathtub." Norquist serves on the board of directors of the National Rifle Association as well as the American Conservative Union and is a contributor to the conservative publication *American Spectator*. In 2008 Norquist published *Leave Us Alone: Getting the Government's Hands Off Our Money, Our Guns, Our Lives* in which he distinguishes between two competing groups: the Leave Us Alone coalition, which advocates greater freedom from government interference, and the Takings Coalition, which is composed of "tax and spend" liberals. Although Norquist is optimistic about the prospects for the Leave Us Alone coalition, greater federal government involvement in economics due to financial difficulties in the private sector and the outcome of the 2008 elections indicate that the competition between the two groups over the role of government will continue.

"Liberalism as Religion: The Culture War Is Between Religious Believers on Both Sides"

- *Document:* An article by Howard P. Kainz that expands the understanding of religion to include the liberal ideology.
- *Date:* May 2006.
- *Where:* *Touchstone* magazine.
- *Significance:* Howard Kainz portrays a certain portion of liberals as religiously committed and close-minded to any appeals from conservatives, constituting, along with Marxism, a secular religion. The possibility that a portion of conservatives also fit this description suggests the makeup of the two armies in the culture war.

DOCUMENT

Many Christians view the "culture war" as a clash between religious believers and secularist "liberals." But there are liberals . . . and there are liberals. Most of the heat of battle occurs where traditional religious believers clash with certain liberals who are religiously committed to secular liberalism.

This explains why talking about abortion or same-sex "marriage," for example, with certain liberals is usually futile. It is like trying to persuade a committed Muslim to accept Christ. Because his religion forbids it, he can only do so by *converting* from Islam to Christianity; he cannot accept Christ as long as he remains firmly committed to Islam. So it is with firmly committed liberals: Their "religion" forbids any concessions to the "conservative" agenda, and as long as they remain committed to their secular ideology, it is futile to hope for such concessions from them.

But can a secular ideology fairly be classified as a religion?

The Ideal Religion

Religion in the most common and usual sense connotes dedication to a supreme being or beings. While one's gods may be demonic, as in Satanic religions, or may be deified humans rather than of an order beyond the human, as in the ancient Roman religions that deified the Caesars—they are understood to be personal beings.

But, especially in the last few centuries, "religion" has taken on the additional connotations of dedication to abstract principles or ideals rather than a personal being. The French Enlightenment, with its worship of Reason, is a prime example of this kind of religion. The god is no longer personal, but abstract, though it may be personified in art or ritual (as, for example, when the actress Mademoiselle Maillard, representing the Goddess of Reason, was enthroned with great festivity in the Cathedral of Notre Dame in 1793).

Hence, modern dictionaries include definitions relating religion to impersonal principles rather than persons. The *Merriam-Webster Collegiate Dictionary* widens the definition to include: "a cause, principle, or system of beliefs held with ardor and faith." So in our day, Scientology is considered a religion, and even an atheist could say proudly, "Humanism is my religion."

Meaning *religion* in only this broad, even purely metaphorical sense, the atheist may bristle at the notion that his "religion" entails anything other than adherence to his core principles, whatever they may be. Yet two movements of the last century, one explicitly atheist and the other vehemently secular if not outright atheist, exhibit many elements strikingly similar to those of more traditional religions.

Marxism as Religion

Until recently, the most notable example of a secular movement that was, for all practical purposes, a religion, was Marxism. During the global expansion of Marxism in the twentieth century, many critics noted its religious and quasi-religious characteristics (see, for instance, chapter XVI, "The Emergence of the Secular Kingdom of God," in my *Democracy and the "Kingdom of God"*).

For example, Marxism had *dogmas*, core teachings that all Marxists embraced. Among these were "economic determinism," the doctrine that politics, culture, and ethics were necessary extensions of economic relations; and the "dictatorship of the proletariat," a necessary historical stage in the inevitable transformation of capitalism into socialism. Such dogmas were laid out in Marxism's *canonical scriptures*, which included *Das Kapital*, *The Communist Manifesto*, *The Little Red Book* of Mao Tse Tung, and other official Marxist-Leninist works of the mid-twentieth century.

Marxist orthodoxy was safeguarded by its *priests* and *theologians*, who taught the requisite dogmas and presided over the *ritualistic observances*, principally workers' strikes, especially general strikes. Throughout Marxist regimes, ideological police and government censors saw that the dogmas found their way into factories and neighborhood organizations and newspapers. Local communes functioned like *parochial congregations*, and vied with one another for fidelity to socialism, while the ideal of the Third International replaced the Christian image of Church Militant.

In academe, philosophy professors studiously promoted adherence to dialectical materialism ("Diamat") as the common *creed*.

Deviations from dogma, i.e., *heresies*, needed to be suppressed. Things associated with the two great heresies, traditional religion and capitalism, were banned and demonized. Traditional religion, the "opiate of the masses" in Karl Marx's famous phrase, had to be religiously abolished for the success of scientific socialism. Capitalism, particularly as expressed through private ownership of the means of production, had to be abandoned in favor of the foresight and "five-year plans" of state-controlled hierarchies. Orthodox Marxists had meticulously to avoid such *sins* as expropriating "surplus value" from an army of oppressed workers, preaching rewards in an afterlife to the proletariat, or settling into the life of a pure consumer removed from the struggles of workers. The wayward were corrected in mandated "reeducation" camps; those found intractable to correction were frequently subjected to *excommunication* from the party, exile, and even execution.

There was even an *eschatology*: After the earlier evolutionary stages of capitalism and the dictatorship of the proletariat, the "end times" would come, characterized by a new state of consciousness in "communist man," who would live in a cooperative, crime-less, international community, without any vestiges of dehumanizing labor; and a *hagiography*, which included generally accepted revolutionary saints, such as Marx, Engels, and Lenin, as well as some venerated by select or local groups, such as Bakunin and Trotsky.

Liberalism as Religion

Not all Marxists, of course, had sufficient "ardor and faith" to qualify them as "religious" in the wide sense. In the West during the Cold War, there were many persons influenced somewhat by progressive ideals of worker solidarity and a new socialist order, but taking their Marxism with a "grain of salt." So also now, in the twenty-first century, there are many people working for social justice, human rights, international solidarity, and other causes commonly regarded as liberal without a deep ideological commitment. But there are also those for whom liberalism is a life commitment, held to with the same ardor and faith as Marxism was for its strongest adherents. Among such liberals can be found a cluster of many of the same religious components:

1. *Dogmas*. The backdrop for the major dogmas of the religiously liberal are those of the eighteenth-century Enlightenment: that mankind must overcome religious superstition by means of Reason; that empirical science can and will eventually answer all the questions about the world and human values that were formerly referred to traditional religion or theology; and that the human race, by constantly invalidating and disregarding hampering traditions, can and will achieve perfectibility.

Contemporary liberalism also includes three ideals selectively borrowed from the New Testament, but with its own suitably revisionist interpretations. The first reinterprets Mark 12:17, Jesus' admonition to "give to Caesar what is Caesar's, and to God what is God's," as a case for absolute secularism, a wall between church and state, religion reduced to something purely private. Also, whereas the traditional

Christian understands Galatians 3:28, "There is neither Jew nor Greek, there is neither slave nor free person, there is neither male nor female," as extolling the new unity of disparate persons through unity in Christ, the liberal sees it, on the one hand, as wiping away distinctions between the sexes in a sweeping egalitarianism, and on the other, as wiping away all salient distinctions between cultures (such as their values and morals) in a vapid celebration of "diversity" and "multiculturalism." Similarly, Matthew 7:1, "Stop judging, that you may not be judged," no longer conveys the mandate of Jesus to leave the judgment of sinners to God, but instead sweepingly condemns "judgmentalism," to the extent that one may not even judge whether something is a sin or not.

2. *Sins.* Yet, ironically, there are sins for the religiously liberal to eschew. In addition to judgmentalism, the most serious sins are racism, which does not simply mean failing to treat members of all races equally, but failing to show special preference for racial minorities; sexism, which does not mean treating members of both sexes with equal dignity, but making any differentiation between male and female roles; and "homophobia," which does not simply cover unjust discrimination against persons with same-sex desires but also any judgment that such desires are disordered or that acting on them is sinful.

Intolerance is also a grave sin—*except* as regards Christian fundamentalism and the adherence of Catholics to the teachings of the magisterium. (Islamic fundamentalism, on the other hand, is considered a regrettable but understandable Islamic reaction to the medieval Christian Crusades.) Public ridicule of Catholic dogmas, moral teachings, and the pope, as well as of fundamentalist Protestants are types of scapegoating and exorcism officially allowed by the standard of "political correctness." Pro-life and pro-family movements can also be demonized as anti-liberal agendas emanating from these Catholic and Protestant religious sources. The vehemence of the denunciations may offer reliable testimony regarding one's religious commitment to liberalism.

3. *Scriptures.* The "classical" scriptures of liberalism fall into two categories: Darwinist and scientistic writings championing materialist and naturalistic explanations for everything, including morals; and feminist writings exposing the "evil" of patriarchy and tracing male exploitation of females throughout history up to the present. For trustworthy day-to-day liberal exegesis of ideas and events, *The New York Times* stands out among newspapers, *The Nation* among magazines.

4. *Priests and Priestesses.* The sacerdotal elite are generally intellectuals with a literary or other media flair and an infectious enthusiasm for the liberal agenda. Exemplars include Stephen Jay Gould as a proponent of Darwinist explanations for life and Carl Sagan as a guru defending naturalistic explanations of the universe; Gloria Steinem as a pathfinder for abortion "rights" and other feminist issues; and dissident Catholics such as Garry Wills, Daniel Maguire, and Charles Curran, and their counterparts in certain Protestant denominations, who, as darlings of the liberal media, are always available to excoriate traditional Christian beliefs and morals.

5. *Congregations.* Over the past several decades, Democratic party leadership has made being pro-abortion a veritable requirement for credibility, and Democratic politicians have vied with one another in asserting their "pro-choice" credentials through such actions as opposing pro-life judicial nominees. Hence, religiously

committed liberals gravitate almost exclusively towards the Democratic party for their political affiliation. Other abortion-centered organizations, such as Planned Parenthood, the ACLU, NOW, and the oxymoronic "Catholics for Free Choice," also help supply a sense of affiliation and commonality for the religiously liberal.

6. *Rites and Rituals*. The most emphatic statements of liberal religiosity are directed against what is considered to be oppressive sexual morality. Like the ancient pagan mystery rites celebrating unrestrained sensuality in honor of the god Dionysus, "gay pride" parades are held to celebrate liberals' liberation from traditional sexual morality. Similarly, pro-abortion groups, like ancient Aztecs and Mayans proudly offering child sacrifices to their gods, feel privileged to participate in the ongoing immolation of human fetuses, including female fetuses, to manifest the emancipation of females from childbearing. Through the distribution of condoms, Planned Parenthood literature, and the like, liberals increase their sense of commitment to the feminist cause while preaching it to others.

7. *Eschatology*. The final goal is not concerned with an afterlife or the "last things," but a this-worldly, and basically utilitarian, objective—the attainment of the greatest possible happiness by the greatest number here and now. In the estimation of the religiously liberal, all lifestyles and all moralities can approximate this goal, as long as the proscribed illiberal "sins" are avoided.

8. *Saints and Martyrs*. Margaret Sanger, although somewhat tainted in her day by racism, has been sainted as the founder of Planned Parenthood. Living saints include radical feminists such as Andrea Dworkin, Catharine MacKinnon, and Gloria Steinmen, who have supplied spiritual inspiration for sisterhood. Kate Michelman, longtime head of NARAL [formerly National Abortion Rights Action League, now called NARAL Pro-Choice America], and Sarah Weddington, the attorney who won *Roe v. Wade*, are revered as pathbreakers for abortion "rights." TV star Ellen De Generes attained reverential status by her courage in "coming out" as a lesbian, and the ordination of the openly homosexual Anglican bishop V. Gene Robinson has been construed as having prophetic significance. Larry Flynt is equally venerated for championing the production and consumption of pornography as a "free speech" issue.

Among the martyrs, Matthew Shepard has lost none of his luster despite the revelation that his 1998 murder was precipitated by a drug dispute rather than the sexual proclivities and practices of the victim. Other liberal martyrs include: (1) pre-*Roe* coathanger-aborted women (estimates of whose deaths have been based on the unreliable figures of Alfred Kinsey, and on the "5,000 to 10,000" deaths a year figure given as testimony by Dr. Bernard Nathanson, who later admitted the figure was fabricated); and (2) those who have been forced to suffer because they live in jurisdictions that have not legalized assisted suicide.

Reasonable Liberals

Of course, religiously committed liberals constitute only a sub-group of contemporary liberals. For many "moderate" liberals, liberalism is a political perspective, not a core ideology. In the culture war it is important for Christians to distinguish between the religiously committed liberal and the moderate liberal. For one thing, Christians should not be surprised when they find no common ground with the former. But they may form occasional, even if temporary, alliances with the latter.

Currently, a moderate liberal may be expected to support human rights, non-discrimination, tolerance, democratization, liberation from political and economic oppression, and similar goals. Even conservatives may identify with such goals, although they may differ in their interpretation of the goals and how best they might be attained. But more important, when specific political and social issues come to the fore, especially controversial ones, moderate liberals will be willing to engage in debate and to consider pros and cons regarding such issues as abortion, same-sex "marriage," affirmative action, capital punishment, assisted suicide, and so forth.

Religiously committed liberals, on the other hand, like their Marxist counterparts, are characterized by unshakable faith in sanctioned *agendas*—abortion on demand, with no restrictions or compromises; the abolition of all strictures, standards, and morals regarding consensual sexual behavior; the mainstreaming of same-sex relationships and legitimization of "gay marriage"; the prioritizing of AIDS research and treatment over other medical concerns, while at the same time rejecting morally based preventive measures (e.g., abstinence); knee-jerk refusal to even consider such embarrassing data as the failure rate of condoms, the statistical connection between contraceptive pills and breast cancer, or the often self-serving motivations of family or health providers in supporting assisted suicide. Such issues as these are considered beyond debate by the religiously committed liberal.

In order to maintain purity, religiously committed liberals will adamantly refuse even to consider any ideas or arguments suspected of being conservative. If you present them with books or articles supporting a conservative position, they may thank you politely, but never give any indication of actually reading the material—as if this were a temptation that must be avoided to preserve their integrity. They will carefully avoid cultivating friendships with conservatives, or supporting the nomination or election of conservatives to any positions where they might have some influence. And they will be on the constant lookout for graphic examples of misogynism, homophobia, sexism, and racism among the *bêtes noires*—Catholics and fundamentalists, as well as prominent conservatives.

It is important that discussion between liberals and conservatives take place, but these are usually only possible with moderate liberals. A conservative can bring up a religiously charged topic with a moderate liberal, with the result that reasonable, multi-sided representations of the topic will be aired in the public square.

But with a religiously committed liberal, calm intellectual debates are rarely possible. For example, the elegant arguments against abortion presented by Hadley Arkes in his 2002 book, *Natural Rights and the Right to Choose*, will invite thoughtful responses from moderate liberals, but religiously committed liberals will dismiss the arguments unread, considering them on par with the doctrines contained in the tracts handed out by Jehovah's Witnesses or Mormon missionaries. In other words, their motivation is a faith-commitment, the abjuring of which will necessarily result in personal guilt, infidelity to their spiritual community, and possible ostracism if they prove to be embarrassments to liberal believers.

There are no professional cult-breakers to rescue victims from this recent and already widespread religious movement. It is ironic that those who most strongly denounce fundamentalism should prove to be such fundamentalists themselves. While they may constitute a minority of all contemporary liberals, theirs may be the dominant liberal voice in the public square. Therefore, for the advancement of family and pro-life values, and rational sexual norms, it is important for Christians to be able to distinguish the moderate liberal from his religiously committed counterpart. Among the former, allies may be found; among the latter, only firm opponents.

SOURCE: Howard P. Kainz. "Liberalism As Religion: The Culture War Is Between Religious Believers on Both Sides." *Touchstone* 19 (May 2006), 22–26. Reprinted courtesy of Howard P. Kainz.

ANALYSIS

In portraying a portion of liberals as "religiously committed" and hence not open to alternative viewpoints, Kainz in effect attributes the culture wars to the unreasonableness of liberals who will not interact with conservatives. He describes these liberals as uncompromising on such issues as contraception, abortion, same-gender marriage, affirmative action, capital punishment, and assisted suicide, which represent many of the points of controversy between liberal and conservative forces in the United States that have been labeled the culture wars. Kainz assigns to "religiously committed" liberals the various characteristics of a religion: rigidly held dogmatic beliefs, a list of sins to be avoided, canonical writings, authority figures, a congregation of true believers, sacred ceremonies, a final goal to which all are aiming, and a pantheon of saints and martyrs. Although Kainz applauds "moderate" liberals with whom conservatives can discuss issues on which they disagree, "religiously committed" liberals refuse to accept the possibility of being persuaded by their ideological opponents. If we add to this description what Kainz omits—the mirror image of extreme liberalism, which is extreme conservatism—the result is two opponents equally committed to their beliefs and unwilling to compromise with the other, and hence the culture war in which each side refuses to accept the possibility of mutual concessions.

"The Politics of Culture"

- **Document:** Michael Parenti presents a progressive view of the culture wars and their political significance.
- **Date:** 2006.
- **Where:** Introductory chapter of Michael Parenti's *The Culture Struggle*, published by Seven Stories Press, New York.
- **Significance:** Michael Parenti provides an alternative interpretation of the culture wars from a perspective that emphasizes the contrast between the capitalist influence on American society and the dissent of those on the left.

DOCUMENT

In the academic social sciences, students are taught to think of *culture* as representing the customs, values, and accumulated practices of a society, including its language, art, laws, and religion. Such a definition has a nice neutral sound to it, but culture is anything but neutral. It is more than just our common heritage, the social glue of society. The eighteenth-century political thinker, Edmund Burke, referred to the imponderable consensual bond that holds society together. But culture is also an arena of conflict as well as consensus. While some of its attributes are shared by practically all of a society's members, certain others are not. Many customary standards operate to benefit particular people and disadvantage others. In other words, culture is often a cloak for privilege and inequity.

In the nineteenth century the Germans coined the world *Kulturkampf*, which eventually passed into the English language, literally meaning "culture struggle." It referred to the conflicts between church and state over the control of education.

Today in the United States we talk of "culture wars" to describe how whole segments of American culture have become politically contested areas.

Culture is not an abstract force that just floats around in space and settles upon us—although given the seemingly subliminal ways it influences us, it often can feel like a disembodied ubiquitous entity. In fact, we get our culture through a social structure, from a network of social relations involving other people in primary groups such as family, peers, and other community associations or, as is increasingly the case, from formally chartered institutions such as schools, media, government agencies, courts, corporations, churches, and the military. Linked by purchase and persuasion to dominant ruling interests, such social institutions are regularly misrepresented as being politically neutral, especially by those who occupy command positions within them or who are otherwise advantaged by them.

Much of what we call "our common culture" is really the selective transmission of elite-dominated values. A society built upon slave labor, for instance, swiftly develops a self-justifying slaveholder culture with its own racist laws, science, mythology, and religious preachments. Likewise, a society based on private corporate enterprise develops supportive values and beliefs that present the business system as the optimal and natural mode of social organization. Antonio Gramsci understood all this when he spoke of *cultural hegemony*, noting that the state is only the "outer trench behind which there [stands] a powerful system of fortresses and earthworks," [1] a network of cultural values and institutions not normally thought of as political, yet political in their impact.

Some parts of culture may be neutral composites of accumulated practices, the "glue of social relations," but other parts often clash with society's ascendant interests. When thinking about "our common culture," we tend to gloss over both the class divisions and the cultural differences that exist. If culture defines a people, a society, or a nation, which group of people and which subculture within that nation are we talking about? In the United States, through much of the nineteenth century, slaveholders and abolitionists held cultural values that were markedly at odds with each other, as did male supremacists and female suffragists.

There are two misunderstandings I should like to put to rest. First is the notion that culture is to be treated as mutually exclusive of, and even competitive with, political economy. An acquaintance of mine who used to edit a socialist journal once commented to me: "You emphasize economics. I deal more with culture." I thought this an odd dichotomization since my work on the news media, the entertainment industry, social institutions, and political mythology has been deeply involved with both culture and economics. In fact one cannot talk intelligently about culture if one does not at some point also introduce the dynamics of political economy and social power. This is why, when I refer to the "politics of culture," I mean something more than just the latest controversy regarding federal funding of the arts.

The other myth is that our social institutions are autonomous entities not linked to each other. In fact, they are interlocked by public and private funding and overlapping corporate elites who serve on the governing boards of universities, colleges, private schools, museums, symphony orchestras, the music industry, art schools, libraries, churches, newspapers, magazines, radio and TV networks, publishing houses, and charitable foundations. Whatever their particular institutional subcultures, they usually share some common elitist values. A conservative newspaper columnist named George Will once asserted that radicals deny the autonomy of culture. Not entirely. Radicals recognize that unexpected forces can emerge and new cultural values and practices develop among the people themselves. Indeed that is my point when I say that culture is not a fixed and finished product. It is not that radicals deny the autonomy of culture, it is that they recognize the conditional nature of that autonomy.

Professions and professional associations offer an example of the limited autonomy of cultural practices. Whether composed of anthropologists, political scientists, physicists, psychiatrists, doctors, lawyers, or librarians, professional associations emphasize their commitment to independent expertise, and fail to recognize that they are wedded to the dominant politico-economic social structure. In fact, many of their most important activities are shaped by corporate interests in a social context that is less and less of their own making, as doctors and nurses are discovering in their dealings with HMOs, and as academic scientists who work on corporate or Pentagon-funded projects discovered long ago.

Generally, publicists, pundits, professors, and politicos can operate freely only as long as they confine themselves to certain ideological parameters. When they stray into forbidden territory, uttering or doing iconoclastic things, they experience the structural restraints imposed on their professional subcultures by the larger social hierarchy. To give an example: In 1996 Gary Webb, a Pulitzer-winning reporter, ignited a national debate with an exposé in the *San Jose Mercury News* that linked the CIA-sponsored Nicaraguan contras [2] to the cocaine trade and to the crack-dealing epidemic in Los Angeles and other American cities. In quick order Webb was hit by an unforgiving barrage laid down by the mainstream press, which relied principally on government sources to whitewash the CIA. Press critics accused him of saying things he never said. They inflated a few minor points that he had not fully documented, while they ignored the devastating corpus of his research and evidence. [3] Despite the disrepute cast upon him, Webb's articles forced both the CIA and Justice Department to conduct internal investigations that belatedly vindicated his findings, namely that there were links between the CIA and drug dealers and that the U.S. government regularly overlooked these connections. CIA Inspector General Frederick Hitz reported as much to Congress in 1998, albeit in somewhat watered down terms. Webb's real mistake was not that he wrote falsehoods but that he went too far into the truth. He was denounced, threatened, drummed out of his profession, and unable to get back into mainstream journalism. As he described it:

If we had met five years ago, you wouldn't have found a more staunch defender of the newspaper industry than me. . . . I was winning awards, getting raises, lecturing college classes, appearing on TV shows, and judging journalism contests. . . . And then I wrote some stories that made me realize how sadly misplaced my bliss had been. The reason I'd enjoyed such smooth sailing for so long hadn't been, as I'd assumed, because I was careful and diligent and good at my job. . . . The truth was that, in all those years, I hadn't written anything important enough to suppress. [4]

Gary Webb never got over having been betrayed by many of his journalistic peers. He knew his work was deserving of their respect, yet he continued to be treated as something of an outcast even after his book had won favorable reviews, which should have put to rest the earlier allegations against him. [5] In December 2004, he committed suicide.

The higher circles of wealth and power instinctively resist any pressure toward social equality, not only in economic status but also in regard to what has been called *identity politics*, which focuses on gender, race, lifestyle, and sexual orientation. But in time leaders learn to make limited accommodations to identity issues, even gleaning some advantages from reforms. The concessions they make usually are confined to personnel and operational style, leaving institutional interests largely intact. Thus when feminists challenged patriarchal militarism, the resulting concession was not an end to militarism but the emergence of female generals.

Eventually we get female political leaders, but of what stripe? Lynn Cheney, Elizabeth Dole, Margaret Thatcher, Jeane Kirkpatrick, and—just when some of us were recovering from Madeleine Albright—we were treated to Condoleeza Rice (who further satisfied a concession to identity politics by being African-American). It is no accident that this type of conservative woman is most likely to reach the top governing circles of conservative administrations. While indifferent or even hostile to the feminist movement, rightist females are not above reaping its benefits.

In short, culture is a changing and evolving thing. And one of the major forces shaping its development is the power of entrenched interests. These interests usually are able to maintain their hegemony while making limited and marginal adjustments to newly evolving social values.

NOTES

[1] Antonio Gramsci, *Selections from the Prison Notebooks*, edited by Quinton Hoare and Geoffry Nowell-Smith (New York: International Publishers, 1971), 238.
[2] A mercenary force dedicated to destroying the Sandinista revolution in Nicaragua mostly by attacking unprotected civilian targets.
[3] See Gary Webb, *Dark Alliance: The CIA, the Contras, and the Crack Cocaine Explosion* (New York: Seven Stories Press, 1998).
[4] Quoted in *LA Weekly*, 16 December 2004.
[5] See the excellent statement by Daniel Simon, http://www.sevenstories.com/Book/index.cfm?GCOI=58322100705890.

SOURCE: Michael Parenti, "The Politics of Culture," from *The Culture Struggle*. Copyright © 2006 by Michael Parenti. Reprinted with permission of Seven Stories Press, www.sevenstories.com.

ANALYSIS

Michael Parenti, a political scientist and progressive activist, offers a view of culture and the culture wars that is distinct from many of the treatments of current cultural conflict in the United States. Although recognizing that the term culture wars accurately describes the current situation in which "whole segments of American culture have become politically contested areas," Parenti argues that to a great extent general American culture has resulted from "the selective transmission of elite-dominated values." Any proper discussion of culture must include an analysis of the interaction of political economy and social power.

Parenti represents an ideological position somewhat in tune with Howard Kainz's analysis. The culture war as Parenti perceives it involves the established order, entrenched in the economic system that exercises basic control of those areas commonly associated with culture—educational institutions (both private and public), the mass media, religious institutions, and the arts—in opposition to those like himself who challenge that conservative hegemony. Those who dominate these established institutions make certain concessions to demands for reform, but without surrendering social, economic, and political control. Although Parenti does not focus on social conservative dissatisfaction with the system, his argument could be extended to those who object to policies that threaten conservative values in such areas as education and immigration. The left and the right have a common objective in challenging the status quo in American society and politics, but definitely come down on opposite sides with regard to many cultural issues—including abortion, sexuality, and the separation of church and state—that characterize the common understanding of the culture wars. We may conclude that, for Parenti, although cultural conflicts arise over such issues as abortion, prayer in the public schools, the teaching of evolution, and embryonic stem cell research, control of the economic, social, and political structures remains firmly in the hands of an elite, which is willing to compromise on these issues as long as their privileged positions are not endangered. Ultimately, the question is whether a pluralist or an elitist conception of American society and politics is correct, a debate that has arisen among political scientists since the 1960s.

DID YOU KNOW?

Who Is Fighting the Culture War?

Much of the debate over whether the United States has been engaged in a culture war revolves around which people can be identified as fighting the war. Researchers such as Morris P. Fiorina, who are skeptical of the culture war thesis, argue that average Americans tend to hold moderate views on the issues commonly thought to comprise the culture war and that the conflict is being waged by relatively small groups composed of the more active citizens. Therefore, "culture warriors" do not represent the vast majority of the population. Other researchers, such as the authors of *The American Voter Revisited* (2008)—Michael S. Lewis-Beck, William G. Jacoby, Helmut Northpoth, and Herbert F. Weisberg—who conducted 1,500 in-depth interviews during the 2000 and 2004 presidential campaigns, conclude that the average American voter lacks basic knowledge about the political process, the major political players, and the issues that attract the attention of government officials. Although other researchers present a less severe evaluation of the average American, arguing that voters know enough to make intelligent decisions, the typical level of knowledge reasonably can lead to the conclusion that if there is a culture war, by default it is waged by the more informed citizens who have a clearer understanding of political ideology, have a greater interest in politics, and possess higher levels of information about political issues.

FURTHER READING

Baker, Ross K. "Sorting Out and Suiting Up: The Presidential Nominations." In *The Election of 1992*, edited by Gerald M. Pomper et al. Chatham, NJ: Chatham House Publishers, 1993.

Bettmann, Otto L. *The Good Old Days—They Were Terrible!* New York: Random House, 1974.

Bode, Carl. *Mencken*. Carbondale, IL: Southern Illinois University Press, 1969.

Boorstin, Daniel. *The Americans: The Democratic Experience*. New York: Random House, 1973.

Buchanan, Patrick J. *Day of Reckoning: How Hubris, Ideology, and Greed Are Tearing America Apart*. New York: St. Martin's Press, 2007.

Buchholz, Rogene A. *America in Conflict: The Deepening Values Divide*. Lanham, MD: Hamilton Books, 2007.

Burns, Eric. *The Spirits of America: A Social History of Alcohol*. Philadelphia: Temple University Press, 2004.

Carr, Craig L. *Polity: Political Culture and the Nature of Politics*. Lanham, MD: Rowman and Littlefield, 2007.

Citrin, Jack. "Political Culture." In *Understanding America*, edited by Peter H. Schuck and James Q. Wilson. New York: Public Affairs Press, 2008.

Finkelman, Paul. *Dred Scott v. Sanford: A Brief History with Documents*. Boston, MA: Bedford/St. Martin's, 1997.

Fiorina, Morris P., Samuel J. Abrams, and Jeremy C. Pope. *Culture War? The Myth of a Polarized America*. New York: Pearson Longman, 2006.

Fowler, Robert Booth. *Enduring Liberalism: American Political Thought Since the 1960s*. Lawrence, KS: University Press of Kansas, 1999.

Freehling, William W. *The Road to Disunion, Volume II: Secessionists Triumphant, 1854–1861*. New York: Oxford University Press, 2007.

Hunter, James Davison, and Alan Wolfe, eds. *Is There a Culture War? A Dialogue on Values and American Public Life*. Washington, DC: Brookings Institution Press, 2006.

Lindsey, Brink. *The Age of Abundance: How Prosperity Transformed America's Politics and Culture*. New York: Harper Collins, 2007.

Mayer, William G. "The Presidential Nominations." In *The Election of 1996*, edited by Gerald M. Pomper, et al. Chatham, NJ: Chatham House Publishers, 1997.

McGough, Michael. *A Field Guide to the Culture Wars: The Battle Over Values from the Campaign Trail to the Classroom*. Westport, CT: Praeger, 2008.

Mencken, H. L. "The Noble Experiment." In *A Choice of Days*, edited by H. L. Mencken. New York: Alfred A. Knopf, 1980.

Parenti, Michael. *Contrary Notions: The Michael Parenti Reader*. San Francisco: City Lights Books, 2007.

Patterson, Orlando. "Black Americans." In *Understanding America*, edited by Peter H. Schuck and James Q. Wilson. New York: Public Affairs Press, 2008.

Perry, Rick. *On My Honor: Why the American Values of the Boy Scouts Are Worth Fighting For*. Macon, GA: Stroud and Hall, 2008.

White, John Kenneth. *The Values Divide: American Politics and Culture in Transition*. New York: Chatham House Publishers, 2003.

Wright, Benjamin Fletcher. *Consensus and Continuity: 1776–1787*. Westport, CT: Greenwood Publishing Group, 1984.

2

DIFFERING RELIGIOUS UNDERSTANDINGS

Document: Douglas LeBlanc, "Two Minds in One Episcopal Body" (2006)

Document: Solange De Santis, "Bishop Gene Robinson Says He Was at Canterbury as a Witness: Know God, Acknowledge Gays, He Asked" (2008)

Document: Evangelical Environmental Network, "Climate Change: An Evangelical Call to Action" (2006)

Document: Cornwall Alliance for the Stewardship of Creation, *excerpts from* "An Open Letter to the Signers of 'Climate Change: An Evangelical Call to Action' and Others Concerned about Global Warming" (2006)

Document: David A. Noebel, "Aikman, Berlinski, Day, and Lennox Versus Dawkins, Hitchens, Dennett, and Harris" (2008)

Document: Ronald Aronson, "All Ye Unfaithful" (2008)

"Two Minds in One Episcopal Body"

- **Document:** Douglas LeBlanc portrays the difficulties that the Episcopal Church has faced following the ordination of an openly gay bishop, V. Gene Robinson, of New Hampshire.
- **Date:** 2006.
- **Where:** *Christian Research Journal*, a publication of the Christian Research Institute.
- **Significance:** The dissension between liberals and conservatives within the Episcopal denomination tend to mirror the conflicts over sexuality and other issues in the general society. Other denominations, including the United Methodist Church, the Presbyterian Church (U.S.A.), and the Evangelical Lutheran Church in America, have faced similar divisions among members and clergy.

DOCUMENT

In the Episcopal Church's three-decade discussion about homosexuality and the church, conservatives and liberals alike have often said that the debate is about far more than sex. Most conservatives have held that the sexuality debate is really about theology—specifically how both sides understand God, the world He created, the meaning of sin, the nature of redemption, and the authority of Scripture over each Christian's life. Liberals generally have held that the sexuality debate is not about theology or the authority of Scripture, but about power—specifically the efforts of privileged, heterosexual, and white men, primarily, to preserve their power over everybody else.

At the church's 75th General Convention, which met in Columbus, Ohio, on June 13–21, 2006, Episcopalians' theological divisions became clearer than ever. This convention was charged with responding to the broader Anglican Communion regarding the decisions of the 74th General Convention, which met in 2003. That convention confirmed the election of Gene Robinson, an openly gay man, as the Bishop of New Hampshire, and said that local churches are "within the bounds of our common life" when they bless gay couples. Anglican leaders across the world protested these decisions, declaring the communion between their churches and the Episcopal Church to be impaired or broken.

"I believe that what we have is one church with two minds," said Bishop Charles Jenkins of Louisiana during a central debate at this year's convention. Bishop Katharine Jefferts Schori of Nevada, who was elected this year to be the church's presiding bishop for the next nine years, took the image further, comparing the church to conjoined twins.

"Some parents have to wrestle with the decision of trying to separate or not trying to separate those twins. They operate with the assumption that it is wrong to attempt to separate those twins unless both can live full lives," Jefferts Schori said when addressing the convention's clergy and lay deputies. "This creature, this body of Christ, is not wholly one and not wholly two."

Jefferts Schori's metaphor was not surprising considering her background in science. She earned a Ph.D. in oceanography in 1983, and worked in that profession until entering seminary in the early 1990s. The real surprise was hearing the newly elected presiding bishop, who has expressed consistently liberal convictions in the sexuality debate, acknowledge the depth of the church's divisions.

For some conservatives, Jefferts Schori not only was acknowledging the problem, but was part of the problem, both in her unprecedented election and in her theology. Bishop Jack Iker of the Diocese of Fort Worth (Texas) asked the Archbishop of Canterbury for "alternative primatial oversight" soon after Jefferts Schori's election. (Iker's diocese does not ordain women as priests.) In the weeks after the convention, another six dioceses made requests similar to Iker's, mostly because of Jefferts Schori's theology or because of the convention's decisions. The convention highlighted the ways in which conservatives and liberals differ in how they speak about the persons of the Holy Trinity, how they understand revelation, how they define evangelism, and how they worship.

Mother Jesus? Jefferts Schori disturbed conservatives on the final morning of the convention, in her first sermon as presiding bishop-elect, by comparing Jesus' crucifixion to a mother's giving birth. "That sweaty, bloody, tear-stained labor of the cross bears new life. Our mother Jesus gives birth to a new creation—and you and I are his children," Jefferts Schori said.

Jefferts Schori later told the *Washington Post* that such language is "straight-down-the-middle orthodox theology," citing the precedent of medieval mystics, including Julian of Norwich and Teresa of Avila. She suggested that her critics are guilty of idolatry. "All language is metaphorical, and if we insist that particular words have only one meaning and the way we understand those words is the only possible interpretation, we have elevated that text to an idol," she told Alan Cooperman of the *Post*. "I'm encouraging people to look beyond their favorite understandings."

Jefferts Schori's sermon itself, however, soon became the subject of varying interpretations. Liberal Episcopalians, like the bishop, saw the message as a harmless reassertion of language used by mystics. Conservatives saw it as a deliberate provocation.

Bishop V. Gene Robinson of the Episcopal Diocese of New Hampshire attends the 75th General Convention of the Episcopal Church, held in Columbus, Ohio, in June 2006; photograph by Donald Vish. (E15 http://flickr.com/photos/86764746@N00/. CC-SA license)

The bishop's language was enough to send the Rev. David Roseberry of the 4,500-member Christ Episcopal Church in Plano, Texas, out of the doors of the denomination he has served as a priest since 1983. He plans to take his congregation and its buildings with him, and so far his bishop, James Stanton of Dallas, has been cooperative.

Roseberry, who has worked for theological reform within the church since the early 1990s, had gathered signatures from more than 1,000 priests in the weeks before the General Convention. Roseberry and the priests who signed his petition pleaded with the convention to reaffirm the church's historic teachings about sexual morality. Addressing an open hearing during the convention, he referred to those priests and the estimated 22,490 years of service they represented. "Can you hear me now?" Roseberry said.

Roseberry stayed on through the duration of the convention. Hearing Jefferts Schori's sermon, however, convinced him that the sexuality debate was part of an inescapable theological package in which the majority of bishops and other decision-makers in the church believe. "When the presiding bishop-elect had a chance to build consensus, she chose to interweave the cross with radical feminism. It seemed Gnostic," said Roseberry, who added that he's aware of Julian's writings.

An Impersonal Holy Spirit. Jesus was not the only person of the Trinity who was the subject of unconventional language at the convention. Deputies—laypeople, deacons, and priests elected to attend the triennial gathering—often invoked the Holy Spirit as the driving force of the church's changing teachings regarding homosexuality.

Louie Crew, an openly gay deputy from Newark, New Jersey, spoke against a resolution that asked the church not to approve any new bishop "whose manner of life presents a challenge to the wider church." Both sides understood the coy language of that resolution to mean withholding approval from any bishop involved in a same-sex relationship.

"It's a bit like telling Samuel that he must choose only from the first [sons] that Jesse brings out," said Crew, who served as cochairman of a committee to nominate candidates for Newark's next bishop. "I speak against this because it attempts to cut the tongue out of the Holy Spirit." (On June 28 the Diocese of Newark announced its slate, which includes the Rev. Canon Michael Barlowe, an openly gay priest who is in charge of congregational development in the Diocese of California.)

Crew and some other deputies referred to the Holy Spirit as *she*. Others avoided personal language, instead calling the Holy Spirit *it*. Most liberal Episcopalians seem unaware that such usage places them in the company of unorthodox sects such as the Jehovah's Witnesses, who consider the Holy Spirit to be an impersonal force, like electricity.

Liberal deputies regularly referred to the Holy Spirit as speaking through the convention's votes. Some compared the convention to the Council at Jerusalem, which agreed to welcome Gentiles into the early church, or to the Council of Nicaea, which agreed on the doctrines in the Nicene Creed.

"I believe that the Holy Spirit speaks through General Convention as it has in church councils throughout history," said Lilith Zoe Cole of Denver. She spoke against resolutions that asked the Episcopal Church to show restraint on consecrating gay bishops or blessing gay couples: "These resolutions represent a compromise of the power of the Holy Spirit."

"The actions of General Convention in 2003 swept down a mighty wall of oppression," said the Rev. Bradley Wirth of Troy, Montana. "Let us bless such actions of the Holy Spirit."

Liberals spoke of the Holy Spirit as constantly leading the church into new truth, with an eye toward a never-ending process of liberation. They also spoke of the Holy Spirit as inhabiting, or perhaps even causing, chaos in the church. "The Holy Spirit often works in moments of chaos," said Rev. Mark Beckwith of Worcester, Massachusetts, who is now among the nominees to become the next bishop of Newark.

Bishop Gene Robinson of New Hampshire, whose approval by the convention in 2003 generated significant chaos in the Anglican Communion, explained the Holy Spirit this way: "It's that part of God that refuses to be confined and contained in the little boxes we have for God."

Robinson was the preacher at a convention Eucharist (Communion) sponsored by the organization Integrity, which describes itself as "a witness of God's inclusive love to the Episcopal Church and the lesbian, gay, bisexual, and transgender community." Robinson's sermon, which included passionate calls for Integrity members to love their enemies, expressed liberal Episcopalians' commitment to the concept of continuing revelation.

"We hear God's calm and loving voice over the noisy din of the church's condemnation," Robinson said about gay and lesbian Episcopalians' decades-long persistence in church debates. "We don't worship a God who is all locked up in the Scripture of 2,000 years ago."

Robinson also quoted from gay author John Fortunato, who described his experience of a personal visit from God. In his book, *Embracing the Exile* (Harper and Row, 1982), Fortunato wrote that during the visit, "God smiled and said quietly, 'How can loving be wrong? All love comes from me.'"

The notion of continuing revelation is not limited to Integrity. Frank Griswold, who in November will complete his nine-year term as the church's 25th presiding bishop, has frequently suggested a foretaste of continuing revelation in Jesus' words at John 16:12-13: "I have much more to say to you, more than you can now bear. But when he, the Spirit of truth, comes, he will guide you into all truth. He will not speak on his own; he will speak only what he hears, and he will tell you what is yet to come" (NIV).

No prominent leader of liberal Episcopalians has yet observed how this notion of continuing revelation places the church in the theological company of the Church of Jesus Christ of Latter-day Saints.

Uncommon Prayer. More optimistic Episcopalians have argued that, whatever the church's theological conflicts, Episcopalians at least could gather around the Communion table and the poetic rites of the church's Book of Common Prayer. The stormy reception of Jefferts Schori's first sermon, however, suggests that Episcopalians' differences followed them straight into the exhibit hall set aside for the daily Eucharist.

The differences manifested not only in the language of the sermons given during those daily celebrations, but also in the varying reactions of participants to the published texts that accompanied the Eucharist. Congregations in the Episcopal Church's more liberal regions consider the opening words of the Eucharist patriarchal (and therefore oppressive) because of two words: *his* and *kingdom*. Most of the Eucharistic texts at the convention, consequently, reflected this assumption and relied on alternative rites authorized by previous conventions; when the texts reflected the more conservative 1979 Book of Common Prayer, however, many bishops and deputies simply ignored them.

The Rev. Lorne Coyle, a conservative priest from Vero Beach, Florida, explained the phenomenon in a message distributed across the Internet:

> *I told my group on day one that I would stay [with them] if they all agreed to abide by the order of worship as printed. I would abide by the language of the experimental liturgies if they would abide by the language of traditional liturgies. They did, and I did. But at the tables around me, when I heard the celebrant say, "Blessed be God: Father, Son, and Holy Spirit," and expected the normal response, "And blessed by his kingdom, now and for ever," I instead heard it changed into "And blessed be God's reign, now and for ever." Common prayer fled before politically correct prayer.*

Coyle also wrote that those who planned the convention's liturgies essentially restored the curse of Babel by trying to appease everyone present. "The morning Eucharists included Scripture read in Italian, Mandarin, Spanish and Navajo, among others. One day's sermon was entirely in Spanish. While an English translation was always included for those, the same was not true of a number of songs, some in Spanish, some in Chippewa, and so on. . . . I speak Spanish comfortably, but by using it in worship I found myself listening more to my pronunciation than to the Holy Spirit. The overall effect may have blessed some present, but it mostly served to emphasize our divisions, not our oneness in Christ."

The months ahead will offer early indications of whether there is still enough oneness in Christ to hold together a church with two minds.

SOURCE: Douglas LeBlanc. "Two Minds in One Episcopal Body." *Christian Research Journal* 29, no. 5 (2006): 6–8. Reprinted courtesy of Douglas LeBlanc and the Christian Research Institute (www.equip.org).

ANALYSIS

In Plato's *Republic*, Socrates proposes an examination of justice in the city in order to identify justice in the soul. Reversing the process, we can attempt to identify the culture war in a smaller organization—a Christian denomination—in order better to understand the culture war in the American society. Douglas LeBlanc comments on the precarious position of mainline churches generally, in which some members appear to be trying to accommodate their church's position on such issues as human sexuality to the trends within the wider society, while others are attempting to maintain their denomination's traditional stands on those issues. The disagreements involve differing interpretations of the importance of scripture in determining religious beliefs and mandating certain modes of behavior, especially in the realm of sexuality and claimed gender discrimination. Christian commentators such as LeBlanc tend to regard critically the attempts on the part of theological liberals to compromise the traditional teachings of the church. They consider conservatives as justified in their discontent and also justified in wishing to separate from the larger church body. These intra-denominational disagreements reflect the clashes over social issues, and hence the culture war, in the wider society.

Douglas LeBlanc's discussion of the Episcopal Church's 75th General Convention in 2006 presents a description of the divisions between the conservative and liberal factions within the Episcopal Church. The Episcopal Church historically has been the locus of dissent from traditional religious belief. For several decades differences over theology and the traditional beliefs of the church contributed to friction between conservatives and liberals. Such figures as bishops James Pike and John Shelby Spong have questioned some of the foundational beliefs of Christianity, including the virgin birth and resurrection of Jesus, and the concept of original sin. As a portent of things to come, in 1997 New York Bishop Paul Moore Jr. stirred

---

DID YOU KNOW?

Divisions in the Episcopal Church

In 2008 the cultural divide within the Episcopal Church continued to widen as congregations considered leaving the denomination. The Episcopal House of Bishops, meeting in March, voted to expel two bishops: John-David Schofield of the Diocese of San Joaquin, California, which had left the Episcopal Church because of the denomination's sexual policies, and retired Bishop William Cox, who had ordained two priests for the primate of Uganda. The question of ownership of church property, worth several million dollars, loomed large as the Diocese of San Joaquin left the Episcopal Church. In April, many of the members of the Church of the Good Shepherd, along with the Reverend Stan Gerber, left the Tomball, Texas, congregation and church property behind to establish a new church that would meet in a junior high school. The new congregation pondered the possibility of affiliating with the Anglican Mission in the Americas under the supervision of the Episcopal Province of Rwanda. In November 2008 the Episcopal Diocese of Fort Worth became the fourth diocese (the first three are the dioceses of Quincy, Illinois, San Joaquin—located in Fresno, California—and Pittsburgh, Pennsylvania) to leave the Episcopal Church. Each diocese initially joined the Anglican province of the Southern Cone, headquartered in Argentina.

---

controversy in the church by ordaining a lesbian woman. A serious division between liberals and conservatives began in 2003 when the Episcopal Diocese of New Hampshire elected V. Gene Robinson, an openly gay priest, as bishop. Later in the year, the clergy and lay deputies to the General Convention, despite the strong objections of conservatives, approved Robinson's elevation to the position of bishop. That action resulted in a crisis not only in the U.S. Episcopal Church, but in the worldwide Anglican Communion, in which many bishops especially from non-Western countries strongly opposed the selection of an openly gay bishop. At the 2006 General Convention delegates elected Katharine Jefferts Schori, who is generally associated with liberal positions, as presiding bishop. Conservatives, who emphasize the sacredness of scripture, object to the intention of liberals to introduce gender-neutral language in the liturgy (for instance, by eliminating the words "his" [referring to God] and "kingdom" from the opening words of the Eucharist) and to proclaim God's love for, and hence approval of, all people, including gay and lesbian church members. Jefferts Schori, recognizing the deep divisions within the church, commented that the denomination was not completely one but also not distinctly two. Observers of the Episcopal Church's internal disputes had to wonder whether the denomination would continue as one body or if it would remain a full member of the Anglican Communion.

"Bishop Gene Robinson Says He Was at Canterbury as a Witness: Know God, Acknowledge Gays, He Asked"

- **Document:** Solange De Santis reports from the 2008 Lambeth Conference of Anglican primates regarding the unofficial presence of V. Gene Robinson, the openly gay bishop of New Hampshire, whom the Archbishop of Canterbury did not invite to attend the conference.
- **Date:** September 2008.
- **Where:** *Episcopal Life*, an official publication of the Episcopal Church.
- **Significance:** Solange De Santis recounts the attempts of Episcopal Bishop of New Hampshire V. Gene Robinson, an unofficial attendee at the Lambeth Conference, to further the cause of gays and lesbians within the Anglican Communion.

DOCUMENT

Like Banquo's Ghost at Macbeth's dinner party, Diocese of New Hampshire Bishop Gene Robinson was perhaps the most prominent uninvited guest at the conference and, notwithstanding, a compelling factor.

Robinson, whose long-term same-gender relationship is a source of controversy in the Anglican world, said he was in Canterbury not to protest his exclusion. He was there, rather, "to witness to the joy I know in my life because I know God and [to] be a constant reminder to the conference that there are gay and lesbian people sitting in their pews in every country in every congregation around the world."

The meeting was in one sense defined by absence, as about 210 of the global Anglican Communion's 880 bishops voluntarily stayed away, many to protest the U.S. and Canada's openly liberal stance toward homosexuality.

Speaking at a news conference, Archbishop of Canterbury Rowan Williams explained that he did not invite Robinson because his participation was "questionable."

Robinson was permitted to be in the Lambeth marketplace (the display and sales area), and attend two receptions hosted by Episcopal church bishops that were intended to allow him to meet colleagues from around the world. He was invited to worship and speak at several other venues in the Canterbury area, including the University of Kent's law school, and wrote a blog, or Internet diary, called Canterbury Tales from the Fringe.

Sitting down for an interview several days before the conference ended, Robinson said he was surprised that "I felt the highs and lows as much as I did. I thought I was spiritually prepared, that I could shield myself from strong feelings, but being separated from my brothers and sisters [in the Episcopal Church House of Bishops] was infinitely more painful than I expected."

He was not allowed to attend his colleagues' Bible study, worship, discussion groups, study and plenary sessions. The emotions of exclusion, he said, "stirs up all of that rejection I felt as a kid, as a teenager, of not feeling a part of the guys."

Robinson said his Episcopal Church colleagues tried to keep in touch with him and let him know what was going on in their discussions about such varied topics as evangelism, interfaith relations and global poverty.

He said he longed to participate in the bishops' sessions on world social issues. "In the north country [of New Hampshire], the unemployment is sky high and alcohol out of control and the men are taking it out on their wives. It breaks my heart not to be part of those discussions," he said.

"Even in just the brief encounters I had with people, I was dying to hear more about this or that or the other in their dioceses."

The focus on sexuality meant that he was identified with only one issue. "You know how committed I am to [same-sex] issues, but when I go back, I don't want to talk about being gay for a month! I don't want it to come up," he said, smiling.

At the two receptions, held on the University of Kent campus where the conference took place, the program opened with a presentation on the process Episcopal Church dioceses use to elect bishops. Bishop Michael Curry of North Carolina spoke on why he consented to Robinson's consecration and Bishop Don Johnson of West Tennessee explained why he voted "no" at the 2003 General Convention.

The events also featured a short video from the people of New Hampshire who elected Robinson. "There were six continents represented, including some people there who took a risk in coming," Robinson said. The reference was to bishops who wanted to meet him, but were from countries where senior clerics have condemned his presence.

"I was moved by a couple of bishops from the Church of India, both north and south. They expressed quite clearly and forcefully that they just didn't get this, that their culture is in a different place than ours. There was no rancor and no judgment—there it is, the holy mess we are in. They thanked me," Robinson said.

The interfaith aspect of his presence is one area, he said, that he'd like to explore further. Bishops from areas where homosexuality is against the law or culturally unacceptable have said that interfaith relations and evangelism have become harder since he was consecrated in 2003.

Robinson said he didn't have an answer. "All I could say to the guy [at one of the receptions] was I am so, so sorry that this has made your life and your ministry harder. . . . But the answer is not for me to give up being who I am and it's not for the Episcopal Church to give up where it feels God is calling it. At the same [time] I would love to have had the opportunity to sit longer with him and just sort of be with one another in that dilemma. He wasn't asking me or us to stop doing what we were doing but it was important to him [for me] to hear how that complicated his life and ministry."

Robinson—who was interrupted by a heckler when he preached in London before the conference—was accompanied by a security guard and stayed at a rented house outside of Canterbury for much of the conference. Individuals, including members of Episcopal parishes, and a foundation donated funds to pay for his security, he said, adding that neither New Hampshire nor the Episcopal Church bore any costs.

He was able to worship each morning with an order of Franciscan brothers in Canterbury that invited him to visit. "In the mornings, I'm able to let go of the negative stuff—just give it to God," he said.

Among the conservative voices at the conference, the primate of the Episcopal Church of the Sudan, Archbishop Daniel Deng Bul, called for his resignation and Bishop Mouneer Anis, of Egypt, North Africa and the Horn of Africa, complained in a statement that "the revisionists . . . push upon us the view that current secular culture, not the Bible, should shape our mission and morals."

Robinson also said he was opposed to any proposed Anglican covenant "that has as its primary focus punishment for anyone who colors outside the lines. I don't see anything about reconciliation in it, but I understand there are people who are working to make it a covenant about theology and mission rather than discipline."

SOURCE: Solange De Santis. "Bishop Gene Robinson Says He Was at Canterbury as a Witness: Know God, Acknowledge Gays, He Asked." *Episcopal Life*, September 2008: 17. Reprinted courtesy of Solange De Santis.

ANALYSIS

Ever since V. Gene Robinson's elevation to the position of Episcopal bishop of New Hampshire, the Episcopal Church in the United States and the worldwide Anglican Communion have experienced deep divisions over the issue of homosexuality, including the ordination of homosexual priests and the blessing of same-gender marriages. Particularly bishops in other parts of the world reacted negatively to Robinson's selection as a bishop. Archbishop of Canterbury Rowan Williams, the titular head of the Anglican Union, worked to maintain unity within the church in the face of strong objections from the minority of conservatives within the Episcopal Church, conservative church leaders in the developing parts of the world,

DID YOU KNOW?

Changing Religious Affiliation

In February 2008 the Pew Forum on Religion and Public Life released the results of the U.S. Religious Landscape Survey which is based on interviews of more than 35,000 Americans. The survey provided basic information about religious affiliation in the United States. For instance, the survey indicated that more than 40 percent of Americans have changed their religious faith since childhood, that 40 percent of marriages involve couples with different religious traditions, that Protestants now compose little more than a majority (51 percent) of the population, and that 16 percent of Americans do not identify with a religion. The last figure is 24 percent for those between the ages of 18 and 29. Although nearly one-third of those raised as Roman Catholics have left the church, the percentage of Catholics has remained steady—at 24 percent—largely because of immigration, particularly from Latin America. Those identifying with a non-Christian religion remain a small proportion of the population—a little more than 3 percent. Researchers speculated that the trend toward changing religious affiliation suggests religious belief as an individual choice and may signal a trend toward greater tolerance of other faiths and possibly a lessening in the intensity of the culture wars.

and the wishes of liberal elements within the Episcopal Church who support a more welcoming policy toward gays and lesbians within the church. There appeared to develop an irresolvable division within the Anglican Union, with churches in western countries on one side and churches in underdeveloped areas of the world on the other. With the latter emphasizing the authority of scripture and the former focusing on the optimistic assumption that all ultimately can fit under the same church umbrella, the battle lines appeared drawn.

Climate Change: An Evangelical Call to Action

- **Document:** A statement on global warming endorsed by 86 evangelical Christian leaders (footnotes have been omitted).
- **Date:** February 8, 2006.
- **Where:** Washington, DC.
- **Significance:** This statement, signed by such prominent evangelical leaders as Rick Warren, pastor of Saddleback Church in Lake Forest, California, and Leith Anderson, former president of the National Association of Evangelicals, demonstrated the increasing concern of many evangelical leaders for issues that transcend such divisive topics as abortion and homosexuality. Responses from other leaders indicated that the evangelical movement did not present a united front on the changing public policy focus.

DOCUMENT

Preamble

As American evangelical Christian leaders, we recognize both our opportunity and our responsibility to offer a biblically based moral witness that can help shape public policy in the most powerful nation on earth, and therefore contribute to the well-being of the entire world. *Whether* we will enter the public square and offer our witness there is no longer an open question. We are in that square, and we will not withdraw.

We are proud of the evangelical community's long-standing commitment to the sanctity of human life. But we also offer moral witness in many venues and on many issues. Sometimes the issues that we have taken on, such as sex trafficking, genocide in the Sudan, and the AIDS epidemic in Africa, have surprised outside observers. While individuals and organizations can be called to concentrate on certain issues, we are not a single-issue movement. We seek to be true to our calling as Christian leaders, and above all faithful to Jesus Christ our Lord. Our attention, therefore, goes to whatever issues our faith requires us to address.

Over the last several years many of us have engaged in study, reflection, and prayer related to the issue of climate change (often called "global warming"). For most of us, until recently this has not been treated as a pressing issue or major priority. Indeed, many of us have required considerable convincing before becoming persuaded that climate change is a real problem and that it ought to matter to us as Christians. But now we have seen and heard enough to offer the following moral argument related to the matter of human-induced climate change. We commend the four simple but urgent claims offered in this document to all who will listen, beginning with our brothers and sisters in the Christian community, and urge all to take the appropriate actions that follow from them.

Claim 1: Human-Induced Climate Change Is Real

Since 1995 there has been general agreement among those in the scientific community most seriously engaged with this issue that climate change is happening and is being caused mainly by human activities, especially the burning of fossil fuels. Evidence gathered since 1995 has only strengthened this conclusion.

Because all religious/moral claims about climate change are relevant only if climate change is real and is mainly human-induced, everything hinges on the scientific data. As evangelicals we have hesitated to speak on this issue until we could be more certain of the science of climate change, but the signatories now believe that the evidence demands action:

- The Intergovernmental Panel on Climate Change (IPCC), the world's most authoritative body of scientists and policy experts on the issue of global warming, has been studying this issue since the late 1980s. (From 1988–2002 the IPCC's assessment of the climate science was Chaired by Sir John Houghton, a devout evangelical Christian). It has documented the steady rise in global temperatures over the last fifty years, projects that the average global temperature will continue to rise in the coming decades, and attributes "most of the warming" to human activities.

- The U.S. National Academy of Sciences, as well as all other G8 country scientific Academies (Great Britain, Germany, Japan, Canada, Italy, and Russia), has concurred with these judgments.

- In a 2004 report, and at the 2005 G8 summit, the Bush Administration has also acknowledged the reality of climate change and the likelihood that human activity is the cause of at least some of it.

In the face of the breadth and depth of this scientific and governmental concern, only a small percentage of which is noted here, we are convinced that evangelicals must engage this issue without any further lingering over the basic reality of the problem or humanity's responsibility to address it.

Claim 2: The Consequences of Climate Change Will Be Significant, and Will Hit the Poor the Hardest

The earth's natural systems are resilient but not infinitely so, and human civilizations are remarkably dependent on ecological stability and well-being. It is easy to forget this until that stability and well-being are threatened.

Even small rises in global temperatures will have such likely impacts as: sea level rise; more frequent heat waves, droughts, and extreme weather events such as torrential rains and floods; increased tropical diseases in now-temperate regions; and hurricanes that are more intense. It could lead to significant reduction in agricultural output, especially in poor countries. Low-lying regions, indeed entire islands, could find themselves under water. (This is not to mention the various negative impacts climate change could have on God's other creatures.)

Each of these impacts increases the likelihood of refugees from flooding or famine, violent conflicts, and international instability, which could lead to more security threats to our nation.

Poor nations and poor individuals have fewer resources available to cope with major challenges and threats. The consequences of global warming will therefore hit the poor the hardest, in part because those areas likely to be significantly affected first are in the poorest regions of the world. **Millions of people could die in this century because of climate change, most of them our poorest global neighbors.**

Claim 3: Christian Moral Convictions Demand Our Response to the Climate Change Problem

While we cannot here review the full range of relevant biblical convictions related to care of the creation, we emphasize the following points:

- Christians must care about climate change because we love God the Creator and Jesus our Lord, through whom and for whom the creation was made. This is God's world, and any damage that we do to God's world is an offense against God Himself (Gen. 1; Ps. 24; Col. 1:16).
- Christians must care about climate change because we are called to love our neighbors, to do unto others as we would have them do unto us, and to protect and care for the least of these as though each was Jesus Christ himself (Mt. 22:34–40; Mt. 7:12; Mt. 25:31–46).
- Christians, noting the fact that most of the climate change problem is human induced, are reminded that when God made humanity he commissioned us to exercise stewardship over the earth and its creatures. Climate change is the latest evidence of our failure to exercise proper stewardship, and constitutes a critical opportunity for us to do better (Gen. 1:26–28).

Love of God, love of neighbor, and the demands of stewardship are more than enough for evangelical Christians to respond to the climate change problem with moral passion and concrete action.

Claim 4: The Need to Act Now Is Urgent. Governments, Businesses, Churches, and Individuals All Have a Role to Play in Addressing Climate Change—Starting Now

The basic task for all the world's inhabitants is to find ways now to begin to reduce the carbon dioxide emissions from the burning of fossil fuels that are the primary cause of human-induced climate change.

There are several reasons for urgency. First, deadly impacts are being experienced now. Second, the oceans only warm slowly, creating a lag in experiencing the consequences. Much of the climate change to which we are already committed will not be realized for several decades. The consequences of the pollution we create now will be visited upon our children and grandchildren. Third, as individuals and as a society we are making long-term decisions today that will determine how much carbon dioxide we will emit in the future, such as whether to purchase energy efficient vehicles and appliances that will last for 10–20 years, or whether to build more coal-burning power plants that last for 50 years rather than investing more in energy efficiency and renewable energy.

In the United States, the most important immediate step that can be taken at the federal level is to pass and implement national legislation requiring sufficient economy-wide reductions in carbon dioxide emissions through cost-effective, market-based mechanisms such as a cap-and-trade program. On June 22, 2005 the Senate passed the Domenici-Bingaman resolution affirming this approach, and a number of major energy companies now acknowledge that this method is best both for the environment and for business.

We commend the Senators who have taken this stand and encourage them to fulfill their pledge. We also applaud the steps taken by such companies as BP, Shell, General Electric, Cinergy, Duke Energy, and DuPont, all of which have moved ahead of the pace of government action through innovative measures implemented within their companies in the U.S. and around the world. In so doing they have offered timely leadership.

Numerous positive actions to prevent and mitigate climate change are being implemented across our society by state and local governments, churches, smaller businesses, and individuals. These commendable efforts focus on such matters as energy efficiency, the use of renewable energy, low CO_2 emitting technologies, and the purchase of hybrid vehicles. These efforts can easily be shown to save money, save energy, reduce global warming pollution as well as air pollution that harm human health, and eventually pay for themselves. There is much more to be done, but these pioneers are already helping to show the way forward.

Finally, while we must reduce our global warming pollution to help mitigate the impacts of climate change, as a society and as individuals we must also help the poor adapt to the significant harm that global warming will cause.

Conclusion

We the undersigned pledge to act on the basis of the claims made in this document. We will not only teach the truths communicated here but also seek ways to implement the actions that follow from them. In the name of Jesus Christ our Lord, we urge all who read this declaration to join us in this effort.

[A list of 86 signatories follows.]

SOURCE: "The Evangelical Climate Initiative." http://christiansandclimate.org/learn/call-to-action. Reprinted courtesy of Jim Ball, president and CEO, Evangelical Environmental Network.

ANALYSIS

In the twentieth century, the evangelical movement in the United States traditionally expressed minimal concern for environmentalism. However, earlier in U.S. history, evangelicals tended to adhere to a postmillenialist viewpoint, the biblical interpretation that held that Jesus would return to earth following a 1,000-year Christian reign. Therefore, the reform efforts of Christians would help to bring about this era of peace and prosperity (Balmer 2007, 145). Partly in response to this emphasis on social reform, as well as a more liberal approach to Christian belief generally, evangelicals began to embrace an alternative interpretation of the end times, called premillenialism. Conditions in the world would continue to worsen until Jesus returned to establish his millenial reign. Therefore, concern for social reform became secondary to concentration on making ready for the second coming.

Although not altering their position on issues of personal morality such as abortion and sexual relations, a segment of the evangelical movement began to express support for assistance to the poor and efforts to ameliorate the claimed ill effects of human-caused climate change. The group of evangelicals who signed the Evangelical Climate Initiative present four basic claims: first, climate change is in fact occurring due to human activities, particularly the use of fossil fuels; second, the negative effects of climate change will be substantial, and will disadvantage the poor more heavily; third, Christian moral principles require that actions be taken in response to the problem; and fourth, governments, businesses, and religious organizations all have a role to play in dealing with this critical problem.

The statement represents a significant shift in perspective by some evangelical leaders that alters the traditional focus on individual salvation as well as on an economic system that emphasizes free enterprise and minimal government action. However, other evangelicals reacted strongly against this new approach, indicating differing religious understandings within this Christian group.

"An Open Letter to the Signers of 'Climate Change: An Evangelical Call to Action' and Others Concerned About Global Warming"

- *Document:* Excerpts from a statement from Cornwall Alliance for the Stewardship of Creation.
- *Date:* July 25, 2006.
- *Where:* Washington, DC.
- *Significance:* This document is a direct response to the Evangelical Climate Initiative and questions the claims that document made regarding the negative effects of human activity on global warming. In addition to disputing factual assertions about the cause and extent of global warming, the signers affirm the value of liberty and private property over any government action to manage the environment.

DOCUMENT

Widespread media reports tell of a scientific consensus that:

- the world is presently experiencing unprecedented global warming;
- the main cause of it is rising atmospheric carbon dioxide because of human use of fossil fuels for energy; and
- the consequences of continuing his pattern will include (1) rising sea levels that could inundate highly populated and often poor low-lying lands, (2) more frequent deadly heat waves, droughts, and other extreme weather events, (3) increased tropical diseases in warming temperate regions, and (4) more frequent and intense hurricanes.

Recently eighty-six evangelical pastors, college presidents, mission heads, and other leaders signed "Climate Change: An Evangelical Call to Action," under the auspices of the Evangelical Climate Initiative. The document calls on the federal government to pass national legislation requiring sufficient reductions in carbon dioxide emissions to fight global warming and argues that these are necessary to protect the poor from its harmful effects.

In light of all this, many people are puzzled by the Interfaith Stewardship Alliance's opposition to such calls. Do we not *care* about the prospect of catastrophic global warming? Do we not *care* that with rising temperatures the polar ice caps will melt, and the sea will inundate low island countries and coastal regions? Do we not *care* that the world's poor might be most hurt by these things?

Yes, we care. But we also believe, with economist Walter Williams, that "truly compassionate policy requires dispassionate analysis." That is the very motive for our opposing drastic steps to prevent global warming. In short, we have the same motive proclaimed by the Evangelical Climate Initiative in its "Call to Action."

But motive and reason are not the same thing. It matters little how well we mean, if what we do actually harms those we intend to help.

That is why we take the positions we do. In the accompanying document, **"A Call to Truth, Prudence, and Protection for the Poor: An Evangelical Response to Global Warming,"** we present extensive evidence and argument against the extent, the significance, and perhaps the existence of the much-touted scientific consensus on catastrophic human-induced global warming. Further, good science—like truth—is not about counting votes but about empirical evidence and valid arguments. Therefore we also present data, arguments, and sources favoring a different perspective:

- Foreseeable global warming will have moderate and mixed (not only harmful but also helpful), not catastrophic, consequences for humanity—including the poor—and the rest of the world's inhabitants.

- Natural causes may account for a large part, perhaps the majority, of the global warming in both the last thirty and the last one hundred fifty years, which together constitute an episode in the natural rising and falling cycles of global average temperature. Human emissions of carbon dioxide and other greenhouse gases are probably a minor and possibly an insignificant contributor to its causes.

- Reducing carbon dioxide emissions would have at most an insignificant impact on the quantity and duration of global warming and would not significantly reduce alleged harmful effects.

- Government-mandated carbon dioxide emissions reductions not only would not significantly curtail global warming or reduce its effects but also would cause greater harm than good to humanity—especially the poor—while offering virtually no benefit to the rest of the world's inhabitants.

- In light of all the above, the most prudent response is not to try (almost certainly unsuccessfully and at enormous cost) to prevent or reduce whatever slight warming might really occur. It is instead to prepare to adapt by fostering means that will effectively protect humanity—especially the poor—not only from whatever harms might be anticipated from global warming but also from harms that might be fostered by other types of catastrophes, natural or manmade.

We believe the harm caused by mandated reductions in energy consumption in the quixotic quest to reduce global warming will far exceed its benefits. Reducing energy consumption will require significantly increasing the costs of energy—whether through taxation or by restricting supplies. Because energy is a vital component in producing all goods and services people need, raising its costs means raising other prices, too. For wealthy people, this might require some adjustments in consumption patterns—inconvenient and disappointing, perhaps, but not devastating. But for the world's two billion or more poor people, who can barely afford sufficient food, clothing, and shelter to sustain life, and who are without electricity and the refrigeration, cooking, light, heat, and air conditioning it can provide, it can mean the difference between life and death.

Along with all the benefits we derive from economic use of energy, another consideration—a Biblical/theological one—points in the same direction. The stewardship God gave to human beings over the earth—to cultivate and guard the garden (Genesis 2:15) and to fill, subdue, and rule the whole earth (Genesis 1:28)—strongly suggests that caring for human needs is compatible with caring for the earth. As theologian Wayne Grudem put it, "It does not seem likely to me that God would set up the world to work in such a way that human beings would eventually destroy the earth by doing such ordinary and morally good and necessary things as breathing, building a fire to cook or keep warm, burning fuel to travel, or using energy for a refrigerator to preserve food."

Whether or not global warming is largely natural, (1) human efforts to stop it are largely futile; (2) whatever efforts we undertake to stem our small contributions to it would needlessly divert resources from much more beneficial uses; and (3) adaptation strategies for whatever slight warming does occur are much more sensible than costly but futile prevention strategies. Therefore, we believe it is far wiser to promote economic growth, partly through keeping energy inexpensive, than to fight against potential global warming and thus slow economic growth. And there is a side benefit, too: wealthier societies are better able and more willing to spend to protect and improve the natural environment than poorer societies. Our policy, therefore, is better not only for humanity but also for the rest of the planet.

We recognize that reasonable people can disagree with our understanding of the science and economics. But this is indeed our understanding.
[A list follows, updated June 11, 2007, that includes the names of 171 endorsers—including Michael Cromartie, vice president, Ethics and Public Policy Center; D. James Kennedy, senior minister, Coral Ridge Presbyterian Church; Tony Perkins, president, Family Research Council; David Ridenour, vice president, National Center for Public Policy Research, and Louis P. Sheldon, chairman, Traditional Values Coalition—of "A Call to Truth, Prudence, and Protection of the Poor: An Evangelical Response of Global Warming."]

SOURCE: "An Open Letter to the Signers of 'Climate Change: An Evangelical Call to Action' and Others Concerned about Global Warming." Reprinted courtesy of Cornwall Alliance for the Stewardship of Creation.

ANALYSIS

This document, as well as the Cornwall Declaration on Environmental Stewardship, issued in 1999, the result of a meeting of 25 conservative religious leaders in West Cornwall, Connecticut, respond to the beginnings of concern for the environment among evangelical Christians. The Cornwall Declaration refers to the "romanticism" of the ideal of the earth "untouched by human hands." Among the concerns the Declaration labels as unfounded are "destructive man-made global warming, overpopulation, and rampant species loss." The Declaration declares that the Judeo-Christian heritage includes the belief that human beings are "called to be fruitful, to bring forth good things from the earth" and affirms a beneficial relationship between stewardship of the earth and private property, which can best be obtained by allowing people's "natural incentive" to look after their own property and thus reduce the need for "collective ownership and control of resources and enterprises." Economic freedom, the foundation of privately owned market economies, supposedly allows for "sound ecological stewardship."

In March 2007 James Dobson, chairman of Focus on the Family and a major conservative religious figure, signed a letter along with two dozen other religious leaders that was addressed to L. Roy Taylor, chairman of the board of the National Association of Evangelicals (NAE). The letter criticized Richard Cizik, NAE vice president of government relations, for emphasizing the issue of global warming. The signers expressed concern that Cizik and others within the NAE were "using the global warming controversy to shift the emphasis away from the great moral issues of our time," including abortion, marriage, and sexual abstinence. Among the signers were Donald Wildmon, chairman of the American Family Association, Tony Perkins, president of the Family Research Council, Gary L. Bauer, president of Coalitions for America and erstwhile candidate for the Republican presidential nomination, and Paul Weyrich, chairman of American Values.

Three factors appear to underlie the strong reaction against some evangelical Christians focusing attention on environmental issues (particularly global warming) that place this controversy within the realm of the culture war. First, biblical interpretation of the role of human beings in creation and the ultimate fate of the world (whether Christians tend to adhere to a premillenial or postmillenial view of the end times) contributes to different understandings of a contemporary Christian's responsibility for environmental policy. Second, there is disagreement over what moral issues (whether more individualized ones such as sexual behavior and abortion, or more general responsibility to society, such as feeding the hungry, providing adequate health care, and assuring social justice) should receive significant attention. Finally, evangelicals tend to disagree over what role government should play in dealing with such social and environmental concerns. Does a commitment to economic freedom trump calls for government to deal with society-wide problems? As in other areas of disagreement, these three factors appear to influence the interpretation of empirical data used as evidence for human-caused global warming.

"Aikman, Berlinski, Day, and Lennox Versus Dawkins, Hitchens, Dennett, and Harris"

- **Document:** Article by David A. Noebel, director of the Christian Anti-Communism Crusade, in response to recent publications advocating atheism.
- **Date:** July 2008.
- **Where:** *The Schwarz Report* (Volume 48, Number 7).
- **Significance:** David A. Noebel reviews responses by Christian authors to recently published works of noted atheist writers, challenging the atheists' arguments against the existence of God.

DOCUMENT

The Delusion of Disbelief (David Aikman) [Carol Stream, IL: Tyndale House 2008]
The Devil's Delusion (David Berlinski) [New York: Crown Forum 2008]
The Irrational Atheist (Vox Day) [Dallas, TX: Benbella Books 2008]
God's Undertaker (John C. Lennox) [Oxford: Lion Publishing 2007]

Our 2008 Australian Summit [of the Christian Anti-Communism Crusade] was conducted in Melbourne at the Deakin University campus. The college bookstore was drenched in Richard Dawkins. His picture was everywhere, promoting his book *The God Delusion*. But nowhere to be found were any works challenging Dawkins' atheism, Darwinism, or humanism (but I repeat myself).

Dawkins teaches at Oxford University, but so does John C. Lennox. Alas, the bookstore had no interest in Lennox, only Dawkins! It wanted nothing to do with Lennox's scientific observation that "the fossil record gives no good examples of macroevolution" (Lennox, p. 110). Also not to be found was Berlinski's *The Devil's Delusion*, "the definitive book of the new millennium," according to George Gilder. And although there wasn't time to check over every book in that bookstore,

I seriously doubt one would find Stephen Hawking's scientific deduction that "it would be very difficult to explain why the universe should have begun in just this way, except as the act of a God who intended to create beings like us."

The evidence clearly shows that many of our institutions of higher learning are cesspools of atheism and hotbeds of radicalism, including sexual radicalism. It's as though we're reliving the pre-French and pre-Bolshevik revolutionary eras.

Prior to the French Revolution, atheism was rampant throughout the nation, along with the sexual radicalism of the Marquis de Sade, Mirabeau, Jean-Paul Marat, the Jacobins, and Robespierre, etc.

The same was true during the years preceding the 1917 Bolshevik Revolution. Communism was founded on the atheism and socialism of Marx and Lenin with Darwin's evolutionary theory thrown in for spice. Remember that it was Marx who wrote Engels saying, "During . . . the past four weeks I have read . . . Darwin's work on Natural Selection . . . this is the book which contains the basis in natural science for our view."

Now we are being assaulted with what is sometimes labeled "New Atheism." Paul Kurtz's Center for Inquiry, for example, is conducting a summer institute for young atheists entitled "The Journey From Religion to Science." One of their course descriptions reads, "Contemporary issues in secular studies; multisecularism, desecularization and the 'new atheism.'"

In reality, however, there are no new arguments for atheism. Unless "new atheism" means "new atheists," it's a misnomer. The arguments that the French and Communist atheists had in their quiver generations ago are the very same arguments Dawkins, Hitchens, Dennett, and Harris (DHDH) have in their quiver. It seems each generation is called upon to face the same issues, and the question of God's existence is a perennial. It wasn't too long ago that Richard Bentley (1662–1742) was invited to give the first Boyle Lectures on Natural Theology. His lectures were entitled "Confutation of Atheism from the Origin and Frame of the World."

Because we, too, must face the issue of atheism head-on, let me recommend the four books listed at the top of this article by Aikman, Berlinski, Day, and Lennox (ABDL). These authors handle all the major arguments, accusations, and assertions of the new atheist crowd. Indeed, it's as if we have two law firms bidding for the hearts and minds of this generation. And so they are because ideas have consequences. Theism and atheism have consequences.

Let's begin with David Aikman, who summarizes the case against these famous four theologians of atheism. Analyzing their writings, he says their errors fall nicely into three major categories: (1) their assertions are too wild to be taken seriously (e.g., "religion poisons everything," "better many worlds than one god," or "Christianity is child abuse."); (2) they stray into unfamiliar territory (biblical studies, theology, philosophy) and prove they are wading in way over their heads (e.g., "Jesus was born in 4 A.D."); and (3) their view that somehow science invalidates religious truth is far from historically true and certainly not scientifically true since religion birthed science (see Berlinski, p. 46). Berlinski goes so far as to state that the faith necessary to do coherent scientific work is debauched by a complacent atheism.

So let's be blunt for a moment. For all the hype given over to the atheists' charges, claims, pronouncements, and fairy tales, I can't think of one thing that Dawkins, Hitchens, Dennett, or Harris preaches that isn't answered in a scholarly, even "fair and balanced" manner, by Aikman, Berlinski, Day, and Lennox. No Christian need be embarrassed by the avalanche of atheistic propaganda, believing that their arguments are really too profound and powerful to challenge. ABDL challenges every one of them with reason, logic, science, common sense, and yes, a sense of humor, too.

Atheists, by the way, seem to lack a sense of humor (although Hitchens has far more than the others combined). Case in point: Harris wants to put to death those he considers truly harmful to society (Aikman, p. 32). I'll let his words speak for him: "The link between belief and behavior raises the stakes considerably. Some propositions are so dangerous that it may be ethical to kill people for believing them. This may seem an extraordinary claim, but it merely enunciates an ordinary fact about the world in which we live" (*The End of Faith*, p. 52).

And these are our modern-day tolerant atheists! Can you imagine if they were the Communist variety that slaughtered millions (see *The Black Book of Communism* by [Stéphane] Courtois). Even one of their own, Theodore Dalrymple, remarks that Harris' statement is "quite possibly the most disgraceful that I have read in a book by a man posing as a rationalist" (*City Journal*, Autumn 2007). Surely the "new atheists" have lost touch with reality.

Hitchens was probably not trying to be funny when he remarked, "We do not rely solely upon science and reason because these are necessary rather than sufficient factors." Berlinski's response is facetious, yet utterly reasonable—"If Hitchens is not prepared to 'rely solely upon science and reason,' why, one might ask, should anyone else?" (Berlinski, p. 5). Hitchens also reasons (in all seriousness) that his belief in the nonexistence of God is not a belief, but my belief in the existence of God is a belief. Go figure!

A question worth asking is this: What triggered such a sudden onslaught of hardcore, mean-spirited, atheistic propaganda? Why now?

Some suggest that perhaps it was George [W.] Bush and his administration that riled up the godless with his evangelical Christianity clearly on display. I personally think the answer is much closer to the atheist camp itself. One of their very own (and not just one of their lightweights) decided after looking at the scientific evidence that atheism is untenable, indefensible, and yes, false! The gang of four (DHDH) decided that such a gap in their Secular Humanist worldview armor needed to be plugged, and since Antony Flew is a heavyweight, so, too, the humanists had to call their remaining heavyweights to arms. Hence, this massive flood of atheist books and TV appearances, college lectures, and radio call-in programs.

DHDH could not stand back and fail to challenge Dr. Flew's admission that it was his study of science and philosophy, not theology and evangelism, that actually led him out of atheism. In his book *There Is A God* (also highly recommended), Flew begins with his early life as an atheist, explaining his reasons why God could not exist, and then moves to his later life and why he changed his mind. He now concludes that indeed there has to be a God, or there would be no universe. Sound like Genesis 1?

Since the flurry over Flew's conversion to deism, a bit of calm has descended and a lot of research and writing has commenced. The authors answering the four purveyors of atheism are handing them their heads on a platter! Regretfully, atheist heads on platters is not graphic enough for coverage on the evening news.

Any fair-minded readers of Aikman, Berlinski, Day, and Lennox will recognize that the atheists' thrusts and daggers have been brilliantly and convincingly defeated.

Berlinski and Lennox, for example, take on the atheistic notion that somehow science proves the nonexistence of God. After examining the scientific method and its various ramifications, Berlinski concludes that he has yet to see how science disproves the existence of God. He notes that physicists seem "remarkably unenthusiastic about welcoming philosophers as fellow scientists" (Berlinski, p. 58). Richard Feynman observes, "The philosophers are always on the outside making stupid remarks." Saying that science somehow proves the nonexistence of God is a stupid remark! Another stupid remark is Dawkins' theological/philosophical claim that "Better many worlds than one god." Equally stupid is his "many worlds" or multiverse theory of not one universe but an infinite number of parallel universes. Such "science so-called" or better, "scientism," is merely Dawkins' atheism and materialism coming to the fore. There is absolutely no scientific evidence for a multiverse, but it seems to be the atheists' last stronghold, even though it puts Occam's razor on its head!

Berlinski's comments about "faith" and "science" are also worth examining. He quotes Stephen Hawking to the effect that "so long as the universe had a beginning, we could suppose it had a creator." It takes faith to accept the proposition that science has discovered a beginning to the universe. In fact, it takes faith in reason to even reason logically about it. Vox Day points out that faith is not the opposite of reason; the opposite of reason is irrationalism.

Berlinski contends (p. xii, xiii) that there have been four profound scientific theories since the great scientific revolution in the West—Newtonian mechanics, electro-magnetic field theory, special and general relativity, and quantum mechanics—and none disproves the existence of God. Stated another way, none proves the atheist claim that science has buried God (note the title of Lennox's book). Einstein said it like this, "Science without religion is lame, religion without science is blind." Dawkins, who constantly claims Einstein as one of his own atheistic brothers, should listen to his scientific superior. (Incidentally, Einstein repeatedly stated, "I'm not an atheist." See Max Jammer, *Einstein and Religion*, p. 48).

Berlinski insists that "no scientific theory touches on the mysteries that the religious tradition addresses" (p. xiv). In fact, he says science has "nothing of value to say on the great and aching questions of life, death, love, and meaning." On the other hand, the religious tradition "has formed a coherent body of thought regarding these subjects" (p. xiv). Berlinski further notes, "Science does not harbor the slightest idea of how the ordered physical, moral, mental, aesthetic, social world in which we live could have ever arisen from the seething anarchy of the world of particle physics."

Aikman, Lennox, and Day do not in any way disagree with Berlinski, but rather add to his basic arguments. Day, for example, addresses in some detail the charge that religion is an enemy of science. He proves why the charge is false and quotes from

Feynman to the effect that "[s]cientific knowledge is an enabling power to do either good or bad—but does not carry instruction on how to use it" (Day, p. 52).

Both Aikman and Day cover the area of atheism's practical outworkings in society. And their examples do not edify the atheist cause. For example, few atheists wish to discuss the relationship of Darwin to Hitler or atheism's role in the former U.S.S.R. Day quotes Lenin and Trotsky to the effect that "atheism is a material and inseparable part of Marxism" and the "very essence of religion is the mortal enemy of Communism" (Day, p. 243).

Day's chapter entitled "The Robespierre of Atheism" is an insightful look at Michel Onfray, the French atheist and hedonist and far-left Nietzschean. Nietzsche, of course, was not only an atheist and nihilist (life has no meaning), but also a warmonger. His famous statement on war: "War is an admirable remedy for peoples that are growing weak and comfortable and contemptible; it excites instincts that rot away in peace." Not surprising, Onfray, although a historian, has nothing to say of the "fifty-two atheist mass murderers of the twentieth century" (Day, p. 202). But he has plenty of nasty things to say about the American Secular Humanists for accepting way too much of the Judeo-Christian morality (e.g., Paul Kurtz says he can accept the Golden Rule in spite of its religious connotations). Onfray, however, would banish Christian morality on the basis that "it is anti-social." Translation: It is anti-Darwin's natural selection/survival of the fittest. Christian morality coddles the weak, the sick, and the helpless instead of allowing them to die (or even assisting in their death), thus enhancing the evolutionary process.

Day's chapter entitled "The End of Sam Harris" is worth the price of the book. He especially takes Harris to the woodshed for his statement that "some propositions are so dangerous that it may be ethical to kill people for believing them" (Day, p. 129).

John C. Lennox's powerful defense of the Christian perspective will be hard to dismiss by any atheist. His overall thrust is to prove that theism as a worldview "sits most comfortably with science." His argument is that the scientific evidence moves toward theism, exactly opposite the argument of Dawkins, Hitchens, Dennett, and Harris.

In fact, Lennox points to immunologist George Klein, who "states categorically that his atheism is not based on science, but is an a priori faith commitment" (Lennox, p. 34). Statements like this are bad news for the fearsome foursome of DHDH! Lennox also points to former atheist Antony Flew, who admits that his "whole life has been guided by the principle of Plato's Socrates [to] follow the evidence wherever it leads." Following the evidence led him to remove himself from the atheist camp (Lennox, p. 38).

Much of Lennox's book covers the issue that "the genetic material DNA carries information" (Lennox, p. 54). Read it to be fully informed on why the existence of "information" spells death to the forces of DHDH. (Hint: Information is a form of language, and language implies a speaker or an author.)

I now return to David Aikman, whose chapter entitled "The Christian World-view Is the Foundation of Liberty" is priceless. Aikman begins by quoting Michael Novak: "Can an atheist be a good citizen? That has been done, many times. Can American liberties survive if most of our nation is atheist? The most common, almost universal judgment of the founders was that it could not" (Aikman, p. 135).

Aikman moves to answer more fully the question of the survivability of freedom under the atheistic worldview. He comes to the founding fathers' conclusion, but offers his analysis in a most interesting way. In fact, Aikman quotes Hitchens, one of the fearsome foursome, to the effect that "secular totalitarianism has actually provided us with the summa of human evil" (p. 98). However, this same Hitchens concludes the founding fathers were not "men of faith" because "almost to a man, none had a priest at his deathbed" (Aikman, p. 137). Aikman replies tongue-in-cheek, "Dying Protestants don't make a habit of calling on priests to attend their departure from this life."

Aikman's comments on Thomas Paine are also worth noting. Though Paine was one of the very few true Deists (most of the founding fathers were either Christian or Unitarian), when he returned to Paris following the American Revolution he went there to "fight against atheism." Paine fought against atheism because he held the atheists of the French Revolution era "responsible for the massacres" (Aikman, p. 141).

Aikman also quotes John Adams' (a Unitarian) answer to the French atheist Condorcet, who was arguing for morality without religion: "There is no such thing [as morality] without the supposition of God. There is no right and wrong in the universe without the supposition of a moral government and an intellectual and moral governor" (Aikman, p. 152).

Not one of the fearsome foursome comes close to challenging Aikman's argument that the founding fathers were in no way establishing an atheistic commonwealth. All of America's founding documents were theistic in one way or another. Thomas Jefferson said, "God who gave us life gave us liberty. Can the liberties of a nation be secure when we have removed a conviction that these liberties are the gift of God?" Our founding fathers knew that atheism could not be the foundation of a free, democratic republic. Dozens of their statements prove this point.

Aikman finds it significant that after atheistic Communist regimes have historically "wreaked suffering and chaos" on a national basis, "it is the secular rationalism of the atheist worldview that is being challenged." In China, most Chinese have lost faith in Marxism-Leninism, sensing that Marxist philosophy is chained to "the iron ball of state atheism, [which] has left it in a moral wasteland" (Aikman, p. 167).

Let me conclude by examining the observations of a former atheist—Sir Fred Hoyle (who, incidentally, was skeptical about Darwin's theory of evolution). Hoyle understood that for life to exist on earth, lots of carbon (C and atomic number 6) is needed. He understood how carbon was formed (combining three helium nuclei or combining helium and beryllium). He also understood that for any of this to happen "the nuclear ground state energy levels have to be fine-tuned with respect to each other" (Lennox, p. 69). If the variation were more than 1 percent either way, the universe could not sustain life. Hoyle says nothing challenged his atheism more than "this scientific discovery." This scientific discovery could well be the Achilles heel ("a small but mortal weakness") of the atheists, and it appears to have all of them reeling in their more quiet moments.

Physicist Freeman Dyson sees it nearly the same way: "The more I examine the universe and study the details of its architecture, the more evidence I find that the universe in some sense must have known that we were coming." Paul Davies likewise concludes, "It seems as though somebody has fine-tuned nature's numbers to make the Universe." Or John A. Wheeler, "Imagine a universe in which one or another of the fundamental dimensionless constants of physics is altered by a few percent one way or the other? Man could never come into being in such a universe." (See also Hugh Ross, *Creation as Science*, p. 96 for additional examples of a finely tuned universe, Martin Rees, *Just Six Numbers*, or even Stephen Hawking, who, in his *A Brief History of Time* insisted that the finely tuned numbers cannot be altered to any degree or the universe collapses.)

Let's hope and pray that DHDH will reach the same conclusion. Let's pray earnestly that they cease and desist their atheistic propaganda machine that weakens Western Civilization's attempt to survive the current onslaught of Islam in its westward march, convinced that the time is right to demolish the decadent "Christian" West. As George Gilder says, "A culture that does not aspire to the divine becomes obsessed with the fascination of evil, reveling in the frivolous, the depraved, and the bestial." (See Gilder's review of *The Devil's Delusion* in *National Review*, May 5, 2008, p. 58.)

Indeed, let's pray for a revitalized and rededicated evangelical Christianity (for a start read Dinesh D'Souza's *What's So Great About Christianity* and Ed Hindson/Ergun Caner's *The Popular Encyclopedia of Apologetics: Surveying the Evidence for the Truth of Christianity*) that can again be the "salt of the earth" and the "light of the world," reflecting its founder and Master—Jesus Christ. Thus ends the homily!

SOURCE: David A. Noebel. "Aikman, Berlinski, Day, and Lennox Versus Dawkins, Hitchens, Dennett, and Harris." *The Schwartz Report* 48 (July 2008): 1–5. Reprinted courtesy of David Noebel.

ANALYSIS

The aggressive arguments of the four well-known atheists to which Noebel refers initiated renewed argumentation between believers and nonbelievers. The responses to these atheist manifestos tend to refer to scientific and philosophical understandings rather than directly to potential political implications, such as the teaching of the theory of evolution in the public schools, abortion, global warming, sex education, and embryonic stem cell research. Nonetheless, these arguments lie at the base of such policies, helping to defend, or to attack, particular positions.

DID YOU KNOW?

Pledge of Allegiance

Francis Bellamy wrote the pledge of allegiance in 1892 and published it in a children's magazine. Congress officially adopted the pledge in 1942. Twelve years later Congress added the words "under God" to the pledge, which became the focus of a legal controversy beginning in 2002 when Michael Newdow, an atheist, brought suit against the Elk Grove Unified School District in Elk Grove, California, arguing that he objected to his daughter having to recite the pledge of allegiance in violation of the establishment clause of the First Amendment of the U.S. Constitution. Since its first appearance, the pledge has become a fundamental part of early education and thus an emotional part of the American identity. Many in government and the general public declared their support for the pledge against what was often considered an unpatriotic attack on a symbol of America. The U.S. Supreme Court agreed to hear the case, and in its unanimous decision (with Justice Antonin Scalia not participating) ruled that Newdow had no right to speak for his daughter because he had never married the mother and thus lacked legal custody. Therefore, the Court sidestepped the question of the constitutionality of the pledge (although Chief Justice William Rehnquist and Justices Sandra Day O'Connor and Clarence Thomas would have found the pledge constitutional). The pledge controversy represents an issue intimately related to the culture wars, with one side challenging the use of the pledge and the other—undoubtedly a large majority of Americans—supporting the pledge as an expression of support for the nation.

It is doubtful that the discussions presented by the four authors that Noebel reviews and finds so compelling would persuade any of the atheist writers to whom they are responding. Scientists would likely agree with Noebel that science cannot prove the nonexistence of God; however, they would be quick to point out that science also cannot prove the positive claim that God exists. Such claims transcend the capabilities of science. Mainstream scientists, for instance, express strong skepticism about so-called Intelligent Design theory as an alternative to the theory of evolution at least in part because it purports to introduce a divine cause to the development of the universe and the occurrence of life on earth. The positions expressed by defenders of Christianity perhaps at best leave the situation as is, but do provide religious believers with arguments to support their stands on public policy issues closely related to the so-called culture war. Hence the differing sides of this debate largely speak to those already committed to their side.

"All Ye Unfaithful"

- *Document:* Opinion piece by Ronald Aronson expressing criticism of both Democrats and Republicans for continuing to introduce religion into the 2008 presidential campaign.
- *Date:* October 27, 2008.
- *Where:* *The Nation.*
- *Significance:* Ronald Aronson responds to the overtures that Democrats have made to the more religious segments of the U.S. population in order to attract electoral support. Aronson argues that secularists deserve to receive greater recognition from the Democratic Party, especially given the claimed influence of the religious right in the George W. Bush administration. No option except a secularization of U.S. politics appears acceptable to Aronson, and hence, unlike mainstream Democrats, who are willing to welcome a certain level of religiosity, he is willing to continue the cultural conflict over the place of religion in public life.

DOCUMENT

As the fading Bush presidency is being greeted with indifference or rolling eyes, one might expect eight years of faith in the White House to have discredited religion in the public square for years to come. But after a generation of the religious right, America is not yet ready to move on to a sensible public understanding of religion. The electrifying arrival of [2008 Republican vice-presidential nominee] Sarah Palin on the national scene demonstrates the continuing vigor of conservative Christianity and the political power of religiosity.

What about the Democrats' approach? In their hands this troubling trend may be softer and sweeter, but there is great danger that religion will continue to invade public life in unacceptable ways. It's not just that Democrats are courting the evangelical vote; they are treating secularists as if they are invisible and have acquiesced to the twenty-first-century "religious test" for public office. They seem blithely willing to undermine our constitutional commitment to the separation of church and state.

In his 2006 speech "Call to Renewal" Barack Obama struck an ambiguous chord, paying homage to the separation of church and state while insisting that religion must not be left "at the door before entering into the public square." He set out what seemed to be a reassuringly sophisticated path for bringing religion into politics:

"Democracy demands that the religiously motivated translate their concerns into universal, rather than religion-specific, values. It requires that their proposals be subject to argument, and amenable to reason. I may be opposed to abortion for religious reasons, but if I seek to pass a law banning the practice, I cannot simply point to the teachings of my church or evoke God's will. I have to explain why abortion violates some principle that is accessible to people of all faiths, including those with no faith at all."

Obama's universalism offered a potentially profound and sensitive vision of community and unity based on acknowledging rather than suppressing differences. The vision drew its energy from his evident capacity to feel empathy and from his demand that we see the world through other people's eyes.

As the presidential campaign unfolds, however, something very different is happening. The Democrats have conducted a highly organized and many-sided effort to attract evangelical and Catholic voters, based on the political arithmetic that even a small increase in their share of that vote may be enough to defeat the Republicans. . . . This strategy entails much more than marketing or pandering. It has encouraged the coming out of many Democrats who are religious and an embrace of a new kind of diversity among others who are not. It is creating openings for the progressive religious political breed long championed by Jim Wallis, the evangelical activist and editor of *Sojourners Magazine* who ran faith-and-politics workshops at the Democratic National Convention in Denver.

As Amy Sullivan points out in her book *The Party Faithful*, Democrats have been learning to respect and appeal to the devout. They are discovering that making religious voters feel welcome means making their faith part of the conversation, bringing their concerns into the formulation of public policy and even accepting their ways of judging candidates. Not only that—progressive evangelicals have worked to show that the environment, poverty and war are values issues, demanding the attention of those guided by religious morality.

None of this should be troubling, except that it is carried out in a way that leaves in the cold America's largest minority, out-and-out secularists, and the even larger number of secular believers who stand by Jefferson's "wall of separation" between church and state. Secular humanists, derided by Republicans and the religious right for the past eight years, are confronting a new consensus-in-the-making. This includes:

§ an informal but clear religious test for public office, to which Obama and John McCain submitted when they were cross-examined by mega-church pastor

Rick Warren at his Saddleback Church. Each had to answer questions about personal as well as political beliefs: "What does it mean to you to trust in Christ? And what does that mean to you on a daily basis? What does that really look like?"

§ widespread social pressure to believe, based on the pervasive myth that "nearly all Americans" do. This was hammered home repeatedly by Leah Daughtry, [Democratic National Committee chairman] Howard Dean's chief of staff and the CEO of the Denver [Democratic national] convention, who explained the religious events there by saying, "Democrats have been, are and will continue to be people of faith." Of course, this leaves out atheists, agnostics, humanists, skeptics and freethinkers, people of no religion and many deists and spiritualists.

§ ever more frequent references to God, faith and religion in public life. In a Labor Day speech in Detroit shortened to nine minutes because of Hurricane Gustav, Obama mentioned God and prayer no fewer than six times, including leading the audience in silent prayer for those in possible danger [from the hurricane].

§ treating secularists as invisible. Obama, who once seemed keenly respectful of them, appears to have forgotten they exist. On Labor Day, he did not say, "For those threatened by Gustav, let's have a moment of silence, whether in prayer or meditation." Planning the Denver interfaith events, Daughtry ignored the Secular Coalition for America's request to participate.

DID YOU KNOW?

Judge Roy Moore and the Ten Commandments

The First Amendment establishment clause and the doctrine of separation of church and state came to the forefront in national politics when on the night of July 31, 2001, Judge Roy Moore, the elected chief justice of the Alabama state supreme court, had a 2 1/2-ton granite monument inscribed with the Ten Commandments and other sayings making reference to God and the Bible installed in the rotunda of the court building in Montgomery. Various organizations, including the Southern Poverty Law Center, sued to have the monument removed. In November 2002 U.S. District Judge Myron Thompson ruled that the monument must be removed. Moore appealed the decision, but in June 2003 the 11th U.S. Circuit Court of Appeals upheld the original ruling ordering the removal of the monument. Moore appealed the case to the U.S. Supreme Court, but the justices declined to hear the case. Claiming that God is the basis of American law and government and that he could not violate his conscience, Moore still refused to comply with the court order and the monument attracted thousands of supporters, including conservative leaders James Dobson, Jerry Falwell, and Alan Keys. Because Moore refused to comply with the law, Alabama's Court of the Judiciary on November 13, 2003, decided unanimously to remove the judge from office. All attempts to overturn the decision failed. If Moore expected his actions to help him politically, he miscalculated. In 2006 Moore ran for governor against incumbent Bob Riley, but lost by a 2-to-1 margin.

Paradoxically, in certain ways this new dispensation reflects the fact that the country has become more tolerant. Seventy percent of Americans believe that there are many different paths to salvation. Former doctrinal antagonisms have dissolved into a multi-denominational religiosity that declares that the specifics of one's faith no longer matter—as long as one believes in God. Talking to Larry King after Saddleback, Warren said he could vote for someone of a different faith, but not an atheist. He proclaimed his tolerance while revealing his bigotry.

No less paradoxical, Obama proclaimed his expertise as a constitutional scholar when announcing a "faith-based initiative" that undermines the spirit if not the letter of the Supreme Court's "Lemon test," which requires that laws must not advance religion and "must not foster 'an excessive government entanglement with religion.'" How will Obama's proposed "Council for Faith-Based and Neighborhood Partnerships" choose among competing religious organizations applying for funding, some of which are very large and powerful and some of which are local storefronts?

And how will he guarantee an end to discrimination and eliminate proselytizing when these have long been features of many faith-based social service agencies? In trying to capitalize on the perceived popularity of faith-based programs, Obama has clearly chosen to ignore the fact that two-to-one majorities recently indicated a preference for government agencies and nonreligious organizations, rather than religious ones, to provide services for the needy.

It may appear odd that Obama and the Democrats are so unconcerned about the dangers of welcoming religion into the public square after so many years of religious-right influence, capped by eight years of Bush and the current Supreme Court. Perhaps it's because they take no notice of the broad community of secularists and believers who strongly support our secular Constitution.

These two streams add up to at least half of all Democratic voters, but Jacques Berlinerblau, who blogs at The God Vote, explains that Obama and other Democrats have concluded that secularists can be safely ignored. Democrats "did the math around 2005 and figured out that the vaunted 'secular base' was underperforming." Berlinerblau sees American secularism's two parts as "organizationally impotent and incapable of forging a meaningful alliance."

A striking indication of this disarray is the lack of any grassroots backlash after years of political attacks on secular humanism, public displays of religiosity, bans on gay marriage and stem-cell research, restrictions on abortion, the promoting of creationism and the campaign to appoint judges who favor weakening the separation of church and state. As a result, Berlinerblau writes, "if there was ever a constituency [Obama] could stomp on while moving to The Center, this may be the one."

Unless religious and irreligious secularists overcome their disarray, find their voices and become a political force, there seems to be little chance that Obama's once inspiring call to find common ground will be any more than words, a cover for him to create common ground with those he needs in order to become president and maintain power.

But how will secularists become mobilized? As a group they share no easily discernible characteristics: they cannot be recognized by such markers as color, gender, class or ethnicity, and while they may be more demographically concentrated in some places—in coastal and Northern cities, for example—they certainly cannot be found according to workplace or neighborhood. In short, unless they go out of their way to proclaim themselves, the irreligious dispersed across America are unable to see themselves as a "we." Although the Secular Coalition for America calculates from a Harris Interactive Survey that there are more than 60 million US atheists and agnostics, this brave lobby's constituent organizations can claim no more than 100,000 members. Why this shocking discrepancy?

Obviously one reason is that nonbelievers have long been one of the most despised groups in America. Another lies in the fact that secularists may be among the last Americans who consider their beliefs private. Unlike churchgoers, their beliefs, usually arrived at individually, require no organizational expression, so they do not easily become part of a structured community.

Secularists are often quite political but not often on behalf of their secularism; other issues seem far more urgent. Why make a big deal about church-state issues when we need to combat war, poverty and global warming? It is hard to feel very motivated about being ignored, given the pressing need to end Republican rule. And can't the constitutional issues get handled by contributing to lobbies, foundations and legal defense organizations rather than by joining and participating in mass organizations?

A no less stubborn problem is the difficulty nonbelievers have in making common cause with secular believers over issues pertaining to religion. We know from experience that secular and religious people work together on peace, justice and environmental issues but usually without discussing their underlying beliefs. We have all experienced the perils of such conversations, especially because of the profound difference between being guided by faith as opposed to science and reason. Each side has enormous difficulty understanding and respecting the other.

The current religious climate poses new dangers but also new possibilities that may rouse secular America. A Republican victory will keep alive, and possibly even worsen, the in-your-face religiosity of the Bush years. But a Democratic victory will not crush the religious right, and it cannot eliminate [Antonin] Scalia, [Clarence] Thomas, [Samuel] Alito and [John] Roberts from the Supreme Court.

Yet the release of Larry Charles and Bill Maher's film *Religulous*, and the recent presence of six books on the bestseller list advocating atheism or attacking religion, suggests that a sizable number of people are sick of public religiosity. The election of either party may generate the urge for nonbelievers to "out" themselves. Imagine that a significant fraction of atheists, agnostics, secular humanists and skeptics overcame their inhibitions and made themselves seen and heard. Imagine that large numbers connected with one another organizationally in ways that multiplied their overall visibility and political heft. Fed-up secularists might become political about their concerns and figure out how to work with the openly religious. Women, blacks and gays were not invited to enter the public conversation—they *made* themselves part of it. And secularists? Who is to say that at the next Democratic National Convention a secular caucus might not suddenly appear, demanding its place alongside the thirteen other caucuses that were a part of the 2008 convention? What would happen if secularists were visible, recognized and speaking out in their own voice?

SOURCE: Ronald Aronson. "All Ye Unfaithful: Atheists, Agnostics and Secularists Could Be a Powerful Force. They Just Need to Get Organized." *The Nation*, October 27, 2008: 52–53. Reprinted with permission from *The Nation*. For subscription information, call 1-800-333-8536. Portions of each week's *Nation* magazine can be accessed at www.thenation.com.

ANALYSIS

Although significant majorities in attitude surveys express a belief in God, contemporary U.S. society can be considered fundamentally secular. In recent decades, Thomas Jefferson's notion of a "wall of separation" between religion and the state has gained increasing support. However, religious groups still exercise a great deal

DID YOU KNOW?

Antony Flew: From Atheist to Theist

Although several noted atheists—including Richard Dawkins, Sam Harris, and Christopher Hitchens—have published books recently supporting their position and criticizing belief in God, one atheist, Antony Flew, in 2004 announced that he has been persuaded of the existence of God. For many years Flew, the son of an English Methodist minister but nonetheless a lifelong atheist, engaged in public debates with theologians and pastors, defending his atheist position and attacking theological claims. In 2007 Flew published *There Is a God: How the World's Most Notorious Atheist Changed His Mind* in which he presents reasons for his new conclusions. For instance, Flew argues that the fact that the universe exists at all, that nature follows precise mathematical laws, and that life and the mind developed from dead matter lead to the conclusion that there is a deity. Some speculate that the aggressive arguments of contemporary atheists also may have played a part in Flew's change of mind. Although Flew does not advocate any particular religious beliefs and asserts that he does not accept the idea of an afterlife, his change of mind represents something to be explained away by atheists and perhaps embraced by Christians in a culture war over religious belief.

of influence in electoral politics, government decision making, and various other areas of public engagement. As a measure of the influence that religious groups have in the political process, the Democratic Party has in recent years expressed a greater sensitivity to appealing to more religious voters. Ronald Aronson expresses his distress with the willingness of Democratic Party candidates to accept a major role for religion in American politics. Aronson calls for nonbelievers to make themselves heard in the public realm. Although Democratic politicians appear to be attempting to reduce the importance of religious divisions, Aronson in effect urges secular people to make their interests heard, by creating effective organizations, as conservative Christians have done, which may increase the cultural divide over issues of importance particularly to evangelical Christians.

FURTHER READING

Balmer, Randall. *Thy Kingdom Come: How the Religious Right Distorts Faith and Threatens America, an Evangelical's Lament.* New York: Basic Books, 2007.

Blaker, Kimberly, ed. *The Fundamentals of Extremism: The Christian Right in America.* New Boston, MI: New Boston Books, 2003.

Burklo, Jim. *Open Christianity: Home by Another Road.* Scotts Valley, CA: Rising Star Press, 2002.

Cromartie, Michael, ed. *Religion and Politics in America: A Conversation.* Lanham, MD: Rowman and Littlefield, 2005.

Flew, Antony, with Roy Abraham Varghese. *There Is a God: How the World's Most Notorious Atheist Changed His Mind.* New York: Harper Collins, 2007.

Free Inquiry. *Imagine There's No Heaven: Voices of Secular Humanism.* Amherst, NY: Council for Secular Humanism, 1997.

Harris, Sam. *The End of Faith: Religion, Terror, and the Future of Reason.* New York: W. W. Norton, 2005.

Hasson, Kevin Seamus. *The Right to Be Wrong: Ending the Culture War over Religion in America.* San Francisco, CA: Encounter Books, 2005.

Jones, Robert P. *Progressive and Religious: How Christian, Jewish, Muslim, and Buddhist Leaders Are Moving Beyond the Culture Wars and Transforming American Public Life.* Lanham, MD: Rowman and Littlefield, 2008.

Keller, Timothy. *The Reason for God: Belief in an Age of Skepticism.* New York: Dutton, 2008.

Kennedy, Sheila. *God and Country: America in Red and Blue.* Waco, TX: Baylor University Press, 2007.

Kreeft, Peter. *How to Win the Culture War: A Christian Battle Plan for a Society in Crisis.* Downers Grove, IL: InterVarsity Press, 2002.

Murray, Iain H. *Evangelicalism Divided: A Record of Crucial Change in the Years 1950 to 2000.* Carlisle, PA: Banner of Truth, 2000.

Spong, John Shelby. *Why Christianity Must Change or Die: A Bishop Speaks to Believers in Exile.* New York: Harper Collins, 1999.

Sugg, John. "A Nation Under God." *Mother Jones* 30 (December 2005): 33–35, 78–79.

Wallis, Jim. *God's Politics: A New Vision for Faith and Politics in America.* New York: Harper Collins, 2005.

Zuckerman, Phil. *Society Without God: What the Least Religious Nations Can Tell Us about Contentment.* New York: New York University Press, 2008.

3

ABORTION, EMBRYONIC STEM CELL RESEARCH, AND THE RIGHT TO DIE

Document: *Excerpts from* Justice Harry Blackmun's majority opinion in *Roe v. Wade* (1973)

Document: *Excerpt from* Justice Anthony Kennedy's majority opinion in *Gonzales v. Carhart et al.* (2007)

Document: *Excerpts from* The National Women's Law Center, *Gonzales v. Carhart: The Supreme Court Turns Its Back on Women's Health and on Three Decades of Constitutional Law* (2007)

Document: *Excerpt from* President George W. Bush, "President Discusses Stem Cell Research" (2001)

Document: President Barack Obama, statement prior to signing the executive order regarding federal funding of embryonic stem cell research (2009)

Document: United States Conference of Catholic Bishops, "On Embryonic Stem Cell Research" (2008)

Document: National Conference of Catholic Bishops, "Statement on Euthanasia" (1991)

Document: *Excerpt from* State of Oregon, Death with Dignity Act (1994)

Roe v. Wade

- **Document:** Excerpts from Justice Harry Blackmun's majority opinion.
- **Date:** Decided January 22, 1973.
- **Where:** U.S. Supreme Court building, Washington, DC.
- **Significance:** Few Supreme Court decisions have initiated such a furor of debate and action as the *Roe v. Wade* ruling on abortion. Subsequently organizations, both supporting and opposing abortion rights, were established to lobby public officials and to engage in public demonstrations for their cause, supporting and opposing congressional and state legislative candidates based on their position on this controversial issue that has divided Americans culturally.

DOCUMENT

The Constitution does not explicitly mention any right of privacy. In a line of decisions, however, going back perhaps as far as *Union Pacific R. Co. v. Botsford*, 141 U.S. 250, 251 (1891), the Court has recognized that a right of personal privacy, or a guarantee of certain areas or zones of privacy, does exist under the Constitution. In varying contexts, the Court or individual Justices have, indeed, found at least the roots of that right in the First Amendment, in the Fourth and Fifth Amendments, in the penumbras of the Bill of Rights, in the Ninth Amendment, or in the concept of liberty guaranteed by the first section of the Fourteenth Amendment. These decisions make it clear that only personal rights that can be deemed "fundamental" or "implicit in the concept of ordered liberty," *Palko v. Connecticut*, 302 U.S. 319, 325 (1937), are included in this guarantee of personal privacy. They also make it clear that the right has some extension to activities relating to marriage, procreation, contraception, family relationships, and child rearing and education.

This right of privacy, whether it be founded in the Fourteenth Amendment's concept of personal liberty and restrictions upon state action, as we feel it is, or, as the District Court determined, in the Ninth Amendment's reservation of rights to the people, is broad enough to encompass a woman's decision whether or not to terminate her pregnancy. The detriment that the State would impose upon the pregnant woman by denying this choice altogether is apparent. Specific and direct harm medically diagnosable even in early pregnancy may be involved. Maternity, or additional offspring, may force upon the woman a distressful life and future. Psychological harm may be imminent. Mental and physical health may be taxed by child care. There is also the distress, for all concerned, associated with the unwanted child, and there is the problem of bringing a child into a family unable, psychologically and otherwise, to care for it. In other cases, as in this one, the additional difficulties and continuing stigma of unwed motherhood may be involved. All these are factors that a woman and her responsible physician necessarily will consider in consultation.

On the basis of elements such as these, appellant and some *amici* argue that the woman's right is absolute and that she is entitled to terminate her pregnancy at whatever time, in whatever way, and for whatever reason she alone chooses. With this we do not agree. Appellant's arguments that Texas either has no valid interest at all in regulating the abortion decision, or no interest strong enough to support any limitation upon the woman's sole determination, are unpersuasive. The Court's decisions recognizing a right of privacy also acknowledge that some state regulation in areas protected by that right is appropriate. As noted above, a State may properly assert important interests in safeguarding health, in maintaining medical standards, and in protecting potential life. At some point in pregnancy, these respective interests become sufficiently compelling to sustain regulation of the factors that govern the abortion decision. The privacy right involved, therefore, cannot be said to be absolute. In fact, it is not clear to us that the claim asserted by some *amici* that one has an unlimited right to do with one's body as one pleases bears a close relationship to the right of privacy previously articulated in the Court's decisions. The Court has refused to recognize an unlimited right of this kind in the past. *Jacobson v. Massachusetts*, 197 U.S. 11 (1905) (vaccination); *Buck v. Bell*, 274 U.S. 200 (1927) (sterilization).

We, therefore, conclude that the right of personal privacy includes the abortion decision, but that this right is not unqualified and must be considered against important state interests in regulation.

We note that those federal and state courts that have recently considered abortion law challenges have reached the same conclusion. A majority, in addition to the District Court in the present case, have held state laws unconstitutional, at least in part, because of vagueness or because of overbreadth and abridgment of rights. . . .

The District Court held that the appellee failed to meet his burden of demonstrating that the Texas statute's infringement upon Roe's rights was necessary to support a compelling state interest, and that, although the appellee presented "several compelling justifications for state presence in the area of abortions," the statutes outstripped these justifications and swept "far beyond any areas of compelling state interest." Appellant and appellee both contest that holding. Appellant, as has been indicated, claims an absolute right that bars any state imposition of criminal penalties in the area. Appellee argues that the State's determination to recognize and protect prenatal life from and after conception constitutes a compelling state interest. As noted above, we do not agree fully with either formulation.

A. The appellee and certain *amici* argue that the fetus is a "person" within the language and meaning of the Fourteenth Amendment. In support of this, they outline at length and in detail the well-known facts of fetal development. If this suggestion of personhood is established, the appellant's case, of course, collapses, for the fetus' right to life is then guaranteed specifically by the Amendment. The appellant conceded as much on reargument. On the other hand, the appellee conceded on reargument that no case could be cited that holds that a fetus is a person within the meaning of the Fourteenth Amendment.

The Constitution does not define a "person" in so many words. Section 1 of the Fourteenth Amendment contains three references to "person." The first, in defining "citizens," speaks of "persons born or naturalized in the United States." The word also appears both in the Due Process Clause and in the Equal Protection Clause. "Person" is used in other places in the Constitution. But in nearly all these instances, the use of the word is such that it has application only postnatally. None indicates, with any assurance, that it has any possible pre-natal application.

All this, together with our observation that throughout the major portion of the 19th century prevailing legal abortion practices were far freer than they are today, persuades us that the word "person," as used in the Fourteenth Amendment, does not include the unborn. This is in accord with the results reached in those few cases where the issue has been squarely presented. . . .

This conclusion, however, does not of itself fully answer the contentions raised by Texas, and we pass on to other considerations.

B. The pregnant woman cannot be isolated in her privacy. She carries an embryo and, later, a fetus, if one accepts the medical definitions of the developing young in the human uterus. The situation therefore is inherently different from marital intimacy, or bedroom possession of obscene material, or marriage, or procreation, or education, with which [prior cases] were respectively concerned. As we have intimated above, it is reasonable and appropriate for a State to decide that at some point in time another interest, that of health of the mother or that of potential human life, becomes significantly involved. The woman's privacy is no longer sole and any right of privacy she possesses must be measured accordingly.

Texas urges that, apart from the Fourteenth Amendment, life begins at conception and is present throughout pregnancy, and that, therefore, the State has a compelling interest in protecting that life from and after conception. We need not resolve the difficult question of when life begins. When those trained in the respective disciplines of medicine, philosophy, and theology are unable to arrive at any consensus, the judiciary, at this point in the development of man's knowledge, is not in a position to speculate as to the answer.

It should be sufficient to note briefly the wide divergence of thinking on this most sensitive and difficult question. There has always been strong support for the view that life does not begin until live birth. This was the belief of the Stoics. It appears to be the predominant, though not the unanimous, attitude of the Jewish faith.

It may be taken to represent also the position of a large segment of the Protestant community, insofar as that can be ascertained; organized groups that have taken a formal position on the abortion issue have generally regarded abortion as a matter for the conscience of the individual and her family. As we have noted, the common law found greater significance in quickening. Physicians and their scientific colleagues have regarded that event with less interest and have tended to focus either upon conception, upon live birth, or upon the interim point at which the fetus becomes "viable," that is, potentially able to live outside the mother's womb, albeit with artificial aid. Viability is usually placed at about seven months (28 weeks) but may occur earlier, even at 24 weeks. The Aristotelian theory of "mediate animation," that held sway throughout the Middle Ages and the Renaissance in Europe, continued to be official Roman Catholic dogma until the 19th century, despite opposition to this "ensoulment" theory from those in the Church who would recognize the existence of life from the moment of conception. The latter is now, of course, the official belief of the Catholic Church. As one brief *amicus* discloses, this is a view strongly held by many non-Catholics as well, and by many physicians. Substantial problems for precise definition of this view are posed, however, by new embryological data that purport to indicate that conception is a "process" over time, rather than an event, and by new medical techniques such as menstrual extraction, the "morning-after" pill, implantation of embryos, artificial insemination, and even artificial wombs. . . .

In view of all of this, we do not agree that, by adopting one theory of life, Texas may override the rights of the pregnant woman that are at stake. We repeat, however, that the State does have an important and legitimate interest in preserving and protecting the health of the pregnant woman, whether she be a resident of the State or a nonresident who seeks medical consultation and treatment there, and that it has still *another* important and legitimate interest in protecting the potentiality of human life. These interests are separate and distinct. Each grows in substantiality as the woman approaches term and, at a point during pregnancy, each becomes "compelling."

With respect to the State's important and legitimate interest in the health of the mother, the "compelling" point, in the light of present medical knowledge, is at approximately the end of the first trimester. This is so because of the now-established medical fact, referred to above at 149, that until the end of the first trimester mortality in abortion may be less than mortality in normal childbirth. It follows that, from and after this point, a State may regulate the abortion procedure to the extent that the regulation reasonably relates to the preservation and protection of maternal health. Examples of permissible state regulation in this area are requirements as to the qualifications of the person who is to perform the abortion; as to the licensure of that person; as to the facility in which the procedure is to be performed, that is, whether it must be a hospital or may be a clinic or some other place of less-than-hospital status; as to the licensing of the facility; and the like.

This means, on the other hand, that, for the period of pregnancy prior to this "compelling" point, the attending physician, in consultation with his patient, is free to determine, without regulation by the State, that, in his medical judgment, the patient's pregnancy should be terminated. If that decision is reached, the judgment may be effectuated by an abortion free of interference by the State.

With respect to the State's important and legitimate interest in potential life, the "compelling" point is at viability. This is so because the fetus then presumably has the capability of meaningful life outside the mother's womb. State regulation protective of fetal life after viability thus has both logical and biological justifications. If the State is interested in protecting fetal life after viability, it may go so far as to proscribe abortion during that period, except when it is necessary to preserve the life and health of the mother. . . .

This holding, we feel, is consistent with the relative weights of the respective interests involved, with the lessons and examples of medical and legal history, with the lenity of the common law, and with the demands of the profound problems of the present day. The decision leaves the State free to place increasing restrictions on abortion as the period of pregnancy lengthens, so long as those restrictions are tailored to the recognized state interests. The decision vindicates the right of the physician to administer medical treatment according to his professional judgment up to the points where important state interests provide compelling justifications for intervention. Up to those points, the abortion decision in all its aspects is inherently, and primarily, a medical decision, and basic responsibility for it must rest with the physician. If an individual practitioner abuses the privilege of exercising proper medical judgment, the usual remedies, judicial and intra-professional, are available.

SOURCE: *Roe v. Wade* 410 U.S. 113; 93 S.Ct. 705; 35 L.Ed. 2d. 147 (1973).

ANALYSIS

Prior to the *Roe* decision, the abortion issue was essentially a matter for individual states to resolve. By 1973, seventeen states had instituted provisions allowing for abortion under certain conditions. Women wishing to undergo an abortion who lived in a state where the procedure was prohibited could travel to a state where the law was more lenient. Undoubtedly a shift in cultural values generally to a more secular society contributed to a more pragmatic view of abortion as a reasonable alternative for women at least under certain circumstances. The issue of abortion became nationalized when a pregnant woman from Texas decided to challenge her state's prohibition on abortion. In finding restrictions on abortion unconstitutional, the Court majority divided a pregnancy into three stages. During the first trimester, states could not limit the right of a woman to undergo an abortion, but during the second and third trimesters state regulation would be entertained as potentially legitimate. The premier issue in the culture war thus came to life with a judicial decision that, at the time, many, including religious leaders, applauded.

Many have criticized the Court for an overly definitive decision that precluded states from dealing with the issue via the political branches of government. An issue that the Court attempted to decide on historical, social, and scientific grounds came to be opposed primarily on moral and religious grounds: that life begins at conception and that human life is sacred and should not intentionally be ended. Thus began

Abortion rights activists demonstrate against an anti-abortion candidate at the 1976 Democratic National Convention in New York City; photograph by Warren K. Leffler. (Library of Congress, Prints & Photographs Division, *U.S. News & World Report* Magazine Photograph Collection, LC-DIG-ppmsca-09733)

DID YOU KNOW?

Unborn Victims of Violence Act

In April 2004 President George W. Bush, in a public ceremony, signed the Unborn Victims of Violence Act, which a Republican-controlled Congress had approved. The legislation makes it a separate federal offense to harm a fetus during the commission of a crime against a pregnant woman. Those supporting the right to choose an abortion strongly opposed the legislation because it defined an "unborn child" as a fetus at "any stage of development," thus potentially preparing the way for outlawing the abortion procedure. Tony Perkins, president of the Family Research Council, applauded the new law, stating the nation was "one step closer to rebuilding a culture of life" in which both born and unborn children are granted "the protections they so clearly deserve." Twenty-nine states had already enacted similar laws. Laura Murphy, director of the Washington legislative office of the American Civil Liberties Union, declared that the ultimate purpose of the legislation was "to create fetal rights" and therefore represented an attack on the legal choices of women, including abortion.

an era of protests and confrontations with abortion clinic doctors and personnel. Clinics were vandalized or destroyed, and on some occasions, doctors who performed abortions were murdered.

States attempted to institute various limitations on the performance of abortions, including establishing such provisions as parental notification requirements for minors, waiting periods before an abortion could be performed, and informed consent requirements mandating that specific information, for instance about fetal development and possible health risks, be provided to women contemplating an abortion. Supporters of abortion rights saw in such laws a reversion to a time when cultural standards viewed women as less capable of making decisions than men, while abortion opponents saw the regulations as means of persuading women to carry their fetuses to term. Various political maneuvers by both sides were, and continue to be, challenged in the courts, and both pro-life and pro-choice groups have used the abortion issue as a litmus test for supporting or opposing candidates for public office.

Gonzales v. Carhart et al., Majority Opinion

- **Document:** Excerpt from Supreme Court Justice Anthony Kennedy's majority opinion.
- **Date:** Decided April 18, 2007.
- **Where:** U.S. Supreme Court building, Washington, DC.
- **Significance:** By a vote of 5 to 4, the U.S. Supreme Court upheld the Partial Birth Abortion Ban Act of 2003. Although not overturning the landmark 1973 *Roe v. Wade* decision, the Court ruled that the legislation was constitutional because it did not "place a substantial obstacle in the path of a woman seeking an abortion before a fetus attains viability." That the act does not include an exception to protect a woman's health was not considered a serious objection.

DOCUMENT

Casey reaffirmed these governmental objectives. The government may use its voice and its regulatory authority to show its profound respect for the life within the woman. . . .

Where it has a rational basis to act, and it does not impose an undue burden, the State may use its regulatory power to bar certain procedures and substitute others, all in furtherance of its legitimate interests in regulating the medical profession in order to promote respect for life, including life of the unborn.

The Act's ban on abortions that involve partial delivery of a living fetus furthers the Government's objectives. No one would dispute that, for many, D&E [dilation and extraction] is a procedure itself laden with the power to devalue human life. Congress could nonetheless conclude that the type of abortion proscribed by the

Act requires specific regulation because it implicates additional ethical and moral concerns that justify a special prohibition. Congress determined that the abortion methods it proscribed had a "disturbing similarity to the killing of a newborn infant," Congressional Findings (14)(L), in notes following 18 U.S.C. §1531 (2000 ed., Supp. IV), p. 769, and thus it was concerned with "draw[ing] a bright line that clearly distinguishes abortion and infanticide." Congressional Findings (14)(G), *ibid.* The Court has in the past confirmed the validity of drawing boundaries to prevent certain practices that extinguish life and are close to actions that are condemned. *Glucksberg* found reasonable the State's "fear that permitting assisted suicide will start it down the path to voluntary and perhaps even involuntary euthanasia." 521 U.S., at 732-735, and n. 23.

Respect for human life finds an ultimate expression in the bond of love the mother has for her child. The Act recognizes this reality as well. Whether to have an abortion requires a difficult and painful moral decision. *Casey, supra,* at 852-853 (opinion of the Court). While we find no reliable data to measure the phenomenon, it seems unexceptionable to conclude some women came to regret their choice to abort the infant life they once created and sustained. See Brief for Sandra Cano et al. As *Amici Curiae* in No. 05-380, pp. 22–24. Severe depression and loss of esteem can follow. See *ibid.*

In a decision so fraught with emotional consequence some doctors may prefer not to disclose precise details of the means that will be used, confining themselves to the required statement of risks the procedure entails. From one standpoint this ought not to be surprising. Any number of patients facing imminent surgical procedures would prefer not to hear all details, lest the usual anxiety preceding invasive medical procedures become the more intense. This is likely the case with the abortion procedures here in issue. See, *e.g., Nat. Abortion Federation,* 330 F. Supp. 2d, at 466, n. 22 ("Most of [the plaintiffs'] experts acknowledged that they do not describe to their patients what [the D&E and intact D&E] procedures entail in clear and precise terms"); see also *id.,* at 479.

It is, however, precisely this lack of information concerning the way in which the fetus will be killed that is of legitimate concern to the State. *Casey, supra,* at 873 (plurality opinion) ("States are free to enact laws to provide a reasonable framework for a woman to make a decision that has such profound and lasting meaning"). The State has an interest in ensuring so grave a choice is well informed. It is self-evident that a mother who comes to regret her choice to abort must struggle with grief more anguished and sorrow more profound when she learns, only after the event, what she once did not know: that she allowed a doctor to pierce the skull and vacuum the fast-developing brain of her unborn child, a child assuming the human form.

It is a reasonable inference that a necessary effect of the regulation and the knowledge it conveys will be to encourage some women to carry the infant to full term, thus reducing the absolute number of late-term abortions. The medical profession, furthermore, may find different and less shocking methods to abort the fetus in the second trimester, thereby accommodating legislative demand. The State's interest in respect for life is advanced by the dialogue that better informs the political and legal systems, the medical profession, expectant mothers, and society as a whole of the consequences that follow from a decision to elect a late-term abortion. . . .

This traditional [discretionary] rule is consistent with *Casey*, which confirms the State's interest in promoting respect for human life at all stages in the pregnancy. Physicians are not entitled to ignore regulations that direct them to use reasonable alternative procedures. The law need not give abortion doctors unfettered choice in the course of their medical practice, nor should it elevate their status above other physicians in the medical community. . . .

Respondents have not demonstrated that the Act, as a facial matter, is void for vagueness, or that it imposes an undue burden on a woman's right to abortion based on its overbreadth or lack of a health exception. For these reasons the judgments of the Courts of Appeals for the Eighth and Ninth Circuits are reversed.

SOURCE: *Gonzales v. Carhart* 550 U.S. ____ (2007).

ANALYSIS

As Fiorina, Abrams, and Pope (2006, 79) note, many have cited the 1973 *Roe v. Wade* decision on abortion as the most crucial issue energizing the culture wars. However, they conclude that "public opinion on abortion does not support militants on either side of the issue" (93). Nonetheless, activists and interest groups on both sides expended great energy in furthering their position. One such effort was the attempt to prohibit a type of late-term abortion called dilation and extraction—which opponents of abortion labeled partial birth abortion—that involves partially delivering the fetus before puncturing or crushing the skull. Consistently over time, majorities of those interviewed in attitude surveys have expressed support for the right of women to have an abortion, but are willing to accept certain limitations on that right. Therefore, abortion opponents followed an astute political strategy, given a general public approval of the right to an abortion, by focusing on a procedure the prohibition of which could gain wider public support.

Following the Republican Party's electoral victory in 1994, Congress passed bills to ban the abortion procedure, but in 1996 and 1997 President Bill Clinton vetoed measures that were sent to him. George W. Bush made clear that he would sign a bill restricting the procedure, the first federal legislation of its kind since the 1973

DID YOU KNOW?

Is There a Right Not to Engage in Certain Medical Procedures for Ethical Reasons?

In spring 2008, as the George W. Bush administration drew to a close, a new skirmish ignited over the issue of abortion and other medical procedures that some medical workers consider morally objectionable. Journalists conceptualized the disagreement as one between the religious freedom of health care workers and the rights of patients. The Department of Health and Human Services began to review a draft regulation that would withdraw funding from any hospital, clinic, or health care plan that does not allow employees to refuse to take part in such activities as providing birth control pills, intrauterine devices (IUDs) and the Plan B emergency contraceptive because they consider them morally objectionable. According to the new regulation, any action taken from conception to natural birth "whether before or after implantation" could be considered an abortion, and thus groups such as Planned Parenthood of America and the National Women's Law Center strongly opposed the regulation as overly ambiguous. Such conservative groups as the U.S. Conference of Catholic Bishops, Concerned Women for American, and the Family Research Council supported the changes.

Roe v. Wade decision. In late September 2003 a Senate and House conference committee reported the bill on a strict party vote (six Republicans in favor and four Democrats opposed). Even though the Supreme Court in *Stenberg v. Carhart* (2000), in a 5-to-4 decision, had invalidated a Nebraska law for failing to include a health exception, the bill expressly declared that "a partial birth abortion is never necessary to preserve the health of a woman" and that the procedure is "outside the standard of medical care."

Even before President Bush signed the bill into law on November 5, 2003, abortion rights groups initiated challenges to the legislation. The legal arguments against the new law claimed that it lacked a health exemption for a woman seeking an abortion and that its language was too broad and therefore could be interpreted as outlawing several other procedures. Opponents of the abortion ban filed suit in San Francisco, New York, and Lincoln, Nebraska, where the Supreme Court three years before had ruled against a state restriction on the procedure. After opponents won in the lower courts, the cases ultimately came before the U.S. Supreme Court, which rejected by a 5-to-4 vote the objections raised by opponents of the legislation. Predictably, many abortion rights supporters lamented the decision while supporters applauded the Court's ruling. However, some on both sides saw the decision by itself as having minimal impact on abortion practices because the number of dilation and extraction abortions performed each year was very small. Nonetheless, many pro-choice advocates saw the decision as potentially the first step in the enactment of further limitations on abortion rights and the possible overturning of *Roe v. Wade*. Clearly the battle over abortion would continue in Congress, in state legislatures, and during election campaigns.

"*Gonzales v. Carhart*: The Supreme Court Turns Its Back on Women's Health and on Three Decades of Constitutional Law"

- *Document:* Excerpts from the National Women's Law Center response to the U.S. Supreme Court's ruling in *Gonzales v. Carhart* regarding a late-term abortion restriction.
- *Date:* May 2007.
- *Where:* National Women's Law Center, Washington, DC.
- *Significance:* This response to the Supreme Court ruling in *Gonzales v. Carhart* upholding a federal law banning a late-term abortion procedure echoes the continuing conflict over the right of a woman to undergo an abortion.

DOCUMENT

On April 18, 2007, the Supreme Court issued a closely-divided opinion in *Gonzales v. Carhart.* [1] In its decision, written by Justice Kennedy, the Court upheld a federal law that prohibits a medically-approved abortion method in every state across the nation with no exception to protect a woman's health. [2] The Court's decision flies in the face of established law, allows the federal government to override the medical decisions of a woman and her doctor, and declares open season on rights that women have relied on since *Roe v. Wade* was decided 34 years ago. Justice [Ruth Bader] Ginsburg made the threat of the decision plain when she said in her dissent that the "Court's hostility to the right *Roe* and *Casey* secured is not concealed." [3]

An Analysis of the Decision

For the first time, the Court upheld an abortion prohibition lacking a safeguard for women's health, undermining a core principle of *Roe v. Wade.*

This case represents the first time the Court approved a government restriction on a woman's access to abortion without an exception to protect the woman's health. As Justice Ginsburg pointed out in her dissent, "the Court has consistently required that laws regulating abortion, at any state of pregnancy and in all cases, safeguard a woman's health." [4] This core principle of *Roe v. Wade* was reaffirmed as recently as seven years ago, in *Stenberg v. Carhart*, when the Court struck down a state law similar to the federal ban in large part because it did not have a health exception. [5]

But the majority of the Court in this case disregarded the medical judgment of the American College of Obstetricians and Gynecologists, the testimony of a host of respected physicians, and all of the lower court findings that the banned procedure can be medically necessary for a woman. Instead, the Court declared that there is not absolute consensus in the medical community about whether prohibiting this procedure would create significant health risks, and that in the face of medical uncertainty, politicians can step in to prohibit access to the procedure altogether. In doing so, the Court allowed the federal government to substitute its opinion for the judgment of medical experts and to trump the medical decisions of individual women and their doctors. This green light to the government severely undermines the health protections for women guaranteed by *Roe v. Wade*.

The Court recognized unproven new State interests to justify government restrictions on a woman's access to abortion.

In this case, the Court recognized new government interests that can justify restrictions on a woman's access to abortion. Most troubling, the majority of the Court held that a woman's decision to follow her physician's advice can be overridden by the government, based on a new principle never advanced or documented by either side in the case: protecting "the bond of love the mother has for her child." [6] The Court determined that abortion has serious harmful effects on women, including severe psychological consequences. Even though the Court admitted that this determination was based on "no reliable data," [7] it decided that criminalizing a medically-approved abortion procedure was an acceptable way for the state to protect women from the "harmful" consequences of their own decisions that it decided to recognize. In other words, the Court deprived women of the right to make the best choice for themselves and their families because it is *for their own good*. Justice Ginsburg recognized that this reasoning "reflects ancient notions about women's place in the family and under the Constitution—ideas that have long since been discredited." [8]

Additionally, the Court accepted Congress's labeling of a medically necessary procedure as "brutal and inhumane" [9] and elevated the interest in prohibiting such a procedure to one that justifies restrictions. The Court also approved Congress's asserted interest in protecting the reputation of the medical profession. [10] The Court therefore not only allowed legislators to act to protect women from themselves, but also allowed politicians to disregard the views of the medical profession and intrude in the day-to-day practice of medicine in order to protect the medical community from itself.

The Court weakened the "undue burden" standard, which has been used for 15 years to determine whether a restriction on abortion is constitutional.

The 1992 *Planned Parenthood of Southeastern Pennsylvania v. Casey* decision established the "undue burden" standard for reviewing whether restrictions on abortion are constitutional. If a "state regulation has the purpose or effect of placing a substantial obstacle in the path of a woman seeking an abortion," [11] it imposes an undue burden and is invalid. After *Roe*, but prior to *Casey*, abortion restrictions were subject to "strict scrutiny"—the highest standard of review. *Casey*'s "undue burden" standard weakened the protection against abortion restrictions put into place by *Roe*, but still represented a heightened standard of review that meant that states and the federal government had a difficult time justifying restrictions on abortion. In this case, the Court claimed to evaluate whether the ban constituted an undue burden, but then said that the government needed only a "rational basis" for enacting the ban. This language indicates that the Court weakened the undue burden standard and replaced it with "rational basis review," the most relaxed standard the Court can apply (and the easiest test for a government to meet) when determining whether a law infringes upon constitutional rights. Justice Ginsburg recognized this troubling change: "Instead of the heightened scrutiny we have previously applied, the Court determines that a 'rational' ground is enough to uphold the Act." [12]

The Court also broke from prior law when deciding which women to consider when evaluating whether a restriction is an undue burden. In the words of Justice Ginsburg, "*Casey* makes clear that, in determining whether any restriction poses an undue burden on a 'large fraction' of women, the relevant class is *not* 'all women,' nor 'all pregnant women,' nor even all women 'seeking abortions.'" [13] Rather, *Casey* said courts must look at the particular women who are burdened by the restriction. In *Casey*, that meant that a requirement that married women notify their husbands before obtaining an abortion was struck down as an undue burden. In so deciding, the Court in that case looked at the impact of the restriction on the women who would be actually affected by such a restriction, including the millions who are victims of regular physical and psychological abuse at the hands of their husbands. [14] The Court in this case retreated from the focus on the women being harmed.

Finally, the Court subjected the lack of a health exception to the undue burden standard. Again, this is a departure from prior law since previously, lack of a health exception was a separate inquiry that did not include the undue burden or women-affected consideration. Justice Ginsburg explained in her dissent why this has been the case: "It makes no sense to conclude that this facial challenge fails because respondents have not shown that a health exception is necessary for a large fraction of second-trimester abortions, including those for which a health exception is unnecessary: The very purpose of a health *exception* is to protect women in *exceptional* cases." [15]

The Court harms women by departing from the long-standing practice of bringing an immediate challenge to abortion restrictions lacking a protection for women's health, before women are actually injured.

The Court stated that the lawsuits brought against the federal ban should not have proceeded as "facial" challenges, or challenges to the entire law as unconstitutional on its face. Instead, the Court said that challenges to the law should have been "as-applied" challenges, which require individuals to stop the law from being applied to them because of their particular circumstances.

As-applied challenges present enormous obstacles for women and doctors. Justice [Ruth Bader] Ginsburg's dissent recognized the real impact of this change on women and their doctors. She said, "The Court's allowance only of an 'as-applied challenge in a discrete case' jeopardizes women's health and places doctors in an untenable position" [16] and noted, '[a] woman suffer[ing] from medical complications' needs access to the medical procedure at once and cannot wait for the judicial process to unfold." [17] This decision therefore puts the burden on individual women when time is of the essence and any delay may have grave consequences for their future well-being.

This is a momentous change from prior practice; for decades, courts have allowed facial challenges by doctors concerned about how an abortion restriction could hurt their patients. In fact, the Court allowed a facial challenge to a law without a health exception just last year in *Ayotte v. Planned Parenthood of Northern New England.* [18] **The Court rewrote principles of settled law and refused to reaffirm *Roe v. Wade*, leaving open the possibility of overruling it at a later date.**

By upholding a prohibition on abortion without a health exception, creating new state interests, changing the standard of review, and limiting the use of facial challenges, the Court implicitly overruled significant portions of its prior decisions. The Court never explicitly acknowledged what it has done. As Justice Ginsburg stated in her dissent, the Court "retreat[ed] from prior rulings" and "refuse[d] to take *Casey* and *Stenberg* seriously." [19]

The Court also made a point of repeatedly saying that it "*assumes*" prior precedent to be controlling. Justice Ginsburg's dissent pointed out the danger inherent in what the majority did: "[M]ost troubling, *Casey*'s principles, confirming the continuing vitality of 'the essential holding of *Roe*,' are merely 'assume[d] for the moment, rather than 'retained' or 'reaffirmed.' " [20] Like last year's *Ayotte* decision, in which the Court pointedly noted that it was not revisiting its abortion precedents "today," [21] this is an ominous sign that the Court might revisit—and overrule—*Roe* at a later date.

The Court used troubling rhetoric that demonstrates hostility to a woman's right to choose and disdain for the medical profession.

In a decision with ramifications for the fundamental constitutional principles underlying a woman's right to choose, the Court did not once mention the words "privacy," "liberty" or "equality." Instead, throughout the decision, the Court used language that indicates hostility to the right. Justice Ginsburg highlighted this in her dissent: "Throughout, the opinion refers to obstetricians-gynecologists and surgeons who perform abortions not by the titles of their medical specialities, but by the pejorative label 'abortion doctor.' A fetus is described as an 'unborn child,' and as a 'baby'; second trimester, previability abortions are referred to as 'late-term'; and the reasoned medical judgments of highly trained doctors are dismissed as 'preferences' motivated by 'mere convenience.' " [22] This language reflects a disdain for a meaningful right to choose—one that respects women's autonomy and doctors' medical judgment—and signals the Court's openness to further restrictions on abortion.

Implications of the Decision

This decision leaves many vulnerable women without access to the safest procedure for them.

Substantial record evidence in the cases showed that the banned procedure is medically necessary for some women. These include women who face serious health issues, like placenta previa, placenta accreta, liver disease, sepsis, heart problems and cancer of the placenta. In addition, the procedure is often safest for women whose fetuses have grave health conditions. The banned procedure was used in such cases to avoid adverse health consequences, including debilitating conditions requiring invasive and expensive medical procedures, problems with future pregnancies, permanent infertility, and other serious health impairments. The ban upheld by the Court therefore has removed an important option for women in choosing the safest healthcare for them. These women facing problem pregnancies must now choose a less-safe procedure or go to court for an exception to the ban.

This ban is in effect in every state in the nation, and states can no longer allow the procedure when it is the safest for a woman.

Because the ban is in federal law, it is now in force in every state in the nation. No matter were a woman lives, and no matter what her health circumstances, she is barred from access to this medically-approved procedure. [23] States may not enact their own law to allow physicians to perform the procedure when medically necessary for women in their own jurisdiction.

The Court's decision is likely to have a chilling effect on doctors who provide abortions.

The ban's definition of the prohibited procedure does not track medical practice, so whether only one procedure is actually banned remains an open question. The ambiguity further created by the Court's decision may create disincentives for doctors who fear ending up in jail or facing fines for practicing reproductive medicine. Medical professionals have spoken out about the chilling effect of the ban, [24] which may dissuade doctors from performing any second trimester abortion procedures at all.

The Court's decision is an open invitation to legislatures to pass new restrictions on abortion.

With changes in core principles of abortion law, this decision serves as an open invitation to state legislatures to pass new restrictions on abortion. Troy Newman, president of Operation Rescue, said that this case "swings the door wide open." [25] According to the *Los Angeles Times*, he and other anti-choice activists plan to introduce legislation in a number of states that would, among other things, ban all abortions of viable fetuses, even when the woman's health is at risk; ban abortion for fetal abnormalities; require women seeking abortions to view ultrasound images; require doctors to warn women that abortions might make them suicidal; and significantly lengthen waiting periods before women can obtain abortions. [26] It is clear that this decision will open the floodgates for anti-choice attempts to restrict access to abortion further.

The decision makes it clear that judicial nominations matter.

There is no doubt that the Court's two new justices appointed by President [George W.] Bush—Chief Justice [John] Roberts and Justice [Samuel] Alito—made a critical difference in these cases. In particular, Justice Alito's replacement of Justice

[Sandra Day] O'Connor, who provided the decisive fifth vote in *Stenberg*, was key. Justice Alito's willingness to disregard core protections of *Roe v. Wade* was not unexpected. His record before joining the Court revealed disdain for the medical judgments of doctors and a lack of support for *Roe v. Wade*. [27] He even wrote a memo while in the Solicitor General's office that offered a roadmap for undermining *Roe* incrementally, which would eventually lead to its reversal. [28] In the clearest possible way, this decision demonstrates how women's rights can be eroded by packing the courts with judges who are hostile to long-standing constitutional decisions like *Roe v. Wade*.

The new Court could be just one vote away from overturning *Roe v. Wade* in its entirety.

In *Casey*, Justice Kennedy stopped short of reversing *Roe* altogether, [29] even though he authored this case's major retreat from *Roe* principles. However, Justices [Antonin] Scalia and [Clarence] Thomas once again made their view on *Roe* known—they believe *Roe* should be overturned altogether. [30] And although Chief Justice Roberts and Justice Alito did not join Scalia and Thomas in that opinion, many expect that Roberts will add a third vote [31] and Alito a fourth [32] to overrule *Roe* when the right case comes along. The average age of the four remaining Justices who have voted to uphold the core principle of *Roe v. Wade*—Justices Ginsburg, [John Paul] Stevens, [David] Souter, and [Steven] Breyer—is 74. Upon the departure of one of these four or Justice Kennedy, his or her replacement could then provide the fifth vote to overturn *Roe* altogether.

Groups on both sides of this issue agree that at least 30 states are poised to make abortion illegal within a year if the Supreme Court reverses *Roe v. Wade*, [33] thereby leaving abortion decisions to the states, or to Congress and a President bent on imposing nationwide rules to take away the discretion of those states that want to protect women's access to abortion. This could force women to resort to unsafe abortions and send doctors to jail.

Conclusion

The decision in *Gonzales v. Carhart* represents a retreat from over three decades of constitutional law protecting women's rights. The newly constituted Supreme Court eroded long-standing protections for women's health and put in jeopardy the fundamental freedom to make important life decisions. It is certainly not an overstatement to say, as Justice Ginsburg did, that the "decision is alarming." [34]

1. This opinion covers two cases—*Gonzales v. Planned Parenthood* and *Gonzales v. Carhart*. The federal abortion ban, known as the Partial Birth Abortion Act of 2003, was struck down by three circuit courts of appeals: the Eighth Circuit, Ninth Circuit and Second Circuit, upholding district court decisions in Nebraska, California and New York, respectively. Carhart v. Gonzales, 413 F.3d 791 (8th Cir. 2005); Planned Parenthood Fed'n of Am. V. Gonzales, 435 F.3d 1163 (9th Cir. 2006); Nat'l Abortion Fed'n v. Gonzales, 437 F.3d 278 (2nd Cir. 2006). The Court accepted the Eighth and Ninth Circuits decision, heard them in tandem, and issued one opinion for both cases.

2. Gonzales v. Carhart, 550 U.S. ____ (2007).

3. Gonzales v. Carhart, No. 05-380, slip op. At 19 (Apr. 18, 2007) (Ginsburg, J., dissenting).

4. *Id.* At 4 (Ginsburg, J., dissenting) (citations omitted).

5. Sternberg v. Carhart, 530 U.S. 914 (2000).

6. Gonzales v. Carhart, No. 05-380, slip op. At 28 (Apr. 18, 2007).

7. *Id.* At 29.

8. *Id.* At 18 (Ginsburg, J., dissenting) (citations omitted).

9. *Id.* at 26.

10. *Id.* At 27.

11. Planned Parenthood of Se. Pa. v. Casey, 505 U.S. 833, 877 (1992).

12. Gonzales v. Carhart, No. 05-380, slip op. At 20 (Apr. 18, 2007) (Ginsburg, J., dissenting) (citation omitted).

13. *Id.* At 21 (Ginsburg, J., dissenting) (citation omitted).

14. *Casey*, 505 U.S. at 887-98.

15. Gonzales v. Carhart, No. 05-380, slip op. At 21-22 (Apr. 18, 2007) (Ginsburg, J., dissenting).

16. *Id.* At 23 (Ginsburg, J., dissenting) (citation omitted).

17. *Id.* At 22 (Ginsburg, J., dissenting) (citation omitted).

18. Ayotte v. Planned Parenthood of N. New England, 546 U.S. 320 (2006). The Court in *Ayotte* did, however, severely limit the remedy for a facial challenge to an abortion restriction, saying that rather than striking the ban in its entirety, it may be possible to strike down the ban only in part.

19. Gonzales v. Carhart, No. 05-380, slip op. At 3 (Apr. 18, 2007) (Ginsburg, J., dissenting).

20. *Id.* At 20 (Ginsburg, J., dissenting) (citations omitted).

21. *Ayotte*, 546 U.S. at 320.

22. Gonzales v. Carhart, No. 05-380, slip op. At 19-20 (Apr. 18, 2007) (Ginsburg, J., dissenting) (citations omitted).

23. The federal ban does permit use of the procedure where the woman's life is in danger. 18 U.S.C. § 1531(a) (2005).

24. *See, e.g.*, Michael F. Greene, M.D., *The Intimidation of American Physicians—Banning Partial Birth Abortion*, NEW ENGLAND J. MED., Apr. 2007; Press Release, Am. College of Obstetricians and Gynecologists, ACOG Statement on the US Supreme Court Decision Upholding the Partial-Birth Abortion Ban Act of 2003 (Apr. 18, 2007), available at http://www.acog.org/from_home/publications/press_releases/nr04-18-07.cfm.

25. Stephanie Simon, *Joyous Abortion Foes to Push for New Limits*, L.A. TIMES, Apr. 19, 2007, at 25.

26. *Id.*

27. *See Judge Alito's Confirmation Would Endanger the Right to Chose* (National Women's Law Center, Washington, D.C.), Jan. 2006, *available at* http://www.nwlc.org/pdf/010306_JudgeAlitoEndangersRighttoChoice.pdf.

28. Memorandum for Samuel A. Alito, Assistant to the Solicitor General, to Charles Fried, Solicitor General, re "*Thornburgh v. American College of Obstetricians & Gynecologists* No. 84-495; *Diamond v. Charles*, No. 84-1379," at 8 (June 3, 1985).

29. Justice Kennedy was one of the authors of the opinion in *Planned Parenthood of Se. Pa. v. Casey*, which reaffirmed the core principles of *Roe v. Wade*. Justices O'Connor and Souter joined Justice Kennedy in writing the opinion of the Court. *Planned Parenthood of Se. Pa. v. Casey*, 505 U.S. 833 (1992).

30. *See* Gonzales v. Carhart, 550 U.S. ____ (2007) (Thomas, J., dissenting, joined by Justice Scalia).

31. *See, e.g., Roberts's Testimony Gives No Assurance That He Will Uphold a Woman's Right to Choose* (National Women's Law Center, Washington, D.C.), Sept. 19, 2005, *available at* http://ww.nwlc.org/pdf/RobertsHearingAnalysisOn Roe_sept2005.pdf; *The Record of John Roberts on Critical Legal Rights for Women* (National Women's Law Center, Washington, DC), August 31, 2005, *available at* http://www.nwlc.org/pdf/NWLCRobertsReport_FINAL_Aug2005.pdf.

32. *See supra* note 27.

33. *See* Center for Reproductive Rights, *What if Roe Fell?*, Sept. 2004, *available at* http://www.crlp.org/pdf/bo_whatifroefell.pdf; Associated Press, *Many States Would Ban Abortion, Report Finds*, Oct. 5, 2004 (saying Tony Perkins, President of the Family Research Council, a leading abortion opponent, agrees with CRR's figure), *available at* http://www.msnbc.msn.com/id/6184949/.

34. Gonzales v. Carhart, No. 05-380, slip op. at 3 (Apr. 18, 2007) (Ginsburg, J., dissenting).

A lone protester outside a women's health clinic casts abortion as a violation of the Sixth Commandment, as proclaimed in the biblical Book of Exodus. (morgueFile.com)

SOURCE: National Women's Law Center. *"Gonzales v. Carhart:* The Supreme Court Turns Its Back on Women's Health and on Three Decades of Constitutional Law." Reprinted courtesy of the National Women's Law Center.

ANALYSIS

Individuals and groups supporting the right of abortion strongly objected to the U.S. Supreme Court's 2007 ruling in *Gonzales v. Carhart* upholding the federal ban on a late-term abortion procedure. The National Women's Law Center's (NWLC) analysis of the decision focuses on criticism of the content of the ruling, potential consequences for women, justices' paternalistic views of women revealed in the ruling, and the possible significance of the decision for women's right to an abortion established in *Roe v. Wade.*

The composition of the Supreme Court is pointed to by both sides in the conflict over abortion as a key political factor in the outcome of Court decisions. That George W. Bush, a conservative and born-again Christian, won the presidential elections of 2000 and 2004 created an opportunity for social and religious conservatives to move toward creating a majority on the Supreme Court that would look more sympathetically on their cause. Bush's appointment of John Roberts as chief justice on the death of William Rehnquist, and of Samuel Alito on the retirement of Sandra Day O'Connor potentially resulted in a four-justice minority in support of overturning *Roe.* The other two justices in opposition to *Roe* are Antonin Scalia, a Ronald Reagan appointee, and Clarence Thomas, a George H. W. Bush appointee. Pro-abortion rights groups fear that one more conservative appointment to the Court could result in the five-vote majority willing to overturn the long precedent on abortion.

The justices most likely to oppose any major change in precedent—Ruth Bader Ginsburg, John Paul Stevens, David Souter, and Steven Bryer—are among the older members of the Court and hence more likely to retire in the near future. Therefore, the 2008 presidential election loomed large for those on both sides of the abortion issue, with the expectation that outcome could determine whether or not the Supreme Court would be willing to revisit the core decision in *Roe* and thus create a critical moment within the so-called culture war.

President Barack Obama's appointment of Sonya Sotomayor to the U.S. Supreme Court to replace retiring Justice David Souter likely will maintain the status quo between liberals and conservatives on such issues as abortion.

DID YOU KNOW?

Anti-Abortion Ballot Measures

Those opposed to abortion have followed a state strategy, attempting to have abortion-limiting measures passed by state legislatures or approved by state voters. In 2008 three states (South Dakota, Colorado, and California) had abortion measures on the November ballot. However, voters rejected all three measures. In Colorado—headquarters of James Dobson's Focus on the Family and other conservative Christian organizations—voters turned down a proposal that would have declared that personhood begins with conception, and in California, voters rejected, for the third time in four years, a parental notification requirement. In South Dakota, voters refused to approve a ballot measure that would have banned abortion except in cases of rape, incest, and grave risk to the woman's health or life. The California measure failed even though voters approved another proposal limiting marriage in the state constitution to a union between one man and one woman.

"President Discusses Stem Cell Research"

- **Document:** President George W. Bush's remarks on embryonic stem cell research.
- **Date:** August 9, 2001.
- **Where:** The Bush Ranch, Crawford, Texas.
- **Significance:** President George W. Bush announces his decision regarding federal funding of embryonic stem cell research, a decision that limits such funding to approximately 60 existing stem cell lines. Some cultural conservatives supported the president's decision while others criticized the president for allowing any federal funding of stem cell research at all, and liberals and medical researchers strongly attacked the new policy for potentially limiting research that could lead to cures for debilitating diseases.

DOCUMENT

The issue of research involving stem cells derived from human embryos is increasingly the subject of a national debate and dinner table discussions. The issue is confronted every day in laboratories as scientists ponder the ethical ramifications of their work. It is agonized over by parents and many couples as they try to have children, or to save children already born.

The issue is debated within the church, with people of different faiths, even many of the same faith coming to different conclusions. Many people are finding that the more they know about stem cell research, the less certain they are about the right ethical and moral conclusions.

My administration must decide whether to allow federal funds, your tax dollars, to be used for scientific research on stem cells derived from human embryos. A large number of these embryos already exist. They are the product of a process called in vitro fertilization, which helps so many couples conceive children. When doctors match sperm and egg to create life outside the womb, they usually produce more embryos than are planted in the mother. Once a couple successfully has children, or if they are unsuccessful, the additional embryos remain frozen in laboratories.

Some will not survive during long storage; others are destroyed. A number have been donated to science and used to create privately funded stem cell lines. And a few have been implanted in an adoptive mother and born, and are today healthy children.

Based on preliminary work that has been privately funded, scientists believe further research using stem cells offers great promise that could help improve the lives of those who suffer from many terrible diseases—from juvenile diabetes to Alzheimer's, from Parkinson's to spinal cord injuries. And while scientists admit they are not yet certain, they believe stem cells derived from embryos have unique potential.

You should also know that stem cells can be derived from sources other than embryos—from umbilical cords that are discarded after babies are born, from human placenta. And many scientists feel research on these type of stem cells is also promising. Many patients suffering from a range of diseases are already being helped with treatments developed from adult stem cells.

However, most scientists, at least today, believe that research on embryonic stem cells offer the most promise because these cells have the potential to develop in all of the tissues in the body.

Scientists further believe that rapid progress in this research will come only with federal funds. Federal dollars help attract the best and brightest scientists. They ensure new discoveries are widely shared at the largest number of research facilities and that the research is directed toward the greatest public good.

The United States has a long and proud record of leading the world toward advances in science and medicine that improve human life. And the United States has a long and proud record of upholding the highest standards of ethics as we expand the limits of science and knowledge. Research on embryonic stem cells raises profound ethical questions, because extracting the stem cell destroys the embryo, and thus destroys its potential for life. Like a snowflake, each of these embryos is unique, with the unique genetic potential of an individual human being.

As I thought through this issue, I kept returning to two fundamental questions: First, are these frozen embryos human life, and therefore, something precious to be protected? And second, if they're going to be destroyed anyway, shouldn't they be used for a greater good, for research that has the potential to save and improve other lives?

I've asked those questions and others of scientists, scholars, bioethicists, religious leaders, doctors, researchers, members of Congress, my Cabinet, and my friends. I have read heartfelt letters from many Americans. I have given this issue a great deal of thought, prayer and considerable reflection. And I have found widespread disagreement.

On the first issue, are these embryos human life—well, one researcher told me he believes this five-day-old cluster of cells is not an embryo, not yet an individual, but a pre-embryo. He argued that it has the potential for life, but it is not a life because it cannot develop on its own.

An ethicist dismissed that as a callous attempt at rationalization. Make no mistake, he told me, that cluster of cells is the same way you and I, and all the rest of us, started our lives. One goes with a heavy heart if we use these, he said, because we are dealing with the seeds of the next generation.

And to the other crucial question, if these are going to be destroyed anyway, why not use them for good purpose—I also found different answers. Many argue these embryos are byproducts of a process that helps create life, and we should allow couples to donate them to science so they can be used for good purpose instead of wasting their potential. Others will argue there's no such thing as excess life, and the fact that a living being is going to die does not justify experimenting on it or exploiting it as a natural resource.

At its core, this issue forces us to confront fundamental questions about the beginnings of life and the ends of science. It lies at a difficult moral intersection, juxtaposing the need to protect life in all its phases with the prospect of saving and improving life in all its stages.

As the discoveries of modern science create tremendous hope, they also lay vast ethical mine fields. As the genius of science extends the horizons of what we can do, we increasingly confront complex questions about what we should do. We have arrived at that brave new world that seemed so distant in 1932, when Aldous Huxley wrote [in the novel *Brave New World*] about human beings created in test tubes in what he called a "hatchery."

In recent weeks, we learned that scientists have created human embryos in test tubes solely to experiment on them. This is deeply troubling, and a warning sign that should prompt all of us to think through these issues very carefully.

Embryonic stem cell research is at the leading edge of a series of moral hazards. The initial stem cell researcher was at first reluctant to begin his research, fearing it might be used for human cloning. Scientists have already cloned a sheep. Researchers are telling us the next step could be to clone human beings to create individual designer stem cells, essentially to grow another you, to be available in case you need another heart or lung or liver.

I strongly oppose human cloning, as do most Americans. We recoil at the idea of growing human beings for spare body parts, or creating life for our convenience. And while we must devote enormous energy to conquering disease, it is equally important that we pay attention to the moral concerns raised by the new frontier of human embryo stem cell research. Even the most noble ends do not justify any means.

My position on these issues is shaped by deeply held beliefs. I'm a strong supporter of science and technology, and believe they have the potential for incredible good—to improve lives, to save life, to conquer disease. Research offers hope that millions of our loved ones may be cured of a disease and rid of their suffering. I have friends whose children suffer from juvenile diabetes. Nancy Reagan has written me about President [Ronald] Reagan's struggle with Alzheimer's. My own family has confronted the tragedy of childhood leukemia. And, like all Americans, I have great hope for cures.

I also believe human life is a sacred gift from our Creator. I worry about a culture that devalues life, and believe as your President I have an important obligation to foster and encourage respect for life in America and throughout the world. And while we're all hopeful about the potential of this research, no one can be certain that the science will live up to the hope it has generated.

Eight years ago, scientists believed fetal tissue research offered great hope for cures and treatments—yet, the progress to date has not lived up to its initial expectations. Embryonic stem cell research offers both great promise and great peril. So I have decided we must proceed with great care.

As a result of private research, more than 60 genetically diverse stem cell lines already exist. They were created from embryos that have already been destroyed, and they have the ability to regenerate themselves indefinitely, creating ongoing opportunities for research. I have concluded that we should allow federal funds to be used for research on these existing stem cell lines, where the life and death decision has already been made.

Leading scientists tell me research on these 60 lines has great promise that could lead to breakthrough therapies and cures. This allows us to explore the promise and potential of stem cell research without crossing a fundamental moral line, by providing taxpayer funding that would sanction or encourage further destruction of human embryos that have at least the potential for life.

I also believe that great scientific progress can be made through aggressive federal funding of research on umbilical cord placenta, adult and animal stem cells which do not involve the same moral dilemma. This year, your government will spend $250 million on this important research.

I will also name a President's council to monitor stem cell research, to recommend appropriate guidelines and regulations, and to consider all of the medical and ethical ramifications of biomedical innovation. This council will consist of leading scientists, doctors, ethicists, lawyers, theologians and others, and will be chaired by Dr. Leon Kass, a leading biomedical ethicist from the University of Chicago.

This council will keep us apprised of new developments and give our nation a forum to continue to discuss and evaluate these important issues. As we go forward, I hope we will always be guided by both intellect and heart, by both our capabilities and our conscience.

I have made this decision with great care, and I pray it is the right one. . . .

SOURCE: "President Discusses Stem Cell Research." http://georgewbush-whitehouse. archives.gov/news/releases/2001/08/20010809-2.html.

ANALYSIS

Much has been said about the potential for embryonic stem cell research to lead to treatments for a wide variety of human ailments, including spinal cord injuries, stroke, cancer, diabetes, Alzheimer's, and Parkinson's. However, social conservatives

DID YOU KNOW?

Stem Cells

The possibility of deriving stem cells from sources other than human embryos promised to defuse the ethical objections of cultural conservatives about stem cell research. For instance, in October 2008 researchers at the University of Tuebingen in Germany announced that they had transformed cells from human testes into stem cells that became specialized types of tissue, such as muscle and nerve cells, when transplanted into mice. Researchers obtained the cells from biopsies conducted on men aged from 17 to 81. The cells then were grown in laboratory dishes and subsequently formed cell groups with characteristics similar to embryonic stem cells.

raise ethical objections to the use of human embryos to obtain stem cells because the process destroys the embryo. Conservatives and the devoutly religious consider this destruction unacceptable because they believe that a human life begins at conception and therefore the destruction of an embryo amounts to the taking of that life. In his statement, Bush expresses concern for the devaluing of life that would result from federal government support of research that destroyed embryos, even though such destruction might lead to effective treatments for various diseases. Because the "life and death decision" had already been made for existing stem cell lines, Bush permitted funding of research involving those lines. The president announced that support also would be given to alternative sources of stem cells that do not raise the same moral objections. Bush raised the specter of human cloning, which the American public generally opposes.

Supporters of stem cell research, including many in the president's own political party, see no objection to using human embryos from in vitro fertilization clinics. These excess embryos will be discarded, and so they could be put to potentially valuable use instead. The president's decision by no means settled the question of embryonic stem cell research, with Congress in 2006 ultimately passing a bill allowing for funding of research on discarded embryos from fertility clinics. However, Bush vetoed the measure and supporters in Congress were unable to muster the two-thirds vote in each house to override the veto.

President Barack Obama's Remarks on Stem Cell Research

- *Document:* President Barack Obama's statement prior to signing the executive order regarding federal funding of embryonic stem cell research.
- *Date:* March 9, 2009.
- *Where:* Washington, DC.
- *Significance:* President Obama overturned the eight-year long limitation on federal funding of embryonic stem cell research that President George W. Bush had instituted. The new policy represents a significant change in fortunes for the differing sides in the culture war, with those having ethically and religiously based reservations about such research losing influence to scientists and others strongly supporting such research.

DOCUMENT

Today, with the executive order I am about to sign, we will bring the change that so many scientists and researchers, doctors and innovators, patients and loved ones have hoped for, and fought for, these past eight years: we will lift the ban on federal funding for promising embryonic stem cell research. We will also vigorously support scientists who pursue this research. And we will aim for America to lead the world in the discoveries it one day may yield.

At this moment, the full promise of stem cell research remains unknown, and it should not be overstated. But scientists believe these tiny cells may have the potential to help us understand, and possibly cure, some of our most devastating diseases and conditions. To regenerate a severed spinal cord and lift someone from a wheelchair. To spur insulin production and spare a child from a lifetime of needles. To treat Parkinson's, cancer, heart disease and others that affect millions of Americans and the people who love them.

But that potential will not reveal itself on its own. Medical miracles do not happen simply by accident. They result from painstaking and costly research—from years of lonely trial and error, much of which never bears fruit—and from a government willing to support that work. From life-saving vaccines, to pioneering cancer treatments, to the sequencing of the human genome—that is the story of scientific progress in America. When government fails to make these investments, opportunities are missed. Promising avenues go unexplored. Some of our best scientists leave for other countries that will sponsor their work. And those countries may surge ahead of ours in the advances that transform our lives.

But in recent years, when it comes to stem cell research, rather than furthering discovery, our government has forced what I believe is a false choice between sound science and moral values. In this case, I believe the two are not inconsistent. As a person of faith, I believe we are called to care for each other and work to ease human suffering. I believe we have been given the capacity and will to pursue this research—and the humanity and conscience to do so responsibly.

It is a difficult and delicate balance. Many thoughtful and decent people are conflicted about, or strongly oppose, this research. I understand their concerns, and we must respect their point of view.

But after much discussion, debate and reflection, the proper course has become clear. The majority of Americans—from across the political spectrum, and from all backgrounds and beliefs—have come to a consensus that we should pursue this research. That the potential it offers is great, and with proper guidelines and strict oversight, the perils can be avoided.

That is a conclusion with which I agree. And that is why I am signing this Executive Order, and why I hope Congress will act on a bi-partisan basis to provide further support for this research. We are joined today by many leaders who have reached across the aisle to champion this cause, and I commend them for that work.

Ultimately, I cannot guarantee that we will find the treatments and cures we seek. No President can promise that. But I can promise that we will seek them—actively, responsibly, and with the urgency required to make up for lost ground. Not just by opening up this new frontier of research today, but by supporting promising research of all kinds, including groundbreaking work to convert ordinary human cells into ones that resemble embryonic stem cells.

I can also promise that we will never undertake this research lightly. We will support it only when it is both scientifically worthy and responsibly conducted. We will develop strict guidelines, which we will rigorously enforce, because we cannot ever tolerate misuse or abuse. And we will ensure that our government never opens the door to the use of cloning for human reproduction. It is dangerous, profoundly wrong, and has no place in our society, or any society.

This order is an important step in advancing the cause of science in America. But let's be clear: promoting science isn't just about providing resources—it is also about protecting free and open inquiry. It is about letting scientists like those here today do their jobs, free from manipulation or coercion, and listening to what they tell us, even when it's inconvenient—especially when it's inconvenient. It is about ensuring that scientific data is never distorted or concealed to serve a political agenda—and that we make scientific decisions based on facts, not ideology.

By doing this, we will ensure America's continued global leadership in scientific discoveries and technological breakthroughs. That is essential not only for our economic prosperity, but for the progress of all humanity.

That is why today I am also signing a Presidential Memorandum directing the head of the White House Office of Science and Technology Policy to develop a strategy for restoring scientific integrity to government decision making. To ensure that in this new administration, we base our public policies on the soundest science: that we appoint scientific advisors based on their credentials and experience, not their politics or ideology; and that we are open and honest with the American people about the science behind our decisions. That is how we will harness the power of science to achieve our goals—to preserve our environment and protect our national security; to create the jobs of the future, and live longer, healthier lives.

As we restore our commitment to science, and resume funding for promising stem cell research, we owe a debt of gratitude to so many tireless advocates, some of whom are with us today, many of whom are not. Today, we honor all those whose names we don't know, who organized, and raised awareness, and kept on fighting—even when it was too late for them, or for the people they love. And we honor those we know, who used their influence to help others and bring attention to this cause—people like Christopher and Dana Reeve, who we wish could be here to see this moment.

One of Christopher's friends recalled that he hung a sign on the wall of the exercise room where he did his grueling regime of physical therapy. It read: "For everyone who thought I couldn't do it. For everyone who thought I shouldn't do it. For everyone who said, 'It's impossible.' See you at the finish line."

Christopher once told a reporter who was interviewing him: "If you came back here in ten years, I expect that I'd walk to the door to greet you."

Now, Christopher did not get that chance. But if we pursue this research, maybe one day—maybe not in our lifetime, or even in our children's lifetime—but maybe one day, others like him might.

There is no finish line in the work of science. The race is always with us—the urgent work of giving substance to hope and answering those many bedside prayers, of seeking a day when words like "terminal" and "incurable" are potentially retired from our vocabulary.

Today, using every resource at our disposal, with renewed determination to lead the world in the discoveries of this new century, we rededicate ourselves to this work.

Thank you, God bless you, and God bless America.

SOURCE: "Signing of Stem Cell Executive Order and Scientific Integrity Presidential Memorandum." Washington, DC, March 9, 2009. www.whitehouse.gov/the_press_office/ Remarks-of-the-President-As-Prepared-for-Delivery-Signing-of-Stem-Cell-Executive-Order-and-Scientific-Integrity-Presidential-Memorandum.

DID YOU KNOW?

The British Parliament Expands Stem Cell Research

Other countries have confronted the contentious issue of embryonic stem cell research. In October 2008 the British Parliament gave final approval to a controversial bill that would allow scientists to create hybrid animal-human embryos to be used in stem cell research. Scientists create the hybrid embryos by injecting an empty cow or rabbit egg with human DNA and then subjecting the egg to a jolt of electricity to induce the egg to divide regularly. Stem cells are then extracted from the egg, which will not be allowed to develop for more than fourteen days. The stem cell research measure was approved by a vote of 355 to 129 after months of heated debate between Prime Minister Gordon Brown's government and scientists who supported the proposal, and religious leaders and anti-abortion activists who strongly opposed the use of human embryos in scientific research. Both liberals and conservatives objected to the failure of the legislation to revise the country's abortion policy, which had not been altered since 1990. The legislation also removed a restriction on in-vitro fertilization clinics which had mandated that such clinics consider the need a child has for a father when deciding whether to offer services to lesbian couples.

ANALYSIS

Among President Barack Obama's reversals of George W. Bush's policies, the removal of limitations on federal funding of embryonic stem cell research stands out as a clear indication of alternative views in the culture wars. On one side are scientists and those suffering from incurable disease and the people close to them, and on the other those who express deep concern for the ethics of destroying human embryos in order to harvest stem cells for research. However, President Obama rejects the basis for the disagreement, speaking of a "false choice between sound science and moral values," and thus indicating at least his hope that a consensus can arise among Americans, regardless of political preferences or religious beliefs, that stem cell research should continue with government support. To assure those with ethical concerns, the president announced that such practices as human cloning should be prohibited.

In addition to the stem cell executive order, President Obama comments more generally on the value of scientific research, claiming that the Bush administration politicized scientific investigation. He speaks of allowing scientists to work "free from manipulation or coercion," "ensuring that scientific data is never distorted or concealed to serve a political agenda," "restoring scientific integrity to government decision-making," and appointing scientific advisers "based on their credentials and experience, not their politics or ideology." However, the response from Republicans suggested that this segment of the culture war was likely to continue. For instance, John Boehner, minority leader in the U.S. House of Representatives, charged that President Obama had removed protections for innocent life, thus further dividing the nation. House minority whip Eric Cantor declared that the president's action will require citizens who regard embryonic stem cell research as "morally reprehensible" to support such research with their tax dollars. Although public opinion polls fairly consistently indicate that a majority of Americans support funding for embryonic stem cell research, the strong opposition on ethical and religious grounds from a substantial minority may portend continuing conflict on this issue in the culture war.

"On Embryonic Stem Cell Research"

- **Document:** A statement of the United States Conference of Catholic Bishops on embryonic stem cell research.
- **Date:** June 13, 2008.
- **Where:** Washington, DC.
- **Significance:** The United States Conference of Catholic Bishops reaffirms the Roman Catholic Church's opposition to the destruction of human embryos for the purpose of deriving stem cells to be used in medical research.

DOCUMENT

Stem cell research has captured the imagination of many in our society. Stem cells are relatively unspecialized cells that, when they divide, can replicate themselves and also produce a variety of more specialized cells. Scientists hope these biological building blocks can be directed to produce many types of cells to repair the human body, cure disease, and alleviate suffering. Stem cells from adult tissues, umbilical cord blood, and placenta (often loosely called "adult stem cells") can be obtained without harm to the donor and without any ethical problem, and these have already demonstrated great medical promise. But some scientists are most intrigued by stem cells obtained by destroying an embryonic human being in the first week or so of development. Harvesting these "embryonic stem cells" involves the deliberate killing of innocent human beings, a gravely immoral act. Yet some try to justify it by appealing to a hoped-for future benefit to others.

The Imperative to Respect Human Life

The Catholic Church "appreciates and encourages the progress of the biomedical sciences which open up unprecedented therapeutic prospects" (Pope Benedict XVI, Address of January 31, 2008). At the same time, it affirms that true service to humanity begins with respect for each and every human life.

Because life is our first and most basic gift from an infinitely loving God, it deserves our utmost respect and protection. Direct attacks on innocent human life are always gravely wrong. Yet some researchers, ethicists, and policy makers claim that we may directly kill innocent embryonic human beings as if they were mere objects of research—and even that we should make taxpayers complicit in such killing through use of public funds. Thus, while human life is threatened in many ways in our society, the destruction of human embryos for stem cell research confronts us with the issue of respect for life in a stark way.

Some Arguments and Our Response

Almost everyone agrees with the principle that individuals and governments should not attack the lives of innocent human beings. However, several arguments have been used to justify destroying human embryos to obtain stem cells. It has been argued that (1) any harm done in this case is outweighed by the potential benefits; (2) what is destroyed is not a human life, or at least not a human being with fundamental human rights; and (3) dissecting human embryos for their cells should not be seen as involving a loss of embryonic life. We would like to comment briefly on each of these arguments.

First, the false assumption that a good end can justify direct killing has been the source of much evil in our world. This utilitarian ethic has especially disastrous consequences when used to justify lethal experiments on fellow human beings in the name of progress. No commitment to a hoped-for "greater good" can erase or diminish the wrong of directly taking innocent human lives here and now. In fact, policies undermining our respect for human life can only endanger the vulnerable patients that stem cell research offers to help. The same ethic that justifies taking some lives to help the patient with Parkinson's or Alzheimer's disease today can be used to sacrifice that very patient tomorrow, if his or her survival is viewed as disadvantaging other human beings considered more deserving or productive. The suffering of patients and families affected by devastating illness deserves our compassion and our committed response, but not at the cost of our respect for life itself.

Second, some claim that the embryo in his or her first week of development is too small, immature, or undeveloped to be considered a "human life." Yet the human embryo, from conception onward, is as much a living member of the human species as any of us. As a matter of biological fact, this new living organism has the full complement of human genes and is actively expressing those genes to live and develop in a way that is unique to human beings, setting the essential foundation for further development. Though dependent in many ways, the embryo is a complete and distinct member of the species *Homo sapiens*, who develops toward maturity by directing his or her own integrated organic functioning. All later stages of life are steps in the history of a human being already in existence. Just as each of us was once an adolescent, a child, a newborn infant, and a child in the womb, each of us was once an embryo.

Others, while acknowledging the scientific fact that the embryo is a living member of the human species, claim that life at this earliest stage is too weak or undeveloped, too lacking in mental or physical abilities, to have full human worth or human rights. But to claim that our rights depend on such factors is to deny that human beings have human *dignity*, that we have inherent value simply by being members of the human family. If fundamental rights such as the right to life are based on abilities or qualities that can appear or disappear, grow or diminish, and be greater or lesser in different human beings, then there are no inherent human rights, no true human equality, only privileges for the strong. As believers who recognize each human life as the gift of an infinitely loving God, we insist that every human being, however small or seemingly insignificant, matters to God—hence everyone, no matter how weak or small, is of concern to us.

This is not only a teaching of the Catholic Church. Our nation's Declaration of Independence took for granted that human beings are unequal in size, strength, and intelligence. Yet it declared that members of the human race who are unequal in all these respects are created equal in their fundamental rights, beginning with the right to life. Tragically, this principle of equal human rights for all has not always been followed in practice, even by the Declaration's signers. But in our nation's proudest moments Americans have realized that we cannot dismiss or exclude any class of humanity—that basic human rights must belong to all members of the human race without distinction. In light of modern knowledge about the continuity of human development from conception onwards, all of us—without regard to religious affiliation—confront this challenge again today when we make decisions about human beings at the embryonic stage of development.

Finally, some claim that scientists who kill embryos for their stem cells are not actually depriving anyone of life, because they are using "spare" or unwanted embryos who will die anyway. This argument is simply invalid. Ultimately each of us will die, but that gives no one a right to kill us. Our society does not permit lethal experiments on terminally ill patients or condemned prisoners on the pretext that they will soon die anyway. Likewise, the fact that an embryonic human being is at risk of being abandoned by his or her parents gives no individual or government a right to directly kill that human being first.

Cloning and Beyond

It is also increasingly clear that such stem cell "harvesting" will not stop with the destruction of "spare" embryos frozen in fertility clinics. The search for a large supply of viable embryos with diverse genetic profiles has already led some researchers to claim a right to create vast numbers of human embryos solely to destroy them for research. Thus human cloning, performed by the same method used to create Dolly the cloned sheep, is now said to be essential for progress in embryonic stem cell research.

Human cloning is intrinsically evil because it reduces human procreation to a mere manufacturing process, producing new human beings in the laboratory to predetermined specifications as though they were commodities. It shows disrespect for human life in the very act of generating it. This is especially clear when human embryos are produced by cloning for research purposes, because new human lives are generated solely in order to be destroyed. Such cloning for research will also inevitably facilitate attempts to produce live-born cloned children, posing a new challenge to each and every child's right to be respected as a unique individual with his or her own future. Some policy makers offer to prevent this result by mandating that all embryos produced by cloning be destroyed at a certain point, so they cannot survive to birth. These proposals wrongly approve human cloning, while compounding the evil further by insisting that the innocent human victim of cloning must die.

Some researchers and lawmakers even propose developing cloned embryos in a woman's womb for some weeks to harvest more useful tissues and organs—a grotesque practice that Congress has acted against through the Fetus Farming Prohibition Act of 2006. Some would solicit women as egg donors for human cloning research, even offering cash payments to overcome these women's qualms about the risk to their own health from the egg harvesting procedure. Other researchers want to use animal eggs for human cloning experiments, creating "hybrid" embryos that disturbingly blur the line between animal and human species.

It now seems undeniable that once we cross the fundamental moral line that prevents us from treating any fellow human being as a mere object of research, there is no stopping point. The only moral stance that affirms the human dignity of all of us is to reject the first step down this path. We therefore urge Catholics and all people of good will to join us in reaffirming, precisely in this context of embryonic stem cell research, that "the killing of innocent human creatures, even if carried out to help others, constitutes an absolutely unacceptable act" (Pope John Paul II, *The Gospel of Life* [*Evangelium Vitae*], no. 63).

A Better Way

Nature in fact provides ample resources for pursuing medical progress without raising these grave moral concerns. Stem cells from adult tissues and umbilical cord blood are now known to be much more versatile than once thought. These cells are now in widespread use to treat many kinds of cancer and other illnesses, and in clinical trials they have already benefited patients suffering from heart disease, corneal damage, sickle-cell anemia, multiple sclerosis, and many other devastating conditions. (In general see the site *www.stemcellresearch.org*. Current clinical trials using adult and cord blood stem cells can be viewed at the site *ClinicalTrials.gov* by using the search term "stem cell.") Researchers have even developed new non-destructive methods for producing cells with the properties of embryonic stem cells—for example, by "reprogramming" adult cells. There is no moral objection to research and therapy of this kind, when it involves no harm to human beings at any stage of development and is conducted with appropriate informed consent. Catholic foundations and medical centers have been, and will continue to be, among the leading supporters of ethically responsible advances in the medical use of adult stem cells.

Conclusion

The issue of stem cell research does not force us to choose between science and ethics, much less between science and religion. It presents a choice as to *how* our society will pursue scientific and medical progress. Will we ignore ethical norms and use some of the most vulnerable human beings as objects, undermining the respect for human life that is at the foundation of the healing arts? Such a course, even if it led to rapid technical progress, would be a regress in our efforts to build a society that is fully human. Instead we must pursue progress in ethically responsible ways that respect the dignity of each human being. Only this will produce cures and treatments that everyone can live with.

RESOURCES

Benedict XVI. Address to the Participants in the International Congress sponsored by the Pontifical Academy for Life, September 16, 2006. *www.vatican.va/holy_father/bene-dict_xvi/speeches/2006/september/index_en.htm.*

Benedict XVI. Address to the Participants in the Plenary Session of the Congregation for the Doctrine of the Faith, January 31, 2008. *www.vatican.va/holy_father/benedict_xvi/ speeches/2008/january/index_en.htm.*

John Paul II. Encyclical Letter. *The Gospel of Life (Evangelium Vitae)*. Washington, DC: United States Conference of Catholic Bishops, 1995. Also available at *www.vatican.va/holy_father/john_paul_ii/encyclicals/index.htm*

USCCB Secretariat of Pro-Life Activities. *Stem Cell Research and Human Cloning: Questions and Answers*. Washington, DC: United States Conference of Catholic Bishops, 2008. *www.usccb.org/prolife/issues/bioethic/stemcell/Q&ABulletinInsert.pdf.*

SOURCE: "On Embryonic Stem Cell Research: A Statement of the United States Conference of Catholic Bishops." www.usccb.org/prolife/issues/bioethic/bishopsESCRstmt.pdf. Reprinted courtesy of the United States Conference of Catholic Bishops.

ANALYSIS

Following President George W. Bush's statement on stem cell research on August 9, 2001, Bishop Joseph A. Fiorenza, president of the United States Conference of Catholic Bishops (USCCB), released a statement criticizing the president's decision to allow federal funding for research using existing lines of embryonic stem cells, calling the decision morally unacceptable. Even though the embryos from which the stem cells were derived had already been destroyed, the bishop concluded that their use in research contributed to a disrespect for human life.

In the statement issued by the USCCB in 2008, the bishops reiterated their opposition to the use of embryonic stem cells in research, calling such an action "deliberate killing of human beings" and "a gravely immoral act." As did President Bush in his 2001 statement, the USCCB raised the issue of cloning: once the extraction of stem cells from human embryos is accepted, there is a slippery slope to human cloning, which the bishops called "intrinsically evil."

The USCCB affirmed support for alternative means of deriving stem cells from adult tissues and umbilical cord blood—methods that have gained publicity in recent years as morally acceptable because they do not involve the destruction of a human embryo. For the USCCB, experimentation using stem cells from adult tissues does not represent the better alternative to embryonic stem cells because the use of the latter is for them no alternative at all.

Although supporters of embryonic stem cell research have argued that there should be no moral objection to using embryos from fertility clinics that will be destroyed in any event, and that the potential is great for discovering cures for devastating illnesses, the USCCB has responded that although at some point each person will die, that fact does not justify killing another human being, and the embryo qualifies for that status.

The timing of the statement, less than five months before the 2008 general election, may have been intended in part to place the issue on the public agenda, given the high probability that the prospective presidential candidates would be less averse to embryonic stem cell research than President Bush.

"Statement on Euthanasia"

- *Document:* Statement on euthanasia issued by the National Conference of Catholic Bishops.
- *Date:* September 12, 1991.
- *Where:* Washington, DC.
- *Significance:* The Administrative Committee of the National Conference of Catholic Bishops in 1991, in response to efforts to have states approve measures to allow terminally ill individuals to end their lives, issued a statement strongly opposing any such legislation. The Catholic Church has remained a strong opponent of any policy that is considered a threat to the right to life.

DOCUMENT

Current efforts to legalize euthanasia place our society at a critical juncture. These efforts have received growing public attention, due to new publications giving advice on methods of suicide and some highly publicized instances in which family members or physicians killed terminally ill persons or helped them kill themselves.

Proposals such as those in the Pacific Northwest, spearheaded by the Hemlock Society, aim to change state laws against homicide and assisted suicide to allow physicians to provide drug overdoses or lethal injections to their terminally ill patients.

Those who advocate euthanasia have capitalized on people's ambivalence, and even fear about the use of modern life-prolonging technologies. Further, borrowing language from the abortion debate, they insist that the "right to choose" must prevail over all other considerations. Being able to choose the time and manner of one's death, without regard to what is chosen, is presented as the ultimate freedom.

A decision to take one's life or to allow a physician to kill a suffering patient, however, is very different from a decision to refuse extraordinary or disproportionately burdensome treatment.

As Catholic leaders and moral teachers, we believe that life is the most basic gift of a loving God—a gift over which we have stewardship but not absolute dominion. Our tradition, declaring a moral obligation to care for our own life and health and to seek such care from others, recognizes that we are not morally obligated to use all available medical procedures in every set of circumstances. But that tradition clearly and strongly affirms that as a responsible steward of life one must never directly intend to cause one's own death, or the death of an innocent victim, by action or omission. As the Second Vatican Council declared, "euthanasia and willful suicide" are "offenses against life itself" which "poison civilization"; they "debase the perpetrators more than the victims and militate against the honor of the creator" (*Pastoral Constitution on the Church in the Modern World*, n.27).

As the Vatican Congregation for the Doctrine of the Faith has said, "nothing and no one can in any way permit the killing of an innocent human being, whether a fetus or an embryo, an infant or an adult, an old person, or one suffering from an incurable disease, or a person who is dying." Moreover, we have no right "to ask for this act of killing" for ourselves or for those entrusted to our care; "nor can any authority legitimately recommend or permit such an action." We are dealing here with "a violation of the divine law, an offense against the dignity of the human person, a crime against life, and an attack on humanity" (*Declaration on Euthanasia*, 1980).

Legalizing euthanasia would also violate American convictions about human rights and equality. The Declaration of Independence proclaims our inalienable rights to "life, liberty and the pursuit of happiness." If our right to life itself is diminished in value, our other rights will have no meaning. To destroy the boundary between healing and killing would mark a radical departure from longstanding legal and medical traditions of our country, posing a threat of unforeseeable magnitude to vulnerable members of our society. Those who represent the interests of elderly citizens, persons with disabilities, and persons with AIDS or other terminal illnesses, are justifiably alarmed when some hasten to confer on them the "freedom" to be killed.

We call on Catholics, and on all persons of good will, to reject proposals to legalize euthanasia. We urge families to discuss issues surrounding the care of terminally ill loved ones in light of sound moral principles and the demands of human dignity, so that patients need not feel helpless or abandoned in the face of complex decisions about their future. And we urge health care professionals, legislators, and all involved in this debate, to seek solutions to the problems of terminally ill patients and their families that respect the inherent worth of all human beings, especially those most in need of our love and assistance.

SOURCE: Administrative Committee of the National Conference of Catholic Bishops. "Statement on Euthanasia," September 12, 1991. http://www.usccb.org/prolife/issues/euthanas/euthnccb.shtml.

ANALYSIS

The Roman Catholic Church has consistently supported positions that can be termed "pro-life," and the church's stand on the "right to die" issue is no exception. In opposition to those who claim that individuals should have the right to make the ultimate decision as to the continuance or ending of their life, the Catholic Church regards that decision to be in the hands of God and therefore either euthanasia or suicide is morally impermissible and should be legally prohibited. The Catholic Church emphasizes providing care for the terminally ill and their families, a strategy that the church believes reflects a basic respect and love for human beings and a desire to assist others. The USCCB holds that the seriously ill are among the most vulnerable persons in society and therefore their right to life should be firmly protected by upholding the legal and medical traditions of the country.

Death with Dignity Act

- *Document:* Excerpt from State of Oregon Death with Dignity Act
- *Date:* 1994
- *Where:* Oregon
- *Significance:* When enacted in 1994 by voters in a statewide referendum, Oregon became the first state to legally permit individuals suffering from terminal illnesses to request medication to end their life. From 1997 through 2007, more than 340 people used the procedure established by the law. Religious leaders argue that suicide even in circumstances of the terminally ill violates God's command to preserve life.

DOCUMENT

127.805 s.2.01. Who may initiate a written request for medication
(1) An adult who is capable, is a resident of Oregon, and has been determined by the attending physician and consulting physician to be suffering from a terminal disease, and who has voluntarily expressed his or her wish to die, may make a written request for medication for the purpose of ending his or her life in a humane and dignified manner in accordance with ORS 127.800 to 127.897.
(2) No person shall qualify under the provisions of ORS 127.800 to 127.897 solely because of age or disability. . . .
127.810 s.2.02. Form of the written request.
(1) A valid request for medication under ORS 127.800 to 127.897 shall be in substantially the form described in ORS 127.897, signed and dated by the patient and witnessed by at least two individuals who, in the presence of the patient, attest that

to the best of their knowledge and belief the patient is capable, acting voluntarily, and is not being coerced to sign the request.

(2) One of the witnesses shall be a person who is not:

(a) A relative of the patient by blood, marriage or adoption;

(b) A person who at the time the request is signed would be entitled to any portion of the estate of the qualified patient upon death under any will or by operation of law; or

(c) An owner, operator or employee of a health care facility where the qualified patient is receiving medical treatment or is a resident.

(3) The patient's attending physician at the time the request is signed shall not be a witness.

(4) If the patient is a patient in a long term care facility at the time the written request is made, one of the witnesses shall be an individual designated by the facility and having the qualifications specified by the Department of Human Services by rule....

127.815 s.3.01. Attending physician responsibilities.

(1) The attending physician shall:

(a) Make the initial determination of whether a patient has a terminal disease, is capable, and has made the request voluntarily;

(b) Request that the patient demonstrate Oregon residency pursuant to ORS 127.860;

(c) To ensure that the patient is making an informed decision, inform the patient of:

(A) His or her medical diagnosis;

(B) His or her prognosis;

(C) The potential risks associated with taking the medication to be prescribed;

(D) The probable result of taking the medication to be prescribed; and

(E) The feasible alternatives, including, but not limited to, comfort care, hospice care and pain control;

(d) Refer the patient to a consulting physician for medical confirmation of the diagnosis, and for a determination that the patient is capable and acting voluntarily;

(e) Refer the patient for counseling if appropriate pursuant to ORS 127.825;

(f) Recommend that the patient notify next of kin;

(g) Counsel the patient about the importance of having another person present when the patient takes the medication prescribed pursuant to ORS 127.800 to 127.897 and of not taking the medication in a public place;

(h) Inform the patient that he or she has an opportunity to rescind the request at any time and in any manner, and offer the patient an opportunity to rescind at the end of the 15 day waiting period pursuant to ORS 127.840 ...

127.820 s.3.02 Consulting physician confirmation.

Before a patient is qualified under ORS 127.800 to 127.897, a consulting physician shall examine the patient and his or her relevant medical records and confirm, in writing, the attending physician's diagnosis that the patient is suffering from a terminal disease, and verify that the patient is capable, is acting voluntarily and has made an informed decision....

127.825 s.3.03. Counseling referral.

If in the opinion of the attending physician or the consulting physician a patient may be suffering from a psychiatric or psychological disorder or depression causing impaired judgment, either physician shall refer the patient for counseling. No medication to end a patient's life in a humane and dignified manner shall be prescribed until the person performing the counseling determines that the patient is not suffering from a psychiatric or psychological disorder or depression causing impaired judgment. . . .

127.845 s.3.07. Right to rescind request.

A patient may rescind his or her request at any time and in any manner without regard to his or her mental state. No prescription for medication under ORS 127.800 to 127.897 may be written without the attending physician offering the qualified patient an opportunity to rescind the request. . . .

127.850 s3.08. Waiting periods.

No less than fifteen (15) days shall elapse between the patient's initial oral request and the writing of a prescription under ORS 127.800 to 127.897. No less than 48 hours shall elapse between the patient's written request and the writing of a prescription under ORS 127.800 to 127.897. . . .

127.885 s.4.01. Immunities; basis for prohibiting health care provider from participation; notification; permissible sanctions.

Except as provided in ORS 127.890 . . .

(2) No professional organization or association, or health care provider, may subject a person to censure, discipline, suspension, loss of license, loss of privileges, loss of membership or other penalty for participating or refusing to participate in good faith compliance with ORS 127.800 to 127.897. . . .

127.897 s.6.01. Form of the request.

A request for medication as authorized by ORS 127.800 to 127.897 shall be in substantially the following form:

REQUEST FOR MEDICATION TO END MY LIFE IN A HUMANE AND DIGNIFIED MANNER

I, _____, am an adult of sound mind.

I am suffering from _____, which my attending physician has determined is a terminal disease and which has been medically confirmed by a consulting physician.

I have been fully informed of my diagnosis, prognosis, the nature of medication to be prescribed and potential associated risks, the expected result, and the feasible alternatives, including comfort care, hospice care and pain control.

I request that my attending physician prescribe medication that will end my life in a humane and dignified manner.

INITIAL ONE:

_____ I have informed my family of my decision and taken their opinions into consideration.

_____ I have decided not to inform my family of my decision.

_____ I have no family to inform of my decision.

I understand that I have the right to rescind this request at any time.

I understand the full import of this request and I expect to die when I take the medication to be prescribed. I further understand that although most deaths occur within three hours, my death may take longer and my physician has counseled me about this possibility.

I make this request voluntarily and without reservation, and I accept full moral responsibility for my actions.

Signed: _____

Dated: _____

DECLARATION OF WITNESSES

We declare that the person signing this request:

(a) Is personally known to us or has provided proof of identity;

(b) Signed this request in our presence;

(c) Appears to be of sound mind and not under duress, fraud or undue influence;

(d) Is not a patient for whom either of us is attending physician.

_____ Witness 1/Date

_____ Witness 2/Date

NOTE: One witness shall not be a relative (by blood, marriage or adoption) of the person signing this request, shall not be entitled to any portion of the person's estate upon death and shall not own, operate or be employed at a health care facility where the person is a patient or resident. If the patient is an inpatient at a health care facility, one of the witnesses shall be an individual designated by the facility.

SOURCE: Oregon Death With Dignity Act, 1994. www.oregon.gov/DHS/ph/pas/ors.shtml.

ANALYSIS

Those favoring a right to physician-assisted suicide argue that the person ought to be granted autonomy over his or her own life, and that governments ought not to make moral edicts regarding a person's autonomous life choices. However, social conservatives and many fundamentalists, Catholics, and evangelical Christians, advocating what they term the culture of life, strongly oppose not only abortion but also the intentional ending of life through active euthanasia. The Oregon Death with Dignity Act represents for them a serious challenge to the sanctity of life. Many others express reservations about legally recognizing a right to die. For instance, Cass R. Sunstein (1997) noted five such reservations. First, individuals suffering from severe and sometimes painful illnesses often do not meet the requirements of rational, autonomous individuals capable of making a clear decision. Second, individuals may confront psychological

DID YOU KNOW?

Right to Die

Two individuals, both suffering from Parkinson's disease, took prominent roles on opposite sides of Initiative 1000, a 2008 ballot proposal to establish a right-to-die law in the state of Washington. Former governor Booth Gardner argued that when facing inevitable death, people should not be forced to experience severe suffering. Chris Carlson, a longtime Democratic Party worker, opposed the measure, stating that suicide is an "irrational and selfish act." Among the groups opposed to the ballot measure were the Catholic Church, conservative Christians, right-to-life organizations, and advocates for the disabled. Voters ultimately approved the ballot measure, with more than 57 percent of voters supporting the initiative, making Washington the second state to institute a "death with dignity" law.

pressures due to the financial costs and emotional strain on family members. Third, physicians might intentionally or unintentionally persuade patients to end their life. Fourth, the line between voluntary and involuntary suicide may become blurred if health care workers misinterpret a patient's intentions. Finally, Sunstein introduces a reservation more relevant to concerns of value: legally sanctioned suicide may erode societal attitudes favoring the sanctity of life.

In contrast to physician assisted suicide, passive euthanasia involves the withholding of extraordinary medical treatment when the likelihood is extremely remote that an individual, perhaps in a persistent vegetative state, will recover. Many speak of a reduced "quality of life" that makes continuing such an existence of questionable value. Social conservatives express doubts about the notion of quality of life, claiming that it involves making a judgment about the worth of another's existence. The Terri Schiavo case represents an exception to the general policy of states, which is to leave to family members the decision whether to withdraw life support. The Florida woman, who for fourteen years had existed in a persistent vegetative state, was the focus of a national struggle over the removal of the feeding tube that kept her alive. A cause-celebre for right to life groups, Schiavo became the focus of congressional legislation to mandate a federal court review of her case, which pitted her husband, who claimed that Schiavo had expressed a verbal wish not to be kept alive in such a condition, and her parents, who desperately wanted her to survive. When the Supreme Court refused to review the case, the Florida court decision was enforced and Schiavo's feeding tube was removed. In response to the Court's decision, then Speaker of the House of Representatives Tom DeLay commented that the judges would be made to answer for their decision.

As medical science continues to advance, life and death decisions may well increase in their complexity. Differing cultural understandings of the ethical and moral dimensions of such decisions promise to keep the issue a controversial one and hence contribute to the continuance of the culture war.

FURTHER READING

Baird, Robert M., and Stuart E. Rosenbaum, eds. *The Ethics of Abortion: Pro-Life vs. Pro-Choice*. Third edition. Amherst, NY: Prometheus Books, 2001.

Baird-Windle, Patricia, and Eleanor J. Bader. *Targets of Hatred: Anti-Abortion Terrorism*. New York: Plagrave, 2001.

Caplan, Arthur L., James J. McCartney, and Dominic A. Sisti, eds. *The Case of Terri Schiavo: Ethics at the End of Life*. Amherst, NY: Prometheus Books, 2006.

Fiorina, Morris P., Samuel J. Abrams, and Jeremy C. Pope. *Culture War? The Myth of a Polarized America*. New York: Pearson Longman, 2006.

Klusendorf, Scott. "Betting the Farm: What Cloning Advocates Really Want." *Christian Research Journal* 29, no. 4 (2006), 22–31.

Park, Alice. "The Quest Resumes: After Eight Years of Political Ostracism, Stem-Cell Scientists Like Harvard's Douglas Melton Are Coming Back into the Light—and Making Discoveries That May Soon Bring Lifesaving Breakthroughs." *Time*, February 9, 2009: 38–43.

Solo, Pam, and Gail Pressberg. *The Promise and Politics of Stem Cell Research*. Westport, CT: Praeger, 2006.

Sunstein, Cass R. "The Right to Die." *Yale Law Journal* 106 (January 1997).

4

GUN CONTROL AND GUN RIGHTS

Document: David Hemenway, *Excerpts from Private Guns, Public Health* (2004)

Document: *Excerpts from* Justice Antonin Scalia's majority opinion in *District of Columbia et al. v. Heller* (2008)

Document: National Rifle Association, "The Second Amendment" (2008)

Document: Legal Action Project of the Brady Center to Prevent Gun Violence, "Unintended Consequences: What the Supreme Court's Second Amendment Decision in *D.C. v. Heller* Means for the Future of Gun Laws" (2008)

Document: Don B. Kates, "The Hopelessness of Trying to Disarm the Kinds of People Who Murder" (2005)

Private Guns, Public Health

- ***Document:*** Excerpts from David Hemenway's book on the public health implications of the large number of guns in the United States.
- ***Date:*** 2004.
- ***Where:*** *Private Guns, Public Health* (Ann Arbor, MI: University of Michigan Press): 1–7; 152–61.
- ***Significance:*** David Hemenway presents a critical view from a public health perspective of the number of guns available in the United States, pointing out that, in contrast to other countries, the United States has a serious problem with firearm-related violence. He argues that the Second Amendment should not present a roadblock to effective gun control legislation.

DOCUMENT

Chapter 1: Guns and American Society

On an average day during the 1990s in the United States, firearms were used to kill more than ninety people and to wound about three hundred more. Each day guns were also used in the commission of about three thousand crimes. The U.S. rates of death and injury due to firearms and the rate of crimes committed with firearms are far higher than those of any other industrialized country, yet our rates of crime and nonlethal violence are not exceptional. For example, the U.S. rates of rape, robbery, nonlethal assault, burglary, and larceny resemble those of other high-income countries (Van Kesteren et al. 2000); however, our homicide rate is far higher than that of other high-income nations (Krug, Powell, and Dahlberg 1998). This chapter discusses the nature and extent of the firearms injury problem in the United States

(Hemenway 1995, 1998a) and describes the prevalence of firearms in contemporary America.

The Scope of the Gun Problem

Perhaps the most appropriate international comparisons are those between the United States and other developed "frontier" countries where English is spoken: Australia, Canada, and New Zealand. These four nations have roughly similar per capita incomes, cultures, and histories (including the violent displacement of indigenous populations). In 1992, the rates of property crime and violent crime were comparable across these four countries (Mayhew and van Dijk 1997); with the decline in U.S. crime, by the end of the century U.S. crime rates were actually lower than in these other countries. What distinguishes the United States is its high rate of lethal violence. In 1992 our murder rate was five times higher than the average of these three other countries (Krug, Powell, and Dahlberg 1998); in 1999–2000 it was still about three times higher. In contrast to these other nations, most of our murderers use guns. Comparisons with other high-income countries make our gun/lethal violence problem look even worse (Killias 1993; Hemenway and Miller 2000).

Canada, Australia, and New Zealand all have many guns, though not nearly as many handguns as the United States. The key difference is that these other countries do a much better job of regulating their guns. Their experience and that of all high-income nations shows that when there are reasonable restrictions on guns, gun injuries need not be such a large public health problem. Their experience also shows that it is possible to live in a society with many guns yet one in which relatively few crimes are committed with guns.

A nation may be judged by how well it protects its children. In terms of lethal violence, the United States does very badly. For example, a comparison of violent deaths of five- to fourteen-year-olds in the United States and in the other twenty-five high-income countries during the 1990s shows that the United States has much higher suicide and homicide rates, almost entirely because of the higher gun death rates. The United States has ten times the firearm suicide rate and the same nonfirearm suicide rate as these other countries, and the United States has seventeen times the firearm homicide rate and only a somewhat higher nonfirearm homicide rate. Our unintentional firearm death rate is nine times higher.

Of particular concern was the rise in children's violent deaths in the early 1990s. For example, between 1950 and 1993, the overall death rate for U.S. children under age fifteen declined substantially (Singh and Yu 1996) because of decreases in deaths from both illness and unintentional injury. However, during the same period, childhood homicide rates tripled and suicide rates quadrupled; these increases resulted almost entirely from gun violence.

Though gunshot wounds often result in death, even nonfatal wounds can be devastating, leading to permanent disability. Traumatic brain injury and spinal cord injuries are two of the more serious firearm-related injuries. For example, nonfatal gunshot injuries are currently the second-leading cause of spinal cord injury in the United States; it is estimated that each year, more than two thousand individuals who are shot suffer spinal cord injuries (DeVivo 1997; Cook and Ludwig 2000).

Spinal cord injuries from gunshot wounds also tend to be quite serious—gunshot wounds are more likely than non-violence-related traumatic spinal cord injuries (e.g., from falls or motor vehicle collisions) to lead to paraplegia and complete spinal cord injury (McKinley, Johns, and Musgrove 1999).

The psychological ravages of firearm trauma can be especially long-lasting. For example, compared to other traumatic injuries, gunshot wounds are more likely to lead to the development of posttraumatic stress disorder (PTSD) in children (Gill 1999). Chronic PTSD following firearm injury is common: in one study, 80 percent of hospitalized gunshot-wound victims reported moderate or severe symptoms of post-traumatic stress eight months after the incident (Greenspan and Kellermann 2002); in another study, 58 percent of firearm assault victims met the full diagnostic criteria for PTSD-3 thirty-six months after the incident (Burnette 1998). Even witnessing firearm violence can have serious psychological consequences. In one study, high school students who witnessed firearms suicides were at higher risk than other demographically similar students to develop psychopathology—specifically, anxiety disorders and PTSD (Brent et al. 1993).

The direct medical costs of gunshot wounds were estimated at six million dollars per day in the 1990s. The mean medical cost of a gunshot injury is about seventeen thousand dollars and would be higher except that the medical costs for deaths at the scene are low (Cook et al. 1999). Half of these costs are borne directly by U.S. taxpayers; gun injuries are the leading cause of uninsured hospital stays in the United States (Coben and Steiner 2003). The best estimate of the cost of gun violence in America, derived from asking people how much they would pay to reduce it, is about one hundred billion dollars per year (Cook and Ludwig 2000).

Fortunately, many reasonable policies can reduce this enormous and, among high-income nations, uniquely American public health problem—without banning all guns or handguns and without preventing responsible citizens from keeping firearms.

The Facts about Gun Ownership

The United States "Almost certainly has more firearms in civilian hands than any other nation in the world."

—Gary Kleck

The role of firearms in American history has been shrouded in myth and legend, none greater than the images of revolutionary militiamen with their trusty rifles defeating the world's most powerful nation and frontier cowboys—tough, brave, and independent—whose remarkable shooting made them memorable and heroic figures. Yet the key firearm in the Revolution was the inaccurate one-shot musket, and the regular army won the war. The militia had very limited success: George Washington considered it to be a "broken reed" (Emory 1904; Peterson 1956; Ropp 1959; Russell 1967; Kennett and Anderson 1975; Higginbotham 1988; Whisker 1997; Gruber 2002; Rakove 2002).

Long the subject of twentieth-century heroic myth, the realistic image of the nineteenth-century cowboy is "a hired hand with a borrowed horse, a mean streak, and syphilis." Cowboys were mostly young, single, itinerant, irreligious, southern-born men who lived, worked, and played in male company. Many were combat veterans, and almost all carried firearms. Youthful irresponsibility, intoxication, and firearms led to so many murders and unintentional injuries at the end of the trail that laws were enacted to force cowboys to check their guns before they entered towns (Courtwright 1996).

For today's gun enthusiasts, the citizen-soldier and the cowboy lawman remain two archetypes of American history (Kohn 2000). But what is not a myth is that America is currently awash with guns. It is estimated that there are more than two hundred million working firearms in private hands in the United States—as many guns as adults.

The total number of firearms in civilian hands has increased rapidly in the past forty years. Seventy percent of all new guns purchased in America during the twentieth century were bought after 1960. The type of gun purchased has also changed. In 1960, only 27 percent of the yearly additions to the gunstock were handguns; by 1994, that number had doubled to 54 percent (Blendon, Young, and Hemenway 1996; Cook and Ludwig 1996; Kleck 1997).

While the number of guns has increased, the percentage of American households reporting that they own guns has declined markedly in recent years, from about 48 percent in 1973 to closer to 35 percent today (Blendon, Young, and Hemenway 1996; T. W. Smith 2001). This decline appears in part to result from the decreasing number of adults in each household and, since 1997, from a decline in the proportion of adults who personally own firearms (T. W. Smith 2001). However, current gun owners have been buying additional firearms; the average number of firearms owned by gun owners has been increasing in recent decades.

Currently, one in four adults owns a gun of some kind, but owners of four or more guns (about 10 percent of the adult population) are in possession of 77 percent of the total U.S. stock of firearms (Cook and Ludwig 1996). Many people, especially women, who live in households with a gun do not own any guns. Approximately 40 percent of adult males and 10 percent of adult females are gun owners (Cook and Ludwig 1996; T. W. Smith 2001). Even though we live in a land of firearms, the majority of males do not own guns, and only about one woman out of ten is a gun owner.

The percentage of households with long guns (rifles and shotguns) fell from 40 percent in 1973 to 32 percent in 1994, but household handgun ownership rose from 20 to 25 percent. Since the mid-1990s, even household handgun ownership has been declining (T. W. Smith 2001). Perhaps 16 percent of U.S. adults currently own handguns.

People report owning guns primarily for hunting, target shooting, and personal protection. The reasons for ownership differ for long guns and handguns. Handguns are owned primarily for protection, while long guns are used mainly for hunting and target shooting. While all guns pose risks for injury, compared to their prevalence in the gun stock, handguns are used disproportionately in crimes, homicides, suicides, and gun accidents. Thus, some proposed gun policies focus on handguns rather than long guns.

Gun ownership varies across geographic regions; it is highest among households in the South and in the Rocky Mountain region and lowest in the Northeast.

It is higher in rural areas than urban areas; it is higher among conservatives than among moderates or liberals (Davis and Smith 1994; T. W. Smith 2001).

One of the most important predictors of gun ownership is whether one's parents had a gun in the home. Gun ownership is highest among those over forty years old and is more prevalent among those with higher incomes. While gun owners come from the entire spectrum of American society, people who admit to having been arrested for a nontraffic offense are more likely to own guns (37 percent versus 24 percent for those without an arrest) (Cook and Ludwig 1996); owners of semiautomatics are more likely than other gun owners to report that they binge drink (Hemenway and Richardson 1997); and combat veterans with PTSD appear more likely than other veterans to own firearms (and to engage in such potentially harmful behavior as aiming guns at family members, patrolling their property with loaded guns, and killing animals in fits of rage) (Freeman, Roca, and Kimbrell 2003).

A few fringe groups of gun owners may someday pose political problems for the United States. The militia movement made the front pages after the Oklahoma City bombing in April 1995 killed 170 innocent people. Armed paramilitary organizations, formed as a result of antigovernment sentiment, interpret the U.S. Constitution for themselves. In effect, they claim liberty as their exclusive right, which sometimes includes the right to attack violently the object of their hate. The existence of independent armed militias, sometimes filled with white supremacist rhetoric, could threaten the peaceful conduct of government and public business. These militia often identify the government itself as the enemy. By contrast, the mission of state sponsored militia of the colonial period was in part to subdue armed insurrections against the state (Halpern and Levin 1996).

Summary

It is often claimed that the United States has a crime problem. We do, but our crime rates, as determined by victimization surveys, resemble those of other high-income countries. It is often claimed that the United States has a violence problem. We do, but our violence rates resemble those of other high-income countries. What is out of line is our lethal violence, and most of our lethal violence is gun violence (Zimring and Hawkins 1997b).

Over the past forty years, the increase in urbanization and the decline in hunting, combined with the fact that fewer adults live in each household, have resulted in a decreasing percentage of households with firearms. At the individual level, about 25 percent of adults currently own guns. On average, these individuals own more firearms than in the past, and the guns are increasingly likely to be handguns. Compared to other high-income nations, Americans own more guns, particularly handguns. And, as we shall see, these guns are readily available to virtually anyone who wants one. . . .

The Second Amendment
[Excerpt from Chapter 8: Policy Background]

Debates about gun policy typically include a discussion of the Second Amendment of the U.S. Constitution. The large majority of Americans (60 to 90 percent) believe that the U.S. Constitution provides for the right of private gun ownership, and the majority of gun owners (55 percent) believe that stricter gun measures would violate that perceived right (Chafee 1992; Blendon, Young, and Hemenway 1996). The media perpetuates these views (Byck 1998), but they are incorrect.

Many of the members of the Continental Congress, which adopted the Articles of Confederation of 1777, distrusted centralized government. The Articles specified that every state "shall always keep up a well regulated and disciplined militia, sufficiently armed and accoutred" to be ready for action, but did not include a proviso on any private right to bear arms (DeConde 2001).

Similarly, the Second Amendment of the U.S. Constitution focused on the militia. The amendment reads, in its entirety, "A well regulated Militia, being necessary to the security of a free State, the right of the people to keep and bear Arms, shall not be infringed." When the National Rifle Association (NRA) placed the words of the Second Amendment near the front door of its former national headquarters, it omitted the first thirteen words.

When the U.S. Constitution was adopted, each state had its own militia, an organized military force comprised of ordinary citizens serving as part-time soldiers. The purpose of the militia was to secure each state against threats from without (e.g., invasions) and threats from within (e.g., riots).

It has been claimed that the Second Amendment provides individual Americans with a constitutional right to have firearms for personal self-defense; some people also argue that this right is crucial to allow individual Americans to rise up to combat government tyranny. While the intellectual and historical records are not completely clear, they seem to provide little support for these positions. Like the Tenth Amendment, the Second Amendment appears to focus on the relationship between the federal government and state governments.

Neither the natural rights tradition of John Locke nor the English constitutional tradition of William Blackstone provides much evidence for an individual rather than a collective interpretation of the Second Amendment. Locke emphasized the importance of the social contract: when an individual enters civil society, "he gives up" his power "of doing whatsoever he thought fit for the preservation of himself." The very notion of political society is that rights should be determined and disputes resolved not through private judgment of each individual backed by private force but rather by the public judgment of the community. By contrast, the unrestrained use of force according to one's own private judgment leads to a war of all against all, which actually undermines rather than furthers the goal of self-preservation (Heyman 2000, 243).

As for resisting tyranny, Locke focused on the right of revolution, which he said belongs to the community, or the people as a whole. Blackstone also rejected a view that would "allow to every individual the right of determining [when resistance is appropriate] and of employing private force to resist even private oppression." Such a doctrine is "productive of anarchy, and in consequence equally fatal to civil liberty as tyranny itself" (Heyman 2000, 258).

Some historians, but not all (Malcolm 1994), also believe that English history provides little support for the individual right to own weapons. The ancient constitution did not include it; it was not in the Magna Carta of 1215 or the Petition of Rights of 1628. No early English government would have considered giving the individual such a right. The Game Act of 1671 limited the right to have a gun to wealthy individuals. Article VII of the Declaration/Bill of Rights of 1689 also restricted the right to the upper classes: "That the Subjects which are Protestants may have Arms for their defence suitable to their Condition and as allowed by Law," with the phrase "suitable to their condition" serving as a euphemism for socioeconomic status. Historian L. G. Schwoerer (2000) concludes that Article VII was a gun control measure drafted by upper-class Protestants. In 1693, the Whigs did introduce a rider to the Game Act "to enable every Protestant to keep a musket in his house for his defence, not withstanding this or any other act" (50). However, the rider was defeated 169 to 65.

The history of the writing of the Second Amendment . . . provides little support for an individual-right interpretation. The Constitutional Convention was called because of the failure of the national government under the Articles of Confederation. The delegates at the Philadelphia convention feared a weak government incapable of repelling foreign invasions or suppressing domestic insurrections. The Federalists, who dominated the convention, wanted a strong central government, including a standing army, which could be supplemented by a trained, well-regulated militia (Finkelman 2000).

At the Pennsylvania ratifying convention, the Antifederalists were soundly defeated. After the convention, they published their reasons for dissent, which included fourteen proposed amendments to the U.S. Constitution. Some of these were later incorporated, almost word for word, into the Bill of Rights. Others were not. One, for example, asserted that "the inhabitants of the several states shall have liberty to fowl and hunt in seasonable times . . . and in like manner to fish in all navigable waters." Another provided "that the people have a right to bear arms for the defense of themselves . . . or for the purpose of killing game . . . ; and as standing armies in the time of peace are dangerous to liberty, they ought not to be kept up." A third declared "that the power of organizing, arming and disciplining the militia . . . remain with the individual states" (Rakove 2000, 134–35).

The same men who wrote the Constitution also wrote the Bill of Rights. The Federalists completely and totally dominated the Congress of 1789. They were not interested in creating or protecting the right to kill game, to hunt in seasonal times, to fish in all navigable waters, or to bear arms for the defense of themselves. The demands for these explicit rights were on the table and could easily have been put into the Bill of Rights. They were not. However, the Federalists were willing to assure the Antifederalists that the national government would not dismantle or disarm the state militias (Finkelman 2000).

Federalist James Madison's first draft of the proposed amendment read, "A well-regulated militia, composed of a body of the people, being the best security of a free state, the right of the people to keep and bear arms shall not be infringed; but no person religiously scrupulous shall be compelled to bear arms." This language clearly concerns the militia. It starts with the militia, it talks about the "body of the people" rather than individual inhabitants, and it excludes conscientious objectors from the requirement of joining the militia. Indeed, much of the debate over the amendment concerned the propriety of exempting religiously scrupulous persons from the obligation to bear arms if summoned to do so (Rakove 2000). Nowhere in the debate concerning this amendment was there the slightest hint about a private or individual right to own a weapon (Finkelman 2000).

The underlying debate concerning the Second Amendment was about limiting the powers of the proposed national government, not about limiting the police powers of individual states. At issue was where the boundaries between national and state responsibilities would lie. Many Americans feared standing armies and hoped that the maintenance of a well-regulated militia would eliminate the need for a substantial national military establishment (Rakove 2000).

The militia was an institution created by government. One of the Antifederalists' fears was that the national government would disarm the state's citizenry, not by confiscating weapons but by failing to provide citizens with military arms, which they rarely possessed or maintained. Antifederalist George Mason argued for an express declaration that the state governments might arm and discipline the militia should Congress fail to do so. Madison argued that the power to arm the militia would in fact remain a concurrent one, shared between federal and state governments (Rakove 2000).

The debate over the Second Amendment also dealt with the role of the militia in suppressing insurrection, and again what was at stake was the question of which level of government—state or national—would be empowered to use the militia. But to all it was clear that the militia was to be used to help defeat insurrections; there was no plan for an armed citizenry, independent of government, acting as a main deterrent against despotism (Rakove 2000). While some of the early state constitutions, written during the revolution, not surprisingly endorsed the right of revolution, the framers of the Constitution did not endorse such a right for their own democratic republic. Every two years there would be an opportunity to participate in an orderly process to replace the existing government (Finkelman 2000).

With the exception of one recent case (*United States v. Emerson*, 270 F. 3d 203 [5th Cir. 2001]), the federal courts have consistently ruled that the Second Amendment concerns a well-regulated (or organized) militia—which the courts currently define as the National Guard—and does not guarantee or protect an individual's right to own or possess a firearm (Vernick and Teret 1993; Henigan, Nicholson, and Hemenway 1995).

In the *Emerson* case, a federal judge in Texas did something that no federal court had done for more than sixty years—he held that the Second Amendment protects an individual's right to keep and bear arms. His decision that an individual under a domestic violence restraining order had a right to own a gun was reversed at the superior court level, but two of the judges expressed their view that the Second Amendment protects an individual's right to possess firearms. Some have argued that this view is dicta—unnecessary to the outcome of the case and not binding on other courts. In 2002, Attorney General John Ashcroft pushed further, reversing Justice Department precedent by proclaiming that the Second Amendment did confer an individual right.

Later in 2002, in *Silveira v. Lockyer* (312 F. 3d 1052 [9th Cir. 2002]), the Ninth Circuit Federal Court of Appeals unanimously upheld California's strict assault weapons ban and rebutted the idea of a constitutionally protected individual right to bear arms. "The [Second] Amendment was not adopted to afford rights to individuals with respect to private ownership or possession."

The U.S. Supreme Court's last word [until 2008] on the Second Amendment came in 1939 (*United States v. Miller*, 307 U.S. 174 [1939]). Defendants in the case had been convicted of transporting an unregistered sawed-off shotgun across state lines. They appealed under the 1934 Firearms Act, claiming that it violated the Second Amendment and was therefore unconstitutional. The Supreme Court rejected that argument, holding that the purpose of the Second Amendment was "to insure the viability of state militias." The unanimous Court stated,

> In the absence of any evidence tending to show that possession or use of a shotgun having a barrel of less than eighteen inches in length at this time has some reasonable relationship to the preservation or efficiency of a well-regulated militia, we cannot say that the Second Amendment guarantees the right to keep and bear such an instrument. (id. at 176)

In subsequent years, the Supreme Court has consistently refused to reopen the issue. In 1983, for example, it let stand a decision upholding a Morton Grove, Illinois, ordinance that banned the possession of handguns within its borders (*Quilici v. Morton Grove*, 695 F. 2d 261 [7th Cir. 1982], *cert. denied* 464 U.S. 863 [1983]). The policy measures to be suggested in the remainder of this book are not nearly as restrictive as the Morton Grove ordinance.

In June 2002, the Supreme Court refused to review the *Emerson* case. It also refused to review a 2001 Oklahoma case (*United States v. Haney*, 264 F. 3d 1161 [10th Cir. 2001]) in which the Tenth Circuit Court of Appeals in Denver ruled, consistent with case law, that a gun control law does not violate the Second Amendment "unless it impairs the state's ability to maintain a well-regulated militia." The militia, it added, is "a governmental organization" (id. at 1165); it is not individuals possessing their own guns. The U.S. Supreme Court may eventually have to weigh in on these recent conflicting interpretations [which the justices finally did in the decision *District of Columbia v. Heller*].

A flavor of the previous consistency and definitiveness of the courts' interpretation of the Second Amendment is provided by some recent rulings:

> "As the language of the [Second] Amendment itself indicates, it was not framed with individual rights in mind. . . . Reasonable gun control legislation is clearly within the police power of the State and must be accepted by the individual though it impose a restraint or burden on him" (*Burton v. Sills*, 86, 106 [1968]).
>
> "Since the Second Amendment right 'to keep and bear arms' applies only to the right of the state to maintain a militia, and not to the individual's right to bear arms, there can be no serious claim to any express constitutional right of an individual to possess a firearm" (*Stevens v. United States*, 440 F. 2d 144, 149 [6th Cir. 1971]).
>
> "Appellant's theory . . . is that by the Second Amendment to the United States Constitution he is entitled to bear arms. Appellant is completely wrong

about that" (*Eckert v. City of Philadelphia*, 477 F. 2d 610, 610 [3d Cir.], *cert. denied*, 414 U.S. 839 [1973]).

"It is clear that the Second Amendment guarantees a collective rather than an individual right" (*United States v. Warin*, 530 F. 2d 103, 106 [6th Cir.], *cert. denied*, 426 U.S. 948 [1976]).

"The Second Amendment guarantees no right to keep and bear a firearm that does not have some reasonable relationship to the preservation or efficiency of a well regulated Militia" (*Lewis v. United States*, 445 US 55, 66 [1980]).

"Construing [the language of the Second Amendment] according to its plain meaning, it seems clear that the right to bear arms is inextricably connected to the preservation of a militia. ... We conclude that the right to keep and bear arms is not guaranteed by the Second Amendment" *Quilici v. Village of Morton Grove*, 695 F. 2d 261, 265 [7th Cir. 1982]).

"Considering this history, we cannot conclude that the Second Amendment protects the individual possession of military weapons" (*United States v. Hale*, 978 F. 2d 1016, 1019 [8th Cir. 1992]).

"The [Second] Amendment protects the people's right to maintain an effective state militia, and does not establish an individual right to own or possess firearms for personal or other use" (*Silveira v. Lockyer*, 312 F. 3d 1052, 1066 [9th Cir. 2002]).

Indeed, even including the *Emerson* case, no federal firearms legislation has been struck down on Second Amendment grounds. When the gun lobby brings cases against federal gun restrictions, it rarely uses the Second Amendment and instead claims unconstitutionality based on the Tenth Amendment, which deals with the separation of power between the federal and state governments, or other constitutional provisions (Vernick and Teret 1999).

Expert interest groups have clearly stated positions in support of the collective interpretation of the Second Amendment. The American Civil Liberties Union (ACLU), the organization that is probably the staunchest supporter of the Bill of Rights, believes that the constitutional right to bear arms is primarily a collective one, designed to protect states' right to maintain militias to assure freedom and security against the central government. "In today's world that idea is somewhat anachronistic and in any case would require weapons much more powerful than handguns or hunting rifles." The ACLU thus believes that the Second Amendment does not prohibit "reasonable regulation of gun ownership, such as licensing and registration" (ACLU 1999). The ACLU's Policy 47 states, "The ACLU agrees with the Supreme Court's long-standing interpretation of the Second Amendment that the individual's right to bear arms applies only to the preservation or efficiency of a well-regulated militia. Except for lawful police and military purposes, the possession of weapons by individuals is not constitutionally protected. Therefore, there is no constitutional impediment to the regulation of firearms" (ACLU 1999).

The American Bar Association, which represents more than four hundred thousand attorneys, has a long-standing position on the Second Amendment that is consistent with the courts' interpretation.

Few issues have been more distorted and cluttered by misinformation than this one. There is no confusion in the law itself. The strictest gun control laws in the nation have been upheld against Second Amendment challenge. . . . Yet the perception that the Second Amendment is somehow an obstacle to Congress and state and local legislative bodies fashioning laws to regulate firearms remains a pervasive myth. . . . As lawyers, as representatives of the legal profession, and as recognized experts on the meaning of the Constitution and our system of justice, we share a responsibility to "say what the law is." . . . The argument that the Second Amendment prohibits all State or Federal regulation of citizens' ownership of firearms has no validity whatsoever. (American Bar Association 1999).

In the past two decades, many legal scholars have claimed that the courts have misinterpreted the intent of the Second Amendment (e.g., Kates 1983; Levinson 1989; Finkelman 2000; Heyman 2000; Rakove 2000; Schwoerer 2000; Uviller and Merkel 2000). Perhaps the most interesting new thesis argues that Madison wrote the Second Amendment to assure the southern states that Congress would not undermine the slave system by disarming the militias, which were the principal instruments of slave control throughout the South (Bogus 1998).

Courts have the power of reinterpreting the law, and the Constitution can be amended. For at least the previous sixty years, courts in the United States have generally held that the U.S. Constitution does not provide individuals with any right to own or carry a firearm, apart from its connection with the "preservation or efficiency" of the militia. Owning a gun is a privilege. Most important, the Constitution does not prevent reasonable gun policies. As summarized by American Bar Association President R. W. Ide III,

It is time we overcome the destructive myth perpetuated by gun control opponents about the Second Amendment. . . . Federal and state courts have reached in this century a consensus interpretation of the Second Amendment that permits the exercise of broad power to limit private access to firearms by all levels of government. (1994)

Even in the aberrant *Emerson* case, the courts ruled that an individual under a restraining order does not have a right to possess a firearm.

It is sometimes claimed that the Second Amendment helps guarantee that an armed citizenry will be able to overthrow potential tyranny of the federal government. However, this notion appears largely ahistorical. American Revolutionary leaders were never of a mind to permit armed rebellions against their governance. For example, in 1786, when debt-ridden farmers, led by Daniel Shays, rose up in arms to demand that the Massachusetts state government reduce their taxes, the federal Congress authorized troops to help suppress the rebellion. Similarly, in 1794, when western Pennsylvania farmers rose in arms to block collection of a federal tax on distilled liquor, the uprising was crushed by troops headed by General George Washington and Light Horse Harry Lee.

On both occasions, self-styled patriots were objecting to what they saw as acts of tyranny. The Second Amendment was not about instigating insurrection—as a Timothy McVeigh might plan—but about enabling government to combat it. In the absence of an organized police force in the eighteenth century, it was expected that the militia's primary responsibility would be internal security rather than defense against invasion (Dorf 2000).

The governmental response to the Whiskey Rebellion, like the earlier Shays uprising, revealed "the establishment's lack of respect for the idea that dissatisfied citizens could keep firearms and use them against the will of the government, even if the insurgents considered the regime tyrannical" (DeConde 2001, 41).

When the Bill of Rights was added to the Constitution, every state had some form of firearms regulation. In the debate about the Second Amendment, no one argued that its passage might hinder the state's authority to regulate firearms, because the Second Amendment was not about individual rights. In 2000, a group of more than forty historians and law professors signed a letter to the NRA president, Charlton Heston, publicized in an advertisement in the *New York Times*, stating that "the law is well-settled that the Second Amendment permits broad and intensive regulation of firearms" (Bogus 2000).

BIBLIOGRAPHY

American Bar Association. 1999. Second Amendment issues. http://www.abanet.org/gunviol/secondamend.html/ (accessed December 2001).

American Civil Liberties Union (ACLU). 1999 [2008]. Gun control. http:www.aclu.org/crimjustice/gen/35904res20020304.html.

Blendon, R., J. Young, and D. Hemenway. 1996. The American public and the gun control debate. *Journal of the American Medical Association* 275:1719–23.

Bogus, C. T. 1998. The hidden history of the Second Amendment. *University of California at Davis Law Review* 31:309–11.

Bogus, C. T. 2000. The history and politics of Second Amendment scholarship. In *The Second Amendment in Law and History*, ed. C. T. Bogus, 1–15. New York: New Press.

Brent, D. A., J. A. Perper, G. Moritz, M. Baugher, and C. Allmann. 1993. Suicide in adolescents with no apparent psychopathology. *Journal of the American Academy of Child and Adolescent Psychiatry* 32:494–500.

Burnette, S. 1998. Post traumatic stress disorder among firearm assault survivors: Risk and resiliency factors in recovering from violent victimization. Ph.D. diss., University of Pittsburgh. AAT 9837559.

Byck, D. L. 1998. The Second Amendment: Do newspapers tell us we have the right to bear arms? Ph.D. diss., Harvard School of Public Health.

Chafee, J. H. 1992. It's time to control handguns: The phantom "right to keep and bears arms" carries a high price tag. *Public Welfare* 50:18–21.

Coben, J. J., and C. A. Steiner. 2003. Hospitalization for firearm-related injuries in the Unites States 1997. *American Journal of Preventive Medicine* 24:1–8.

Cook, P. J., and J. Ludwig. 1996. *Guns in America: Results of a Comprehensive National Survey on Firearms Ownership and Use.* Washington, DC: Police Foundation.

Cook, P. J., and J. Ludwig. 2000. *Gun Violence: The Real Costs.* New York: Oxford University Press.

Cook, P. J., B. A. Lawrence, J. Ludwig, and T. R. Miller. 1999. The medical costs of gunshot injuries in the United States. *Journal of the American Medical Association* 282:447–54.

Courtwright, D. T. 1996. *Violent Land.* Cambridge, MA: Harvard University Press.

Davis, J. A., and T. W. Smith. 1994. General Social Surveys 1972–1994. Chicago, IL: National Opinion Research Center. Machine-readable data file.

DeConde, A. 2001. *Gun Violence in America: The Struggle for Control.* Boston: Northeastern University Press.

DeVivo, M. J. 1997. Causes and costs of spinal cord injury in the United States. *Spinal Cord* 35:809–13.

Dorf, M. C. 2000. What does the Second Amendment mean today? *Chicago-Kent Law Review* 76:291–348.

Emory, U. 1904. *The Military Policy of the United States.* Washington, DC: U.S. Government Printing Office.

Finkelman, P. 2000. A well regulated militia: The Second Amendment in historical perspective. *Chicago-Kent Law Review* 76:195–236.

Freeman, T. W., V. Roca, and T. Kimbrell. 2003. A survey of gun collection and use among three groups of veteran patients admitted to veterans affairs hospital treatment programs. *Southern Medical Journal* 96:240–43.

Gill, A. S. C. 1999. Factors predictive of pediatric post traumatic stress disorder one year post traumatic injury. M. S. Texas Women's University. ATT 13949908.

Greenspan, A. I., and A. L. Kellerman. 2002. Physical and psychological outcome eight months after serious gunshot injury. *Journal of Trauma* 53:709–16.

Gruber, I. D. 2002. Of arms and men: Arming America and military history. *William and Mary Quarterly* 59:217–22.

Halpern, T., and B. Levin. 1996. *The Limits of Dissent: The Constitutional Status of Armed Civilian Militias.* Amherst, MA: Aletheia Press.

Hemenway, D. 1995. Guns, public health, and public safety. In *Guns and the Constitution: The Myth of Second Amendment Protection for Firearms in America,* ed. D. A. Henigan, E. B. Nicholson, and D. Hemenway, 49–76. Northampton, MA: Aletheia Press.

Hemenway, D. 1998a. Regulation of firearms. *New England Journal of Medicine* 339:843–45.

Hemenway, D., and M. Miller. 2000. Firearm availability and homicide rates across twenty-six high-income countries. *Journal of Trauma* 49:985–88.

Hemenway, D., and E. Richardson. 1997. Characteristics of automatic or semiautomatic firearm ownership. *American Journal of Public Health* 87:286–88.

Henigan, D. A., E. B. Nicholson, and D. Hemenway. 1995. *Guns and the Constitution: The Myth of Second Amendment Protection for Firearms in America.* Northampton, MA: Aletheia Press.

Heyman, S. J. 2000. Natural rights and the Second Amendment. *Chicago-Kent Law Review* 76:237–90.

Higginbotham, D. 1988. *War and Society in Revolutionary America: The Wider Dimensions of Conflict.* Columbia: University of South Carolina Press.

Ide, R. W. III. 1994. Remarks to the National Press Club. April 15.

Kates, D. B. Jr. 1983. Handgun prohibition and the original meaning of the Second Amendment. *Michigan Law Review* 82:204–73.

Kennett, L., and J. L. Anderson. 1975. *The Gun in America: The Origin of a National Dilemma.* Westport, CT: Greenwood Press.

Killias, M. 1993. International correlations between gun ownership and rates of homicide and suicide. *Canadian Medical Association Journal* 148:1721–25.

Kleck, G. 1997. *Targeting Guns: Firearms and Their Control*. Hawthorne, NY: Aldine de Gruyter.

Kohn, A. A. 2000. Shooters: The moral world of gun enthusiasts. Ph.D. diss., University of California, San Francisco.

Krug, E. G., K. E. Powell, and L. L. Dahlberg. 1998. Firearm-related deaths in the United States and thirty-five other high- and upper-middle-income countries. *International Journal of Epidemiology* 27:214–21.

Levinson, S. 1989. The embarrassing Second Amendment. *Yale Law Review* 99:637–59.

Malcolm, J. 1994. *To Keep and Bear Arms: The Origins of an Anglo-American Right*. Cambridge, MA: Harvard University Press.

Mayhew, P., and J. J. M. van Dijk. 1997. *Criminal Victimization in Eleven Industrialized Countries: Key Findings from the International Crime Victimization Surveys*. London: Information and Publications Group.

McKinley, W. O., J. S. Johns, and J. J. Musgrove. 1999. Clinical presentations, medical complications, and functional outcomes of individuals with gunshot wound-induced spinal cord injury. *American Journal of Physical Medicine and Rehabilitation* 78:102–7.

Peterson, H. L. 1956. *Arms and Armor in Colonial America: 1526–1783*. Harrisburg, PA: Stackpole.

Rakove, J. N. 2000. The Second Amendment: The highest stage of originalism. *Chicago-Kent Law Review* 76: 103–66.

Rakove, J. N. 2002. Words, deeds, and guns: Arming America and the Second Amendment. *William and Mary Quarterly* 59:205–10.

Ropp, T. 1959. *War in the Modern World*. Durham, NC: Duke University Press.

Russell, C. P. 1967. *Firearms, Traps, and Tools of the Mountain Men*. New York: Knopf.

Schwoerer, L. G. 2000. To hold and bear arms: The English perspective. *Chicago-Kent Law Review* 76:27–60.

Singh, G. K., and S. M. Yu. 1996. U.S. childhood mortality, 1950 through 1993: Trends and socioeconomic differentials. *American Journal of Public Health* 86:505–12.

Smith, T. W. 2001. *National Gun Policy Survey of the National Opinion Research Center: Research Findings*. Chicago: National Opinion Research Center.

Uviller, H. R., and W. G. Merkel. 2000. The Second Amendment in context: The case of the vanishing predicate. *Chicago-Kent Law Review* 76:403–600.

Van Kesteren, J. N., P. Mayhew, and P. Nieuwbeerta. 2000. Criminal Victimisation in Seventeen Industrialised Countries: Key Findings from the 2000 International Crime Victims Survey. The Hague, Ministry of Justice.

Vernick, J. S., and S. P. Teret. 1993. Firearms and health: The right to be armed with accurate information about the Second Amendment. *American Journal of Public Health* 83:1773–77.

Vernick, J. S., and S. P. Teret. 1999. New courtroom strategies regarding firearms: Tort litigation against firearm manufacturers and constitutional challenges to gun laws. *Houston Law Review* 36:1715–54.

Whisker, J. B. 1997. *The American Colonial Militia*. Lewiston, NY: Edwin Mellon Press.

Zimring, F. E., and G. Hawkins. 1997b. *Crime Is Not the Problem: Lethal Violence in America*. New York: Oxford University Press.

SOURCE: David Hemenway, *Private Guns, Public Health*, 1–7, 152–161. Ann Arbor, MI: University of Michigan Press, © 2004 by David Hemenway. Reprint permission courtesy of the University of Michigan Press.

DID YOU KNOW?

Guns on Campus

Following the tragic April 2007 shooting at Virginia Tech University in which a gunman killed 32 people, proposals began to surface that would allow students to carry concealed weapons on campus. Although 38 states specifically ban weapons at schools, in 2004 Utah became the first state to allow carrying concealed weapons at public colleges. In 2003 Colorado enacted a law that allowed universities to adopt their own policies regarding the carrying of firearms. Acting under the assumption that possibly only a student with a concealed weapon could protect innocent classmates from a gunman, in March 2008 the Oklahoma state house of representatives approved a measure by a vote of 65 to 36 that would allow people with firearms training to carry concealed weapons on public college campus. By July 2008 bills had been introduced in seventeen states to allow concealed handguns on college campuses. Measures failed in fifteen of those states, including Oklahoma.

ANALYSIS

David Hemenway's analysis of firearm ownership represents an approach to the subject, developed in the 1980s and 1990s, that emphasizes the adverse medical consequences of widespread gun ownership. Comparisons with other western democracies indicate that although the U.S. crime rate does not vary much from other countries, violent crime involving the use of firearms occurs far more frequently in the United States. Trends in firearm ownership indicate that although the percentage of the U.S. population that own firearms has been decreasing, the number of guns in private hands continues to increase. Handguns appear to be the major culprit when it comes to violent crime (hence recent legislation to prevent those with criminal and mental health records from purchasing these weapons). The Second Amendment to the U.S. Constitution, which involves the protection of a right to "keep and bear arms" has been the focus of much debate between gun rights advocates and those who support more stringent limitations on gun ownership. Health care researchers such as Hemenway tend to advocate greater limitations on gun ownership in order to reduce gun-related injuries and death related to criminal acts, suicide, and accidents, and argue that such limitations do not run counter to the meaning of the Second Amendment, which they have claimed protects not an individual right but a collective right of states to maintain a militia. Gun control advocates interpret the historical events leading up to the ratification of the Second Amendment very differently from gun rights supporters. They perceive the emphasis to have been primarily on preventing the new federal government from disarming state militias. However the early policy makers might have viewed the use of firearms for such purposes as hunting, sport, and self defense, the wording of the Second Amendment, gun control supporters have contended, dealt exclusively with a collective right of states to maintain a militia. Although some groups in the United States assert that the Second Amendment also protects the right of private individuals to form citizen militias in order to defend themselves against, and possibly to overthrow, tyrannical government, gun control supporters assert emphatically that any right to revolutionary action could not have been the intent of the framers of the U.S. Constitution nor the Second Amendment.

For advocates of greater restrictions on the ownership of firearms, some weapons are more likely to be used in the commission of crimes than are others. Gun rights supporters, on the other hand, resist the idea that particular weapons are inherently more likely to attract criminal use. Jerry Adler (2007) has focused on one particular weapon—the 9-millimeter handgun—as a uniquely dangerous firearm that has found increasing use in the military, by police officers, among criminals, and by average citizens concerned about self-protection. Although a gun-rights supporter tends to conclude that criminals will obtain firearms any way they can and therefore law-abiding citizens should be able to obtain the same weapons to deter criminal activity, advocates of gun control measures assert that the use of certain weapons in any circumstance—whether by law enforcement officers or the average citizen—presents a heightened probability of serious harm. Gun-rights supporters view loaded guns in the home a significant deterrent to crime, while those on the other side of the issue regard such weapons as an invitation to tragic accidents and are liable to be used in domestic disputes. As Adler observes, with the expiration of the 1994 assault weapons ban in 2004, the Virginia Tech shooter could purchase 15-round clips for his Glock pistol, thus making it a simpler task for him to shoot his victims. However, gun rights advocates emphasize that less stringent restrictions on the carrying of firearms would have meant an increased likelihood of someone on campus having a firearm with which to stop the shooter and thus to reduce the extent of the tragedy. Advocates as well as opponents of gun control often observe the same data regarding firearm-related crime and deaths, but arrive at very different conclusions: either that additional measures must be taken to reduce the violence, or that individuals must be granted greater latitude in exercising their right of self-defense. The disagreement likely will continue in the political realm of interest group politics backed by fundamentally distinct cultural understandings and conflicting interpretations of events, with one side or the other gaining at best transitory victories.

District of Columbia et al. v. Heller

- *Document:* Excerpts from Justice Antonin Scalia's majority opinion.
- *Date:* June 26, 2008.
- *Where:* U.S. Supreme Court building, Washington, DC.
- *Significance:* The Supreme Court's majority decision, invalidating a restrictive Washington, DC, handgun law, affirms an individual's right to possess a firearm for self-defense. Questions remain for those on both sides of the gun rights issue regarding the extent of that right and of the ability of national, state, and local decision-makers to place limits on the right.

DOCUMENT

The District of Columbia generally prohibits the possession of handguns. It is a crime to carry an unregistered firearm, and the registration of handguns is prohibited. . . . Wholly apart from that prohibition, no person may carry a handgun without a license, but the chief of police may issue licenses for 1-year periods. . . . District of Columbia law also requires residents to keep their lawfully owned firearms, such as registered long guns, "unloaded and disassembled or bound by a trigger lock or similar device" unless they are located in a place of business or are being used for lawful recreational activities. . . .

Respondent Dick Heller is a D.C. special police officer authorized to carry a handgun while on duty at the Federal Judicial Center. He applied for a registration certificate for a handgun that he wished to keep at home, but the District refused. He thereafter filed a lawsuit in the Federal District Court for the District of Columbia seeking, on Second Amendment grounds, to enjoin the city from enforcing the bar on the registration of handguns, the licensing requirement insofar as it prohibits the carrying of a firearm in the home without a license, and the trigger-lock requirement insofar as it prohibits the use of "functional firearms within the home." . . .

The two sides in this case have set out very different interpretations of the [Second] Amendment. Petitioners and today's dissenting Justices believe that it protects only the right to possess and carry a firearm in connection with militia service. . . . Respondent argues that it protects an individual right to possess a firearm unconnected with service in a militia, and to use that arm for traditionally lawful purposes, such as self-defense within the home. . . .

The Second Amendment is naturally divided into two parts: its prefatory clause and its operative clause. The former does not limit the latter grammatically, but rather announces a purpose. The Amendment could be rephrased, "Because a well regulated Militia is necessary to the security of a free State, the right of the people to keep and bear Arms shall not be infringed." . . .

[The phrase "the people"] contrasts markedly with the phrase "the militia" in the prefatory clause. . . . "[T]he militia" in colonial America consisted of a subset of "the people"—those who were male, able bodied, and within a certain age range. Reading the Second Amendment as protecting only the right to "keep and bear Arms" in an organized militia therefore fits poorly with the operative clause's description of the holder of that right as "the people." . . .

The phrase "keep arms" was not prevalent in the written documents of the founding period that we have found, but there are a few examples, all of which favor viewing the right to "keep Arms" as an individual right unconnected with militia service. . . .

Putting all of these textual elements together, we find that they guarantee the individual right to possess and carry weapons in case of confrontation. This meaning is strongly confirmed by the historical background of the Second Amendment. We look to this because it has always been widely understood that the Second Amendment, like the First and Fourth Amendments, codified a *pre-existing* right. The very text of the Second Amendment implicitly recognizes the pre-existence of the right and declares only that it "shall not be infringed." As we said in *United States v. Cruikshank*, 92 U.S. 542, 553 (1876), "[t]his is not a right granted by the Constitution. Neither is it in any manner dependent upon that instrument for its existence. The Second amendment declares that it shall not be infringed. . . . "

By the time of the founding, the right to have arms had become fundamental for English subjects. . . .

There seems to be no doubt, on the basis of both text and history, that the Second Amendment conferred an individual right to keep and bear arms. Of course the right was not unlimited, just as the First Amendment's right of free speech was not, see, *e.g.*, *United States v. Williams*, 553 U.S. ____ (2008) . Thus, we do not read the Second Amendment to protect the right of citizens to carry arms for *any sort* of confrontation, just as we do not read the First Amendment to protect the right of citizens to speak for *any purpose* . . .

We reach the question, then: Does the preface fit with an operative clause that creates an individual right to keep and bear arms? It fits perfectly, once one knows the history that the founding generation knew and that we have described above.

That history showed that the way tyrants had eliminated a militia consisting of all the able-bodied men was not by banning the militia but simply by taking away the people's arms, enabling a select militia or standing army to suppress political opponents. This is what had occurred in England that prompted codification of the right to have arms in the English Bill of Rights. . . .

It is therefore entirely sensible that the Second Amendment's prefatory clause announces the purpose for which the right was codified: to prevent elimination of the militia. The prefatory clause does not suggest that preserving the militia was the only reason Americans valued the ancient right; most undoubtedly thought it even more important for self-defense and hunting. But the threat that the new Federal Government would destroy the citizens' militia by taking away their arms was the reason that right—unlike some other English rights—was codified in a written Constitution. . . .

Our interpretation is confirmed by analogous arms-bearing rights in state constitutions that preceded and immediately followed adoption of the Second Amendment. Four States adopted analogues to the Federal Second Amendment in the period between independence and the ratification of the Bill of Rights. Two of them—Pennsylvania and Vermont—clearly adopted individual rights unconnected to militia service. . . .

Blacks were routinely disarmed by Southern States after the Civil War. Those who opposed these injustices frequently stated that they infringed blacks' constitutional right to keep and bear arms. Needless to say, the claim was not that blacks were being prohibited from carrying arms in an organized state militia. A Report of the Commission of the Freedmen's Bureau in 1866 states plainly: "[T]he civil law [of Kentucky] prohibits the colored man from bearing arms. . . . Their arms are taken from them by the civil authorities. . . . Thus, the right of the people to keep and bear arms as provided in the Constitution is *infringed*." H.R. Exec. Doc. No. 70, 39th Cong., 1st Sess., 233, 236. . . .

. . . The judgment in [*United States v. Miller*, 307 U.S. 174 (1939)] upheld against a Second Amendment challenge two men's federal indictment for transporting an unregistered short-barreled [sawed-off] shotgun in interstate commerce, in violation of the National Firearms Act, 48 Stat. 1236. It is entirely clear that the Court's basis for saying that the Second Amendment did not apply was *not* that the defendants were "bear[ing] arms" not "for . . . military purposes" but for "nonmilitary use," *post*, at 2. Rather, it was that the *type of weapon at issue* was not eligible for Second Amendment protection: "In the absence of any evidence tending to show that the possession or use of a [short-barreled shotgun] at this time has some reasonable relationship to the preservation or efficiency of a well regulated militia, we cannot say that the Second Amendment guarantees the right to keep and bear *such an instrument*" 307 U.S., at 178 (emphasis added). "Certainly," the Court continued, "it is not within judicial notice that this weapon is any part of the ordinary military equipment or that its use could contribute to the common defense." *Ibid*. Beyond that, the opinion provided no explanation of the content of the right.

This holding is not only consistent with, but positively suggests, that the Second Amendment confers an individual right to keep and bear arms (though only arms that "have some reasonable relationship to the preservation or efficiency of a well regulated militia") . . .

We conclude that nothing in our precedents forecloses our adoption of the original understanding of the Second Amendment. It should be unsurprising that such a significant matter has been for so long judicially unresolved. For most of our history, the Bill of Rights was not thought applicable to the States, and the Federal Government did not significantly regulate the possession of firearms by law-abiding citizens. Other provisions of the Bill of Rights have similarly remained unilluminated for lengthy periods. . . .

. . . Although we do not undertake an exhaustive historical analysis today of the full scope of the Second Amendment, nothing in our opinion should be taken to cast doubt on longstanding prohibitions on the possession of firearms by felons and the mentally ill, or laws forbidding the carrying of firearms in sensitive places such as schools and government buildings, or laws imposing conditions and qualifications on the commercial sale of arms.

We also recognize another important limitation on the right to keep and carry arms. *Miller* said, as we have explained, that the sorts of weapons protected were those "in common use at the time." 307 U.S., at 179. We think that limitation is fairly supported by the historical tradition of prohibiting the carrying of "dangerous and unusual weapons." . . .

. . . It may well be true today that a militia, to be as effective as militias in the 18th century, would require sophisticated arms that are highly unusual in society at large. Indeed, it may be true that no amount of small arms could be useful against modern-day bombers and tanks. But the fact that modern developments have limited the degree of fit between the prefatory clause and the protected right cannot change our interpretation of the right.

We turn finally to the law at issue here. As we have said, the law totally bans handgun possession in the home. It also requires that any lawful firearm in the home be disassembled or bound by a trigger lock at all times, rendering it inoperable.

As the quotations earlier in this opinion demonstrate, the inherent right of self-defense has been central to the Second Amendment right. The handgun ban amounts to a prohibition of an entire class of "arms" that is overwhelmingly chosen by American society for that lawful purpose. The prohibition extends, moreover, to the home, where the need for defense of self, family, and property is most acute. Under any of the standards of scrutiny that we have applied to enumerated constitutional rights, banning from the home "the most preferred firearm in the nation to 'keep' and use for protection of one's home and family," 478 F. 3d, at 400, would fail constitutional muster.

Few laws in the history of our Nation have come close to the severe restriction of the District's handgun ban. And some of those few have been struck down. . . .

It is no answer to say, as petitioners do, that it is permissible to ban the possession of handguns so long as the possession of other firearms (*i.e.*, long guns) is allowed. It is enough to note, as we have observed, that the American people have considered the handgun to be the quintessential self-defense weapon. There are many reasons that a citizen may prefer a handgun for home defense: It is easier to store in a location that is readily accessible in an emergency; it cannot easily be redirected or wrestled away by an attacker; it is easier to use for those without the upper-body strength to lift and aim a long gun; it can be pointed at a burglar with one hand while the other hand dials the police. Whatever the reason, handguns are the most popular weapon chosen by Americans for self-defense in the home, and a complete prohibition of their use is invalid.

We must also address the District's requirement (as applied to respondent's handgun) that firearms in the home be rendered and kept inoperable at all times. This makes it impossible for citizens to use them for the core lawful purpose of self-defense and is hence unconstitutional. . . .

In sum, we hold that the District's ban on handgun possession in the home violates the Second Amendment, as does its prohibition against rendering any lawful firearm in the home operable for the purpose of immediate self-defense. Assuming that Heller is not disqualified from the exercise of Second Amendment rights, the District must permit him to register his handgun and must issue him a license to carry it in the home.

We are aware of the problem of handgun violence in this country, and we take seriously the concerns raised by the many *amici* who believe that prohibition of handgun ownership is a solution. The Constitution leaves the District of Columbia a variety of tools for combating that problem, including some measures regulating handguns. . . . But the enshrinement of constitutional rights necessarily takes certain policy choices off the table. These include the absolute prohibition of handguns held and used for self-defense in the home. Undoubtedly some think that the Second Amendment is outmoded in a society where our standing army is the pride of our Nation, where well-trained police forces provide personal security, and where gun violence is a serious problem. That is perhaps debatable, but what is not debatable is that it is not the role of this Court to pronounce the Second Amendment extinct.

We affirm the judgment of the Court of Appeals.

SOURCE: *United States v. Heller* 554 U.S. _____ (2008).

ANALYSIS

For many decades the Second Amendment to the U.S. Constitution has contributed to clashes between those who advocate placing additional limitations on gun ownership and those who insist on an extensive right to own and carry firearms. The Second Amendment states ambiguously: "A well regulated militia, being necessary to the security of a free state, the right to keep and bear arms, shall not be infringed." In his majority decision supporting an individual right to possess firearms, Justice Antonin Scalia labeled the first clause of the Second Amendment that refers to a "well regulated militia" a statement of purpose for codifying the preexisting right to keep and bear arms.

The struggle over firearm policy at the national, state, and local levels tends to divide urban residents from rural residents, liberals from conservatives, and libertarians from communitarians. Gun rights advocates have established politically influential interest groups, the National Rifle Association being the dominant group with a claimed membership of four million. These organizations generally oppose various policy proposals to reduce gun-related violence by limiting gun ownership and use. On the other side, organizations such as the Brady Center to Prevent Gun Violence advocate additional restrictions on the ownership and use of firearms.

Prior to 2008, the U.S. Supreme Court last issued a decision involving firearms in 1939 in *United States v. Miller*, a case involving an appeal of a violation of the National Firearms Act of 1934, a law limiting weapons generally associated with criminal activities, such as machine guns, sawed-off shotguns, and silencers. Two individuals who had been indicted and convicted for transporting an unregistered sawed-off shotgun across state lines appealed their conviction. The Supreme Court, in upholding the conviction, ruled that the federal regulation of firearms can be justified by Congress's taxing power.

Although subsequent commentary on the *Miller* case interpreted it as a rejection of an individual right to own a firearm, Scalia declared that the decision involved only "those weapons not typically possessed by law-abiding citizens for lawful purposes, such as short-barreled shotguns." Scalia stated that the Court's 2008 decision applied to "law-abiding, responsible citizens" who wished to possess firearms "in defense of hearth and home."

The decision left open many questions that would result in a continuing struggle over this aspect of the culture war. The National Rifle Association lawyer Chuck Michel quickly announced that the organization would challenge the San Francisco prohibition on the sale of firearms and ammunition in city housing projects. Challenges to similar laws in other cities, including Chicago, appeared imminent.

However, a constitutional question remained unresolved by the *Heller* decision. Does the Second Amendment apply to state and local governments as well as to the federal government (the decision immediately applied to the District of Columbia as federal territory)? Supporters of gun rights and advocates of gun control perceive the same data regarding the level of criminal violence in the United States but interpret the evidence very differently; one side concludes that more firearms in the hands of law-abiding citizens can be part of the solution to this violence by providing a means of defense, while the other views firearms as a major part of the problem and therefore further restrictions are justified.

The *Heller* decision notwithstanding, many gun rights supporters continued to express concerns about future gun control policy. For instance, James H. Warner (2008), an attorney and retired official of the National Rifle Association, argued during the 2008 presidential campaign that firearm owners still needed to cast their presidential ballot according to the

DID YOU KNOW?

The Castle Doctrine

In recent years the National Rifle Association has lobbied state legislatures to adopt laws to allow citizens greater leeway in the use of armed force to deal with threats. The so-called castle doctrine removes the criterion that individuals first attempt to flee before resorting to deadly force in responding to a threat in their homes, automobiles, or possibly in the workplace. From 2003 to 2008, 23 states adopted some version of the castle doctrine. The NRA argues that such laws appropriately eliminate the legal liability associated with exercising a constitutional right to protect oneself in a life-threatening situation. As evidence mounted that the number of self-defense killings has risen, questions arose regarding the legal application of the new laws. Police investigators and prosecutors are placed in the position of having to demonstrate beyond a reasonable doubt that deadly force was not justified. One criterion used is that the person against whom deadly force was used possessed a weapon.

candidates' stands on the issue of gun control and gun rights. Warner argued that, despite disagreements with Republican presidential candidate John McCain on other issues, gun owners should cast their ballots for him as the candidate more likely to oppose gun control legislation and to appoint Supreme Court justices who would support an individual right to keep and bear arms. However, economic issues dominated the last weeks of the campaign, and gun owners, like the rest of the electorate, may well have decided that those issues trumped gun rights in determining their vote decision even though, according to Warner, Barack Obama likely would appoint a Supreme Court justice less willing to support gun rights in future cases. Warner's position reflects the role that attitudes toward guns have have played in the culture war. For gun rights advocates, that one issue supposedly should dominate all other considerations in electoral politics.

"The Second Amendment"

- **Document:** National Rifle Association statement commenting on the U.S. Supreme Court decision in *District of Columbia v. Heller*.
- **Date:** July 15, 2008.
- **Where:** National Rifle Association headquarters, Fairfax, Virginia.
- **Significance:** For many years the National Rifle Association has played a significant role in the politics of gun control and gun rights, devoting its resources to electing public officials who support their interpretation of the Second Amendment, defeating those candidates who do not, and lobbying Congress and state legislatures to enact policies conducive to the interests of firearms owners. In this statement, the organization expresses its support for the Supreme Court decision in *Heller*.

DOCUMENT

On June 26, the Supreme Court ruled in *District of Columbia v. Heller* that the Second Amendment—"A well regulated Militia, being necessary to the security of a free State, the right of the people to keep and bear Arms, shall not be infringed"—protects a purely individual right, as do the First, Fourth and Ninth Amendments. "Nowhere else in the Constitution does a 'right' attributed to 'the people' refer to anything other than an individual right," the court said. "The term ['the people'] unambiguously refers to all members of the political community."

The court's 5–4 majority rejected the notion pushed by D.C. officials and gun control supporters in *Heller*—taken from the Kansas Supreme Court's decision in *Salina v. Blaksley* (1905)—that the amendment protects only a privilege to possess arms when serving in a militia. All nine justices rejected gun control supporters' alternate and mutually exclusive idea—invented by the U.S. Court of Appeals for the 3rd Circuit in *U.S. v. Tot* (1942)—that the amendment protects only a state power (a so-called "collective right") to maintain a militia.

Citing a previous decision by the court, recognizing that the right to arms is individually-held, the court noted, "As we said in *United States v. Cruikshank* (1876), '[t]his is not a right granted by the Constitution. Neither is it in any manner dependent upon that instrument for its existence. The Second Amendment declares that it shall not be infringed.'"

The court also declared that the Second Amendment protects "the individual right to possess and carry weapons in case of confrontation," including "all instruments that constitute bearable arms." It said that people have the right to keep and bear handguns (the type of arm at issue in *Heller*), because "[T]he inherent right of self-defense has been central to the Second Amendment right.... Under any of the standards of scrutiny that we have applied to enumerated constitutional rights, banning from the home 'the most preferred firearm in the nation to 'keep' and use for protection of one's home and family,' would fail constitutional muster."

As demonstrated by the vast majority of research on the subject, the court's ruling is consistent with the Second Amendment's history and text, the statements and writings of the amendment's author, James Madison, and other statesmen of the founding period, and the writings of respected legal authorities of the 19th century. Constitutional scholar Stephen Halbrook has noted that there is no evidence that anyone associated with drafting, debating and ratifying the amendment considered it to protect anything other than an entirely individual right.

Madison, who introduced the Bill of Rights in Congress, said that the amendments "relate first to private rights." In *The Federalist #46*, he wrote that the federal government would not be able to tyrannize the people, "with arms in their hands, officered by men chosen from among themselves, fighting for their common liberties, and united and conducted by [state] government possessing their affections and confidence." In *The Federalist #29*, Alexander Hamilton wrote, "if circumstances should at any time oblige the government to form an army of any magnitude that army can never be formidable to the liberties of the people while there is a large body of citizens, little, if at all, inferior to them in discipline and the use of arms, who stand ready to defend their own rights and those of their fellow-citizens."

Supreme Court Justice Joseph Story, in his *Commentaries on the Constitution* (1833), still regarded as the standard treatise on the subject, wrote, "the right of the citizens to keep and bear arms has justly been considered, as the palladium of the liberties of the republic."

In *U.S. v. Miller* (1939), the most recent of the important Second Amendment-related Supreme Court cases prior to *Heller*, the court recognized, as it did in *U.S. v. Cruikshank* (noted above), that the right to arms is individually-held and not dependent upon militia service. Had the court believed the amendment protected only a militiaman's privilege or a state power, it would have rejected the case on the grounds that the defendants were neither actively-serving militiamen or states. As the *Heller* court noted, the *Miller* court never questioned the defendants' standing. It questioned only whether a short-barreled shotgun had "a reasonable relationship to the preservation or efficiency of a well regulated militia," which it described as private citizens "bearing arms supplied by themselves and of the kind in common use at the time."

As indicated in the *Heller* decision, the Supreme Court has always recognized that the Second Amendment protects, and was intended by the Framers to protect, a purely individual right of individuals to keep and bear arms useful for defense, hunting, training and all other legitimate purposes.

SOURCE: National Rifle Association, "The Second Amendment," http://www.nraila.org/Issues/FactSheets/Read.aspx?id=177. Reprinted courtesy of the National Rifle Association.

ANALYSIS

The National Rifle Association and other gun rights organizations expressed their enthusiastic support for the Supreme Court decision in *District of Columbia et al. v. Heller.* In its official comment on the decision, the organization stated the long-standing position of the organization on the issue of firearm ownership and use. For gun rights groups and individual supporters of the right to keep and bear arms, attempts to limit gun ownership and use represents an attempt by a tyrannical power to squash the prime protection of liberty. Advocates consider the right to keep and bear arms to predate the Constitution, which essentially recognizes the existence of a right that must be vehemently protected against what are labeled the misdirected intentions of gun control supporters.

Critics of the Supreme Court's decision noted that Justice Scalia spent inordinate space in the Court's majority opinion attempting to explain away the first thirteen words of the Second Amendment as essentially unimportant to the fundamental meaning of the amendment. They considered the justice's interpretation as an attempt by the Court's conservatives to satisfy the agenda of the political right. Critics—including Justice Stephen Breyer in a dissenting opinion—referred to the Court's denial to the District of Columbia the authority to deal with "a serious, indeed life-threatening, problem" in its own way. For critics, the decision represented an example of judicial activism engaged in by conservative justices who otherwise advocate judicial restraint.

> ## *DID YOU KNOW?*
>
> ### Black Friday in South Carolina
>
> In 2008 the South Carolina state legislature granted a tax break to gun purchasers by adding an amendment to a measure to establish a tax incentive for energy-efficient appliances. The amendment suspended state and local sales taxes on purchases of handguns, rifles, and shotguns on Black Friday (the day after Thanksgiving) and on the following Saturday. The tax holiday was referred to as "Second Amendment Weekend." Republican state representative Mike Pitts, a retired police officer who introduced the amendment, stated that Alabama has a gun-owning and hunting tradition and that often people will purchase a shotgun or rifle for "their pop or grandpop" for Christmas. Although Republican Governor Mark Sanford is a devoted hunter and gun supporter, he opposed the measure, calling it a stunt that may affect the timing of a firearm purchase but not overall gun ownership or demand. The tax break measure was introduced at a time when Alabama had to reduce annual spending by $448 million, but state officials estimated that the measure would cost the state only about $15,000 in revenue.

"Unintended Consequences: What the Supreme Court's Second Amendment Decision in *D.C. v. Heller* Means for the Future of Gun Laws"

- *Document:* A public response from the Legal Action Project of the Brady Center to Prevent Gun Violence to the U.S. Supreme Court Ruling in *District of Columbia v. Heller*.
- *Date:* October 20, 2008.
- *Where:* Washington, DC.
- *Significance:* The Brady Campaign, an organization calling for additional regulations on firearms, responds to the U.S. Supreme Court's decision holding that the Second Amendment protects an individual's right to possess firearms. This analysis disagrees with the Court's interpretation of the Second Amendment and focuses on the organization's intention to continue calling for additional "sensible gun laws" to prevent gun violence.

DOCUMENT

The Supreme Court's 5-4 decision in *District of Columbia v. Heller* declared a private right to arms, dramatically changing the long-settled meaning of the Second Amendment, struck down the District of Columbia's ban on handguns as unlawful, and inspired lawsuits against similar bans in other cities. The *Heller* decision, and its questionable reasoning, creates risks to gun laws that criminal defendants and the gun lobby will likely attempt to exploit. Nonetheless, the long-term effects of the decision are at odds with the day-after headlines proclaiming a seminal victory for "gun rights."

The Court went out of its way to make clear that most gun laws are "presumptively" constitutional while also putting to rest gun owners' fears of a total ban or ultimate confiscation of all firearms. By taking the extremes of the gun policy debate off the table,

Heller has the potential to allow genuine progress in implementing reasonable gun restrictions, while protecting basic rights to possess firearms. The unintended consequence of *Heller* is that it may end up "de-wedgeifying" one of the more divisive "wedge" issues on the political landscape: guns. The net result of *Heller* would then be positive by leading to the enactment of the strong gun laws that we need—and the vast majority of Americans want—to protect our communities from gun violence.

The Limited Direct Effect of the Heller Decision

A narrow 5–4 majority of the Supreme Court in *Heller* held that the Constitution provides private citizens with a right to arms, rejecting the view—held by virtually every previous court in our nation's history—that the Second Amendment's militia clause and history limit the right of arms to service in a "well-regulated militia." But the practical effect of the decision is likely to help, not hurt, the cause of preventing gun violence in America.

The direct effect of *Heller* is that the District of Columbia's ban on handguns was invalidated. As Justice Scalia put it in the Court's opinion, the Second Amendment protects "the right of law-abiding, responsible citizens to use arms in defense of hearth and home." *D.C. v. Heller*, 554 U.S.___. Slip op. at 63 (2008). However, other than the Washington, D.C. law struck down by the Court, only Chicago, and a handful of suburban Chicago jurisdictions, have a handgun ban. And even those bans may not be struck down under *Heller*. Because the District is a federal enclave, whether the Second Amendment is "incorporated" against the states was "a question not presented by this case," and the Court cited to its earlier decisions that "reaffirmed that the Second Amendment applies only to the Federal Government." *Heller*, slip op. at 48, n.23. Therefore, unless and until the Court holds otherwise, the Second Amendment does not restrict state or local laws. As direct precedent, *Heller* could not be used to support the invalidation of any other gun law in America.

Not only are gun bans impacted by *Heller* few and far between, but they are the only gun violence prevention proposals that do not consistently garner overwhelming public support. *Compare* Pew Research Center for the People & the Press, April 23–27, 2008, finding that 59% of Americans oppose a handgun ban [1] *with* Greenberg Quinlan Rossner & The Tarrance Report poll finding that 67% of Americans favor an assault weapon ban [2]. Taking such bans off the table of policy options will have little effect on the national debate over what effective, politically viable gun violence prevention proposals should be enacted. . . .

"De-Wedgefying" the Gun Issue

There is a reason that guns—along with God and gays—has been among the most divisive wedge issues in the political playbook. There are many law-abiding citizens in America who care deeply about their guns, and do not want their guns taken away. The proposals that the Brady Campaign advocates (from universal background checks to anti-trafficking measures) are aimed at keeping dangerous weapons out of the hands of dangerous people, and would not deprive law-abiding citizens of conventional pistols, rifles, or shotguns. Nonetheless, the gun lobby has been successful

Sarah Brady speaks at a White House press conference attended by her husband, James Brady (center), and President and Mrs. Ronald Reagan. James Brady was severely injured in a March 1981 assassination attempt in which Reagan himself was wounded. (Ronald Reagan Library)

in arguing that any Brady Campaign proposal is "anti-gun," and could lead to a total gun ban or confiscation of all guns in private hands. Every election, the gun lobby tells gun owners that the politicians they oppose are "going to take away your guns." As then-NRA President Charlton Heston famously told the NRA Convention in 2000, with a rifle held aloft his head, "As we set out this year to defeat the divisive forces that would take freedom away, I want to say those words again for everyone within the sound of my voice to hear and to heed, and especially for you, Mr. Gore: 'From my cold, dead hands!'" [3] The fact that Al Gore only supported reasonable gun violence prevention proposals, not far-reaching gun bans, did not stop the NRA from employing some slippery slope sleight of hand to convert those modest proposals into a broad attack on gun owners' "freedom." In 2004, the NRA recycled those attacks against John Kerry, as the Annenberg Political Fact Check explained:

The National Rifle Association began airing a TV ad Oct. 26 falsely accusing Kerry of voting to ban deer-hunting ammunition. In fact, what Kerry voted for was a proposal to outlaw rifle ammunition "designed or marketed as having armor piercing capability." The NRA ad also claims Kerry is co-sponsoring a bill "that would ban every semiautomatic shotgun and every pump shotgun." That's false. Kerry co-sponsored extension of the now-expired assault-weapon ban, a measure that would have expanded the ban to cover military-style shotguns but specifically *exempts* pump-action shotguns. [4]

In 2008, the name on the top of the Democratic ticket changed, but the NRA script remained the same: Barack Obama supports gun control, ergo, they say, he is after your guns. [5]

These gun lobby attacks are—and always have been—patently false. While there have been some in America who favor far-reaching gun bans, Al Gore, John Kerry, and Barack Obama are not among them. The Brady Campaign, too, has not supported broad bans on conventional handguns, sporting rifles or shotguns, but that has not stopped some in the gun lobby to falsely drum up fears of a nefarious secret agenda. Indeed, the gun lobby's fear-mongering tends to be selective. For example, John McCain supported closing the gun show loophole, and George W. Bush and [Senator] John Warner supported renewing the assault weapon ban, but the NRA has not suggested they had ulterior motives—at least not when they were on a general election ballot.

After *Heller*, the fears that the gun lobby tries to drum up are not simply false— they are impossible. For *even if* supporters of gun control *wanted* to bar law-abiding citizens from possessing guns to defend themselves in the home, the Constitution, as interpreted by *Heller*, would not permit it. The law-abiding citizen's hunting rifle and handgun are safe. Once the fact that the slippery slope is dead settles into our political consciousness, the "wedgeification" of guns should lose its salience.

Now that the Supreme Court has removed the fears and Constitutional concerns that have clouded our national discourse on gun policy, gun owners have no more reason to fear that reasonable gun laws could lead to confiscation of their guns—for the Supreme Court has made clear that the Constitution will not allow it. Supporters of reasonable gun laws need not fear that the laws they desire are not permitted under the Constitution—for the Court has made clear that they are permitted. *Heller* has left us in a world where the debate over our nation's gun policy should be necessarily constrained within these limits. After *Heller*, the issue is: What reasonable gun laws should be passed that will make our families and communities more safe, without infringing on the right of law-abiding persons to possess guns for self-defense? This framing of the issue will move the debate from the extremes to the middle and, as such, is highly favorable to progress toward a new, sensible, national gun policy.

Heller's Shaky Precedent

Despite the potentially positive effects of *Heller*, its shaky legal reasoning should not be ignored. Especially when the gun lobby and criminals attempt to extend the opinion far beyond its language, courts must be reminded that the right discovered by five Justices in *Heller* was not supported by the Second Amendment's text or history. Many legal scholars still firmly believe that the decision by Justice Scalia and four fellow Justices that the Second Amendment protects a right to bear arms unrelated to participation in a state militia was incorrect. Virtually every court in American history that had construed the Amendment had been swayed by the historical record that makes the militia-centric purpose of James Madison and the other framers undeniable, as well as by the inconvenient fact that the Amendment begins by expressly referencing its one purpose—"a well-regulated militia, being necessary to the security of a free State." The last time the Court considered the Amendment's meaning, in *U.S. v. Miller*, 307 U.S. 174 (1939), it unanimously stated that it "must be interpreted and applied" in accord with its "obvious purpose to assure the continuation and render possible the effectiveness" of a well regulated militia. Nonetheless, Justice Scalia somehow found that the Amendment served purposes unstated in its text, stating "[t]he prefatory clause does not suggest that preserving the militia was the only reason Americans valued the ancient right * * *." Unencumbered by history, the *Miller* precedent, or the militia-centric language chosen by the Framers, Scalia read the Second Amendment as if its first 13 words didn't exist. So much for "judicial restraint," "original intent," and "respect for precedent."

As Justice [John Paul] Stevens aptly noted in his dissent, "the right the Court announces was not 'enshrined' in the Second Amendment by the Framers; it is the product of today's law-changing decision." Judicial scholars from across the political spectrum have roundly criticized Justice Scalia's majority opinion. One of the most noted conservative legal scholars of our day, Judge Richard Posner, likened the opinion to a "snow job," stating that "It is questionable in both method and result, and it is evidence that the Supreme Court, in deciding constitutional cases, exercises a freewheeling discretion strongly flavored with ideology." [6] Judge J. Harvie Wilkinson III, a perennial on the short-lists of potential Republican Supreme Court nominees, railed against Scalia's decision as driven by the Justices' policy views, and as evidencing a "failure to adhere to a conservative judicial methodology." [7] Judge Wilkinson wrote that the losers in *Heller* "have cause to feel they have been wrongfully denied the satisfaction of a fair hearing and an honest fight."

The questionable basis for the ruling should counsel against its extension, much like another controversial decision, *Bush v. Gore*.

DID YOU KNOW?

Gun Sales across the Southern Border

The border between El Paso, Texas, and Juárez, Mexico has become the focus of concern about the increasing level of violence in Mexico spilling over to the United States. Although El Paso registered about 15 murders in 2008, Juárez logged more than 1,300 killings. The drug war among Mexican drug-trafficking groups, including six cartels, more than 125 subordinate organizations, and at least 606 local gangs, are responsible for much of the violence. A factor keeping in check the violence on the U.S. side of the border is that although law enforcement agencies in Mexico have failed to address the crime problem, often due to corruption, officials from various federal agencies, including Immigration and Customs Enforcement, the Federal Bureau of Investigation, and the Drug Enforcement Administration, regularly monitor the violence in Mexico. Although reports of violence in Mexico raise fears that the violence may spread to border areas in the United States, reports indicate that firearms purchased in the United States are responsible for much of the violence in Mexico. For instance, the Bureau of Alcohol, Tobacco, Firearms, and Explosives has reported that of the guns recovered in Mexico—a country with very stringent gun control laws—in 2007, 1,131 were purchased in Texas, 436 in California, and 238 in Arizona. Mexican officials claim that 90 percent of approximately 27,000 weapons recovered from crime scenes and criminal storage locations originated in the United States, where firearms are available in plentiful numbers.

Conclusion

As students of the Constitution and American history, we believe that Justice Stevens' opinion, also representing the views of Justice [Steven] Breyer, [David] Souter, and [Ruth Bader] Ginsburg, better reflects the meaning of the Second Amendment and the intent of its framers than the majority opinion of Justice Scalia. However, in the real world, the *Heller* decision will likely mark an historic example of another law—the law of unintended consequences. By making clear that the Constitution does not permit broad gun bans such as the District's, while allowing for strong reasonable gun laws, the *Heller* decision could well mark a turning point that leads to our nation finally addressing our gun violence problem in a sane and sensible way.

NOTES

[1] See poll at http://people-press.org/reports/pdf/419.pdf, last accessed on 10/8/08.

[2] See poll at http://www.mayorsagainstillegalguns.org/downloads/pdf/polling_memo.pdf, last accessed on 10.8.08.

[3] http://www.Youtube.com/watch?v=5ju4Gla20dw.

[4] http://www.factcheck.org/article296.html.

[5] NRA anti-Obama mailing at http://marcambinder.theatlantic.com/archives/2008/09/nra_hits_obama_hed_be_the_most.php.

[6] Richard A. Posner, "In Defense of Looseness," *The New Republic*, August 27, 2008.

[7] J. Harvie Wilkinson III, "Of Guns, Abortion, and the Unraveling of the Rule of Law," forthcoming and at http://ssrn.com/abstract=1265118....

SOURCE: Legal Action Project of the Brady Center to Prevent Gun Violence, "Unintended Consequences: What the Supreme Court's Second Amendment Decision in *D.C. v. Heller* Means for the Future of Gun Laws" (October 20, 2008). http://www.bradycenter.org/xshare/pdf/heller/post-heller-white-paper.pdf. Reprinted courtesy of the Legal Action Project of the Brady Center to Prevent Gun Violence.

ANALYSIS

The Brady Campaign to Prevent Gun Violence, in responding to the U.S. Supreme Court decision in *Washington, D.C. v. Heller* invalidating a law in the nation's capital that prohibited the ownership of handguns—disagreed with the Court's interpretation of the Second Amendment but also attempted to find in the decision promising elements for the organization's goal of limiting firearm violence. According to the Brady Campaign, although the Court's majority decision proclaimed an individual's right to keep and bear arms, the decision also allows various restrictions on types of weapons, on the sale of firearms, and on the carrying of concealed weapons. The organization anticipates that the decision, by recognizing a constitutionally protected right to own firearms, could result in gun control becoming less of a "wedge issue," and thus increase the likelihood of instituting reasonable limitations on firearms and also reducing the issue's divisive role in the culture wars. Less optimistically, the Brady Campaign anticipates that individuals and groups opposed to gun control measures will begin bringing additional suits in state and federal courts challenging various regulations. A question that still remains unanswered is whether the Second Amendment applies to state and local governments as well as to the federal government. The Brady Campaign, considering gun violence a major problem for the nation, remains committed to passing additional gun control laws, especially where the organization considers legislation weak or nonexistent.

"The Hopelessness of Trying to Disarm the Kinds of People Who Murder"

- *Document:* Don B. Kates's article arguing that attempts to ban fire-arms are futile.
- *Date:* 2005.
- *Where:* *Bridges*, an interdisciplinary journal of theology, philosophy, history, and science (Volume 12, numbers 3/4): 313–30.
- *Significance:* Don Kates, a longtime advocate of gun rights and the advantages of gun ownership, argues against any attempt to pro-hibit the ownership of firearms. Kates claims that such a legal prohibition would be bound to fail, given the enterprising nature of the underworld. The key to deterring crime is allowing the aver-age citizen to possess a firearm for self-protection and the defense of family and home.

DOCUMENT

I have two replies when—as a criminologist studying firearms issues—I am asked: Would the world not benefit if there were no guns? First, 1,200 years ago there were no guns. Yet, for excellent reasons, that period in Europe has been called the Dark Ages. Firearms are the only weaponry by which the weak can resist the strong. Their absence was characterized by oppression and massacre, not peace.

Second, I advise those wanting a world without guns to pray. If there is a God, He can eliminate guns. All banning guns to the general populace can accomplish is disarming the law-abiding, leaving the lawless armed.

Ducking the Enforcement Problem

There are literally thousands of articles proclaiming how wonderful it would be if guns just disappeared. I know of none undertaking to explain how nations can successfully confiscate guns from a resistant citizenry, much less from thugs. Only a very few of these thousands of articles even mention the enforcement problem. One 10,000-word article devotes just a paragraph to the problem—and just two words to solving it: that illuminating solution is "strict enforcement." [1]

Typical of the very few discussions treating the problem seriously is one by a former head of the American Civil Liberties Union (ACLU). His philippic against guns ends by woefully admitting bans are unenforceable within our Bill of Rights. [2] Others, less dedicated to civil liberties, implicitly or explicitly admit the same by advocating "*unlimited* search and seizure . . . the police will have to be given the right to frisk anyone for hidden guns at any time and any place." [3] The ardently anti-gun *Journal of the American Medical Association* (JAMA) reports without demurrer a call by the president of the Los Angeles Medical Association for a "'military attack'" on minority areas: " 'make a sweep through those neighborhoods, take all the weapons . . . ' " [4]

A Dubious Assumption, An Erroneous Assertion

Some gun ban advocates frankly concede that "No amount of control will stop a determined assassin—or a determined street robber—from getting a gun." [5] To blunt the force of this, they blithely assume enforcement will be unnecessary to disarm the millions of ordinary American gun owners since they will voluntarily surrender the guns they think essential to family defense in a nation beset with violence. From this dubious assumption, anti-gun advocates reason that disarming ordinary people will diminish murders that they (wrongly) think are primarily "not committed by felons or mentally ill people, but are acts of passion that are committed using a handgun that is owned for home protection. That gun in the closet to protect against burglars will most likely be used to shoot a spouse in a moment of rage. . . . The problem is you and me—law-abiding folks." [6]

Actually killers are virtually never "law-abiding folks." So all disarming such folks accomplishes is reducing their capacity to protect their families. Perpetrator studies invariably show persons involved in life-threatening violence " . . . *almost always* have a long history of involvement in criminal behavior," [7] and/or psychopathology and substance abuse. Studies by the Kennedy School at Harvard University suggest that as many as 95% of killers are violent gang members or were arrested for prior crimes; 89% had been arrested for armed violent crime. [8] And unlike ordinary people, the other 5% (and many of the 95% as well) have sanity problems [9] or were under restraining orders for prior violence or threats. [10]

Whether ordinary, responsible adults have guns or not, their incidence of serious violent crime is virtually nil. The contrary assertions pervading anti-gun articles usually appear *sans* supporting evidence. The few articles purporting to cite supporting criminological evidence actually cite irrelevancies, *e.g.*, most killers "are neither felons nor crazy" but rather are "people who are sad or depressed"; [11] that: many killings arise out of arguments and/or occur in the home, among relatives or acquaintances, and "typically involve people who loved, or hated, each other;" [12] "murder is almost always an act of blind rage or illogical passion;" [13] "most shootings are not committed by felons or mentally ill people, but are acts of passion." [14]

To accept these irrelevancies as proving murderers are ordinary people and not criminals or lunatics, one must think criminals and lunatics have no relatives or acquaintances nor do criminals or lunatics get sad or angry, love or hate people, or act out of passion. As to many murders occurring in homes, suffice it to note that in handgun murders occurring between acquaintances in a home "the most common victim-offender relationship was that between persons involved in drug dealing, where *both parties were criminals who knew one another because of prior illegal transactions.*" [15].

In short, murderers are overwhelmingly extreme aberrants with life histories of violence, psychopathology, and/or substance abuse. So gun bans can only reduce murder if they disarm precisely those whom even anti-gun advocates admit they will not disarm. (**Note:** my argument does not apply against our existing laws banning guns to people with serious criminal or sanity records. Though such people will disobey those laws, the laws have marginal utility in providing a basis for incarcerating such people in the rare event they are discovered having guns.) [16]

Unenforceability of Gun Bans

Experience in several nations confirms that gun bans do not disarm even a resistant general populace, much less lunatics and criminals.

a. The American Example

From the 1920s forward, American state laws generally forbade those with prior felony convictions possessing handguns. The federal Gun Control Act of 1968 went further, prohibiting any gun to people who were convicted of felony or involuntarily committed to mental institutions. The crime history of 20th-century America makes it obvious that these laws are regularly flouted.

As to whether the normally law abiding populace can be disarmed, polls show owners responding that they would not comply with a firearms ban. That is verified by actual behavior. Despite often ferocious penalties, gun owners will not register their firearms because they fear this paves the way for eventual confiscation.

In recent years, several states and municipalities passed laws mandating the registration of assault rifles [or banning them outright]. These laws were overwhelmingly ignored. In Boston and Cleveland the rate of compliance ... is estimated at 1%. Out of the 100,000 to 300,000 assault rifles estimated to be in private hands in New Jersey, 947 were registered, an additional 888 rendered inoperable and 4 turned over to authorities. In California, nearly 90% of the approximately 300,000 assault weapons owners did not register their weapons. [17]

b. The British Example

Foreign observers dismiss gun control in America as hopeless, given America's enormous civilian gunstock. [18] But experience in nations with much less gun ownership suggests gun control is unworkable there as well. As early as the 1970s, a senior police official's study for the Cambridge Institute of Criminology described the effect of the 1920 handgun permit requirement: "Half a century of strict controls has ended, perversely, with a far greater use of this class of weapon in crime than ever before." [19] Extending these remarks the same official, Chief Superintendent Greenwood, stated some years later:

> At first glance it may seem odd, or even perverse, to suggest that statutory controls on the private ownership of firearms are irrelevant to the problem of armed crime, yet that is precisely what the evidence shows. Armed crime and violent crime generally are products of ethnic and social factors unrelated to the availability of any particular type of weapon. *The numbers of firearms required [to arm criminals] are minute, and these are supplied no matter what controls are instituted.* Controls have had serious effects on legitimate users of firearms, but there is no case either in the history of this country or in the experience of other countries, in which controls have been shown to have restricted the flow of weapons to criminals or in any way to have reduced armed crime. [20]

Despite the policies then in force and the progressively more stringent steps that followed, violent crime soared through and after the end of the 20th century. The ever more stringent policies culminated in England's 1997 total handgun ban and confiscation—from owners law abiding enough to surrender them. Despite this, by the 2000s England's violent crime rate was double that of the U.S. [21] News headlines began to mirror American headlines from prior decades, *e.g.*, *London Times*, Jan. 16, 2000: "Killings Rise As 3 Million Illegal Guns Flood Britain"; *Punch*, May 3–16, 2000, "Britain's Tough Gun Control Laws Termed Total Failure: Land of Hope and Gunrunning"; *London Telegraph*: August 17, 2001, "Gun killings double as police claim progress"; *New Statesman*, Nov. 5, 2001, "The British Become Trigger Happy"; *London Telegraph*, Feb. 24, 2002, "Gun crime trebles as weapons and drugs flood British cities"; *London Times*, October 13, 2002, "Murder rate soars to highest for a century." As of 2004 while the rate at which violent crime was accelerating had greatly slowed, English violent crime rates remained enormous and were still growing. One 2005 article was headlined "Violent Crime 'Out of Control'." [22] Another quoted a police chief who has to beg chiefs from adjacent jurisdictions to lend his over-worked department detectives as saying, " 'We are reeling with the murders, we are in a crisis with major crime'." *News Telegraph*, Feb. 14, 2005.

Under the 1997 handgun ban, 166,000 handguns were turned in by law-abiding owners. Yet that left untold numbers in criminal hands. Nor has England been able to prevent illegal importation of millions more guns. As of 2002, a report of England's National Crime Intelligence Service lamented, that while "Britain has some of the strictest gun laws in the world [i]t appears that anyone who wishes to obtain a firearm [illegally] will have little difficulty in doing so." [23]

c. The Belgian Example

In 2002, Belgium enacted what an anti-gun advocacy group described as the "World's Strictest Gun Law." Under it, gun possession was only by a permit which required a showing of need and all guns had to be registered. [24] As of 2005, however, Belgium's Justice Minister was proposing further legislation because of the apparent flouting of the 2002 registration/permission law. Though more than 641,000 guns had been registered, an estimated two million more (approximately 70% of the total) were being possessed without permit or registration. [25]

Two million illegal guns is an enormous number for a nation whose total population is little over 10 million. Perhaps this massive evasion of the gun laws was impelled by the 1997 British experience in which owners who had registered and gotten permits had their handguns later confiscated while illegal owners did not. Whatever the cause, the effect is that, once again, stringent gun control proved unenforceable against even the general citizenry, much less criminals.

d. *The Canadian Example*

In 1995, Canada required every civilian-owned firearm to be registered as of year-end 2002. This was enacted with promises that implementation would cost about two million dollars and be processed by ordinary civil servants without diverting police resources from handling dangerous crimes. Two years after the deadline the registry was still woefully incomplete—and it was estimated to have already cost at least two *billion* dollars and to have diverted tens of thousands of hours of police time. (A full cost estimate could not be made because the Justice Ministry had ceased cooperating with the Auditor-General in 2002 after she reported that costs already exceeded one billion dollars.) What these expenditures have so far wrought is a gun registry that covers less than half of Canadian guns. The rest (estimated by the government at seven million guns and by its critics at 20 million) have gone unregistered by defiant owners. [26]

Some General Observations

Those who recognize the futility of gun control enforcement in the gun-dense U.S. are certainly correct as far as that goes. But there is no basis for their assumption that gun controls are enforceable in nations that are less gun-dense. While there is a distinction between very gun-dense nations and those less gun-dense, it is a distinction without a difference: where guns are less dense there will be a thriving black market. Where guns are plentiful, the black market is smaller because criminals can get guns easily from multiple sources. In either case criminals get ready access to guns illegally.

This was epitomized by an incident in which English police discovered a covert shipment of 30 Croatian-made Mini-Uzis *without serial* numbers. [27] To obtain those guns, an English drug gang or organized gun trafficker had to have the resources and connections in distant Croatia to special-order 30 Mini-Uzis to be taken off the assembly line before being inscribed with serial numbers and then covertly shipped to England. This could not have happened in the U.S.—because the easy availability of guns here means there is no high-end black market in guns. Sometimes low-level criminal entrepreneurs go to states where handguns are legal, buy 30 or more, and smuggle them back to New York where handguns are banned. But low-level American gun runners would not have the resources or connections to special order Mini-Uzis from a Croatian factory. Nor would they want to do so because there is no market. Why would an American robber pay $3,000 for a Mini-Uzi when for $150 or less he can buy a 12-gauge, double-barrel shotgun on the street and saw down the barrels, thereby producing a weapon just as concealable and even more awesome looking than a Mini-Uzi?

In England, severe anti-gun laws make firearms unavailable to the general public—but not to those willing to defy gun laws. All that is accomplished by the scarcity of guns to the general public is to make obtaining and selling them more profitable. The English National Crime Information Service report notes, "Pistols and even machine guns are now freely available on the black market, often coming from the war-ravaged Balkans." [28] To reiterate, in either the U.S. or England "anyone who wishes to obtain a firearm [illegally] will have little difficulty in doing so." [29]

There is no way of sealing off the borders even of a nation surrounded by water. Thousands of illegal emigrants are smuggled by boat into both England and the U.S. A *fortiori* millions of guns could be smuggled in—if there were a market for them. At the time of John Lennon's murder nearly 25 years ago I noted that if all 54 million handguns then in the U.S. suddenly evaporated, they could be more than replaced in only 3 years of smuggling at the rate U.S. authorities estimated that marijuana was being smuggled in. [30]

Nor would it matter even if the smuggling of guns could somehow be eliminated. All that would do is create a market for organized crime manufacture of black market guns. During the Vietnam and Afghan Wars (respectively) Pakistani and Vietnamese peasants regularly produced crude but workable copies of modern handguns and full-auto rifles. Anyone with access to the far superior metal working machinery and energy resources that millions of Europeans and Americans have in home workshops can manufacture for the black market pot metal copies of modern firearms. These would actually cost less than legal guns do now being much cheaper to produce and because the black market is not burdened by taxes, record keeping requirements, and safety standards. [31] Thus despite severe Philippine anti-gun laws it is reported that "cottage manufactured" submachine guns sell for $215.00 or less while .38 revolvers sell there for $27.00. [32] (By way of contrast, the cheapest legally sold U.S. .38 would cost about 10 times that.) Cottage-manufactured guns have also been observed in considerable numbers in Jamaica and Chechnya.

Conclusion

Anti-gun advocates fervently intone the mantra that **more guns = more murder, fewer guns = fewer murders**. Twenty-five years ago, a U.S. Government-sponsored study of the entire literature on gun control found "no persuasive evidence" supporting the mantra. [33]

In 2003 and 2004, studies by the Centers for Disease Control (CDC) and the National Academy of Sciences (NAS) respectively, it was found that no gun control initiative had reduced murder or suicide. [34]

Nor can the mantra be

squared with U.S. experience since 1946, the earliest time for which reliable figures exist on murder and gunstock rates. That year those rates were:

34,430 guns, and six murders, per 100,000 population. As of 2000 the gunstock rate had [almost tripled, swelling] to 95,500 but the murder rate [had increased only 1/10th of 1% to] 6.1 per 100,000. [35]

The mantra is supposedly validated by comparing U.S. murder rates to those of a few specially selected other nations. But when large numbers of nations (including the U.S.) are compared no correlation appears between nations having greater per capita gun ownership and higher murder rates. [36]

Since ordinary people virtually never kill, the overall number of guns they have is virtually irrelevant. What is relevant is the number of guns possessed by the violent aberrants who do kill. Unfortunately there seems no effective way to disarm them. Just as they are unwilling to obey laws against violence so are they unwilling to obey laws against guns. Just as we are largely unable to prevent them from committing murders so are we largely unable to prevent them from getting illegal guns.

Attempting to disarm the general population will make things much worse. First, it would promote crime by depriving victims of the means of self-defense and, thereby, remove a major deterrent to violent crime. [37] Moreover, as noted in the study done for Oxford University Press by James Jacobs, Director of the Center for Research in Crime and Justice at New York University (NYU):

Any serious effort to pass a firearms disarmament plan would trigger massive gun acquisition [during the pre-enactment period while it was under discussion] and expand and radicalize a resistance movement. The last thing the U.S. government needs is endless conflict with a large segment of the population that has never committed a gun crime. A war on civilian gun ownership would undermine crime prevention by unnecessarily diverting resources from preventing and solving crime. [38]

ENDNOTES

[1] R. J. Riley, "Shooting to Kill the Handgun: Time to Martyr Another American 'Hero' " 51 *J. Urb L.* 491, 524 (1974).

[2] Aryeh Neier, *Crime and Punishment: A Radical Solution* (1975). To the same effect see Donald T. Lunde, *Murder and Madness.*

[3] Columbia (Mo.) *Daily Tribune*, Dec. 22, 1980.

[4] Quoted in P. Cotton, "CDC investigators explore new territory in aftermath of unrest in Los Angeles," JAMA 267 (1992):3001–2.

[5] Editorial "Controlling Guns" *National Law Journal*, April 13, 1981, p. 14. To the same effect see *e.e.*, Richard Harding, "Firearms Ownership and Accidental Misuse in S. Australia," 6 *Adelaide L. Rev.* 271, 272 (1978).

[6] Such false assertions are repeated throughout anti-gun literature, *e.g.* Frank J. Vandall "A Preliminary Consideration of Issues Raised in the Firearms Sellers Immunity Bill" 38 *Akron L. Rev.* 113, 118–19 and footnote 28 (2005) recycling the quotes set out above from Katherine Christoffel, "Toward Reducing Pediatric Injuries from Firearms: Charting a Legislative and Regulatory Course," 88 *Pediatrics* 294, 300 (1991) and Prof. David Kairy's article "A Carnage in the Name of Freedom," *Philadelphia Inquirer*,

September 12, 1988. Accord: Etzioni & Remp supra, p. 107, Daniel Webster, *et al.*, "Reducing Firearms Injuries," *Issues in Science and Technology*, Spring, 1991: 73–9, p. 73; Bruce R. Conklin & Richard H. Seiden, "Gun Deaths: Biting the Bullet on Effective Control" *Public Affairs Report*: Bulletin of the Institute of Governmental Studies [U.C. Berkeley] vol. 22 (1981), p. 4, George Pickett & John J. Hanlon, *Public Health: Administration and Practice* 496 (Times-Mirror: 1990), Frederick P. Rivara & F. Bruder Stapleton, "Handguns and children: a dangerous mix." 3 *Developmental and Behavioral Pedriatrics* 35, 37 (1982).

[7] Emphasis added—Delbert Elliott, "Life Threatening Violence is *Primarily* a Crime Problem: A Focus on Prevention," 69 *Colo. L. Rev.* 1081–1098 at 1089 (1998) (collecting studies).

[8] Anthony A. Brage, *et al.*, "Understanding and Preventing Gang Violence: Problem Analysis and Response Development," forthcoming in 8 *Politice Quarterly #3* (2005). Prior consistent Kennedy School studies include Braga, *et al.* "Youth Homicide in Boston: An Assessment of the Supplementary Homicide Report Data," 3 *Homicide Studies* 277, 283–84 (1999), Kennedy supra and, also by David M. Kennedy, *et al.*, "Homicide in Minneapolis: Research for Problem Solving," 2 *Homicide Studies* 163, 269 (1998), "Youth Violence in Boston: Gun Markets, Serious Youth Offenders and a Use Reduction Strategy," 59 *Law & Contemp Probs* 147, 159–60 (1997) and "Pulling Levers, Chronic Offenders, High Crime Settings, and a Theory of Prevention," 31 *Valparaison L. Rev.* (1997).

[9] See *e.g.*, Wade C. Myers & Kerrilyn Scott, "Psychotic and Conduct Disorder Symptoms in Juvenile Murderers," 2 *Homicide Studies* 160 (1998) (citing psychological studies finding 80–100% of juvenile murderers variously psychotic or have psychotic symptoms), Sheilagh Hodgins, "Mental Disorder, Intellectual Deficiency, and Crime," 49 *Arch. Gen. Psychi.* 476 (1992) (collecting U.S. and foreign studies showing persons suffering major mental disorder and substance abusers are each several times more likely to engage in violent crime than are ordinary people), and Pekka Santilla & Jaana Haapasalo, "Neurological and Psychological Risk Factors Among Young Homicidal, Violent, and Nonviolent Offenders in Finland," 1 *Homicide Studies* 234 (1997) (summarizing American and foreign studies on the extensive psychiatric histories of murderers).

[10] See *e.g.*, Linda Langford, Nancy Isaac & Sandra Adams, "Criminal and Restraining Order Histories of Intimate Partner-Related Homicide Offenders in Massachusetts, 1991–95" in Paul H. Blackman, *et al.*, *The Varieties of Homicide and Its Research* (Quantico, Va.: F.B.I. Academy, 2000) ("According to preliminary analysis, at least 74.7% of perpetrators had a prior criminal history in Massachusetts. . . . Nearly a quarter of perpetrators (23.6%) were under an active restraining order at the time of the homicide. Forty percent of perpetrators had a history of having been under a restraining order at some time prior to the homicide, taken out by the victim or some other person.")

[11] Calhoun, supra, at p. 15.

[12] Spitzer, as quoted above.

[13] Picket & Hanlon, supra at 496.

[14] Christoffel, supra, 88 *Pediatrics* at 300.

[15] Gary Kleck, *Targeting Guns: Firearms and Their Control* 236 (1997) (emphasis added) based on U.S. Bureau of Justice Statistics data run on murder defendants being prosecuted in the 33 largest urban countries in 1988.

[16] See the discussion by a career U.S. federal agent-turned criminal justice professor, William J. Vizzard, *Shots in the Dark: The Policy, Politics, and Symbolism of Gun Control* (New York: Rowman & Littlefield, 2000) at 167–69.

[17] James B. Jacobs, *Can Gun Control Work?* (Oxford, 2002) 150 (footnotes omitted).

[18] Reuters N. America Wire Service, Aut. 1, 1994, "Britain's Police Chief Calls for Gun Crackdown"; M. L. Friedland, "Gun Control: The Options," *Crim. L. Q.* 18 (1975–76) 29, 34–35.

[19] Colin Greenwood, *Firearms Control: Armed Crime and Firearms Control in England and Wales* 243 (London: Routledge, Kegan Paul, 1972).

[20] From Greenwood & Magaddino, "Comparative Statistics" in Don B. Kates, ed., *Restricting Handguns* (1979) at 39, emphasis added.

[21] John van Kesteren, *et al.*, *Criminal Victimization in 17 Industrialised Countries: Key Findings from the 2000 International Crime Victimization Surveys* (Feb. 23, 2001).

[22] *Sky News*, July 21, 2001.

[23] Report as quoted in "Guns, Crack, and Child Porn—UK's Growing Crimes," Reuters, July 22, 2002.

[24] "Belgium Ready to Pass World's Strictest Gun Law," an article posted on the anti-gun Website, Join Together Online, August 28, 2002.

[25] "Tough new gun law promised." February 2005. http://www.expatica.com/source/site_articles.asp?subchannel_id=48&story_id=16553&name=Government+pledges+tough+new+gun=law.

[26] Jacobs, *Can Gun Control Work* 149, second footnote, Gary A. Mauser: "Misfire: Firearm Registration in Canada (Vancouver, B.C.: Fraser Institute, 2001. Also available from Prof. Mauser at the Institute for Canadian Urban Research Studies, Simon Fraser University, Burnaby, British Columbia).

[27] Darius Bazargan, "Balkan Gun Traffickers Target UK," BBC, Dec. 5, 2003, http://news.bbc.co.uk/1/hi/programmes/correspondent/3256318.stm.

[28] Quoting the English government report as summarized in the article cited at note 23 supra.

[29] Ibid.

[30] "If handguns were illegally imported at the same volume as marijuana [it] is estimated [that] approximately 20 million of the size used to slay John Lennon would enter the country each year." Don B. Kates, "Handgun Banning in Light of the Prohibition Experience" in D. Kates (ed.), *Firearms and Violence* (Cambridge, Mass: Ballinger, 1984) at 157–58.

[31] See discussion *Ibid*. At 158–59.

[32] See, *e.g.*, *Taipei Times*, Dec. 8, 2003: "Illegal Guns Flourish in the Trigger-Happy Philippines" (Notwithstanding severe Philippine anti-gun laws makers of cottage manufactured guns sell .38 revolvers for $27.00; submachince guns for up to $215.00.).

[33] James D. Wright, *et al.*, Executive Summary to *Weapons, Crime and Violence in America: A Literature Review and Research Agenda* (Washington, D.C.: Government Printing Office, 1981) at p. 2.

[34] "First Reports Evaluating the Effectiveness of Strategies for Preventing Violence: Firearms Laws" cdc.gov/mmwr/preview/mmwrhtml/rr5214a2.htm (CDC, 2003) and Charles F. Wellford, *et al.* (Eds.), *Firearms and Violence: A Critical Review* (National Academy of Sciences, 2004).

[35] Don B. Kates, "The Limits of Gun Control: A Criminological Perspective" in Timothy Lytton, ed., *Suing the Firearms Industry: A Legal Battle at the Crossroads of Gun Control and Mass Torts* 62 (Ann Arbor: University of Michigan Press, 2005).

[36] See 36-nation study reported in *Targeting Guns*, supra p. 254, and Martin Killias, *et al.* "Guns, Violent Crime, and Suicide in 21 Countries," *Canadian J. of Criminology* 43 (2001): 429–448.

[37] The deterrent effect has been verified in multiple studies, particularly two conducted under the auspices of the National Institute of Justice in state prisons and juvenile incarceration facilities across the nation. Many protective uses of firearms were shown: upwards of 70% of inmates questioned "said they had [either] been 'scared off, shot at, wounded or captured by an armed victim,' [quoting the actual question asked] . . . [or] had at least one acquaintance who had had this experience." As to the deterrent effect, over 70% of the felons said that in contemplating a crime they either "often" or "regularly" worried that they "Might get shot at by the victim"; and 57% agreed that "Most criminals are more worried about meeting an armed victim than they are about running into the police." James D. Wright & Peter Rossi, *Armed and Considered Dangerous: A Survey of Felons and Their Firearms* (New York: Aldine de Gruyter, 1986) and Joseph F. Sheley & James D. Wright, *In the Line of Fire: Youth, Guns and Violence in Urban America* 63 (New York: Aldine de Gruyter, 1995). Significantly, "the felons most frightened 'about confronting an armed victim' were from states with the greatest relative number of privately owned firearms" (Sheley & Wright at 63; Wright & Rossi at 151)—while the robbery rate is highest in states with severe gun controls. Philip J. Cook, "The Effect of Gun Availability on Robbery and Robbery-Murder: A Cross Section Study of 50 Cities" 3 (1979) *Policy Studies Review Annual* at 776–778.

[38] *Can Gun Control Work?* at 221.

DID YOU KNOW?

Pre-Election Gun Sales

State and federal data indicated that firearms and ammunition sales rose 8 to 10 percent in 2008. In support of these figures, the National Shooting Sports Foundation reported that quarterly excise taxes on sales of firearms and ammunition increased by about 10 percent from the previous year. Also, the number of background checks conducted under the National Instant Criminal Background Check System (NICS) for those intending to purchase a firearm increased by 9 percent from 2007 to 2008. Many dealers and buyers attributed this trend in part to the anticipation that if Barack Obama won the presidency, he would join congressional Democrats in enacting additional gun control legislation. In addition, concerns about the economy may have resulted in fear of increasing crime and possible civil unrest, and hence the need for personal protection. A similar increase in gun purchases occurred in 1994 when President Bill Clinton advocated a ban on semiautomatic (assault) rifles, and in 2007 following the Virginia Tech shooting in which several students and faculty were shot and killed by a lone gunman.

SOURCE: Don B. Kates, "The Hopelessness of Trying to Disarm the Kinds of People Who Murder." *Bridges* 12 (numbers 3/4, 2005), 313–330. Reprinted courtesy of Don B. Kates and Robert Seitz Frey, editor of *Bridges.*

ANALYSIS

Don B. Kates, a constitutional law and civil liberties lawyer and professor in the School of Criminology and Criminal Justice at Florida State University, has for many years supported the right of individuals to own firearms, both on constitutional grounds and on the pragmatic basis that firearms ownership contributes to self-defense and tends to deter crime. In this article, Kates focuses on the "worst case scenario" for the gun rights advocate: a complete ban on the ownership of firearms. Certainly the Brady Campaign to Prevent Gun Violence does not advocate such an extreme measure, which would represent the most radical policy recommendation to deal with gun-related violence in the United States. The Brady Campaign recognizes uses of firearms—for instance, hunting and target practice—that the organization does not wish to prohibit.

Kates's argument about the futility of banning all firearms brings to mind the Prohibition era of the 1920s that led to widespread lawbreaking with illegal manufacture and importation of alcoholic beverages and the consumption of these beverages by large segments of the population. Supporters of more stringent gun control legislation argue that existing laws are not effective because they fail to include effective enforcement mechanisms. The Brady Campaign in particular lobbied for background checks to prevent those not legally eligible—those convicted of a felony and those with mental problems—from legally purchasing a handgun. However, even such a measure is opposed by many gun rights advocates because it places a restriction on law-abiding citizens who wish to purchase a handgun. With regard to alcoholic beverages following Prohibition, the federal government did not opt for a total elimination of any controls, but rather for controls on the manufacture of such beverages and the introduction of liquor taxes to raise revenue and also to discourage the use of liquor. A complete elimination of any controls on firearms would mean the criminals as well as law-abiding citizens concerned about self-defense would be able to purchase as many firearms as they wished. Laws would be in place that punished crimes committed with firearms more heavily than other crimes. In any event, Kates's argument represents the position of many gun rights advocates who consider the possession of firearms as a fundamental right of individuals in a free society, contrary to gun control advocates who regard the widespread possession of firearms as a fundamental social problem that requires regulation.

FURTHER READING

Adler, Jerry. "Story of a Gun." *Newsweek* (April 30, 2007), 37–39.

Bender, David L., and Bruno Leone, eds. *Gun Control: Opposing Viewpoints*. San Diego, CA: Greenhaven Press, 1997.

Cook, Philip J., and Jens Ludwig. *Gun Violence: The Real Costs*. New York: Oxford University Press, 2000.

Goss, Kristin A. *Disarmed: The Missing Movement for Gun Control in America*. Princeton, NJ: Princeton University Press, 2009.

Kates, Don B., and Gary Kleck. *The Great American Gun Debate: Essays on Firearms and Violence*. San Francisco, CA: Pacific Research Institute for Public Policy, 1997.

Kopel, David B. *The Samurai, the Mountie, and the Cowboy: Should America Adopt the Gun Controls of Other Democracies?* Buffalo, NY: Prometheus Books, 1992.

Warner, James H. "Why Gun Owners Must Vote for McCain." *The Blue Press*. Issue no. 197 (November 2008). Dillon Precision Products, Inc.

5

IMMIGRATION

Document: National Immigration Forum, "Comprehensive Reform of Our Immigration Laws" (2008)

Document: David A. Hartman, "Reflections on Immigration Reform: The Battle for America's Communities" (2007)

Document: Heidi Ernst, "The Question of Undocumented Immigrants" (2008)

Document: Gregory McNamee, *Excerpt from* "Immigration, the Border, and the Fate of the Land: Notes on a Crisis" (2007)

Document: The Lynde and Harry Bradley Foundation, "Becoming Americans," *Excerpts from* Chapter 4 of the report *E Pluribus Unum* (2008)

Document: Thomas Fleming, "Violent Revolution" (2006)

"Comprehensive Reform of Our Immigration Laws"

- **Document:** Statement by the National Immigration Forum supporting immigration into the United States.
- **Date:** September 2008.
- **Where:** *Backgrounder*, a publication of the National Immigration Forum, Washington, DC.
- **Significance:** The National Immigration Forum supports immigration reform that would allow greater legal immigration, establish a more efficient immigration system, and introduce a more lenient policy to permit present illegal immigrants to obtain legal status.

DOCUMENT

Introduction: Symptoms of a Broken System

Any look at the nation's immigration policy reveals a system greatly in need of reform. Outdated policies keep American families separated from loved ones in other countries. Employers, faced with an insufficient pool of legal workers, increasingly rely on hard-working but unauthorized workers. Immigrants trekking through remote desert territory to gain entry to the U.S. die from the heat and lack of water. The rights of American workers are undermined when unscrupulous employers have their way with unauthorized workers who risk deportation if they stand up for their rights. Our enforcement personnel, who should be focused on security threats and criminals, instead are chasing farmworkers, busboys, and nannies. States and communities, in the absence of federal action to fix the broken system, must figure out on their own how to deal with a growing undocumented population. The frustration of the American people grows as politicians, rather than solving the problem, play politics with the issue.

For more than two decades, American policy makers have taken the approach of spending ever greater sums of money trying to enforce our broken immigration laws. This approach simply has not worked. It has been the failure to face economic and social realities, not failure to provide enforcement resources, that has led to the current chaotic, deadly system. We need a new approach to managing migration, one that recognizes reality and regulates it effectively; an approach that will make the immigration flow safe, orderly, and legal instead of deadly, chaotic, and operating outside the bounds of the law.

The Problem: Our Immigration Laws Are Broken

Currently, there are estimated to be more than twelve million immigrants here without legal papers. Each year, an estimated 300,000 or more join that population. These people are coming here to work, to join family members, or both. Many ask: why don't they just apply to come legally? Some Americans believe that good laws are being violated by bad, selfish, impatient people. That point of view, however, may come from the misunderstanding that legally immigrating to the United States is a relatively easy process. In fact, people trying to come here to work or join family find themselves caught in a hodge-podge of outdated immigration laws and a famously inept and unpredictable immigration bureaucracy. Many rational people are making the decision to risk being in the U.S. illegally in order to work and make money at abundantly available jobs in the U.S. These are not bad people violating good laws; they are rational people making difficult choices to improve their lives and assist their families.

In the decade and a half since our immigration laws were last updated, the number of immigrant visas available has remained static, while the demand has grown—from American families seeking to reunite with loved ones in other countries and from American employers seeking workers. Waits can be as long as 22 years for some categories of immigrants in the family preference system. Faced with years or decades of waiting to reunite with family members, some immigrants attempt to enter the U.S. illegally or use temporary visas for permanent immigration.

Those coming for work face similar obstacles to coming here legally. America's economy and demographic shifts demand more workers, while our economic ties to Latin America and the rest of the world provide the economy with reserves of willing workers desiring nothing more than honest work and honest pay. However, there are very few visas available for immigrants to come here and work if they don't have particular skills—only 5,000 per year. Meanwhile, our economy has been absorbing hundreds of thousands. A father seeking work so he can make a better life for his family must choose to wait in a decades-long line or risk capture, humiliation, second-class status—and even his own life—in order to provide for his family.

The disconnect between the need for worker and family visas on the one hand, and what our immigration system provides on the other, has serious consequences not only for immigrants, but for the country as a whole. A black market for fake documents has grown tremendously. Smuggling cartels have become big businesses, with smugglers becoming more violent as the stakes have grown. The rights of

American workers are undermined when there are so many unauthorized workers in the workforce fearful of deportation; unscrupulous employers are able to use this fear to limit the rights and undercut the wages of all workers. In the context of the threat of terrorism, policies that drive the undocumented further underground will have enormous consequences for our ability to detect and deter terrorism.

Immigrants want to follow the rules and would choose to immigrate legally if that were a realistic option. The question for us then becomes, should we continue to restrict immigration ineffectively or should we embrace reality, update our laws, and manage immigration effectively?

Solution: Comprehensive Immigration Reform

We cannot solve our immigration problems through enforcement alone. We must step back and re-think our immigration system, and make the changes we need to give American families the opportunity to be united with immigrant members in a timely manner, satisfy the needs of our economy for workers, and effectively focus our enforcement resources on fighting terrorism and criminals.

Reform that will make our laws more realistic, so they can be effectively enforced, must adhere to the following principles:

- **It must Reunite Families**: Immigration reform will not succeed if public policy does not recognize one of the main factors driving migration: family unity. Outdated laws and bureaucratic delays have undermined this cornerstone of our legal immigration system. Those waiting in line should have their admission expedited, and those admitted on work visas should be able to keep their nuclear families intact. Reform should also ensure that in the future, more legal opportunities are provided for the immigration of close family members, so they are not forced to wait years and even decades to reunite with loved ones living in the U.S.

- **It Must Protect Workers**: Wider legal channels must be created so needed workers can be admitted legally to fill available jobs. The admission of immigrant workers in the future must be accompanied by a set of rules that will adequately protect the wages and working conditions of U.S. and immigrant workers. It must also allow workers to change jobs, provide for adequate enforcement of both the program's rules and existing labor laws, protect law-abiding employers from unscrupulous competitors, and provide an option for workers to gain permanent status independent of an employer sponsor.

- **It Must Give Undocumented Workers a Chance to Get Right by the Law**: It does not make sense to try to arrest, jail, and deport 12 million people who have integrated into our workplaces and communities. If we let these immigrants get on the right side of the law, they will. When they do, we will be able to run background and security checks on them. If no problems are uncovered, those with clean records should be allowed to continue working and living here.

- **It Must Restore the Rule of Law and Enhance Security**: Enforcement only works when the law is realistic and enforceable. A comprehensive overhaul will make our immigration laws more realistic, permitting an intelligent enforcement regime that should include smart inspections and screening practices aimed to keep out those who intend to harm us, fair proceedings, efficient processing, and strategies that focus on detecting and deterring terrorists and cracking down on criminal smugglers and lawbreaking employers. Such a system will better enable the nation to know who is already here and who is coming in the future, and will bring our system back into line with our tradition as a nation of immigrants and a nation of laws.

- **It Must Promote Citizenship and Civic Participation and Help Local Communities**: Immigration to America works because newcomers are encouraged to become new Americans. It is time to renew our nation's commitment to the full integration of newcomers by providing adult immigrants with quality English instruction, promoting and preparing them for citizenship, and providing them with opportunities to move up the economic ladder. The system should also offer support to local communities working to welcome newcomers.

Conclusion: We Can No Longer Afford the Failed Status Quo

Our immigration system will continue to be troubled until our laws more closely reflect reality. It has now been several years since the dysfunction in our immigration system has brought the issue to the top tier of problems Americans want their leaders to solve. Policy makers in Washington have been stalemated. States and localities across the country have been left to their own devices in dealing with their undocumented population and the local businesses that rely on undocumented workers.

An exclusive focus on enforcement has turned out to be disastrous throughout the country. Immigrant enforcement officers have staged large-scale raids, going into workplaces and homes with guns drawn, terrifying and tearing apart whole communities, hauling away immigrant workers in chains, and leaving children without the care of their mothers. People whose crime has been to work without papers are herded through fast-track deportation proceedings in trials that cast a pall over our tradition of equal justice. Those who are not deported on a fast track are held in institutions with little concern for their health or safety. Some jailed immigrants have paid for this neglect with their lives.

This is all happening in the context of a system that will eventually replace these workers with others who are willing to risk all to provide a better opportunity for themselves and their family. It simply makes no sense to require continued reliance on this illegality.

Across the country, voices are being raised in support of rational solutions. Business groups worry about the ability of our economy to continue expanding without more worker visas to match up employers with willing workers in the future. Labor groups want workers to be brought out of the shadows so that they can enjoy the same labor protections as other workers. Religious and ethnic groups are calling for reform to speed the reunification of families and end the deaths in the desert and inhuman treatment of immigrant workers. Security experts point out that having undocumented workers get on the right side of the law will allow us to know who is here and check their background, while an expanded number of entry visas will allow us to better screen people who are entering our country. Finally the American people, in poll after poll, have indicated that they prefer a realistic, comprehensive, and fair approach to immigration reform—one that includes a path to citizenship for immigrants who, though undocumented, are otherwise obeying our laws.

With a new Congress and new President [in January 2009], there will be a new opportunity to reform our immigration laws in a realistic manner. Harsh enforcement

DID YOU KNOW?

Illegal Immigrant Raid

In August 2008 government agents from Immigration and Customs Enforcement (ICE) conducted a raid of a Howard Industries transformer manufacturing plant in Laurel, Mississippi, to arrest nearly 600 immigrants working at the plant who were suspected of being in the country illegally. Agents transferred approximately 475 of the workers to an ICE facility in Jena, Louisiana. Approximately 100 others were released, many of them mothers who were allowed to return home to care for children, after being fitted with electronic monitoring bracelets. Nine juveniles were transferred to the Office of Refugee Resettlement. At least eight of the workers faced federal criminal charges for allegedly using false Social Security and other identification. Following the raid, hundreds of people reportedly came to the plant to apply for jobs. The raid occurred as a result of union members complaining to federal officials about the employment of undocumented immigrants and represented an increase in enforcement efforts by the George W. Bush administration, which faced strong criticism from conservatives concerned about the failure to enforce immigration policy.

alone has not worked as policy. It is time for our leaders to get past the stalemate of the past four years and overhaul the immigration system in a comprehensive manner.

SOURCE: National Immigration Forum, "Comprehensive Reform of Our Immigration Laws," September 2008. www.immigrationforum.org. Reprinted courtesy of National Immigration Forum.

ANALYSIS

Immigration traditionally has been a sensitive issue for the United States, and has become increasingly complex as the number of illegal immigrants has steadily increased.

The National Immigration Forum expresses what many consider a practical approach to immigration. People come to the United States seeking employment, and employees welcome these new workers. The Forum focuses primarily on the problem of illegal immigration, which the group identifies with an inefficient policy that results in law enforcement officers seeking out people who came to the United States illegally but are otherwise gainfully employed, rather than protecting the country against potential terrorists who wish to cross into the United States. Providing legal status to these workers, it is claimed, would end much of the exploitation that some employers engage in. The Forum urges that Congress end the recent stalemate over immigration policy by instituting comprehensive immigration reform so that families may be reunited and workers may find employment without the prospect of exploitation.

"Reflections on Immigration Reform: The Battle for America's Communities"

- *Document:* Article by David A. Hartman recommending a more stringent immigration policy.
- *Date:* November 2007.
- *Where:* *Chronicles* magazine.
- *Significance:* David Hartman expresses many of the concerns and reservations that conservatives have about immigration policy and offers some of the recommendations they make for dealing with illegal immigration. These concerns help to explain why Congress has been unable to institute immigration reforms.

DOCUMENT

The most significant event in President George W. Bush's second term (thus far) has been the defeat of the Comprehensive Immigration Reform Act of 2007 (S.1348). This bill was initiated by President Bush in collaboration with the Democratic congressional majority, over the opposition of the Republicans and a few rebellious Democrats. The real winners of this battle were the usually silent majority of conservative Americans who rose to protest the next wave of illegal-alien invasion, which would have followed the amnesty proposed by S.1348. The subsequent resignation of Bush's senior Machiavellian, Karl Rove, was not surprising.

It is difficult to know if conservatives were primarily concerned with the sheer magnitude of immigrants or with the threat of terrorism. Both problems would have been exacerbated by the S.1348 amnesty, which could have resulted in as many as 100 million more immigrants, as estimated by Robert Rector of the Heritage Foundation. After being double-crossed by the immigration acts of 1965, 1986, and 1996, our dissident conservatives seem to be saying, "What's wrong with taking control of our borders by enforcing the laws we already have?"

Among its key proposals, S.1348 offered a virtual fence to monitor our Southern border, presumably as a replacement for the physical fence ordered by both houses last year [2006], which remains unconstructed. It also proposed the use of biometric IDs [for instance, finger printing] in visa-entry, monitoring, and exit procedures, which would be administered by the Department of Homeland Security. Of course, the most important way to reduce the chief incentive for illegal immigration—restricting employment to legally approved aliens—is already provided for by present law. That law simply is not enforced with reasonable policing, a conclusion that is supported by the fact that there were only 718 employer arrests in 2006, despite estimates that more than half of the 13 million illegal aliens here are employed. The amnesty of 1996 only served to swell the flood of illegal aliens and increased pressure for additional legal immigration of relatives (who account for 83 percent of those naturalized every year). These figures validate conservative concerns about the prospects of yet another (and greater) flood tide.

In Washington, the political pressure for increases in immigration allowances is, first and foremost, a matter of supply and demand for cheap labor (both salaried and hourly). As of 2003, foreign-born workers made up one sixth of the U.S. civilian workforce. Since the Immigration and Nationality Act of 1965, according to U.S. Department of Labor statistics, real compensation per unit of output (including fringe benefits) for workers in the private sector declined by one quarter, while real paycheck earnings per unit of output declined by one half. Before 1965, however, earnings and compensation per unit of output were relatively stable, so it is not difficult to conclude that immigration has had a negative effect on returns to labor. Admittedly, in the medical and high-tech fields, immigration has helped relieve inflationary shortages. In general, however, the massive flow of migrants has depressed middle-class wages. In addition, immigration enables employers to risk less capital in exchange for more return. Yes, as the mantra goes, the immigrants "are doing the jobs Americans won't do"—but that is because *Americans want reasonable living wages*. The historically low U.S. unemployment rate (4.5 percent), which is regularly cited as proof that the current demand for labor is unsatisfied, does not reflect declines in both female and male workforce participation: 17 percent of American males, ages 16 to 26, refuse to take jobs that pay less than babysitting, but, when combined with welfare benefits, those jobs look good to unskilled immigrants. American workers—who, since Colonial times, were among the highest-paid laborers in the world—are being marginalized by the globalists' manipulation of immigration and trade.

Why shouldn't Americans at least take advantage of the bargain-priced services offered by unskilled aliens? The answer is simple: The immigrants and their employers may be better off for getting the business, but only at the expense of the average working and tax-paying citizen. The low-income aliens pay little or no income or FICA taxes, either by taking advantage of the Earned Income Tax Credit or by avoiding paying taxes altogether. On average, these aliens have double the poverty rate and criminality of the rest of the population, and they secure substantial welfare benefits from both legal and illegal sources, including free medical care and education, paid for by U.S. taxpayers. Eventually, many of them become citizens and then qualify for Social Security and Medicare at a total net cost to taxpayers of over $150,000 per family (after comparing taxes paid to benefits accrued or received).

The fury of the grassroots at the soaring numbers of illegal aliens is warranted, but somewhat misdirected. After all, it is hard to blame aliens when they walk through an open door and help themselves to a better standard of living—and when it is obvious to them that the immigration police could not care less. The traffickers who locate and deliver them, those who employ them illicitly, and the border patrol and the federal overseers who do not enforce the law are at least as guilty as the aliens—perhaps more so.

Of equal or greater importance is the loss of the successful American way of life. For decades, conservatives have warned that excessive immigration would result in the loss of traditional communities, on which American success has been built; now these predictions are becoming realities. Michael Barone, in an op-ed published in the *Wall Street Journal* ("The Realignment of America"), shows that masses of native-born Americans are migrating from the East and West Coast cities to the cities of the Heartland. The population loss on both coasts is being driven and replaced by immigrants. It would appear that the prospects for the "pursuit of happiness" by native-born Americans—who have seen their former communities increasingly overrun by immigrant strangers—have deteriorated to such an extent that it warranted seeking new communities where they could live among other native-born Americans. In another *Wall Street Journal* op-ed, Daniel Henninger records the findings of Prof. Robert Putnam of Harvard University, who studied the effects of "diversity" by conducting 30,000 interviews in 41 U.S. communities: "Short version: People in ethnically diverse settings don't want to have much of anything to do with each other. 'Social capital' erodes. Diversity has a downside." Putnam's composite findings are disturbing:

> Inhabitants of diverse communities tend to withdraw from collective life, to distrust their neighbors, regardless of the color of their skin, to withdraw even from close friends, to expect the worst from their community and its leaders, to volunteer less, give less to charity and work on community projects less often, to register to vote less, to agitate for social reform more, but have less faith that they can actually make a difference, and to huddle unhappily in front of the television.

It appears that the vaunted "diversity" provided by increased immigration has proved no friend either to American communities or to America's middle class, which has been the pride of our republic since its founding. Low-wage illegal-alien workers and their welfare subsidies are really subsidies to their U.S. employers—subsidies that drive up profits while depressing middle-class earnings.

The Christian churches of America, particularly the traditional denominations, represent the potential swing vote of the electorate, which could restore limited immigration. The leaders of these denominations have been purveyors of socialism and globalism for over a century. As a result, their congregations have been brainwashed into believing that taking in the world's poor through an open-borders policy is the requirement of a good Samaritan. But consider the sobering picture painted by Peter Brimelow, in his comprehensive overview of immigration, *Alien Nation*:

> The Census Bureau predicts that, by 2050, the U.S. population will be 392 million; Leon Bouvier of Tulane University estimates that 139 million of them will be post-1970 immigrants and their descendants; and, David A. Coleman of Oxford University estimates that, currently, 60 million people wish to emigrate from the Third World to the United States. Should each of them be followed by seven relatives, as is the present trend, the result of our *de facto* open-borders policy could be an influx of as many as 480 million new arrivals— quite a burden for America's good Samaritans. At some point, these good Samaritans will have to wake up to the fact that open borders mean putting their incomes, standards of living, culture, governance, and even law and order at risk. No country has ever survived when its citizens have given charity to mankind priority over the wellbeing of their families, friends, and neighbors.

Realistically, the 13 million illegal aliens who are currently residing in the United States cannot be abruptly returned to their native countries *en masse*. Their status should be resolved by our adoption of the temporary legal categories of alien-labor quotas proposed in S.1348, in agriculture, high-tech, and services, but not on the terms proposed by S.1348—that is, not by amnesty. Present illegal employees who "surrender" should be allowed to apply for these temporary jobs. Their employment should be contracted on an annual basis, and, after each year, they should be required to return home. Temporary residency should be monitored by biometric IDs. Alien workers' wages and their numbers should be regulated to prevent any further depression of domestic compensation levels. Aliens without criminal records (other than border violations) who are granted temporary employment should be allowed to apply for naturalization, but with no promises and with no priority placed on their applications. Naturalization should require not only proficiency in English, civics, and history but a high school degree or the completion of a GED taken in English. The Constitution should be amended so that citizenship is not automatically extended to those born to noncitizens in the United States, and so that English is established as the national language. As employers of illegal aliens are identified when their illegal employees surrender, they should be convicted and fined or incarcerated, as required by law. Hereafter, no illegal alien should be allowed employment in the United States or given any other basis for staying.

The Democratic and Republican parties have been content to use the immigration invasion to their political benefit, providing empty rhetoric to their respective bases, without regard for the tragic consequences for America and Americans. The Bush Republican machine has pandered to Central Americans and Mexicans, the principal source of illegal immigrants, with offers of bilingual education and citizenship, an approach that promises to turn the American Southwest into Kosovo. After all, President Felipe Calderón of Mexico has all but endorsed a *reconquista* by declaring that "Mexico does not end at its borders." Meanwhile, the Democrats have worked toward a broad expansion of Third World immigration, in order to increase their voting base and thereby displace the Bush Republican regime. The rebellion of congressional Republicans in response to the demands of their core electorate could signal a movement toward sound immigration reform that would protect American communities and workers. Such a movement might even be joined by Democratic rebels intent on returning their party to its populist roots. Unfortunately, it is more likely that both parties, financed by corporate and Wall Street greed, will continue to profit from excessive immigration, making a mockery of the American experiment and its once optimistic prospects—both for Americans and, by example, for the rest of the world.

SOURCE: David A. Hartman, "Reflections on Immigration Reform: The Battle for America's Communities," *Chronicles*, 31, no. 11 (November 2007): 24–25. Reprinted courtesy of the Rockford Institute—Chronicles Press.

ANALYSIS

The United States, referred to as "a nation of immigrants," nonetheless often in its past instituted policies hostile to immigration, at least from certain parts of the world. In the 1850s the Know-Nothing party opposed immigration, especially from Catholic countries. In 1875 Congress established the first official limit on immigration. These limitations were expanded in the last quarter of the nineteenth century. The Immigration Act of 1921, passed over President Woodrow Wilson's veto, established annual limits on immigration, including a 3 percent limit on each country of origin based on that country's number of foreign-born U.S. residents as of the 1910 census. In 1924 the Johnson-Reed (National Origins) Act established an annual limit of 150,000 Europeans, a ban on Japanese immigration, and quotas on immigration from particular nations based on each nation's proportion of the U.S. population in 1890, a policy meant to preserve the existing ethnic balance. In 1952 Congress passed, over President Harry Truman's veto, the McCarran-Walter Act, which maintained the national origins quotas. The act repealed the Japanese exclusion and established a limited quota for Asia and the Pacific region. In 1965 Congress abolished the national origins quotas, establishing instead family and skills categories, and preferences for refugees. Subsequently, immigration, both legal and illegal, from Latin America, the Caribbean, and Asia increased significantly, and presently more than 35 million persons born outside the United States now live in the country (Schuck 2008, 344–45). Many Americans remain concerned about immigration, especially about groups that have more recently immigrated (Schuck 2008, 349). Congress passed additional legislation in 1986 (the Immigration Reform and Control Act) and 1990 (the Immigration Act). The latter legislation significantly liberalized immigration policy. Legislation passed following the 1996 Oklahoma City bombing was intended to place limitations on immigration, but was not successful in the face of a largely pro-immigration majority in Congress (Schuck 2008, 354).

DID YOU KNOW?

Border Patrol

In 2006 there were 12,000 agents patrolling areas along the border with Mexico. The Bush administration announced a target of 18,000 border agents, but that number has proved difficult to maintain. The agents must patrol in rural areas, work long hours, and endure high temperatures that often reach more than 100 degrees. In 2008 it was estimated that 30 percent of agents resign after less than 18 months on the job. The Government Accountability Office estimates that the government invests $14,700 to train each recruit at the Border Patrol Academy in Artesia, New Mexico. In addition, senior agents must continue to train new hires during a two-year probationary period. The training period, which lasts as long as 95 days, includes Spanish lessons. Approximately 20 percent of recruits fail to complete the academy training course. Among the reasons mentioned for resignations is boredom: agents spend hours waiting in parked vehicles for migrants who cross the border. With the long border and many people attempting to cross into the United States, border patrol agents have a formidable task maintaining border security, which undoubtedly will remain a central issue in the culture wars.

In attitude surveys, Americans tend to regard past immigration as having had a positive effect on the country, but many express concern for the negative influence that illegal immigrants are having on local public services such as schools and hospitals, on fluency in English, and on employment opportunities. Illegal immigration tends to provoke the most heated reaction from Americans. The failure to institute immigration reform in 2007, partially because of conservative concern that reform proposals were too lax and the perception that immigration threatens the traditional culture of the United States, means that the problems of immigration remain, including a large group of undocumented aliens in the country, the lack of effective control of the southern border, and ineffective enforcement of rules limiting employment of undocumented immigrants (Schuck 2008, 368). Given continuing disagreements over immigration, this issue promises to remain a key part of the culture wars.

"The Question of Undocumented Immigrants"

- **Document:** Article by Heidi Ernst on differing Lutheran perspectives.
- **Date:** March 2008.
- **Where:** *The Lutheran* magazine.
- **Significance:** Heidi Ernst discusses the immigration issue from a Lutheran perspective, noting the position of many Lutherans and adherents of other mainline denominations that immigrants, whether legal or not, should be offered assistance, based on "respecting humanity" and scriptural imperatives to "welcome one another" and "to love the stranger as yourself." Many within the church who support the position of immigrants question the morality of current immigration laws.

DOCUMENT

Undocumented immigrants. Illegal aliens. Unauthorized residents. The sometimes politically charged monikers are often the only public names given to the estimated 12 million people living in the U.S. against federal immigration laws. In the shadows, yet equal to about 4 percent of our population, they're the focus of a considerable amount of energy—both positive and negative—in border states and the interior, in presidential debates and town meetings, in think tanks and living rooms, on airwaves and city streets.

And in Lutheran churches? The position of the ELCA [Evangelical Lutheran Church in America], related organizations like Lutheran Immigration and Refugee Service [LIRS] and many ELCA members is one of advocacy for undocumented immigrants. But opinions on the issue do vary (somewhat as a reflection of the rest of the country) among ELCA members—from clergy to elected public officials to lay people to academics.

Ultimately, many people want the same goal: to fix a broken federal immigration system while respecting humanity.

The *ELCA Message on Immigration* states: "Newcomers without legal documents . . . are among the most vulnerable. Congregations are called to welcome all people, regardless of their legal status." This resource for congregational deliberation— rather than moral imperative—derives its tenets from the Bible, such as Romans 15:7: "Welcome one another, therefore, just as Christ has welcomed you, for the glory of God."

U.S. Rep. Tom Latham, R-Iowa, a member of Nazareth Lutheran Church, Coulter, Iowa, said: "I have great empathy for people trying to better their lives and take care of their families. But as someone sworn to uphold the Constitution, we can't ignore the fact that people are breaking national laws by coming into the country without documents."

Such a dichotomy has been part of Lutheran thinking for centuries. "The notion of caring for people without any discrimination as to their origins, that's part of the Christian tradition," said Jean Bethke Elshtain, an ELCA member who is professor of social and political ethics at the University of Chicago and Georgetown University, Washington, D.C.

Emphasis on civic order

"That said, there's a very strong emphasis from [Martin] Luther on down in traditional Lutheran theology on the need for civic order in society," Elshtain said.

"There is no barrier in Lutheranism for states to say we need to protect our border, to make the process as orderly as we can. So you could see there would at times be tension between the two strands: As a Christian, I'm obliged toward welcoming; as a citizen, admitting and accepting that the state has the function of maintaining civic order."

In the past few years, a desire for civic order has come with an increase in activities that aren't "welcoming." According to U.S. Immigration and Customs Enforcement, a record 237,000 immigrants were deported in 2007—about 16 percent more than in 2006—and work-site arrests rose almost eightfold between 2002 and 2007. In addition, Detention Watch Network, co-founded in 1997 by LIRS, says the U.S. detained 280,000-plus people in 2006, more than triple the number of people a decade ago.

The federal government has focused on these and other enforcement efforts in recent years just as legislation to solve the issue has stalled. Five years ago, President George W. Bush called for a comprehensive overhaul of immigration laws, the first since 1986. (The visa program was last changed significantly in 1990, even though the demand for workers increased yearly.) But division within the Republican Party quashed his proposal.

Three bipartisan bills addressing illegal immigrants were defeated in the past two years—McCain-Kennedy in 2006, the DREAM act (Development, Relief, and Education for Alien Minors) and the Senate's immigration reform bill in 2007.

Border patrol agents train on ropes to execute rapid-response missions. Heightened tensions over illegal immigration have led to increased efforts to enforce border security. (U.S. Customs & Border Protection)

"This is an issue that cuts across political parties," said Ralston H. Deffenbaugh Jr., president of LIRS, a cooperative advocacy and justice agency of the ELCA, the Lutheran Church—Missouri Synod and the Latvian Evangelical Lutheran Church in America. "Because of the upcoming election, we don't expect any comprehensive immigration reform until late 2009 or 2010. In the meantime, we're going to have more suffering and dysfunction, more enforcement, more families being separated."

About 5 million children in the U.S. have at least one parent who is undocumented, according to the Urban Institute and the National Council of La Raza [a national Hispanic civil rights and advocacy group], and kids are sometimes left behind when parents are detained or deported.

In February 2007, LIRS co-wrote a report called *Locking Up Family Values* after observing immigrant families in two federal detention centers. The visits revealed activities—mostly at the T. Don Hutto Residential Center (a former Texas prison) —from children as young as 6 sleeping in cells separated from parents to pregnant women and others receiving what visitors considered inadequate medical care.

The report recommended that ICE [Immigration and Customs Enforcement] "discontinue the detention of families in prison-like institutions." It led the American Civil Liberties Union to sue the Department of Homeland Security over conditions. According to DHS, "ICE not only made significant changes prior to [the settlement] agreement, it ensured that the remaining issues were reviewed and issued required modifications to ensure compliance at Hutto."

ACLU said "conditions at Hutto have gradually and significantly improved."

In addition, families that included 25 children, plus an additional child, were released, according to LIRS.

ELCA Goal: Family Reunification

"Our advocacy will continue to insist that family reunification should be the primary objective of immigration laws," states the *ELCA Message on Immigration*.

Approved in 1998, that message is currently getting a face-lift, which is expected to be presented by year's end to the ELCA Church Council. "We're dealing with things—like 9/11 and the overwhelming flux of immigrants—that weren't on the radar in '98," said Roger A. Willer, director for the Department of Studies with ELCA Church in Society, who is overseeing the development of the message. "The new message will be congruent with the theological basis set forth in 1998."

Drawing on Bible passages such as "You shall love the stranger as yourself, for you were strangers in the land of Egypt" (Leviticus 19:34), Luther's question "How do we know that the love of God dwells in us? If we take upon ourselves the need of the neighbor," and the ELCA history as a "church of immigrants and with roots in immigrant churches in a nation of immigrants," the message is designed as a tool for reflection.

"It is expected to guide church policy," Willer said. "But we don't expect that every member will believe everything a message says. We expect church members to give it careful consideration as they think through their life of faith."

The ELCA's 19 state public policy advocacy offices, in addition to LIRS and other agencies, use official messages to lobby legislatures and inform and involve congregations. Many members don't read messages or know they exist, said Teri J. Traaen, assistant to the bishop of the Grand Canyon Synod and director of Lutheran Advocacy Ministry in Arizona. And many aren't aware of how they come about, said Norene

N. Goplen, director of Lutheran Advocacy Ministry of Oregon. A small survey of bishops, clergy and lay people says they're right.

Both Traaen and Goplen have also noted from visits to many congregations in their synods that opinions on illegal immigration are diverse.

"Within our congregations, at least on a quiet level, there is disagreement," said Bishop Kevin S. Kanouse of the 120 churches in the Northern Texas-Northern Louisiana Synod. "That really played itself out in a very concrete way at Good Shepherd."

The Irving, Texas, congregation had been offering space to *Iglesia Luterana Santa Maria de Guadalupe* for a monthly usage donation for more than six years. Recently, *Santa Maria*'s pastor, Pedro B. Portillo, had been publicly working with city officials to reduce the number of arrests of undocumented immigrants.

(*The Dallas Morning News* reported in November that "Irving has drawn attention for the vigorous manner in which city police cooperate with federal immigration officials" and that "more than 1,600 people have been deported following their arrests by Irving police." The city's population is 191,000.)

Portillo had scheduled a town-hall meeting at the church in November with some city officials to "help the entire community understand city services and ask the chief of police why Irving had been arresting so many illegal aliens," he said. Some members of Good Shepherd's council voted to cancel it.

"I don't speak for others," said Art Schneewind, council president. "I didn't want our sanctuary being used for that kind of thing."

Santa Maria decided to move out the day before Good Shepherd members voted to renew its contract, each without knowing the other's actions.

Breaking the Law?

Opinion nationwide varies among parishioners and clergy on a number of topics on this issue. Breaking the law—on the part of immigrants—is probably most apparent. *Called to Be a Public Church*, the ELCA's civic participation guide, notes in a section written by LIRS that being an illegal immigrant is a civil offense, not a criminal one.

"If our country doesn't have any laws, then you need to let me know that," Schneewind said.

"The law is clear," said Cynthia E. Nance, dean of the University of Arkansas School of Law in Fayetteville and member of the LIRS board of directors. "But there are some moral and fairness issues, and it reminds me of Jim Crow: The law was clear—you could not enter through that door—but that doesn't mean it's right in the higher sense."

From the advocacy arms of the ELCA to pastors leading educational efforts, the church tries to use facts as a basis for discussion, such as: The number of undocumented immigrants has risen by 3.5 million since 2000, reflecting a favorable economic climate in the U.S. and an unprecedented backlog for applications for people to take the legal route; and the jobs they take are often those in the service sector that most Americans don't want.

Nevertheless, people won't always agree on how to fix the broken system and what to do with the immigrants who are already here illegally. Perhaps we are called to struggle with why we don't agree.

"We are not a law-based religion," ethics professor Elshtain said. "One of the interesting things about the Christian tradition is that people have a lot of interpretation and soul searching to do."

SOURCE: Heidi Ernst, "The Question of Undocumented Immigrants," *The Lutheran* (March 2008): 12, 14, 16. Reprinted courtesy of Heidi Ernst.

ANALYSIS

While more conservative groups express concern for maintaining their traditional understanding of the cultural foundations of the United States and hence for limiting immigration especially from underdeveloped regions of the world, mainline churches have tended to provide assistance to those, both documented and undocumented, who immigrate to the United States, providing a biblical justification for such assistance. These churches emphasize the human suffering that such immigrants have experienced and wish to alleviate that suffering. Those opposing extensive immigration consider such sentiment naive in the face of what they consider the ultimate consequences of widespread immigration. Nonetheless, mainline churches apparently do not speak with a unified voice on the matter of immigration. Heidi Ernst, in her discussion of the Lutheran perspective on immigration, acknowledges that the members of Lutheran churches tend to disagree about what should be the denomination's position especially on illegal immigration. Although Cynthia E. Nance, a member of the Lutheran Immigration and Refugee Service, is quoted as comparing immigration law with past segregation rules in Southern states, many church members undoubtedly consider illegal immigrants as unjustifiably having violated U.S. law. In effect, this aspect of the culture wars is playing out within mainline churches.

Immigration, the Border, and the Fate of the Land: Notes on a Crisis

- **Document:** Excerpt from Gregory McNamee's article.
- **Date:** 2007.
- **Where:** Chilton Williamson Jr., editor, *Immigration and the American Future* (Rockford Institute—Chronicles Press).
- **Significance:** Gregory McNamee raises several concerns about legal and illegal immigration into the United States, especially from Mexico and Latin America, and focuses on the claimed causes and possible consequences of unrestricted immigration in the next 40 years. McNamee encourages action to improve the condition of those who live in other countries in order to decrease the attractiveness of the United States to potential immigrants.

DOCUMENT

Population Shock

On or about October 15, 2006, the population of the United States of America reached 300 million.

When the population reached 200 million, in 1967, Hispanics numbered less than five percent of the population. In 2006, the figure was close to 14 percent, larger than the African American population. In 2046, when the population is expected to be 400 million, the figure will reach 25 percent—that is, if current trends continue and the nation's population grows by 2.8 million immigrants a year, as well as by natural increases. [1] One hundred million new inhabitants is a strain on any human community. One hundred million new Americans, living in a society organized not on consuming—such a nicely neutral word—but devouring, will be a planetary catastrophe.

Is there any way to keep that flood of newcomers from crashing on these shores?

Short of a militarized, environmentally neutral border, perhaps not. That is, not unless one of the environmental causes of immigration over the southern border is remedied: the collapse of private agriculture in Mexico as a result of the spectacularly ill-advised North American Free Trade Agreement [NAFTA]. That treaty, signed under Clinton and endorsed by both former and current Presidents Bush, had the effect of making official Mexico's newfound role as America's southerly breadbasket, as the provider of fresh produce to New England in the dead of winter, of cheap foods to the rest of the continent at all times of the year. (The long distance from Mexican fields to Alaskan supermarkets is one reason, of course, that it takes 65 calories of fossil fuel to produce one calorie of food energy for the American market.) The treaty also helped complete the thoroughgoing industrialization of Mexican agriculture, introducing laborsaving, profit-maximizing machinery while removing people from the land—a sure cause of economic and social catastrophe in any farming community, as development economists such as Charles Hall, Gregoire Leclerc, and Hernando de Soto will tell you. [2]

In the last decade, those displaced farmers have tended to move in two directions. Some have gone to the conurbation of Mexico City, the population of which is now unofficially estimated to be 30 million, a great part of which lives in oceanic wildcat slums that stretch from the capital for scores of miles. Others have gone to el Norte, where, if nothing else, the slums tend to be a touch more congenial, the prospects a little better, and the cities less vast, at least for the time being. I was reminded of this recently when I complained about the size of Phoenix, which has a population of about three million. A friend who lives in Los Angeles retorted, "Three million? That's fewer than the number of illegals here alone."

Getting that crop of farmers back to the farm is likely an impossibility, but developing the economic structures that would make it possible to feed a family in the abundantly fertile nation of Mexico is not. This is a problem to which, I very much hope, American agricultural economists will turn in earnest, for the result can only be beneficial to all concerned on many different levels.

Even with such sweeping changes, illegal immigrants will come. They will come from the south, for, as Jorge Castañeda writes in *The Mexican Shock*, mass migration is unlikely to end so long as radical inequalities exist between the United States and Mexico; inequalities that NAFTA, as it is now constructed, does nothing to solve. [3]

If immigration laws are to acquire the sense of fair play on which we as a nation pride ourselves, then we are going to have to look beyond our southern frontier and onto the larger world and declare our intentions. There is either room, or there is not, or there is some: The fundamental question is whether the American lifeboat is overcrowded and will sink if it takes on more passengers. By many measures, not least of them American patterns of consumption, it is and it will.

On all this my friend Edward Abbey had much to say. Abbey fired his opening shot in a long debate in a letter to the *New York Review* of Books of December 17, 1981, in which, arguing from just that "overcrowded lifeboat" theory, he called for

In desperate attempts to cross the border illegally, many would-be immigrants put their lives at risk. Border Patrol enforcement actions sometimes become rescue missions. (U.S. Customs & Border Protection)

an immediate halt to all immigration into America. A harsh formula, but especially when Abbey added that we be especially vigilant about immigration from Mexico and Central America. Abbey proposed that the Border Patrol be expanded to a force of at least 20,000 heavily armed guards, so that the American way of life might be made safe from threats "to degrade and cheapen [it] downward to the Hispanic standard."

In a series of letters to southern Arizona newspapers, Abbey later suggested that what he really wanted was for the Border Patrol to issue rifles and ammunition, gratis, to would-be immigrants at the border and to point them southward to Mexico City, where they might complete the aborted revolution begun 75 years earlier. Until his death in 1989, Abbey further elaborated this argument, [4] happily urging that the tide of immigrants from Latin America be turned away at the American frontier, while leftists, liberals, businesspeople, Mexican American groups, and so-called conservatives alike joined battle against him, each for their own reasons.

That was in a more innocent time, of course. Things are different now. Abbey is buried in the Cabeza Prieta [the national wildlife refuge on Arizona's southern border with Mexico], and I imagine that he is busily turning over in his grave even as thousands of footsteps erode it away.

In an overcrowded lifeboat, it does not necessarily matter who is drawing the rations. If we agree that there is no room at the inn, immigration must halt or at least be radically curtailed from everywhere. And, quite apart from deciding whether our immigration laws will be made fair and rational, it is in the national interest to reduce pressures to emigrate, no matter from where, and particularly by those who have no skills. In the case of Mexico, as I have said, this means agitating for a thorough program of land reform so that smallholders are not displaced and forced into the cities or across the border, as is now occurring in record numbers. In the case of other countries, it similarly involves encouraging agricultural self-sufficiency. At a time when huge numbers of the world's too-abundant people live in poverty—by some estimates, there are perhaps 3.5 billion poor on the planet today—we should be encouraging population controls and the broader distribution of resources within the limits of carrying capacity.

Another postulate: Happy people do not emigrate. Leaving family and homeland to enter a strange country and speak a strange language is among the most unsettling of experiences a human can undergo. My ancestors came from Ireland and Sweden to escape grinding poverty and hunger, not on a lark. Yours probably came here for similar reasons. Americans who have not traveled or lived abroad can scarcely imagine how difficult this is, but most can understand the economic desires that prompt people to make that difficult decision in the first place: In a world of haves and have-nots, the have-nots will naturally want to go where the haves live. Call me a raving socialist for saying so, but if we can do something to attend to those economic desires where they arise, then we may do much to reduce the impulse to leave home.

One thing everyone agrees on is that it is exceedingly difficult to conduct a rational discussion on the whole issue of immigration, let alone legislate it fairly. By raising that issue, the conservative senator Alan Simpson of Wyoming once remarked, "You'll trod on every segment of American society and be called everything from xenophobe to racist." He was right, and things are worse today. And so we have the politics Abbey described thus: "The conservatives love their cheap labor; the liberals love their cheap cause." (But, he added, "neither group, you will notice, ever invites the immigrants to move into their homes.")

Faced with such conundrums, many environmentalists have chosen to remain altogether silent on the question of immigration, perhaps hoping that it will go away on its own. Immigration is, after all, a cyclical issue in American politics, one that rises and falls every ten or 20 years. I have the feeling, though, that this time it will not disappear: There are too many ruined canyons, tracts of desert land, and streambeds for that. So raise it environmentalists must. At a time when our society seems to be tapped dry, with 60 million poor and unemployed and a national debt in the trillions, the lifeboat may well have sprung one too many leaks to allow more passengers, regardless of where they board. If it is to take on more, determining just how will require informed, dispassionate debate on many fronts: social, economic, cultural, and environmental. If it is not, then the question remains how to become a fortress without walling itself off in the manner of a Chinese dynasty or Stalinist state, and without our becoming prisoners within. There are no easy answers.

In the meanwhile, what remains is to protect our garden.

NOTES

[1] On the occasion of the publication of his book, *An Empire Wilderness* (Random House, 1998), journalist Robert Kaplan told me, "It won't be the old America, and this will be dislocating and upsetting for some people. But it won't happen overnight. Historians will wonder, in a hundred years, just when it was that the United States as we know it disappeared. The answer will be that it happened so gradually that no one really noticed." This is gradualism as mithridatism.

[2] See the essays collected in Hall and Leclerc's edited volume, *Making Development Work* (University of New Mexico Press, 2007); de Soto, *The Mystery of Capital: Why Capitalism Triumphs in the West and Fails Everywhere Else* (Basic Books, 2003); and David S. Landes, *The Wealth and Poverty of Nations* (Norton, 1998).

[3] Castañeda, *The Mexican Shock*, p. 13. See also Carlos Fuentes, *A New Time for Mexico* (Farrar, Straus & Giroux, 1996); Andres Oppenheimer, *Bordering on Chaos: Guerrillas, Stockbrokers, Politicians, and Mexico's Road to Prosperity* (Little, Brown, 2003); Joseph Stiglitz, *The Roaring Nineties: A New History of the World's Most Prosperous Decade* (Norton, 2003).

[4] See, for example, Abbey's essay, "Immigration and Liberal Taboos," collected in *One Life at a Time, Please* (Henry Holt, 1988).

SOURCE: Gregory McNamee, "Immigration, the Border, and the Fate of the Land: Notes on a Crisis," in *Immigration and the American Future*, edited by Chilton Williamson (Rockford, IL: Chronicles Press, 2007), 244–249. Reprinted courtesy of the Rockford Institute—Chronicles Press.

ANALYSIS

Gregory McNamee bases his discussion of immigration into the United States on the premise that the country cannot absorb indefinitely new immigrants at the present rate of influx. McNamee refers to the various consequences, social, economic, cultural, and environmental, that he argues requires action to be taken to

DID YOU KNOW?

The New Sanctuary Movement

In the 1980s, due largely to political unrest particularly in Central American countries, many people from those countries immigrated to the United States illegally, and a number of American churches participated in granting sanctuary to refugees, declaring a moral obligation to assist those in need. With the renewed controversy over illegal immigration and government attempts to enforce laws regarding illegal immigration, faith-based organizations in several states—including California, New York, Illinois, Arizona, and Washington—are advocating a similar moral obligation to help families facing separation due to immigration proceedings. Those supporting such assistance face the question whether those trying to escape poverty merit the same consideration as those fleeing political violence. California churches offering sanctuary have been picketed by the Minutemen organization which opposes illegal immigration. While conservatives assert that the immigration laws should be enforced, those supporting the New Sanctuary Movement hold that concern for fellow humans overrides laws that result in injustice. Although the movement potentially can become involved in few of the many cases of illegal immigration, it likely has contributed to increasing conflict over the issue.

reduce the flow of immigrants into the United States. One suggestion is to provide assistance especially to countries to the south in order to alleviate the reasons—economic want, lack of employment, and disparities of wealth between the United States and these nations—for continued immigration. McNamee calls for revised immigration policy and for an altered North American Free Trade Agreement, but expresses pessimism about such changes given that both conservatives—because of their "love of cheap labor"—and liberals—because they "love their cheap cause"—benefit from the present situation. McNamee claims that anyone advocating effective immigration reform invites being called a xenophobe or racist. The dilemma comes down to gaining control of the nation's borders without making citizens prisoners in their own country. The author concludes that the issue of immigration will not subside, and therefore can be expected to continue to contribute to the intensity of the culture wars.

"Becoming Americans"

- **Document:** Excerpts from a statement issued by the Lynde and Harry Bradley Foundation on past and present immigration.
- **Date:** June 2008.
- **Where:** Chapter 4 of the report, *E Pluribus Unum*
- **Significance:** Although not recommending limitations on immigration, this report from the conservative Lynde and Harry Bradley Foundation recommends that new immigrants be socialized into the traditional values of American society so that they will share in a uniquely American identity.

DOCUMENT

Among those who signed the Declaration of Independence were eight first-generation immigrants; among those who led Americans in the Revolutionary War were John Paul Jones, born in Scotland, and Alexander Hamilton, born in the West Indies. Americans welcomed immigrants—and immigrants came by the millions: before and after the Revolution, during the Irish Potato Famine and the European revolutions of 1848, during the period of European population growth in the late 1800s, and when steamships shortened the passage to America. Immigrants built the Erie Canal and the Transcontinental Railroad. They fought in Union armies. A Hungarian immigrant, Joseph Pulitzer, founded the *St. Louis Post-Dispatch*; a Scottish immigrant, Alexander Graham Bell, invented the telephone. Frances Cabrini came to America from Italy to organize schools and orphanages and became the Catholic Church's Patron Saint of Immigrants. From all over the world, America lured the ambitious, talented and enterprising. From the beginning, America has been, among other things, "a nation of immigrants," and today the Statue of Liberty and Ellis Island are some of our most cherished national symbols.

This large-scale immigration was not without friction. New England Protestants shunned Catholics and claimed immigrants brought diseases and crime. Workers in California said the Chinese were the wrong color and worked for low wages. At the same time, some immigrants found it difficult to adjust to the norms and mores of their new home. Prejudice and strife are clearly part of the historical record. Equally important—and astonishing from an historical perspective—was that prejudice did not lead to ethnic wars, that toleration prevailed over bigotry, and that the overwhelming number of immigrants, a short-time removed from their native countries, became identified with America's culture and institutions. German-speaking soldiers fought on the Union side in the Civil War, Japanese-American units had exemplary combat records in World War II, and today Americans whose ethnic heritages span the globe are defending America abroad.

Many Americans accepted, even welcomed immigrants. And most immigrants embraced America, enjoying its many freedoms and often relishing their newfound identity. What made relative harmony possible was the combination of economic opportunity and a self-conscious effort to become Americans. Not merely a nation of immigrants, America was a nation of immigrants who were expected to—and usually did—fully embrace their new country. Assimilated immigrants rapidly became Americans, not only grateful for land and jobs, but also loyal to the ideals of democracy—political equality, private property, and religious freedom—and eagerly embracing the American proposition.

First-Generation Americans

Those who arrived in the early decades of the twentieth century were intensely committed to becoming Americans. When one immigrant wrote his autobiography, he proudly titled it *The Americanization of Edward Bok*, and his story mirrored that of many of his fellow immigrants. In the open response section of the Harris survey [commissioned by the Bradley Project], one respondent wrote, "I am told that my great-great grandfather said the proudest day of his life was when he legally became a United States citizen." These newcomers insisted their children learn English and they quickly became known as among the nation's most patriotic citizens.

New immigrants and citizens alike understood that a common language and common loyalties promoted social peace, facilitated commerce, grounded civic participation, and mitigated social conflict. Their insight is still valid as our newspapers attest today. Divided societies—Serbia, Lebanon, and Kenya, for example—are fraught with tragic conflict. No nation is immune from such divisions; it requires effort to avoid them. And in an era of terrorism, national unity is not just desirable, it may be a condition of survival.

"America's genius has always been assimilation, taking immigrants and turning them into Americans," observes journalist Charles Krauthammer, himself a Canadian immigrant. [48] Becoming a full partner in a new country is not easy on the immigrant. This change requires not only passing a naturalization examination to qualify, but learning a new language, navigating a new culture, and obeying unfamiliar laws. "This is what we as a country did a century ago with eastern European immigrants," former cabinet member Henry Cisneros explains. "Americans in the early 1900s were not shy about asking the new immigrants to learn to speak English and commit to their new country." [49]

It may not be easy, but full involvement in American life can offer enormous advantages: upward mobility and economic opportunity. While immigrants often start at the bottom of the economic ladder, they tend not to stay there for long. "Perhaps the most striking pattern among American ethnic groups," notes economist Thomas Sowell, "is their general rise in economic conditions with the passage of time." [50]

The Challenge Today

Today, it is estimated that one in eight people living in the United States is an immigrant, the highest level since the 1920s. The more people who come to this country, the more crucial it is that all become full participants in American civic life and culture. This goal is supported by 89 percent of the public, according to the Harris survey. America has successfully met this challenge in the past and can do so again, but it will take effort.

In New York City the Gilder-Lehrman Institute of American History welcomes new citizens with a compilation of historical documents and images as a tribute to their new status. Similar programs should be established across the country.

Newcomers to America should be encouraged to participate fully in American social, economic, and civic life. Efforts by government, as well as schools and colleges, businesses, and civic organizations should be promoted to ensure new citizens learn English, understand democratic institutions, and participate fully in the American way of life.

Americans rightly prize their pluralism, but pluralism presents a challenge as well as a blessing. Harvard sociologist Orlando Patterson warns that, for all its benefits, ". . . pluralism is socially divisive. No society can survive for long without a common set of values whereby other members can be judged and consensus can be achieved." [51] Walter Lippmann spoke of "the public philosophy" as that framework of values and ideas that, broadly speaking, Americans hold in common, and which provides a reference point for resolving our debates and disagreements. [52]

Today a new philosophy, almost the opposite of Lippmann's, seems to be taking hold. With single-minded emphasis on our differences, every group is encouraged to retain its separate identity. The United States is no longer "we the people," but "we the peoples." To this way of thinking, loyalty to one's native land is as important as loyalty to America, and the rewards of being in this country need not be repaid in undivided allegiance.

The new attitude sanctions dual citizenship, multilingual ballots, and bilingual instruction rather than English immersion. Instead of one America, there are voices for many Americas, or even no America at all. Few would intend this result, but it may be the inevitable consequence of citizens not being able to communicate in a common language and placing other loyalties above their allegiance "to the flag and the republic for which it stands."

According to various studies, social fragmentation results in recent immigrants more likely to date and marry only within their own community, more likely to have divided loyalties, and more often indifferent to becoming full partners in American society. [53]

Historical ignorance, civic neglect, and social fragmentation might achieve what a foreign invader could not.

As we celebrate our diversity, we should not adopt policies that perpetuate division or that compromise our pledge of allegiance to "one nation indivisible."

Overcoming Separatism

We look to the public schools to fulfill their civic mission. In 2001, sociologists Alejandro Portes and Ruben Rumbaut published a massive longitudinal study of 5,000 students with immigrant parents from all over the world. Their study reveals an astounding fact: After four years in an American high school, immigrant youths were not more but less likely to consider themselves Americans. [54] This is not their fault; it is ours.

The tendency to separatism is sometimes unintended, the by-product of well-meaning efforts to make minorities comfortable. Some universities, for example, have separate freshmen orientations for different ethnic groups. Colleges, in turn, set aside separate housing for students of various backgrounds, One university, for example, boasts four such dorms: Casa Zapata (Chicano, Mexican-American), Muwekma-tah-ruk (American Indian/Alaska Native American), Okada (Asian-American), and Ujamaa (Black/African-American). [55] And, as their farewell to campus life, students now participate in separate graduation ceremonies at many universities, receiving ethnic symbols as their parting gift. [56] Students often report warm bonds with their fellow ethnics, in part because of these experiences, but one wonders how well they prepare the students to think of themselves as Americans. University of California linguistics professor John McWhorter, himself an African-American, is concerned: "Campuses are precisely where many black students learn a new separatist conception of being 'black' that they didn't have." [57]

Universities, businesses, and civic associations should avoid policies and arrangements that may tend to stereotype and divide Americans. Instead, they should encourage programs and practices that emphasize what unites us.

"The Process of Becoming American"

Reflecting the new way of thinking, the head of the Office of New Americans in Illinois—the official in charge of drawing new citizens into American culture—was quoted in the *Chicago Tribune* as saying, "The nation-state concept is changing. You don't have to say, 'I am Mexican,' or, 'I am American.' You can be a good Mexican citizen and a good American citizen and not have that be a conflict of interest. Sovereignty is flexible." [58]

For the late Congresswoman Barbara Jordan, sovereignty was not flexible, nor was being an American optional if you wanted to be a citizen. In 1995 she wrote a powerful essay in the *New York Times* that addressed the question head-on, not afraid to use a now unfashionable term. "There's a word for all this," she said, "It's Americanization. It's the process of becoming American." [59] She understood that becoming an American is not just a matter of having your paperwork in order. It is also a matter of head and heart.

While public policy may sometimes be muddled on these issues, public opinion is not. In the Harris survey, respondents overwhelmingly supported assimilation and Americanization. Eighty-nine percent agreed that "Americanization, including learning English and embracing American culture and values is important in order for immigrants to successfully fulfill their duties as U.S. citizens." The same poll revealed that 73 percent of respondents agreed that individuals should be required to give up loyalty to their former country when they become American citizens, and 84 percent believed that English should be the official language of the United States.

In a recent Rasmussen poll, 77 percent of Americans said that those who move to America from other countries should adopt American culture. Only 13 percent indicated they believe immigrants should maintain the culture of their home country. Most significantly, the Rasmussen report noted that these figures have changed little over time. [60]

Unlike Europe, America welcomes and integrates immigrants who fully identify with their new country. This does not require that they give up customs their families may have brought with them from other lands. The kind of unity Americans celebrate does not demand uniformity. On the contrary, it provides opportunities within which our distinctive family traditions can flourish. From St. Patrick's Day to Cinco de Mayo, Americans are proud of ethnic festivals, food, parades, and newspapers. It is fine if we all together celebrate our mutual differences—E Pluribus Unum with the Pluribus alive and well—but it can be a problem if each group just celebrates its own differences—Pluribus without the Unum. Whatever our attachments may be to family, neighborhood, or heritage, our allegiance must be to the nation that protects us and our freedoms. America is enriched by diversity. It is preserved by unity.

While appreciating the benefits of diversity, Americans should affirm their commitment to national unity, a shared culture, a common language, and defining ideals.

ENDNOTES

[48] Charles Krauthammer, "Assimilation Nation," *The Washington Post*, 7 June 2005, A31.

[49] Henry Cisneros, quoted in Stewart Lytle, Henry Cisneros—"Homeownership is key for Hispanics," *The Dallas Morning News*, 8 Oct. 2007.

[50] Thomas Sowell, *Ethnic America: A History* (New York: Basic Books, 1981), 275.

[51] Orlando Patterson, *Ethnic Chauvinism: The Reactionary Impulse* (New York: Stein and Day, 1977), 172.

[52] Walter Lippmann, *The Public Philosophy* (New York: New American Library, 1955).

[53] See Daniel T. Lichter, J. Brian Brown, Zhenchao Qian, Julie H. Carmalt, "Marital Assimilation Among Hispanics: Evidence of Declining Cultural and Economic Incorporation?" *Social Science Quarterly* 88 (2007): 745–65 and Zhenchao Qian and Daniel

Lichter, "Social Boundaries and Marital Assimilation: Interpreting Trends in Racial and Ethnic Intermarriage," *American Sociological Review* 72 (2007): 68–94.

[54] Alejandro Portes and Rubén G. Rumbaut, *Legacies: The Story of the Immigrant Second Generation* (Berkeley: University of California Press, 2001), 157–158.

[55] Stanford University Housing, http://stanford.edu/dept/resed/Residences/ (accessed May 1, 2008).

[56] Michael A. Fletcher, "Minority Graduation Galas Highlight a Timely Issue," *The Washington Post*, 19 May, 2003, A01.

[57] Ibid.

[58] Jose Luis Gutierrez, quoted in Antonio Olivo and Oscar Avila, "Influence on both sides of the border," *Chicago Tribune*, 6 Apr. 2007.

[59] Barbara Jordan, "The Americanization Ideal," *New York Times*, 11 Sept. 1995.

[60] Rasmussen Reports, "America's Best Days," April 29, 2008, http://rassmus senreports.com/public_content/politics/general_politics/november_2007/ 77_say_employers_can_require_english_only_on_the_job (accessed May 1, 2008).

SOURCE: The Bradley Project on America's National Identity, *E Pluribus Unum* (June 2008), 31–37. Reprinted courtesy of the Lynde and Harry Bradley Foundation.

ANALYSIS

Immigration represents one of the chief concerns of this report on the status of social and cultural unity in the United States. The authors conjecture that the national identity is disintegrating in the face of the increasing diversity of the population and the failure of the educational system to socialize residents to an understanding of fundamental American values. Unlike other conservative commentaries on immigration, this report does not recommend limiting immigration, but emphasizes the long history of immigrants coming to the United States and the success they achieved in merging with existing social and cultural values. Although the report expresses concern for the unity of the nation, it offers steps that should be taken to reestablish and increase that unity. An aspect of the exceptionalism of the United States is that the country's unity is not based on a common ethnicity, but instead on a set of common ideas as found in the Declaration of Independence and the Constitution. According to the Bradley report, the continuance of American society depends crucially on educating new generations to the values upon which the nation was founded. With regard to the culture war, this report asserts that what unites Americans should override the various issues about which many express opposing views based on differing ethnic origin and cultural values.

"Violent Revolution"

- **Document:** Opinion piece on Mexican immigration by Thomas Fleming.
- **Date:** July 2006.
- **Where:** *Chronicles* magazine.
- **Significance:** Thomas Fleming, who emphasizes the cultural differences between the United States and Mexico, expresses little hope that the immigration issue will be resolved quickly.

DOCUMENT

This past spring [2006], while Congress was engaging in its usual mock debate about tightening immigration, hundreds of thousands of Mexican-Americans took their case to the streets. In the first round of demonstrations, Chicanos, waving Mexican flags, demanded rights for illegals and declared that all those who favored enforcing the law were racists.

We all heard and read the same arguments. Mexicans make an indispensable contribution to the American economy, yet they are treated with disrespect and hostility. The same propaganda appeared in the Mexican press. It had a common source: the speeches of President George W. Bush, who has been widely cited in Mexico as an advocate for the illegals.

Although conservative commentators criticized the demonstrators, they were far more hard on the members of Congress who wanted to criminalize illegal entry into the United States. Across the country, however, rank-and-file conservatives and even some liberals deluged talk radio and newspaper editorial pages with complaints. "Doesn't anybody care," argued the conservatives, "that illegal aliens are in fact *illegal?*" Between the rhetoric of the demonstrators and the rhetoric of their critics, there was and is a broad gap. Part of the gap is the result of the basic disagreement of the two sides; part of it derives from the different loyalties of the two groups—conservatives to their vision of "America the way it oughta be," and the Latinos to their Mexican-American identity. But just as apparent in the attitudes of the two groups was a divergent approach to legal and political questions. For the conservatives, the value of law and order and the U.S. Constitution is taken for granted, like the self-evident truths proclaimed in the Declaration. For the Mexicans, loyalty to family and nation, love and honor, seemed to take precedence over the conservatives' 18th-century abstractions.

Every Mexican-rights group complains about the racism and bigotry of Anglo-Americans, and their complaints are not without justification. Whatever we may say in public, most of us do not much like Mexicans, whom we regard as too irrational, too violent, too passionate. Americans are hardly unique in having ethnic prejudices. There has probably never been a time in human history when members of different ethnic groups respected each other. Greeks despised Romans as crude; Romans despised Greeks as effeminate; and the French and English, many centuries later, played out the same little drama of chauvinism and contempt. A people defines itself, in part, by rejecting the qualities it attributes to foreigners. Anglo-Americans display their respect for cleanliness, self-restraint, and lawfulness by deriding Mexicans as dirty, violent, and lawless. And Mexicans return the compliment, making fun of *gringos* as stiff, unspiritual, and sexless.

The *gringo* stereotype is not restricted to ignorant peasants who have never met educated Americans. Carlos Fuentes, Mexico's most important novelist, has spent a great deal of time in America and speaks excellent English. Although Fuentes has picked up many American friends and admirers, his fiction still perpetuates the familiar self-serving stereotypes and clichés. In *The Old Gringo*, the old American (Ambrose Bierce) is a joyless writer who comes to Mexico seeking a beautiful death; the lovely American schoolmarm, whose family has lived the lie of respectability, only finds erotic fulfillment in the embrace of a peasant who has become one of Pancho Villa's officers. Colonel Arroyo feels he can share his deepest feelings with the *gringuita*, because she is

> from a land as far away and strange as the United States, the Other World, the world that is not Mexico, the foreign and distant and curious, eccentric, and marginal world of the Yankees who did not enjoy good food or violent revolution or women in bondage, or beautiful churches, and broke with all traditions just for the sake of it, as if there were good things only in the future and in novelty ...

Since the frontier between Mexico and the United States is moving ever northward, the best snapshot of the American future can be taken in the series of frontier towns that ring the border. From the West, where San Diego—epitome of American opulence and consumerism—is faced by tacky and squalid Tijuana, which every year launches tens of thousands of illegal immigrants into California's underground labor markets; to El Paso and Juárez, a common city divided by historical conflicts and a border that is more irritating than relevant; to Del Rio and Acuña, Laredo and

Nuevo Laredo, McAllen and Reynosa, Brownsville and Matamoros, America and Mexico are redefining themselves and each other in a cultural equivalent of Spanglish.

Mexico and the United States are both known as violent countries, but there are important differences in the style—and the incidence—of criminal violence. Both are complex countries with varying ethnic and regional traditions. For example, the states of the American South are proverbial for their high homicide rates, but, in contrast with the large cities of the North, much of the killing in the South is done for personal motives. Crimes of violence in the United States can also be broken down by ethnicity: Blacks and Hispanics account for well over half the violent crimes, while the rate for white Americans is in line with those in Western Europe.

In 1999, the U.S. homicide rate was 5.7 per 100,000. This is two to eight times the rate of most countries in Western Europe, but America seems safe when compared with Mexico, which, despite very strict gun laws, has a homicide rate of 17.58. According to the Overseas Security Advisory Council, "In the categories of murder, rape and robbery, Mexico's Distrito Federal posts 3 to 4 times the incidence of these crimes than does New York City, greater Los Angeles or Washington, D.C."

What this means when Mexicans enter the United States can be measured by Ed Rubenstein's calculations in an important article on *VDare.com*: In 2003, while about 27 percent of the inmates in federal prisons were aliens, 67 percent of that figure were Mexican—or 18 percent of the total prison population. When other Latin Americans were added in, the Latino percentage of the federal prison population reached 23 percent. These aliens are very costly to feed, house, and protect, but since most (as Rubenstein points out) are repeat offenders, they cost taxpayers less in prison than on the outside.

In Europe, America is condemned as a nation of homicidal cowboys, but, as Roger McGrath has shown in his classic *Gunfighters, Highwaymen, and Vigilantes*, the well-armed Old West was a peaceful place. The old America had her share of tough-guy heroes, but, for the most part, they did their own killing in what were regarded as fair fights. Men such as Jim Bowie and even John Wesley Hardin did not have men shot in the back, seal off trains in tunnels by dynamiting both sides, or terrorize whole towns—some of Pancho Villa's more notorious escapades.

Mexico and the United States share a reputation for political violence, but, while America's ill fame rests largely on four assassinated presidents and several well-publicized riots and police crackdowns (Haymarket Riot, Kent State, the 1968 Democratic Convention), Mexican history is awash in blood. Among the more famous political killings in Mexico, one might name the last two Aztec rulers, Moctezuma and Cuauhtémoc; the two clerical leaders of uprisings against Spain (Father Hidalgo and Father Morelos); emperors Agustín de Iturbide and Maximilian; presidents Madero, Carranza, and Obregón—to say nothing of a more recent string of high-profile killings that includes a Catholic cardinal murdered by drug lords in Guadalajara in 1993; a PRI [Institutional Revolutionary Party] presidential candidate (Luis Donaldo Colosio) in 1994; a PRI secretary general and majority leader-elect of the lower house (José Francisco Ruíz Massieu) killed by the brother of President Salinas in 1994; [and] a congressman implicated in drugs and murder (Manuel Muñoz Rocha).

These few names do not begin to exhaust a very long list that includes rival political candidates murdered by the PRI, journalists killed by drug lords, thousands of students gunned down in demonstrations (in 1968 and 1971), and the massive suppression of the Chiapas Indians in the 1990's.

The most celebrated victims of political violence were the two outstanding military leaders of the Mexican Revolution, Elimiano Zapata and Francisco Villa. General Villa is one of the most remarkable men produced by Mexico. A reckless and daring cavalryman, he was nicknamed the "Centaur of the North" for his exploits in the saddle. He and his lieutenants also acquired an unsavory reputation for cruelty. Even before Woodrow Wilson decided to recognize Villa's rival Venustiano Carranza as the legitimate president of Mexico, Villa had made a habit of killing *gringos*. Outraged by what he regarded as American treachery, he launched a punitive expedition against the people of Columbus, New Mexico. Villa's men killed about 18 Americans, mostly civilians, but they would have killed many more, had they not been distracted by looting.

Despite his many acts of wanton killing, including (perhaps) the murder of Ambrose Bierce, Villa is unquestionably a great hero in his own country. In Chihuahua, his house has been turned into a museum of the revolution, and, although the cruelty of his lieutenant Fierro is several times mentioned, the general of the Division of the North is treated with the respect he demanded in life.

There is no hero quite like "Pancho" Villa in American history. To match his career, one would have to combine the cavalry exploits of Bedford Forrest with Andrew Jackson's harsh temper and the postwar activities of the Jameses and Youngers, but this hybrid would still lack Villa's homicidal volatility.

Our mass killers are of a different stamp from either American gunfighters or Mexican bandit-revolutionaries: Villa was unquestionably brave and resourceful, admirable in his own way. Our homicidal maniacs are respectable men such as William Tecumseh Sherman and the president [Abraham Lincoln] who sent him on his mission, and Harry S. Truman, who dropped the big ones—not on the Japanese politicians and officers who deserved it, but on civilians. Ours are men with clean hands who kill with a few words.

When reporters began grilling [Secretary of Defense] Donald Rumsfeld about possible war crimes and abuses, his stock response was that "we don't do those things." Indeed, [Iraqi prison] Abu Ghraib is exceptional. Nonetheless, the United States government has an appalling record of what would be called war crimes if they were committed by any other nation. To name only a few examples of war against civilians: the conquest of the Philippines; the bombing of Belgrade and Novi Sad; and the burning of Columbia, South Carolina. Who knows what decent people will say of the nearly one million civilian deaths attributed to the Gulf War and subsequent embargo, or the total mess we have made of Iraq over the past three years?

American violence was summed up for me by the words of a little girl playing fire-control officer on a submarine during the bombing of civilian centers in Yugoslavia. She explained to the cameras that she just sent the missiles and did not think about where they landed. Judges and politicians display a similar insouciance in not thinking about the tens of millions of infants murdered with their permission. Mexican-American immigrants, by contrast, are generally more pro-life than American natives, and some even refused to vote for their would-be Democratic *patrón*, [2004 presidential candidate] John Kerry, because of his outspoken support for a woman's right to kill her child.

Some American Catholics think we should welcome the hordes of pro-life Catholics swarming across our southern border, but this is a mistake. Mexicans quickly become acclimated to America's culture of consumerism and infanticide. What they do not appear to relinquish is their own traditional style of violence.

Unfortunately, Americans, who have lost faith in their traditions and in their God, are as likely to resist the invasion from the south as they are to combat Islamic terrorism. Liberal to the core, we lack the most basic survival instincts. Nearly five years after September 11, our leaders still think they are "fighting terrorism" in Iraq, while they are refusing either to defend our borders or to contain the spreading virus of Islam in our society.

Many Mexican immigrants know who they are. They can name their grandparents; they love their country; and, in their own passionate way, they worship their God and love their Church. If you attack what they love, some Mexicans, instead of acknowledging your right to disagree, just give you a taste of rough justice. If only we could convince them that their real enemies are the Muslims who have slandered Our Lord and His Mother. Then they could fight the battle we are afraid to fight, and, when they have reconquered North America, they would have earned it.

SOURCE: Thomas Fleming, "Violent Revolution." *Chronicles* 30 (July 2006), 10–11. Reprinted courtesy of the Rockford Institute—Chronicles Press.

ANALYSIS

Unlike the authors of the Bradley Project report, Thomas Fleming perceives little indication that Mexican immigrants—legal or illegal—will integrate easily into the American society and culture. Fleming emphasizes the cultural differences between Anglo Americans and Hispanics and the resentments that Mexicans hold against what they consider racist Americans. Fleming focuses especially on the issue of differential levels of violent behavior by Anglo Americans and Mexicans. Although both nations are regarded as violent, the author claims that

DID YOU KNOW?

Border Violence

Trepidation increased among U.S. residents over the issue of immigration, both legal and illegal, as violence close to the U.S.-Mexican border reached alarming levels in 2008, when more than 6,000 people in Mexico were killed in drug-related violence. Drug gangs, becoming more brazen, engaged in gun battles with military units and the police, and threatened public officials. For instance, the police chief of Ciudad Juarez, the largest city in Chihuahua, a state bordering on Texas and New Mexico, stepped down from his position when criminal gangs threatened to kill at least one police officer every 48 hours if he did not resign. Gangs also threatened to behead the mayor and members of his family who reside on either side of the border. In February 2009 gunmen fired on an automobile convoy in which Chihuahua Governor Jose Reyes Baeza was riding. Governor Baeza was unhurt, but two security agents and one of the attackers were wounded. Earlier in February, retired General Mauro Enrique Tello Quiñones, along with a bodyguard and driver, were kidnaped in downtown Cancun. The general was tortured (his arms and legs were broken) and shot in the head. Cancun mayor Gregorio Sánchez had hired Tello to head a recruitment and training program for an elite police organization to combat drug cartel operations. Thomas Fleming's analysis of the different cultural attitudes toward violence in Mexico and the United States gained added credence as killings and attacks on government officials in Mexico continued to spread.

more than half of the violent crimes are committed by blacks and Hispanics, while the rate of violent crime committed by whites is comparable to those of Western Europe. Fleming concludes that, despite what he sees as differing attitudes toward violence, nonetheless Mexican immigrants, who have close family ties, are committed to their religion, and have a better sense of cultural identity than do white Americans, ultimately may prove to be defenders of the United States against what he perceives to be the "real enemies" of Western culture: Islam.

FURTHER READING

Abramsky, Sasha. "Gimme Shelter: What the New Sanctuary Movement Offers, Beyond a Safe Space, for the Undocumented." *The Nation*, February 25, 2008, 24–28.

Buchanan, Patrick J. *State of Emergency: The Third World Invasion and Conquest of America.* New York, St. Martin's Press, 2006.

Rivera, Geraldo. *His Panic: Why Americans Fear Hispanics in the U.S.* New York: Penguin Group, 2008.

Schlesinger Jr., Arthur M. *The Disuniting of America: Reflections on a Multicultural Society.* Second edition. New York: W. W. Norton, 1998.

Schuck, Peter H. "Immigration." In *Understanding America: The Anatomy of an Exceptional Nation*, edited by Peter H. Schuck and James Q. Wilson. New York: Public Affairs, 2008.

Tancredo, Tom. *In Mortal Danger: The Battle for America's Border and Security.* Nashville, TN: Cumberland House, 2006.

Williamson, Chilton, Jr., editor. *Immigration and the American Future.* Rockford, IL: Chronicles Press, 2007.

6

SEX EDUCATION, HOMOSEXUALITY, AND GAY MARRIAGE

"Red Sex, Blue Sex: Why Do So Many Evangelical Teen-Agers Become Pregnant?"

- **Document:** Margaret Talbot reviews the literature on abstinence-only sex education.
- **Date:** November 3, 2008.
- **Where:** *The New Yorker* magazine.
- **Significance:** Margaret Talbot investigates a major cultural difference in the approach toward sex education and sexuality between conservative Christians and social liberals, which appears to result in differential consequences for young people.

DOCUMENT

In early September, when Sarah Palin, the Republican candidate for Vice-President, announced that her unwed seventeen-year-old daughter, Bristol, was pregnant, many liberals were shocked, not by the revelation but by the reaction to it. They expected the news to dismay the evangelical voters that John McCain was courting with his choice of Palin. Yet reports from the floor of the Republican Convention, in St. Paul, quoted dozens of delegates who seemed unfazed, or even buoyed, by the news. A delegate from Louisiana told CBS News, "Like so many other American families who are in the same situation, I think it's great that she instilled in her daughter the values to have the child and not to sneak off someplace and have an abortion." A Mississippi delegate claimed that "even though young children are making that decision to become pregnant, they've also decided to take responsibility for their actions and decided to follow up with that and get married and raise this child." Palin's family drama, delegates said, was similar to the experience of many socially conservative Christian families. As Marlys Popma, the head of evangelical outreach for the McCain campaign, told *National Review*, "There hasn't been one evangelical family that hasn't gone through some sort of situation." In fact, it was Popma's own "crisis pregnancy" that had brought her into the movement in the first place.

During the campaign, the media has largely respected calls to treat Bristol Palin's pregnancy as a private matter. But the reactions to it have exposed a cultural rift that mirrors America's dominant political divide. Social liberals in the country's "blue states" tend to support sex education and are not particularly troubled by the idea that many teenagers have sex before marriage, but would regard a teen-age daughter's pregnancy as devastating news. And the social conservatives in "red states" generally advocate abstinence-only education and denounce sex before marriage, but are relatively unruffled if a teen-ager becomes pregnant, as long as she doesn't choose to have an abortion.

A handful of social scientists and family-law scholars have recently begun looking closely at this split. Last year, Mark Regnerus, a sociologist at the University of Texas at Austin, published a startling book called *Forbidden Fruit: Sex and Religion in the Lives of American Teenagers*, and he is working on a follow-up that includes a section titled "Red Sex, Blue Sex." His findings are drawn from a national survey that Regnerus and his colleagues conducted of some thirty-four hundred thirteen-to-seventeen-year-olds, and from a comprehensive government study of adolescent health known as Add Health. Regnerus argues that religion is a good indicator of attitudes toward sex, but a poor one of sexual behavior, and that this gap is especially wide among teenagers who identify themselves as evangelical. The vast majority of white evangelical adolescents—seventy-four percent—say that they believe in abstaining from sex before marriage. (Only half of mainline Protestants, and a quarter of Jews, say that they believe in abstinence.) Moreover, among the major religious groups, evangelical virgins are the least likely to anticipate that sex will be pleasurable, and the most likely to believe that having sex will cause their partners to lose respect for them. (Jews most often cite pleasure as a reason to have sex, and say that an unplanned pregnancy would be an embarrassment.) But, according to Add Health data, evangelical teenagers are more sexually active than Mormons, mainline Protestants, and Jews. On average, white evangelical Protestants make their "sexual début"—to use the festive term of social-science researchers—shortly after turning sixteen. Among major religious groups, only black Protestants begin having sex earlier.

Another key difference in behavior, Regnerus reports, is that evangelical Protestant teenagers are significantly less likely than other groups to use contraception. This could be because evangelicals are also among the most likely to believe that using contraception will send the message that they are looking for sex. It could also be because many evangelicals are steeped in the abstinence movement's warnings that condoms won't actually protect them from pregnancy or venereal disease. More provocatively, Regnerus found that only half of sexually active teenagers who say that they seek guidance from God or the Scriptures when making a tough decision report using contraception every time. By contrast, sixty-nine percent of sexually active youth who say that they most often follow the counsel of a parent or another trusted adult consistently use protection.

The gulf between sexual belief and sexual behavior becomes apparent, too, when you look at the outcomes of abstinence-pledge movements. Nationwide, according to a 2001 estimate, some two and a half million people have taken a pledge to remain celibate until marriage. Usually, they do so under the auspices of movements such as True Love Waits or the Silver Ring Thing. Sometimes, they make their vows at big rallies featuring Christian pop stars and laser light shows, or at purity balls, where girls in frothy dresses exchange rings with their fathers, who vow to help them remain virgins until the day they marry. More than half of those who take such pledges—which, unlike abstinence-only classes in public schools, are explicitly Christian—end up having sex before marriage, and not usually with their future spouse. The movement is not the complete washout its critics portray it as: pledgers delay sex eighteen months longer than non-pledgers, and have fewer partners. Yet, according to the sociologists Peter Bearman, of Columbia University, and Hannah Brückner, of Yale, communities with high rates of pledging also have high rates of S.T.D.s. This could be because more teens pledge in communities where they perceive more danger from sex (in which case the pledge is doing some good); or it could be because fewer people in these communities use condoms when they break the pledge.

Bearman and Brückner have also identified a peculiar dilemma: in some schools, if too many teens pledge, the effort basically collapses. Pledgers apparently gather strength from the sense that they are an embattled minority; once their numbers exceed thirty percent, and proclaimed chastity becomes the norm, that special identity is lost. With such a fragile formula, it's hard to imagine how educators can ever get it right: once the self-proclaimed virgin clique hits the thirty-one-percent mark, suddenly it's Sodom and Gomorrah.

Religious belief apparently does make a potent difference in behavior for one group of evangelical teenagers: those who score highest on measures of religiosity—such as how often they go to church, or how often they pray at home. But many Americans who identify themselves as evangelicals, and who hold socially conservative beliefs, aren't deeply observant.

Even more important than religious conviction, Regnerus argues, is how "embedded" a teenager is in a network of friends, family, and institutions that reinforce his or her goal of delaying sex, and that offer a plausible alternative to America's sexed-up consumer culture. A church, of course, isn't the only way to provide a cohesive sense of community. Close-knit families make a difference. Teenagers who live with both biological parents are more likely to be virgins than those who do not. And adolescents who say that their families understand them, pay attention to their concerns, and have fun with them are more likely to delay intercourse, regardless of religiosity.

A terrific 2005 documentary, "The Education of Shelby Knox," tells the story of a teenager from a Southern Baptist family in Lubbock, Texas, who has taken a True Love Waits pledge. To the chagrin of her youth pastor, and many of her neighbors, Knox eventually becomes an activist for comprehensive sex education. At her high school, kids receive abstinence-only education, but, Knox says, "maybe twice a week I see a girl walking down the hall pregnant." In the film, Knox seems successful at remaining chaste, but less because she took a pledge than because she has a fearlessly independent mind and the kind of parents who—despite their own conservative leanings—admire her outspokenness. Devout Republicans, her parents end up driving her around town to make speeches that would have curled their hair before their daughter started making them. Her mother even comes to take pride in Shelby's efforts, because while abstinence pledges are lovely in the abstract, they don't acknowledge "reality."

Like other American teens, young evangelicals live in a world of Internet porn, celebrity sex scandals, and raunchy reality TV, and they have the same hormonal urges that their peers have. Yet they come from families and communities in which sexual life is supposed to be forestalled until the first night of a transcendent honeymoon. Regnerus writes, "In such an atmosphere, attitudes about sex may *formally* remain unchanged (and restrictive) while sexual activity becomes increasingly common. This clash of cultures and norms is felt most poignantly in the so-called Bible Belt." Symbolic commitment to the institution of marriage remains strong there, and politically motivating—hence the drive to outlaw gay marriage—but the actual practice of it is scattershot.

Among blue-state social liberals, commitment to the institution of marriage tends to be unspoken or discreet, but marriage in practice typically works pretty well. Two family-law scholars, Naomi Cahn, of George Washington University, and June Carbone, of the University of Missouri at Kansas City, are writing a book on the subject, and they argue that "red families" and "blue families" are "living different lives, with different moral imperatives." (They emphasize that the Republican-Democrat divide is less important than the higher concentration of "moral-values voters" in red states.) In 2004, the states with the highest divorce rates were Nevada, Arkansas, Wyoming, Idaho, and West Virginia (all red states in the 2004 election); those with the lowest were Illinois, Massachusetts, Iowa, Minnesota, and New Jersey. The highest teen-pregnancy rates were in Nevada, Arizona, Mississippi, New Mexico, and Texas (all red); the lowest were in North Dakota, Vermont, New Hampshire, Minnesota, and Maine (blue except for North Dakota). "The 'blue states' of the Northeast and Mid-Atlantic have lower teen birthrates, higher use of abortion, and lower percentages of teen births within marriage," Cahn and Carbone observe. They also note that people start families earlier in red states—in part because they are more inclined to deal with an unplanned pregnancy by marrying rather than by seeking an abortion.

Of all variables, the age at marriage may be the pivotal difference between red and blue families. The five states with the lowest median age at marriage are Utah, Oklahoma, Idaho,

DID YOU KNOW?

Federally Funded Abstinence-Only Sex Education Program

By December 2007, several states had reconsidered the acceptance of federal funds for abstinence-only sex education programs. At least fourteen states had notified the federal government that they would no longer request funds or were not expected to apply for a portion of the $50 million the federal government was offering to the states. Two other states, Ohio and Washington, submitted applications, but indicated that they wished to use the funds for comprehensive sex education, which violated the conditions of the program. William Smith, spokesman for the Sexuality Information and Education Council of the United States, declared that states rejecting the funding indicated the end of the funding program, but Valerie Huber of the National Abstinence Education Association stated that the abstinence approach is the best education tool for teenagers and should be emphasized even more. Cecile Richards of the Planned Parenthood Federation of America claimed that the abstinence education program is ideologically motivated and lacks scientific support. States were bypassing the federal funds for various reasons, including the requirement that states match federal funds and the results of studies that suggest abstinence-only sex education has not been demonstrated to be effective.

Arkansas, and Kentucky, all red states, while those with the highest are all blue: Massachusetts, New York, Rhode Island, Connecticut, and New Jersey. The red-state model puts couples at greater risk for divorce; women who marry before their mid-twenties are significantly more likely to divorce than those who marry later. And younger couples are more likely to be contending with two of the biggest stressors on a marriage: financial struggles and the birth of a baby before, or soon after, the wedding.

There are, of course, plenty of exceptions to these rules—messily divorcing professional couples in Boston, highschool sweethearts who stay sweetly together in rural Idaho. Still, Cahn and Carbone conclude, "the paradigmatic red-state couple enters marriage not long after the woman becomes sexually active, has two children by her mid-twenties, and reaches the critical period of marriage at the high point in the life cycle for risk-taking and experimentation. The paradigmatic blue-state couple is more likely to experiment with multiple partners, postpone marriage until after they reach emotional and financial maturity, and have their children (if they have them at all) as their lives are stabilizing."

Some of these differences in sexual behavior come down to class and education. Regnerus and Carbone and Cahn all see a new and distinct "middle-class morality" taking shape among economically and socially advantaged families who are not social conservatives. In Regnerus's survey, the teenagers who espouse this new morality are tolerant of premarital sex (and of contraception and abortion) but are themselves cautious about pursuing it. Regnerus writes, "They are interested in remaining free from the burden of teenage pregnancy and the sorrows and embarrassments of sexually transmitted diseases. They perceive a bright future for themselves, one with college, advanced degrees, a career, and a family. Simply put, too much seems at stake. Sexual intercourse is not worth the risks." These are the kids who tend to score high on measures of "strategic orientation"—how analytical, methodical, and fact-seeking they are when making decisions. Because these teenagers see abstinence as unrealistic, they are not opposed in principle to sex before marriage—just careful about it. Accordingly, they might delay intercourse in favor of oral sex, not because they cherish the idea of remaining "technical virgins" but because they assess it as a safer option. "Solidly middle- or upper-middle-class adolescents have considerable socioeconomic and educational expectations, courtesy of their parents and their communities' lifestyles," Regnerus writes. "They are happy with their direction, generally not rebellious, tend to get along with their parents, and have few moral qualms about expressing their nascent sexuality." They might have loved Ellen Page in "Juno," but in real life they'd see having a baby at the wrong time as a tragic derailment of their life plans. For this group, Regnerus says, unprotected sex has become "a moral issue like smoking or driving a car without a seatbelt. It's not just unwise anymore; it's wrong."

Each of these models of sexual behavior has drawbacks—in the blue-state scheme, people may postpone childbearing to the point where infertility becomes an issue. And delaying childbearing is better suited to the more affluent, for whom it yields economic benefits, in the form of educational opportunities and career advancement. But Carbone and Cahn argue that the red-state model is clearly failing on its own terms—producing high rates of teen pregnancy, divorce, sexually transmitted disease, and other dysfunctional outcomes that social conservatives say they abhor. In "Forbidden Fruit," Regnerus offers an "unscientific postscript," in which he advises social conservatives that if they really want to maintain their commitment to chastity and to marriage, they'll need to do more to help young couples stay married longer. As the Reverend Rick Marks, a Southern Baptist minister, recently pointed out in a Florida newspaper, "Evangelicals are fighting gay marriage, saying it will break down traditional marriage, when divorce has already broken it down." Conservatives may need to start talking as much about saving marriages as they do about, say, saving oneself for marriage.

"Having to wait until age twenty-five or thirty to have sex *is* unreasonable," Regnerus writes. He argues that religious organizations that advocate chastity should "work" more creatively to support younger marriages. This is not the 1950s (for which I am glad), where one could bank on social norms, extended (and larger) families, and clear gender roles to negotiate and sustain early family formation."

Evangelicals could start, perhaps, by trying to untangle the contradictory portrayals of sex that they offer to teenagers. In the Shelby Knox documentary, a youth pastor, addressing an assembly of teens, defines intercourse as "what two dogs do out on the street corner—they just bump and grind awhile, *boom boom boom*." Yet a typical evangelical text aimed at young people, "Every Young Woman's Battle," by Shannon Ethridge and Stephen Arterburn, portrays sex between two virgins as an ethereal communion of innocent souls: "physical, mental, emotional, and spiritual pleasure beyond description." Neither is the most realistic or helpful view for a young person to take into marriage, as a few advocates of abstinence acknowledge. The savvy young Christian writer Lauren Winner, in her book *Real Sex: The Naked Truth About Chastity*, writes, "Rather than spending our unmarried years stewarding and disciplining our desires, we have become ashamed of them. We persuade ourselves that the desires themselves are horrible. This can have real consequences if we do get married." Teenagers and single adults are "told over and over not to have sex, but no one ever encourages" them "to be bodily or sensual in some appropriate way"—getting to know and appreciate what their bodies can do through sports, especially for girls, or even thinking sensually about something like food. Winner goes on, "This doesn't mean, of course, that if only the church sponsored more softball leagues, everyone would stay on the chaste straight and narrow. But it does mean that the church ought to cultivate ways of teaching Christians to live in their bodies well—so that unmarried folks can still be bodily people, even though they're not having sex, and so that married people can give themselves to sex freely."

Too often, though, evangelical literature directed at teenagers forbids all forms of sexual behavior, even masturbation. "Every Young Woman's Battle," for example, tells teenagers that "the momentary relief" of "self-gratification" can lead to "shame, low self-esteem, and fear of what others might think or that something is wrong with you." And it won't slake sexual desire: "Once you begin feeding baby monsters, their appetites grow bigger and they want MORE! It's better not to feed such a monster in the first place."

Shelby Knox, who spoke at a congressional hearing on sex education earlier this year, occupies a middle ground. She testified that it's possible to "believe in abstinence in a religious sense," but still understand that abstinence-only education is dangerous "for students who simply are not abstaining." As Knox's approach makes clear, you don't need to break out the sex toys to teach sex ed—you can encourage teenagers to postpone sex for all kinds of practical, emotional, and moral reasons. A new "abstinence-plus" curriculum, now growing in popularity, urges abstinence while providing accurate information about contraception and reproduction for those who have sex anyway. "Abstinence works," Knox said at the hearing. "Abstinence-only-until-marriage does not."

It might help, too, not to present virginity as the cornerstone of a virtuous life. In certain evangelical circles, the concept is so emphasized that a girl who regrets having been sexually active is encouraged to declare herself a "secondary" or "born-again" virgin. That's not an idea, surely, that helps teenagers postpone sex or have it responsibly.

The "pro-family" efforts of social conservatives—the campaigns against gay marriage and abortion—do nothing to instill the emotional discipline or the psychological smarts that forsaking all others often involves. Evangelicals are very good at articulating their sexual ideals, but they have little practical advice for their young followers. Social liberals, meanwhile, are not very good at articulating values on marriage and teen sexuality—indeed, they may feel that it's unseemly or judgmental to do so. But in fact the new middle-class morality is squarely pro-family. Maybe these choices weren't originally about values—maybe they were about maximizing education and careers—yet the result is a more stable family system. Not only do couples who marry later stay married longer; children born to older couples fare better on a variety of measures, including educational attainment, regardless of their parents' economic circumstances. The new middle-class culture of intensive parenting has ridiculous aspects, but it's pretty successful at turning out productive, emotionally resilient young adults. And its intensity may be one reason that teenagers from close families see child-rearing as a project for which they're not yet ready. For too long, the conventional wisdom has been that social conservatives are the upholders of family values, whereas liberals are the proponents of a polymorphous selfishness. This isn't true, and, every once in a while, liberals might point that out.

Some evangelical Christians are starting to reckon with the failings of the preaching-and-pledging approach. In "The Education of Shelby Knox," for example, Shelby's father is uncomfortable, at first, with his daughter's campaign. Lubbock, after all, is a town so conservative that its local youth pastor tells Shelby, "You ask me sometimes why I look at you a little funny. It's because I hear you speak and I hear tolerance." But as her father listens to her arguments he realizes that the no-tolerance ethic simply hasn't worked in their deeply Christian community. Too many girls in town are having sex, and having babies that they can't support. As Shelby's father declares toward the end of the film, teenage pregnancy "is a problem—a major, major problem that everybody's just shoving under the rug."

SOURCE: First printed in *The New Yorker*, November 8, 2008. Copyright © 2008 by Margaret Talbot, reprinted with permission of the Wylie Agency, LLC.

ANALYSIS

Several issues, including sexual behavior, homosexuality, marriage, and the related subject of abortion coalesce to form a powerful point of conflict within the culture wars. Liberals and conservatives advocate competing policies to deal with the problem of teenage pregnancy. Many conservative parents have criticized sex education programs, especially the inclusion of such topics as contraception and homosexuality. Conservatives and liberals disagree about the effectiveness of sex education programs, at times interpreting the available data selectively to support their positions. In 1992 groups such as the American Family Association and Focus on the Family began calling for abstinence-only curricula to replace more comprehensive sex education in the public schools. Various local school districts began to alter sex education courses to comply with the wishes of conservative groups, and in 1996 Congress established a funding program within welfare reform legislation, entitled the Personal Responsibility and Work Opportunity Reconciliation Act, to assist states in creating abstinence-only sex education programs. The funds were to be used for school classes, community groups, state and local health departments, and media campaigns that focus on promoting sexual abstinence. The key issue revolved around the question of whether such programs are effective in preventing teenage pregnancy and limiting the occurrence of sexually transmitted diseases. While some advocates of sex education have called for "abstinence-plus" programs, which include discussions of information about such topics as contraception for those students who do not practice abstinence, supporters of abstinence-only curricula tend to oppose such a compromise. In addition to lobbying for abstinence-only education programs, supporters formed such organizations as True Love Waits (established in 1993) to encourage teenagers to sign pledges to refrain from sexual relations. Critics of abstinence-only programs claim that such programs are ineffective, or at least no more effective than comprehensive sex education curricula. They also argue that such programs disseminate incorrect information, including the claim that condoms do not protect against sexually transmitted diseases.

Federal Defense of Marriage Act

- *Document:* Excerpt from the Federal Defense of Marriage Act.
- *Date:* Passed the U.S. House of Representatives July 12, 1996; passed the U.S. Senate September 10, 1996; signed by President Bill Clinton, September 21, 1996.
- *Where:* Washington, DC.
- *Significance:* The possibility that certain state legislatures would pass legislation to recognize same-gender marriages, or that state court systems would mandate the recognition of such marriages, led Congress to pass by wide margins (342 to 67 in the House and 85 to 14 in the Senate) an act defining marriage in federal policy as a legal union of one man and one woman and declaring that states need not legally recognize same-gender marriages performed in other states.

DOCUMENT

One Hundred Fourth Congress of the United States of America AT THE SECOND SESSION

Begun and held at the City of Washington on Wednesday, the third day of January, one thousand nine hundred and ninety-six

An Act

To define and protect the institution of marriage.

Be it enacted by the Senate and House of Representatives of the United States of America in Congress assembled,

SECTION 1. SHORT TITLE.

This act may be cited as the 'Defense of Marriage Act.'

SECTION 2. POWERS RESERVED TO THE STATES.

(a) IN GENERAL—Chapter 115 of title 28, United States Code, is amended by adding after section 1738B the following:

"Section 1738C. Certain acts, records, and proceedings and the effect thereof

"No state, territory, or possession of the United States, or Indian tribe, shall be required to give effect to any public act, record, or judicial proceeding of any other State, territory, possession, or tribe respecting a relationship between persons of the same sex that is treated as a marriage under the laws of such other State, territory, possession, or tribe, or a right or claim arising from such relationship." . . .

SECTION 3. DEFINITION OF MARRIAGE

(a) IN GENERAL—Chapter 1 of title 1, United States Code, is amended by adding at the end the following:

"Section 7. Definition of 'marriage' and 'spouse'

"In determining the meaning of any Act of Congress, or of any ruling, regulation, or interpretation of the various administrative bureaus and agencies of the United States, the word 'marriage' means only a legal union between one man and one woman as husband and wife, and the word 'spouse' refers only to a person of the opposite sex who is a husband or a wife." . . .

SOURCE: Federal Defense of Marriage Act. Pub. L. 104–199, 100 Stat. 2419 (September 21, 1996).

ANALYSIS

How individuals view homosexuality certainly influences their position on the legal recognition of same-gender marriage. The range of positions varies from total acceptance of gay marriage, to support for gay unions and domestic partnerships, to allowing states to decided individually policies on the question but not requiring a state to recognize a gay marriage sanctioned in another state, to supporting an amendment to the U.S. Constitution defining marriage as a union between one man and one woman and prohibiting states and the federal government from legally recognizing same-gender marriage.

The push for a Defense of Marriage Act (DOMA) on the national level began in earnest when the state supreme court of Hawaii, in *Baehr v. Lewin* (1993), ruled that, unless the state could demonstrate a compelling reason, laws

DID YOU KNOW?

"The Cabinet" and Gay Politics

By 2008 a small group of individuals had begun to influence the outcome of electoral races by opposing anti-gay conservative candidates and favoring liberal candidates who support gay rights. The low-profile group, which came to be known as "the Cabinet," was composed of seven major benefactors, including David Bohnett of Beverley Hills, California, Timothy Gill of Denver, Colorado, James Hormel of San Francisco, Jon Stryker of Kalamazoo, Michigan, and Henry van Ameringen of New York. The group invited Linda Ketner, heiress to the Food Lion fortune, to join the group, and in 2008 she ran for Congress against Republican Representative Henry Brown Jr. of South Carolina. The seventh member of the Cabinet is Jonathan Lewis, son of Progressive Insurance co-founder Joseph Lewis. Conservative estimates placed the total contributions from the group from 2004 to 2008 at $7.8 million. Formation of the group allowed members to share information and coordinate contributions where they could have the greatest effect. The Cabinet's activities are seen as a shift in culture war strategy in which significant amounts of money can be used to shift the advantage toward liberal groups and political candidates while signaling to conservatives that they may suffer the consequences of taking anti-gay stands.

prohibiting same-gender couples from marrying violated the right within the state constitution of equal protection. Because states generally have recognized marriages conducted in other states, interests concerned with preserving the traditional family as a union of one man and one woman began to lobby Congress for passage of legislation stating that the federal government may not regard same-gender relationships as marriage, and that no state must recognize a relationship between two individuals as marriage even if another state legally sanctions the relationship.

Representative Bob Barr (R-GA), responding to the demands of conservative groups, authored the Defense of Marriage Act, which ultimately became law. In November 2003 the Massachusetts Supreme Judicial Court ruled that prohibiting same-gender couples from marrying violated the state constitution's protection of equal rights. Subsequently the court offered the opinion that any action by the state legislature to establish a category of same-gender unions distinct from marriage would be unacceptable. Thus Massachusetts, in May 2004, began issuing marriage licenses to same-gender couples.

Opponents of gay marriage (including President George W. Bush), upset by the Massachusetts Supreme Judicial Court's ruling, began to push for an amendment to the U.S. Constitution defining marriage exclusively as a union of one man and one woman. Representative Marilyn Musgrave (R-CO) submitted a proposed amendment in May 2003, but neither it nor various subsequent proposals so far have gained the required two-thirds vote in both houses of Congress to be submitted to the states for ratification. In 2008 the following proposed amendment was introduced in the Senate: "Marriage in the United States shall consist of the union of a man and a woman. Neither this Constitution, nor the constitution of any State, shall be construed to require that marriage or the legal incidents thereof be conferred upon any union other than the union of a man and a woman."

As of 2008, 41 states had approved Defense of Marriage acts and 27 states had placed a definition of marriage in their state constitutions. With continuing political and legal battles over the right to marry, the question of same-gender marriage promises to remain on the agenda of culture warriors.

Lawrence et al. v. Texas, Majority Opinion

- **Document:** Excerpt from Justice Anthony Kennedy's majority U.S. Supreme Court decision regarding a challenge to a Texas sodomy law.
- **Date:** June 26, 2003.
- **Where:** U.S. Supreme Court building, Washington, DC.
- **Significance:** At the time the U.S. Supreme Court issued the 6–3 decision, 13 states still had laws in effect that prohibited private consensual homosexual conduct, generally referred to as sodomy. The Court's decision, in overturning the 1986 decision in *Bower v. Hardwick*, invalidated the Texas sodomy law as well as similar laws in other states, thus raising anew the concern among cultural conservatives that gay marriage would be an issue over which they would be contending with liberal forces.

DOCUMENT

Liberty protects the person from unwarranted government intrusions into a dwelling or other private places. In our tradition the State is not omnipresent in the home. And there are other spheres of our lives and existence, outside the home, where the State should not be a dominant presence. Freedom extends beyond spatial bounds. Liberty presumes an autonomy of self that includes freedom of thought, belief, and certain intimate conduct. The instant case involves liberty of the person both in its spatial and more transcendent dimensions.

The question before the Court is the validity of a Texas statute making it a crime for two persons of the same sex to engage in certain intimate sexual conduct.

In Houston, Texas, officers of the Harris County Police Department were dispatched to a private residence in response to a reported weapons disturbance. They entered an apartment where one of the petitioners, John Geddes Lawrence, resided. The right of the police to enter does not seem to have been questioned. The officers observed Lawrence and another man, Tyron Garner, engaging in a sexual act. The two petitioners were arrested, held in custody over night, and charged and convicted before a Justice of the Peace....

The petitioners exercised their right to a trial *de novo* in Harris County Criminal Court. They challenged the statute as a violation of the Equal Protection Clause of the Fourteenth Amendment and of a like provision of the Texas Constitution.... Those contentions were rejected. The petitioners, having entered a plea of *nolo contendre*, were each fined $200 and assessed court costs of $141.25....

The Court of Appeals for the Texas Fourteenth District considered the petitioners' federal constitutional arguments under both the Equal Protection and Due Process Clauses of the Fourteenth Amendment. After hearing the case en banc the court, in a divided opinion, rejected the constitutional arguments and affirmed the convictions.... The majority opinion indicates that the Court of Appeals considered our decision in *Bowers v. Hardwick*, 478 U.S. 186 (1986), to be controlling on the federal due process aspect of the case. *Bowers* then being authoritative, this was proper.

We granted certiorari, *537 U. S. 1044* (2002), to consider three questions:

"1. Whether Petitioners' criminal convictions under the Texas "Homosexual Conduct" law —which criminalizes sexual intimacy by same-sex couples, but not identical behavior by different-sex couples—violate the Fourteenth Amendment guarantee of equal protection of laws?

"2. Whether Petitioners' criminal convictions for adult consensual sexual intimacy in the home violate their vital interests in liberty and privacy protected by the Due Process Clause of the Fourteenth Amendment?

"3. Whether *Bowers v. Hardwick*, 478 U.S. 186 (1986) should be overruled?" Pet. for Cert. i.

The petitioners were adults at the time of the alleged offense. Their conduct was in private and consensual.

We conclude the case should be resolved by determining whether the petitioners were free as adults to engage in the private conduct in the exercise of their liberty under the Due Process Clause of the Fourteenth Amendment to the Constitution. For this inquiry we deem it necessary to reconsider the Court's holding in *Bowers*....

Laws prohibiting sodomy do not seem to have been enforced against consenting adults acting in private. A substantial number of sodomy prosecutions and convictions for which there are surviving records were for predatory acts against those who could not or did not consent, as in the case of a minor or the victim of an assault. As to these, one purpose for the prohibitions was to ensure there would be no lack of coverage if a predator committed a sexual assault that did not constitute rape as defined by the criminal law. Thus the model sodomy indictments presented in a 19th-century treatise, see 2 Chitty, *supra*, at 49, addressed the predatory acts of an adult man against a minor girl or minor boy. Instead of targeting relations between consenting adults in private, 19th-century sodomy prosecutions typically involved relations between men and minor girls or minor boys, relations between adults involving force, relations between adults implicating disparity in status, or relations between men and animals. . . .

Equality of treatment and the due process right to demand respect for conduct protected by the substantive guarantee of liberty are linked in important respects, and a decision on the latter point advances both interests. If protected conduct is made criminal and the law which does so remains unexamined for its substantive validity, its stigma might remain even if it were not enforceable as drawn for equal protection reasons. When homosexual conduct is made criminal by the law of the State, that declaration in and of itself is an invitation to subject homosexual persons to discrimination both in the public and in the private spheres. The central holding of *Bowers* has been brought in question by this case, and it should be addressed. Its continuance as precedent demeans the lives of homosexual persons. . . .

The rationale of *Bowers* does not withstand careful analysis. In his dissenting opinion in *Bowers* Justice Stevens came to these conclusions:

Seven years after the Stonewall Riots of 1969 launched the gay rights movement, a group of gay rights protesters staged an informal demonstration at the July 1976 Democratic National Convention, despite the heat of a New York City summer; photograph by Warren K. Leffler. (Library of Congress, Prints & Photographs Division, *U.S. News & World Report* Magazine Photograph Collection, LC-DIG-ppmsca-09729)

Our prior cases make two propositions abundantly clear. First, the fact that the governing majority in a State has traditionally viewed a particular practice as immoral is not a sufficient reason for upholding a law prohibiting the practice; neither history nor tradition could save a law prohibiting miscegenation from constitutional attack. Second, individual decisions by married persons, concerning the intimacies of their physical relationship, even when not intended to produce offspring, are a form of 'liberty' protected by the Due Process Clause of the Fourteenth Amendment. Moreover, this protection extends to intimate choices by unmarried as well as married persons. 478 U.S., at 216 . . .

Justice Stevens' analysis, in our view, should have been controlling in *Bowers* and should control here.

Bowers was not correct when it was decided, and it is not correct today. It ought not to remain binding precedent. *Bowers v. Hardwick* should be and now is overruled.

The present case does not involve minors, it does not involve persons who might be injured or coerced or who are situated in relationships where consent might not easily be refused. It does not involve public conduct or prostitution. It does not involve whether the government must give formal recognition to any relationship that homosexual persons seek to enter. The case does involve two adults who, with full and mutual consent from each other, engaged in sexual practices common to a homosexual lifestyle. The petitioners are entitled to respect for their private lives. The State cannot demean their existence or control their destiny by making their private sexual conduct a crime. Their right to liberty under the Due Process Clause gives them the full right to engage in their conduct without intervention of the government. "It is a promise of the Constitution that there is a realm of personal liberty which the government may not enter." *Casey, supra*, at 847. The Texas statute furthers no legitimate state interest which can justify its intrusion into the personal and private life of the individual.

Had those who drew and ratified the Due Process Clauses of the Fifth Amendment or the Fourteenth Amendment known the components of liberty in its manifold possibilities, they might have been more specific. They did not presume to have this insight. They knew times can blind us to certain truths and later generations can see that laws once thought necessary and proper in fact serve only to oppress. As the Constitution endures, persons in every generation can invoke its principles in their own search for greater freedom.

The judgment of the Court of Appeals for the Texas Fourteenth District is reversed, and the case is remanded for further proceedings not inconsistent with this opinion.

SOURCE: Supreme Court of the United States. No. 02–102. *John Geddes and Tyron Garner, Petitioners v. Texas* 539 U.S. 558 (2003). On Writ of Certiorari to the Court of Appeals of Texas, Fourteenth District. Majority opinion of Justice Anthony Kennedy.

ANALYSIS

Society's perceptions of homosexual acts were reflected in laws making it a crime to participate in such activity, at times even if they involved consenting adults. As long as some states were free to exercise the option of criminalizing sodomy, the question of same-gender marriage appeared to present a diminished threat to those who objected to such marriages on religious and moral grounds. Changes in attitudes toward homosexual individuals in recent decades are reflected in this Supreme Court decision, which recognizes a right to privacy in those situations that involve the private actions of consenting adults. However, with the Supreme Court decision, conservative individuals and groups, viewing the decision as auguring the ultimate judicial sanctioning of same-gender marriage, began to push for laws and constitutional amendments at the state and federal levels to ban such marriages, while advocates lobbied for the right of same-gender couples to marry as a basic right of equal treatment.

Lawrence et al. v. Texas, Dissenting Opinion

- **Document:** Excerpt from Justice Antonin Scalia's dissenting opinion, joined by Chief Justice William Rehnquist and Justice Clarence Thomas.
- **Date:** June 26, 2003.
- **Where:** U.S. Supreme Court building, Washington, DC.
- **Significance:** Justice Scalia strongly disagreed with the majority decision, reflecting the views of social conservatives and fundamentalist Christians. Scalia accused the majority of taking sides in the culture war, supporting a particular view of homosexuality that supposedly pervades the legal profession.

DOCUMENT

"Liberty finds no refuge in a jurisprudence of doubt." *Planned Parenthood of Southeastern Pa. v. Casey, 505 U.S. 833, 844* (1992). That was the Court's sententious response, barely more than a decade ago, to those seeking to overrule *Roe v. Wade, 410 U.S. 113* (1973). The Court's response today, to those who have engaged in a 17-year crusade to overrule *Bowers v. Hardwick, 478 U.S. 186* (1986), is very different. The need for stability and certainty present no barrier.

Most of the rest of today's opinion has no relevance to its actual holding—that the Texas statute "furthers no legitimate state interest which can justify" its application to petitioners under rational-basis review. *Ante*, at 18 (overruling *Bowers* to the extent it sustained Georgia's anti-sodomy statute under the rational-basis test). Though there is discussion of "fundamental proposition[s]," *ante*, at 4, and "fundamental decisions," *ibid.* nowhere does the Court's opinion declare that homosexual sodomy is a "fundamental right" under the Due Process Clause; nor does it subject the Texas law to the standard of review that would be appropriate (strict scrutiny) if homosexual sodomy *were* a "fundamental right." Thus, while overruling the *outcome* of *Bower*, the Court leaves strangely untouched its central legal conclusion: "[R]espondent would have us announce . . . a fundamental right to engage in homosexual sodomy. This we are quite unwilling to do." *478 U.S., at 191*. Instead the Court simply describes petitioners' conduct as "an exercise of their liberty"— which it undoubtedly is—and proceeds to apply an unheard-of form of rational-bases review that will have far-reaching implications beyond this case. *Ante, at 3*. . . .

Today's opinion is the product of a Court, which is the product of a law-profession culture, that has largely signed on to the so-called homosexual agenda, by which I mean the agenda promoted by some homosexual activists directed at eliminating the moral opprobrium that has traditionally attached to homosexual conduct. I noted in an earlier opinion the fact that the American Association of Law Schools (to which any reputable law school *must* seek to belong) excludes from membership any school that refuses to ban from its job-interview facilities a law firm (no matter how small) that does not wish to hire as a prospective partner a person who openly engages in homosexual conduct. . . .

One of the most revealing statements in today's opinion is the Court's grim warning that the criminalization of homosexual conduct is "an invitation to subject homosexual persons to discrimination both in the public and in the private spheres." *Ante, at 14*. It is clear from this that the Court has taken sides in the culture war, departing from its role of assuring, as neutral observer, that the democratic rules of engagement are observed. Many Americans do not want persons who openly engage in homosexual conduct as partners in their business, as scout-masters for their children, as teachers in their children's schools, or as boarders in their home. They view this as protecting themselves and their families from a lifestyle that they believe to be immoral and destructive. The Court views it as "discrimination" which it is the function of our judgments to deter. So imbued is the Court with the law profession's anti-anti-homosexual culture, that it is seemingly unaware that the attitudes of that culture are not obviously "mainstream"; that in most States what the Court calls "discrimination" against those who engage in homosexual acts is perfectly legal; that proposals to ban such "discrimination" under Title VII have repeatedly been rejected

DID YOU KNOW?

The Fall of Conservative Christian Leader Ted Haggard

In 2006, soon after Alexandra Pelosi, daughter of U.S. House of Representatives Speaker Nancy Pelosi, completed the documentary film about evangelical Christians, *Friends of God*, for HBO, Ted Haggard, founder and pastor of New Life Church in Colorado Springs, Colorado, and leader of the 30-million-member National Association of Evangelicals, was forced to resign his church positions due to a scandal involving charges of having purchased crystal meth from a male prostitute. In an agreement with church leaders, Haggard received approximately $140,000 in severance pay and pledged never to return to Colorado and New Life Church. Pelosi, who interviewed Haggard in 2005 for her first film, spoke with the fallen pastor for a new film, *The Trials of Ted Haggard*, about the difficulties he faced following the scandal. At the film's conclusion, Pelosi notes that Haggard and his wife were allowed to return to Colorado, which they did in July 2008. Now an insurance salesman, Haggard has no plans to resume a pastoral ministry. Haggard appears to remain uncertain about his sexual identity, but continues to oppose gay marriage, claims that God's plan involves unions between one man and one woman, and holds that homosexuality is a learned behavior. In January 2009 the present pastor of New Life Church announced that in 2006 a young male member of the church had revealed information about a consensual sexual relationship he had with Haggard. Haggard admitted to an "inappropriate relationship," but stated that it did not include physical contact.

by Congress , see Employment Non-Discrimination Act of 1994, S. 2238, 103d Cong., 2d Sess. (1994f); Civil Rights Amendments, H.R. 5452, 94th Cong., 1st Sess. (1975); that in some cases such "discrimination" is *mandated* by federal statute, see 10 U.S.C. §654(b)(1) (mandating discharge from the armed forces of any service member who engages in or intends to engage in homosexual acts); and that in some cases such "discrimination" is a constitutional right, see *Boy Scouts of America v. Dale*, 530 U.S. 640 (2000).

Let me be clear that I have nothing against homosexuals, or any other group, promoting their agenda through normal democratic means. Social perceptions of sexual and other morality change over time, and every group has the right to persuade its fellow citizens that its view of such matters is the best. That homosexuals have achieved some success in that enterprise is attested to by the fact that Texas is one of the few remaining States that criminalize private, consensual homosexual acts. But persuading one's fellow citizens is one thing, and imposing one's views in absence of democratic majority will is something else. I would no more *require* a State to criminalize homosexual acts—or, for that matter, display *any* moral disapprobation of them—than I would *forbid* it to do so. What Texas has chosen to do is well within the range of traditional democratic action, and its hand should not be stayed through the invention of a brand-new "constitutional right" by a Court that is impatient of democratic change. It is indeed true that "later generations can see that laws once thought necessary and proper in fact serve only to oppress,' *ante*, at 18; and when that happens, later generations can repeal those laws. But it is the premise of our system that those judgments are to be made by the people, and not imposed by a governing caste that knows best.

One of the benefits of leaving regulation of this matter to the people rather than to the courts is that the people, unlike judges, need not carry things to their logical conclusion. The people may feel that their disapprobation of homosexual conduct is strong enough to disallow homosexual marriage, but not strong enough to criminalize private homosexual acts—and may legislate accordingly. The Court today pretends that it possesses a similar freedom of action, so that we need not fear judicial imposition of homosexual marriage, as has recently occurred in Canada (in a decision that the Canadian Government has chosen to appeal). . . . At the end of its opinion—after having laid waste the foundations of our rational-basis jurisprudence—the Court says that the present case "does not involve whether the government must give formal recognition to any relationship that homosexual persons seek to enter." *Ante*, at 17. Do not believe it. More illuminating than this bald, unreasoned disclaimer is the progression of thought displayed by an earlier passage in the Court's opinion, which notes the constitutional protections afforded to "personal decisions relating to *marriage*, procreation, contraception, family relationships, child rearing, and education," and then declares that "[p]ersons in a homosexual relationship may seek autonomy for these purposes, just as heterosexual persons do." *Ante*, at 13 (emphasis added). Today's opinion dismantles the structure of constitutional law that has permitted a distinction to be made between heterosexual and homosexual unions, insofar as formal recognition in marriage is concerned. If moral disapprobation of homosexual conduct is "no legitimate state interest" for purposes of proscribing that conduct, *ante*, at 18; and if, as the Court coos (casting aside all pretense of neutrality), "[w]hen sexuality finds overt expression in intimate conduct with another person, the conduct can be but one element in a personal bond that is more enduring," *ante*, at 6; what justification could there possibly be for denying the benefits of marriage to homosexual couples exercising "[t]he liberty protected by the Constitution." *ibid.*? Surely not the encouragement of procreation, since the sterile and the elderly are allowed to marry. This case "does not involve" the issue of homosexual marriage only if one entertains the belief that principle and logic have nothing to do with the decisions of this Court. Many will hope that, as the Court comfortingly assures us, this is so.

The matters appropriate for this Court's resolution are only three: Texas's prohibition of sodomy neither infringes a "fundamental right" (which the Court does not dispute), nor is unsupported by a rational relation to what the Constitution considers a legitimate state interest, nor denies the equal protection of the laws. I dissent.

SOURCE: Supreme Court of the United States. *John Geddes Lawrence and Tyron Garner, Petitioners v. Texas* 539 U.S. 558 (2003). Justice Antonin Scalia, dissenting opinion.

ANALYSIS

Justice Antonin Scalia's dissenting opinion in *Lawrence v. Texas* reflects the concerns of conservative individuals and groups regarding the decision's possible consequences regarding the potential recognition of same-gender marriage. In fact, Scalia claims a direct relationship between the present decision and the legal status of such marriages, since the Court has eliminated the primary basis upon which to prohibit such marriages. Scalia, explicitly using the term "culture war," asserts that the Court, and the legal profession in general—through the American Association of Law Schools—have taken sides in that war. Scalia objects to the Court majority, which he charges is "impatient of democratic change," largely on the ground that democratic processes have been overridden, and he counsels those favoring the "so-called homosexual agenda" to use the democratic process to alter the policies of states regarding such matters as sexual conduct. Democratic majorities, unlike the courts, have the option of stopping short of the "logical conclusion"—in this case, not criminalizing private homosexual acts while disallowing homosexual marriage. Scalia agrees that subsequent generations may conclude that earlier laws served to oppress, but that decision should be left to the later generation, a position that likely gives little comfort to those who conclude that they are experiencing such "oppression," and who are likely to comment, as did economist John Maynard Keynes, "in the long run we'll all be dead."

"Bans of Matrimony: A Constitutional Amendment Is the Only Way to Protect Marriage"

- **Document:** An article by Gerard V. Bradley and William L. Saunders Jr. that supports a constitutional amendment to restrict marriage to a union between one man and one woman.
- **Date:** November 2005.
- **Where:** *Touchstone* magazine.
- **Significance:** Following the U.S. Supreme Court decision in *Lawrence v. Texas*, which found unconstitutional state sodomy laws, and the 2003 Massachusetts Supreme Judicial Court decision in *Goodridge v. Department of Health* declaring that a Massachusetts restriction on same-gender marriage violates the state constitution, many conservatives, including President George W. Bush, began calling for an amendment to the U.S. Constitution restricting marriage to a union between one man and one woman.

DOCUMENT

The legal revolution in favor of same-sex "marriage" has been uncommonly swift. In the nineteenth century, it took the federal government four decades to effectively prohibit polygamy in Utah. By 1856, one national political party (the Republicans) had a platform plank denouncing polygamy, along with slavery, as a "relic of barbarism," but decisive action came only with the Supreme Court cases in the 1890s.

Smashing Victory

Starting in 1896, it took civil rights lawyers nearly sixty years to undo the constitutional doctrine of "separate but equal" facilities for African-Americans, the doctrine established in *Plessy v. Ferguson* in 1896 and not overturned until *Brown v. Board of Education* in 1954 (a decision that featured so prominently in the Senate hearings on the nomination of John Roberts to be Chief Justice). It took thirteen more years, from 1954 to the *Loving v. Virginia* decision in 1967, to persuade the Supreme Court that putting people in jail for marrying someone of a different color was unconstitutional.

In less time than that, lawyers for homosexuals have taken same-sex "marriage" from an exotic suggestion to a smashing victory in the Massachusetts case *Goodridge v. Department of Health* in 2003. The judges there declared that "extending civil marriage to same-sex couples *reinforces* the importance of marriage to individuals and communities" (emphasis supplied).

The Massachusetts decision could scarcely have been more radical. Not only did it cast aside the wisdom of the ages; it declared that our perennial understanding of marriage as the union of man and woman was *irrational*—in other words, *utterly* without a foundation *in reason*. The court even likened opposition to same-sex "marriage" to the racist prejudice against interracial marriage. The date the court appointed for the first same-sex weddings—May 17, 2004—was fifty years to the day after segregation was forbidden in *Brown v. Board of Education*.

The only remaining question is how long it will take for same-sex "marriage" to spread from Massachusetts across the rest of the nation. If the history of this revolution is any guide, the answer is that it will not be long—*unless* the Congress and the people act to put an effective legal block in place.

There are various ways in which same-sex "marriage" might spread across the country. The first is piecemeal: one state at a time, as one state supreme court or perhaps, though this is unlikely, state legislature, establishes the "right." That is how no-fault divorce laws spread during the 1960s. Lawsuits pending in several states make the same claims as those accepted in *Goodridge*.

The other two ways by which same-sex "marriage" might spread are (1) by migration of couples who demand recognition in the 49 states of their Massachusetts "marriages" or (2) by a Supreme Court opinion declaring that the Constitution *requires* the recognition of same-sex "marriage."

On the straightforward question of whether there is a constitutional right to same-sex "marriage," as well as on the question whether there must be *interstate* recognition of same-sex "marriage," the Supreme Court will have the last word. The best way to ensure that the Supreme Court reaches the correct decision(s) is by amending the US Constitution. Similarly, the only way to ensure that *state* judges and/or legislatures do not provide legal recognition of same-sex "marriage" is by amending the US Constitution, which is the supreme law of the land and displaces inconsistent state laws.

One Bar

One way in which same-sex "marriage" might spread is by homosexual couples who have been "married" in Massachusetts moving to another state and demanding that their Massachusetts "marriage" be recognized there. One possible bar is the Defense of Marriage Act (DOMA). Enacted in 1996, this federal statute establishes that, for all federal purposes (such as tax returns, veterans' benefits, etc.), only one husband and one wife count as spouses.

But DOMA also addresses the travel question. It says that no state "shall be required to give effect" to any act "respecting a relationship between persons of the same sex treated as a marriage under the laws of [any] other state." The idea is to bolster states that do not want to have same-sex "marriage" forced upon them because "spouses" from other states have moved into the state.

DOMA is an exercise of a very specific Congressional power, related to the "full faith and credit" required by Article IV of the Constitution. (The provision in its entirety reads: "Full faith and credit shall be given in each State to the public acts, records, and judicial proceedings of every other State. And the Congress may, by general laws, prescribe the manner in which such acts, records, and proceedings shall be proved, and the effect thereof.")

Under our Constitution, each state must to some degree recognize the laws of other states. Congress can prescribe the "effect" given to, for example, a state judgment from Illinois in Ohio, and there are exceptions and limitations to the "extraterritorial" effect of state law, but marriages are entirely portable: Get married in one state, and you will be married in all the rest. People get a new driver's license and re-register to vote when they move from state to state. But they are not required to get married again. DOMA makes an exception for same-sex "marriages."

But DOMA does not "reverse" *Goodridge*. It does nothing to relieve the citizens of Massachusetts of same-sex "marriage," and would not do so in any other state that adopted same-sex "marriage." It performs the limited but valuable service of protecting states from involuntary introduction of same-sex "marriage" through interstate portability.

A state saddled by its activist courts with same-sex "marriage"—the Massachusetts situation—would have to look elsewhere for help. That state's citizens would have to enact a state constitutional amendment correcting the activist decision . . . or pitch in to pass an amendment to the US Constitution, settling the definition of marriage throughout the country once and for all.

DOMA Challenged

There are three reasons to doubt that DOMA will be upheld when challenged in court. Two apply particularly to the question of interstate portability.

First, we simply do not know what difference Congress's *saying* that states need not recognize out-of-state marriages makes. There is no precedent for DOMA. Congress has used its power to prescribe the "effects" of state acts, but in all these cases it required states to recognize other states' acts. DOMA tells states that they do not have to.

Constitutional scholars are divided on DOMA's constitutionality. Harvard Law School professor Laurence Tribe vehemently denies that DOMA is constitutional because Congress lacks the power to legislate a "categorical exemption" from full faith and credit. Yale law professor Lea Brilmayer testified before a Senate Committee that Congress does have that power. But the full extent of her reassurance was this: "Marriages entered into in one state have never been constitutionally entitled to automatic recognition in other states."

Even if Brilmayer is correct, all that means is that Massachusetts "marriages" *might possibly* be denied recognition in other states because the meaning of the constitutional provisions will be decided by the Supreme Court. If it holds that DOMA does not bar the interstate portability of same-sex "marriage," it will be too late. The issue will have been settled. Homosexual "marriage" can then spread unobstructed across the nation. Thus, it would not be wise to wait.

The second reason to question whether DOMA will be upheld has to do with the standard exception to interstate recognition: a state's public policy. States are not obliged to recognize an out-of-state marriage contrary to a strong (in-state) public policy. Many people suppose that so long as a state makes clear that marriage is intended to be for a man and a woman, its "public policy" is "strong" enough to enable it to deny legal recognition to Massachusetts' same-sex "marriages."

Unfortunately, the simple assertion that traditional marriage is a "strong public policy" does not make it so. After all, courts in Vermont, Massachusetts, Hawaii, and other states have (in varying ways) overturned their marriage laws despite both long-established legal practice and custom defining marriage as reserved to a man and a woman.

The underlying problem in those states and in almost every state is that so many concessions have been made to *de facto* "gay unions"—adoption, spousal benefits, and other incidents of marriage—that courts readily conclude that the states do not consistently act on any coherent understanding of marriage. The *Goodridge* court, for example, said that the "gay" wedding aspirants were already treated as "families" capable of being "excellent parents."

The court asked: If these folks are already families doing an excellent job raising children, why exactly cannot they "marry," as do other couples who head families with kids? It is not a trivial question.

DOMA Overruled

Let us illustrate how a court might examine the issue. A judge hearing a Massachusetts couple's challenge to DOMA in, say, Indiana, will ask the state's attorney to identify the rational basis for limiting marriage to a man and a woman.

The most likely first answer will be: "because marriage is procreative." In that case, the court will say, "How is it that sterile couples marry, and that there is no noticeable legal difference between how kids born to married couples and kids born to single women are treated under the law?"

The court, hearing no cogent response, will then likely declare: "It is not really the state's intent to promote marriage because of its link to procreation. That ostensible ground is instead a cover for mere moral disapproval, or simple prejudice, even 'animus' of the kind prohibited by the Supreme Court in *Romer v. Evans*—none of these is a legitimate *rational* basis."

The state's attorney general might advance a second response: "The husband-wife marital home is where the state wishes to have childrearing take place." The court's reply could will be: "Then why does the state permit adoption by unmarried individuals, and even by same-sex couples?" And so on.

This is, in fact, the reasoning employed in *Goodridge* and in *Baker v. State*, the Vermont civil unions case from 1999. It will be employed in any state that has conceded anything to "gay unions" or "domestic partnerships" or in any way treated homosexual people as if they were married (by granting them the right to adopt children, for example).

In summary, we cannot know how the courts will settle the question of the interstate portability of Massachusetts' same-sex "marriages." But everyone agrees that DOMA will be challenged all across the country and that it may well be overturned.

The only way to ensure that states are not forced to accept Massachusetts' same-sex "marriages" is to establish law so clear—and whose constitutionality is so solid—that even judges disinclined to follow it will have to. DOMA (a federal statute whose "validity" depends upon whether or not it violates the constitution) does not, and cannot, do that. A well-drafted constitutional amendment, however, can.

No State Interest

Like every other law in this country, state or federal, DOMA has to pass basic constitutional tests. Every law must serve a "legitimate" state purpose and "rationally" serve that end. Here is the third reason to doubt DOMA's legal effectiveness: the Supreme Court's latest decision on "gay rights."

In a six-to-three ruling in *Lawrence v. Texas*, issued in June 2003, the [Supreme] Court struck down a state law against homosexual sodomy. For the first time, it ruled that states may not forbid people to engage in non- or extra-marital sex acts.

The Court did not rely upon the narrow grounds offered by some opponents of the law, i.e., that Texas could outlaw sodomy as long as unmarried heterosexuals as well as homosexuals were covered. The Court directly overruled one of its precedents, the 1986 case of *Bowers v. Hardwick*, because it "demeans the lives of homosexual persons." The justices said that the Texas law served *no* legitimate state interest and lacked any basis in reason.

The Court seemed eager to make a significant statement about constitutional protection for homosexual relationships. The *reason* homosexual acts are protected, the Court said, is precisely because such acts *may constitute a person's identity*; because sexual conduct "can be but one element in a personal bond that is more enduring"; because penalizing sodomitical acts could lead to "discrimination both in the public and the private spheres."

The Court said that "persons in a homosexual relationship" have the *same* constitutional liberty to marriage, procreation, and family that "heterosexual persons do." *Lawrence* is not about sodomy and privacy. It is about homosexual "bonds" and a state's obligation to respect them.

No wonder that the dissenting justices said of this reasoning that it would "dismantle the structure of constitutional law" that has kept legal marriage a matter of the bond of a man and a woman. *Lawrence* is a very forbidding warning that any law against same-sex "marriage"—*DOMA included*—is unlikely to survive in the

Supreme Court. (This is true regardless of the confirmation of John Roberts as Chief Justice. *Lawrence* was a six-to-three decision, and Roberts is replacing one of the three dissenters [Chief Justice William Rehnquist]. Even when [Sandra Day] O'Connor's successor [Samuel Alito] is confirmed, and even if Roberts and that person turn out to be "conservatives" on this issue, that still leaves a majority for the result in *Lawrence*.)

Only Sure Way

The only sure way to stop the movement toward same-sex "marriage" is by amending the Constitution. Serious proposals to do so are many. They break down into two types, although there are important differences within each type, often having to do with the extent to which the amendment impedes the judicial creation of civil unions (i.e., legally recognized relationships that are, nonetheless, not treated as "marriages").

One kind addresses only the interstate travel problem. These proposals would tolerate same-sex "marriage" in Massachusetts and in any other state where it arose as a result of legal developments *within* that state. Each state would decide (for itself alone) what marriage is. The other kind defines marriage solely as the union of a man and a woman, and thus, nothing else could be a legal marriage in the United States.

The major argument for the first kind of amendment is "federalism." Its advocates argue that in our "federal" system states are, have always been, and should be in charge of marriage.

Rather than straightjacket the whole nation with a single legal template, its advocates argue, states should be allowed to experiment with different legal solutions to social problems. They argue also that problems vary from state to state, and local variations demand different responses. One response might be appropriate for Utah, another for Arizona, and still a third for New Jersey.

The argument for the first kind of amendment misses some obvious facts. First, same-sex couples who are also homosexual activists will simply move from one state (where same-sex "marriage" is permitted) to a second state (where it is not). By living in the second state, these activist couples will create "facts on the ground" that state legislatures may find hard to resist. ("How can Johnny's same-sex 'parents' not be recognized at school events or in the PTA when Suzy's opposite-sex parents are? It is unfair to the child. Wouldn't it be better to recognize as marriage the relationship that already exists between Johnny's 'parents'?")

Second, there already is a national definition of marriage: Everywhere in the United States, no one may submit to the Internal Revenue Service a form 1040 as "married, filing jointly" except a male husband and a female wife. We still have one definition at the state level, too, with, at the moment [2005], a single exception.

But *Lawrence* already signals that we *will* soon have a single national definition of marriage, and it will be a new one: Every state will have to recognize same-sex couples as "married." As Judge Robert Bork noted in *The Wall Street Journal*, "One way or another, federalism is going to be overridden. The only question is whether the general rule will permit or prohibit marriage of same-sex couples."

Indeed, marriage is not simply a matter for the states, and has not been for more than a generation. The strongest statement that marriage is a matter of state law was made in an 1878 Supreme Court case called *Pennoyer v. Neff*: A state has an "absolute" right to decide the "conditions upon which the marriage relation shall be created." (Even in this case, the Court did *not* say the state has the right to decide what marriage *is*.) By 1971, the Supreme Court found (in *Boddie v. Connecticut*) the states's power to be much less "absolute": States controlled marriage "*absent some specific federal constitutional or statutory provision*" (emphasis added).

False Analogy

Before considering the defining features of marriage, and because same-sex "marriage" proponents usually rely on this purported analogy, we will examine a special case of national intervention in marriage. In 1967, in *Loving v. Virginia*, the Supreme Court held that states could not ban interracial marriage. The language of the case, as well as constitutional logic, extends the ruling to prohibit ethnic, national, and color barriers to marriage. *Loving* means that these characteristics have nothing to do with the definition of marriage and that no state can act as if they do.

The Massachusetts court in *Goodridge* fundamentally misunderstood *Loving*. As we noted, the judges likened opposition to same-sex "marriage" to the racist prejudice against interracial marriage. They said in their ruling: "Recognizing the right of an individual to marry a person of the same sex will not diminish the value or the dignity of opposite sex marriage, any more than recognizing the right of an individual to marry a person of a different race devalues the marriage of a person who marries someone of her own race."

This is a distinction based on a fundamentally flawed analogy. One's race (or ethnicity or national origin or color) is irrelevant to whether one possesses the characteristics (being a man or a woman) necessary to enter into marriage, while one's sex is obviously relevant. The *Goodridge* decision thus underlines the necessity of an amendment to the Constitution before other courts issue similarly misguided rulings.

Let us examine the defining features of marriage and the extent to which states have authority over them. Traditionally, marriage has been held in law to be: (1) monogamous; (2) sexually exclusive; (3) the morally legitimate context for raising children; and (4) permanent. What is the autonomy of the states with regard to each of these?

Monogamy was imposed upon Mormon-controlled territories by the national government toward the end of the nineteenth century, in the course of the protracted struggle over polygamy. While it may be true that a state could, at least theoretically, recognize plural marriages (no Supreme Court case squarely holds otherwise), no one has a right, even on the basis of sincere religious belief, to enter a polygamous marriage.

That is the certain effect of the late nineteenth century polygamy cases decided by the Supreme Court. But if, as the Supreme Court held in *Lawrence*, one's sexual acts make up a crucial part of one's identity, why can't two men marry? And if two men can marry, why not three, if they feel group sex crucial to their identity? Or more?

Why not a group of men and women? If the Supreme Court decides to follow the logic of its *Lawrence* decision, states would be powerless to limit marriage to *couples*—of any sort.

The sexual exclusivity of marriage as the only morally legitimate context in which to have and raise children is the central presupposition of many Supreme Court cases. Among them is the Court's condemnation (in 1942) of an Oklahoma law that punished certain career criminals with sterilization, in which it referred to "marriage and procreation" as "one of the basic civil rights of man."

Before *Lawrence*, the states had protected marriage through laws against non- and extra-marital sex *of any sort*, heterosexual as well as homosexual. This protective mantle originally included laws about illegitimacy designed to limit procreation to married couples. The two types of laws are mutually reinforcing: Limit sex to marriage and increase the chances that kids will be born to married couples; discourage procreation outside of marriage and discourage non-marital intercourse, too.

The Law Changed

But again, the national government changed the law. In the first wave of disruption, the Supreme Court ruled that most legal distinctions based upon illegitimacy are unconstitutional. The seminal case was *Levy v. Louisiana* in 1968. The laws challenged were justified by Louisiana as attempts to make marriage the basis of family relationships. The Court's reasoning is opaque, but the main idea seems to have been that these burdens had no social value at all.

The Court stated that the illegitimate person "certainly is subject to all the responsibilities of a citizen, including the payment of taxes and conscription under the Selective Service Act. How under our constitutional regime can he be denied correlative rights which other citizens enjoy?" In support it cited *King Lear*: "Why bastard, wherefore base? When my dimensions are as well compact, my mind as generous, and my shape as true, as honest madam's issue? Why brand they us with base? With baseness? Bastardy? Base, base?"

Finally, although the permanency of marriage had long been assumed in American law, the principle of no-fault divorce is in place all across the country, with minor variations between states, because the states chose it. The homogeneous pattern is *not* the result of an overriding Supreme Court decision. No High Court decision or controlling federal law says that such divorce law is a national rule.

Nonetheless, the extraordinary statements in the *Lawrence* decision about the individual's right to express himself sexually without state interference or disapproval strongly suggest that federal constitutional doctrine now *blocks* any return to *fault*-based divorce by a state legislature. In other words, no-fault divorce arose without the Constitution, but it may be sustained by the Constitution (as interpreted by the current Supreme Court). To this extent, the non-permanency of marriage is, like all the other defining features of marriage, a national principle an individual state cannot change.

The fundamental objection to the first kind of amendment, that addresses only the interstate travel problem, for those who want to defend marriage, is that the question we face is whether men can marry men and women can marry women.

The common justifications for federalism do not apply to marriage. Nothing peculiar to New York or to Wyoming makes any difference.

The common good requires everywhere a single answer to whether a person can marry another, or several others, of the same sex, and that answer is no. Marriage is . . . a social institution with an inherent meaning. Thus, only the second kind of amendment, the kind that defines marriage as the union of a man and a woman, will adequately protect marriage in the United States.

Saving Marriage

Today, for better or worse, the national government, principally the courts, have mostly taken the power to define marriage out of the states' hands, as discussed above. The Supreme Court's promissory note in *Lawrence v. Texas*—that it will require same-sex "marriage" as part of everyone's liberty to express himself sexually, without suffering discrimination—signals the final state of this takeover.

To save marriage, that is, to ensure marriage remains reserved to one man and one woman, it is necessary to amend the US Constitution. If the Constitution is not amended, it is almost certain that marriage will be fundamentally transformed through the judicial recognition of same-sex "marriage."

It could happen in either of two ways. First, homosexuals from other states who marry in Massachusetts will return to their home state and demand through legal action that their Massachusetts "marriage" be recognized despite DOMA (under the Full Faith and Credit Clause) and the Supreme Court will agree. As we have seen, the traditional bar under the Full Faith and Credit Clause—that it would, in a particular case, violate the public policy of the second state—seems no longer viable.

Second, the rationale of the *Lawrence* decision that sexual acts are fundamental to a person's identity could lead the Supreme Court to hold that the Constitution itself *requires* the recognition of same-sex "marriage." (The Court would do so by holding that the language of the Fifth and Fourteenth Amendments—"nor shall any State deprive any person of life, liberty, or property, without due process of law"—creates a substantive "liberty" interest to marry someone of the same sex).

Thus, it is all but certain the Supreme Court will legalize, nationally, same-sex "marriage." The Defense of Marriage Act (DOMA) cannot prevent it. It is a federal statute subject to judicial interpretation, which interpretation will be informed by the language of *Lawrence* about the fundamental importance of sexual behavior. Thus, DOMA is sure to fall, either under the Full Faith and Credit Clause or under a substantive due process "liberty" interest.

It is hardly conceivable that the Supreme Court will allow a federal statute to bar people from exercising such a "fundamental right." The only way to prevent this is to amend the Constitution.

SOURCE: Gerard V. Bradley and William L. Saunders, "Bans of Matrimony: A Constitutional Amendment Is the Only Way to Protect Marriage," *Touchstone*, 18, no. 9 (November 2005): 37–42. Reprinted courtesy of Gerard V. Bradley and William L. Saunders.

ANALYSIS

Unlike Antonin Scalia in his dissenting opinion in *Lawrence et al. v. Texas*, Gerard V. Bradley and William L. Saunders Jr. are less sanguine about allowing the people of individual states individually, through democratic processes, determine policy regarding same-gender marriage. Bradley and Saunders argue that anything short of an amendment to the national Constitution will prevent the trend toward sanctioning such marriage, given the Full Faith and Credit Clause (Article IV, section 1), which specifies that each state shall recognize the legal validity of "the public Acts, Records, and judicial Proceedings" of all other states. They do not expect that those states that prohibit same-gender marriage will be able to refuse to recognize the marriages of same-gender couples who were married in a state that sanctions such marriages and then move to another state. In addition, they do not believe that the U.S. Supreme Court, given the *Lawrence* decision, ultimately will permit individual states to ban such marriage. Thus, gay marriage will spread throughout the country simply through the mobility of same-gender couples despite the 1996 federal Defense of Marriage Act, which in any event, Bradley and Saunders conclude, is destined to be declared unconstitutional by the U.S. Supreme Court. Therefore, to those who fervently believe that monogamous marriage defined as a union between one man and one woman is fundamental to Western civilization and hence who adamantly oppose gay marriage, a constitutional amendment appears to be the surest method of restricting marriage to one man and one woman. Conservatives consider the traditional conception of marriage so fundamental to Western civilization that changing that understanding is considered a serious threat to the contemporary culture.

DID YOU KNOW?

A Gay Bishop and a Civil Union

Ever since the Episcopal Diocese of New Hampshire chose V. Gene Robinson, an openly gay Episcopal priest, to be their bishop, the Episcopal Church in the United States and the entire world Anglican Union have been divided over the propriety of having an openly homosexual member of the priesthood. Despite the strong objections of conservatives within the church, Robinson remained the bishop of the New Hampshire Diocese, and when civil unions for same-gender couples became legal in New Hampshire—which grant all the rights and obligations of marriage—Robinson and his partner Mark Andrew were legally joined in a civil ceremony in June 2008. A religious service of thanksgiving was held at St. Paul's Church in Concord, New Hampshire, following the civil ceremony. Although Robinson and his partner initially planned a public ceremony, they changed plans reportedly out of respect for the Anglican conference scheduled for the next month in England. Due to strong objections to Robinson's open homosexuality, he did not receive an invitation to the conference from the Archbishop of Canterbury.

In re Marriage Cases

- *Document:* Excerpt from the California Supreme Court decision on same-gender marriage (footnotes omitted).
- *Date:* May 15, 2008.
- *Where:* California Supreme Court, Sacramento, California.
- *Significance:* With this ruling, California became the second state to permit same-gender marriages. The ruling went into effect 30 days after issuance (June 16). However, opponents of same-gender marriage worked to have an anti-gay marriage measure placed on the November 2008 ballot, which California voters approved, setting off protests in several cities across the country.

DOCUMENT

Although the understanding of marriage as limited to a union of a man and a woman is undeniably the predominant one, if we have learned anything from the significant evolution in the prevailing societal views and official policies toward members of minority races and toward women over the past half-century, it is that even the most familiar and generally accepted of social practices and traditions often mask an unfairness and inequality that frequently is not recognized or appreciated by those not directly harmed by those practices or traditions. It is instructive to recall in this regard that the traditional, well-established rules and practices of our not-so-distant past (1) barred interracial marriage, (2) upheld the routine exclusion of women from many occupations and official duties, and (3) considered the relegation of racial minorities to separate and assertedly equivalent public facilities and institutions as constitutionally equal treatment. As the United States Supreme Court observed in its decision in *Lawrence v. Texas, supra,* 539 U.S. 558, 579, the expansive and protective provisions of our constitutions, such as the due process clause, were drafted with the knowledge that "times can blind us to certain truths and later generations can see that laws once thought necessary and proper in fact serve only to oppress." For this reason, the interest in retaining a tradition that excludes an historically disfavored minority group from a status that is extended to all others—even when the tradition is long-standing and widely shared—does not necessarily represent a compelling state interest for purposes of equal protection analysis.

After carefully evaluating the pertinent considerations in the present case, we conclude that the state interest in limiting the designation of marriage exclusively to opposite-sex couples, and in excluding same-sex couples from access to that designation, cannot properly be considered a compelling state interest for equal protection purposes. To begin with, limitation clearly is not necessary to preserve the rights and benefits of marriage currently enjoyed by opposite-sex couples. Extending access to the designation of marriage to same-sex couples will not deprive any opposite-sex couple or their children of any of the rights and benefits conferred by the marriage statutes, but simply will make the benefit of the marriage designation available to same-sex couples and their children. As Chief Judge Kaye of the New York Court of Appeals succinctly observed in her dissenting opinion in *Hernandez v. Robles, supra*, 855 N.E. 2d a, 30 (dis. opn. of Kaye, C.J.): "There are enough marriage licenses to go around for everyone." Further, permitting same-sex couples access to the designation of marriage will not alter the substantive nature of the legal institution of marriage; same-sex couples who choose to enter into the relationship with that designation will be subject to the same duties and obligations to each other, to their children, and to third parties that the law currently imposes upon opposite-sex couples who marry. Finally, affording same-sex couples the opportunity to obtain the designation of marriage will not impinge upon the religious freedom of any religious organization, official, or any other person; no religion will be required to change its religious policies or practices with regard to same-sex couples, and no religious officiant will be required to solemnize a marriage in contravention of his or her religious beliefs. (Cal. Const., art. I, § 4.)

While retention of the limitation of marriage to opposite-sex couples is not needed to preserve the rights and benefits of opposite-sex couples, the exclusion of same-sex couples from the designation of marriage works a real and appreciable harm

DID YOU KNOW?

The Mormon Church and Proposition 8 in California

Although same-gender marriage appeared to have gained significant momentum by 2008, with courts in three states having ruled in its favor, Proposition 8 on the 2008 California ballot, which would amend the state's constitution to limit marriage to a union of one man and one woman, threatened to reverse that state's new policy of sanctioning gay marriage. Protect Marriage, the major group supporting the proposition, appealed for financial assistance to campaign for the measure. Much of the volunteer and monetary support emanated from the leadership and membership of the Church of Jesus Christ of the Latter-day Saints, popularly known as the Mormon Church, who joined with Catholics, evangelical Protestants, and conservative black and Latino pastors in the effort to pass the proposed amendment. Roy Otterson, the managing director of public affairs for the Mormon Church, admitted that although his religious organization had taken conservative stands on other issues, the church's involvement in the California gay marriage issue was exceptional. Protect Marriage estimated that approximately half of the $40 million the organization raised was donated by Mormons. Alan Ashton, grandson of former Mormon president David McKay, contributed $1 million to the successful campaign to pass Proposition 8. Those opposed to Proposition 8 protested involvement of the Mormon Church in the electoral process, and boycotts of some Mormon-owned businesses were reported.

upon same-sex couples and their children. . . . [B]ecause of the long and celebrated history of the term "marriage" and the widespread understanding that this word describes a family relationship unreservedly sanctioned by the community, the statutory provisions that continue to limit access to this designation exclusively to opposite-sex couples—while providing only a novel, alternative institution for same-sex couples—likely will be viewed as an official statement that the family relationship of same-sex couples is not of comparable stature or equal dignity to the family relationship of opposite-sex couples. Furthermore, because of the historic disparagement of gay persons, the retention of a distinction in nomenclature by which the term "marriage" is withheld only from the family relationship of same-sex couples is all the more likely to cause the new parallel institution that has been established for same-sex couples to be considered a mark of second-class citizenship. Finally, in addition to the potential harm flowing from the lesser stature that is likely to be afforded to the family relationships of same-sex couples by designating them domestic partnerships, there exists a substantial risk that a judicial decision upholding the differential treatment of opposite-sex and same-sex couples would be understood as *validating* a more general proposition that our state by now has repudiated: that it is permissible, under the law, for society to treat gay individuals and same-sex couples differently from, and less favorably than, heterosexual individuals and opposite-sex couples.

In light of all of these circumstances, we conclude that retention of the traditional definition of marriage does not constitute a state interest sufficiently compelling, under the strict scrutiny equal protection standard, to justify withholding that status from same-sex couples. Accordingly, insofar as the provisions of sections 300 and 308.5 draw a distinction between opposite-sex couples and same-sex couples and exclude the latter from access to the designation of marriage, we conclude these statutes are unconstitutional.

Having concluded that sections 300 and 308.5 are unconstitutional to the extent each statute reserves the designation of marriage exclusively to opposite-sex couples and denies same-sex couples access to that designation, we must determine the proper remedy.

When a statute's differential treatment of separate categories of individuals is found to violate equal protection principles, a court must determine whether the constitutional violation should be eliminated or cured by extending to the previously excluded class the treatment or benefit that the statute affords to the included class, or alternatively should be remedied by withholding the benefit equally from both the previously included class and the excluded class. A court generally makes that determination by considering whether extending the benefit equally to both classes, or instead withholding it equally, would be most consistent with the likely intent of the Legislature, had that body recognized that unequal treatment was constitutionally impermissible. (See, e.g., *Kopp v. Fair Political Practices Com.* (1995) 11 Cal.4th 607, 626–662; *Arp v. Workers' Comp. Appeals Bd.*, supra, 19 Cal.4th 395, 401–410.)

In the present case, it is readily apparent that extending the designation of marriage to same-sex couples is more consistent with the probable legislative intent than withholding that designation from both opposite-sex couples and same-sex couples in favor of some other, uniform designation. In view of the lengthy history of the use of the term "marriage" to describe the family relationship here at issue, and the importance that both the supporters of the 1977 amendment to the marriage statutes and the electors who voted in favor of Proposition 22 unquestionably attached to the designation of marriage, there can be no doubt that extending the designation of marriage to same-sex couples, rather than denying it to all couples, is the equal protection remedy that is most consistent with our state's general legislative policy and preference.

Accordingly, in light of the conclusions we reach concerning the constitutional questions brought to us for resolution, we determine that the language of section 300 limiting the designation of marriage to a union "between a man and a woman" is unconstitutional and must be stricken from the statute, and that the remaining statutory language must be understood as making the designation of marriage available both to opposite-sex and same-sex couples. In addition, because the limitation of marriage to opposite-sex couples imposed by section 308.5 can have no constitutionally permissible effect in light of constitutional conclusions set forth in this opinion, that provision cannot stand.

Plaintiffs are entitled to the issuance of a writ of mandate directing the appropriate state officials to take all actions necessary to effectuate our ruling in this case so as to ensure that county clerks and other local officials throughout the state, in performing their duty to enforce the marriage statutes in their jurisdictions, apply those provisions in a manner consistent with the decision of this court.

SOURCE: California Supreme Court, *In re Marriage Cases*, www.courtinfo.ca.gov/opinions/archive/S147999.PDF.

ANALYSIS

The issue of homosexuality and same-gender marriage gained increasing salience among social and religious conservatives following the 2003 decision of the Massachusetts Supreme Judicial Court resulting from a suit (*Goodrich v. Massachusetts Department of Public Health*, 440 Mass. 309, 798 NE2d 941 [November 18, 2003]) that seven gay couples brought before the judicial system, arguing that the state prohibition on gay marriage violated the state constitution's protection of equal rights. The court found restrictions on gay marriage to be contrary to the state constitution's protection of equal rights. In June of that year the U.S. Supreme Court had ruled that state anti-sodomy laws were unconstitutional. In spring 2004 Mayor Gavin Newsom of San Francisco decided to allow same-gender marriages in the city. Subsequently marriage licenses were issued to gay couples and approximately 4,000 such marriages were performed. However, the California state supreme court ruled that the city lacked the authority to sanction the marriages, which were contrary to current state law. The court's decision focused only on the question of

Demonstrators and counterdemonstrators clash over the issue of gay marriage. Highly polarized public opinion is reflected in inflamed rhetoric on both sides, as the banner at this march indicates. (Shutterstock)

whether Mayor Newsom could legitimately allow gay marriages under existing statutes, not on the larger question of the constitutionality of legally prohibiting such unions.

These events led to intense political and legal activity by both sides in the struggle over the legal recognition of same-gender unions as marriage. President George W. Bush reacted by stating that "Marriage is a sacred institution between a man and a woman." Massachusetts Governor Mitt Romney stated that he would ask members of the state legislature to begin a state constitutional amendment process to overturn the Massachusetts court's decision. Gay marriage supporters were intent on pushing law suits to challenge state prohibitions on such marriages, and opponents lobbied for approval of state laws and constitutional amendments that prohibited these marriages. Following the California state supreme court's ruling that same-gender couples could not be denied the equal right to marry, supporters of the traditional conception of marriage placed on the November 2008 ballot a state constitutional amendment (Proposition 8) which defined marriage as a union between one man and one woman. After California voters approved the proposition, gay marriage supporters held protests against the new constitutional provision, and gay rights organizations filed suit in state court challenging the constitutionality of the initiative process, a challenge that the courts ultimately rejected. Thus, gay marriage promised to remain a key issue in the U.S. culture wars.

"Why Is Polygamy Illegal?"

- **Document:** Article by Wendy Kaminer questioning various limitations on the right to marry.
- **Date:** August/September 2008.
- **Where:** *Free Inquiry* magazine.
- **Significance:** Wendy Kaminer's argument about polygamy can be considered a response to the fears that supporters of traditional marriage raise regarding the acceptance of same-gender marriage: that such acceptance will lead to demands that other unions be considered legal marriages, including polygamy.

DOCUMENT

Opponents of gay rights often warn that legalizing same-sex marriage would inexorably lead to legalizing polygamy. Maybe it would, and maybe it should. Denying gay couples the right to marry violates state constitutional guarantees of equality, as the California and Massachusetts high courts have rightly ruled. (The Supreme Court of California also held that the right to marry is fundamental). Surely Mormons have the same rights to equal treatment under law—and of course, they have a substantial First Amendment claim to engage in multiple marriages according to the dictates of their faith.

So why is polygamy illegal? Why don't Mormons have the right to enter into multiple marriages sanctified by their church, if not the state? There's a short answer to this question but not a very good one: polygamy is illegal and unprotected by the Constitution because the Supreme Court doesn't like it. Over one hundred years ago, the Court held in *Reynolds v. U.S.* that polygamy was "an offence against society." The *Reynolds* decision upheld the criminal conviction of a man accused of taking a second wife in the belief that he had a religious duty to practice polygamy, a duty he would violate at risk of damnation. The Court compared polygamy to murders sanctified by religious belief, such as human sacrifice or the burning of women on their husbands' funeral pyres.

Even in Victorian America, this comparison made little sense. (Most Victorian women, I suspect, would have chosen polygamous marriages over death by burning.) Today the Court's analogy is as anachronistic as a ban on adultery. After all, what's the difference between an adulterer and a polygamist? And if it's not illegal for a married man to support a girlfriend or two and father children out of wedlock with them, how can it be illegal for him to bind himself to them according to the laws of his church? Why is a practicing Mormon with two wives a criminal while Staten Island Congressman Vito Fosella, recently embarrassed by the discovery of his second family, is simply a punchline? What's the moral and practical difference between a man who maintains multiple families without the approval of any church and a man who maintains multiple families with his church's approval?

Nontheists who favor civil unions for everyone—taking the state out of the business of approving or disapproving religious matrimonial rites—should be especially supportive of the First Amendment right to engage in polygamous marriages sanctified by any faith. Whether or not polygamy should be legalized so that people in polygamous marriages enjoy equal rights and entitlements (like Social Security benefits), it should at least be decriminalized. Why should we care about other people's private religious ceremonies? How dare we criminalize them?

"Polygamy encourages child abuse," people say, citing instances involving the marriage of older men to underage girls. Assuming for the sake of argument that this is true, it still doesn't justify categorical prohibitions on polygamy. Alcohol consumption may encourage sexual violence; it's often blamed for date rape. Should we prohibit its use, as members of the Women's Christian Temperance Union demanded over one hundred years ago? Or should we prosecute alcohol-fueled violence whenever we find it?

We rightly prohibit violence, not drunkenness, even though some drunks are violent; we should prohibit child abuse, not polygamy, even though some polygamists are abusers. To do otherwise is to court worse abuses than we seek to prevent, as the raid on the Search for Zion compound in Texas this past April demonstrated [2008]. On the basis of one anonymous phone call (that later appeared to be a hoax), Texas authorities forcibly removed more than 460 children from their parents without evidence of actual abuse in each case. Parents and children were ordered to undergo DNA testing (Who knows how long the state will maintain the DNA database, or to what uses it will be put?), and the children were summarily consigned to the notorious Texas foster-care system. They were subsequently reunited with their parents on order of Texas courts, which rightly held that the state had acted unlawfully, but who knows how much damage was done?

It's hard to explain the relative complacency or cautiousness that initially greeted this extraordinary abuse of power, except with reference to religious bigotry or squeamishness about polygamy. Members of the Search for Zion sect tried taking their case to the public—some attorneys defended their rights, and the American Civil Liberties Union eventually expressed more than cautious concern for them—

but predictably, the national conversation generally reflected little sympathy for the civil liberties of people involved in a religious group far outside the mainstream. Imagine the reaction had the state instead invaded a community of Christian Scientists and removed all their children after receiving an anonymous tip that one child had been harmed by the refusal of his or her parents to provide medical care.

The Search for Zion case is different, some reply, because polygamy is illegal. Exactly. Polygamy's illegality doesn't make the state's actions less abusive—imagine the reaction if the state summarily removed all the children from a commune in which parents were suspected of smoking dope—but it does provide authorities with an argument, however flawed.

Of course, I'm not suggesting that any parent have a religious right to harm their children by denying them medial care, subjecting them to sexual molestation, or otherwise abusing them. I'm simply pointing out that the state should not abuse the power to prosecute people or forcibly remove their children because authorities don't approve of their "life-style." Gay men were once routinely suspected of being pedophiles, a suspicion that persists today but with considerably less prevalence and respectability. Indeed, opposition to gay marriage still relies on specious arguments about the harm it poses to children. Some fools still compare homosexuality to bestiality, just as the Supreme Court once compared polygamy to human sacrifice. We progress when we base the extension of rights on reason, not bias or judicial hyperbole.

SOURCE: Wendy Kaminer, "Why Is Polygamy Illegal?" *Free Inquiry*, August/September 2008: 16–17. © Wendy Kaminer. Reprinted courtesy of Wendy Kaminer.

ANALYSIS

Wendy Kaminer confronts one of the arguments that conservatives make regarding the sanctioning of gay marriage: that once gay marriage is accepted on the grounds of equal rights, then other practices, including polygamy, cannot logically be prohibited either. If a group of three or more individuals of whatever gender decide to formalize their relationship as marriage, legally they could not be prevented from doing so. Kaminer simply accepts the possibility of polygamy, arguing that the constitutional rights of Mormons were violated when authorities, including the U.S. Supreme Court, prohibited them from entering into polygamous marriages. In response to the question, why were nineteenth-century Mormons denied this right, Kaminer claims there is no good answer. Conservatives refer to the overall culture of our society which generally views monogamy as the only valid moral standard (as long as any additional wives or husbands are acquired following the dissolution of the previous marriage). More devout Christians are unwilling to accept the possibility of divorce, believing that a marriage should extend through a lifetime. Nonetheless, members of American society as a whole, including many evangelical Christians, have become more accepting of divorce, likely because divorce has become such a common phenomenon. As for Kaminer's argument about polygamy, liberals will more likely accept her logic, while conservatives will view the logic as confirming their contention that marriage should remain a union, instituted and blessed by God, between one man and one woman. Conservatives concerned about "activist judges" would disagree with Kaminer's assertion that the U.S. Supreme Court made the decision regarding the prohibition on polygamy. Rather, the Supreme Court simply upheld a law prohibiting polygamy, thus in a sense exercising judicial restraint, an avenue recommended by Justice Antonin Scalia.

FURTHER READING

Beil, Laura. "Just Saying No to Abstinence Ed." *Newsweek*, October 27, 2008:, 58.

Doan, Alesha E., and Jean Calterone Williams. *The Politics of Virginity: Abstinence in Sex Education*. Westport, CT: Praeger, 2008.

Fleming, Thomas. "Sex and Marriage in San Francisco." *Chronicles*, August 2008: 5.

Hertzog, Dagmar. *Sex in Crisis: The New Sexual Revolution and the Future of American Politics*. New York: Basic Books, 2008.

Hirsch, H. N. *The Future of Gay Rights in America*. Oxford: Taylor and Francis, 2005.

Lane, Frederick S. *The Decency Wars: The Campaign to Cleanse American Culture*. Amherst, NY: Prometheus Books, 2006.

Stein, Rob. "Not That Kind of Sex Ed: More States Are Turning Down Federal Money for Abstinence-Only Programs." *Washington Post National Weekly Edition*, December 24, 2007–January 6, 2008: 34.

Strasser, Mark, Traci C. West, Martin Dupuis, and William A. Thompson, eds. *Defending Same-Sex Marriage*. 3 volumes. Westport, CT: Praeger, 2006.

Wildmon, Don. "Consequences of Same-Sex 'Marriage' Will Be Far Reaching." www.afajournal.org/2004/april/404don.asp (accessed July 7, 2008).

7

SCIENCE AND EDUCATION

Document: *Excerpts from* Judge John E. Jones's ruling in *Kitzmiller et al. v. Dover Area School District et al.* (2005)

Document: William A. Dembski and Sean McDowell, "Objection: Responding to the Top Ten Objections Against Intelligent Design" (2008)

Document: John G. West, "Debate Over Evolution Not Going Away," (2006)

Document: Matthew C. Nisbet, "Ben Stein's Trojan Horse: Mobilizing the State House and Local News Agenda" (2008)

Document: National Academy of Sciences Institute of Medicine, "Creationist Perspectives," *Excerpt from Science, Evolution, and Creationism* (2008)

Kitzmiller et al. v. Dover Area School District et al.

- *Document:* Excerpts from Judge John E. Jones's ruling on the question of introducing the theory of Intelligent Design into the Dover, Pennsylvania, public school curriculum as an alternative to the theory of evolution.
- *Date:* December 20, 2005.
- *Where:* U.S. District Court for the Middle District of Pennsylvania, Scranton, Pennsylvania.
- *Significance:* Various groups, including the Discovery Institute, have attempted to challenge Darwin's theory of evolution by advocating the presentation in the public schools of alternative explanations for the existence of complex life forms, including human beings. The Dover Area School District in Pennsylvania passed a policy requiring teachers to read a statement to students in ninth grade biology classes mentioning Intelligent Design as an alternative scientific theory to that of evolution. In a suit filed by those opposed to the new policy, Judge John E. Jones declared the policy an unconstitutional violation of the First Amendment protection against the establishment of religion.

DOCUMENT

On October 18, 2004, the Defendant Dover Area School Board of Directors passed by a 6–3 vote the following resolution:

Students will be made aware of gaps/problems in Darwin's theory and of other theories of evolution including, but not limited to, intelligent design. Note: Origins of Life is not taught.

On November 19, 2004, the Defendant Dover Area School District announced by press release that, commencing in January 2005, teachers would be required to read the following statement to students in the ninth grade biology class at Dover High School:

The Pennsylvania Academic Standards require students to learn about Darwin's Theory of Evolution and eventually to take a standardized test of which evolution is a part.

Because Darwin's Theory is a theory, it continues to be tested as new evidence is discovered. The Theory is not a fact. Gaps in the Theory exist for which there is no evidence. A theory is defined as a well-tested explanation that unifies a broad range of observations.

Intelligent Design is an explanation of the origin of life that differs from Darwin's view. The reference book, *Of Pandas and People*, is available for students who might be interested in gaining an understanding of what Intelligent Design actually involves.

With respect to any theory, students are encouraged to keep an open mind. The school leaves the discussion of the Origins of Life to individual students and their families. As a Standards-driven district, class instruction focuses upon preparing students to achieve proficiency on Standards-based assessments.

On December 14, 2004, Plaintiffs filed the instant suit challenging the constitutional validity of the October 18, 2004 resolution and November 19, 2004 press release (collectively, "the ID Policy"). It is contended that the ID policy constitutes an establishment of religion prohibited by the First Amendment to the United States Constitution, which is made applicable to the states by the Fourteenth Amendment, as well as the Constitution of the Commonwealth of Pennsylvania. Plaintiffs seek declaratory and injunctive relief, nominal damages, costs, and attorneys' fees. . . .

Conclusion

The proper application of both the endorsement and *Lemon* tests to the facts of this case makes it abundantly clear that the Board's ID Policy violates the Establishment Clause. In making this determination, we have addressed the seminal question of whether ID is science. We have concluded that it is not, and moreover that ID cannot uncouple itself from its creationist, and thus religious, antecedents.

Both Defendants and many of the leading proponents of ID make a bedrock assumption which is utterly false. Their presupposition is that evolutionary theory is antithetical to a belief in the existence of a supreme being and to religion in general. Repeatedly in this trial, Plaintiffs' scientific experts testified that the theory of evolution represents good science, is overwhelmingly accepted by the scientific community, and that it in no way conflicts with, nor does it deny, the existence of a divine creator.

To be sure, Darwin's theory of evolution is imperfect. However, the fact that a scientific theory cannot yet render an explanation on every point should not be used as a pretext to thrust an untestable alternative hypothesis grounded in religion into the science classroom or to misrepresent well-established scientific propositions.

The citizens of the Dover area were poorly served by the members of the Board who voted for the ID Policy. It is ironic that several of these individuals, who so staunchly and proudly touted their religious convictions in public, would time and again lie to cover their tracks and disguise the real purpose behind the ID Policy.

With that said, we do not question that many of the leading advocates of ID have *bona fide* and deeply held beliefs which drive their scholarly endeavors. Nor do we controvert that ID should continue to be studied, debated, and discussed. As stated, our conclusion today is that it is unconstitutional to teach ID as an alternative to evolution in a public school science classroom.

Those who disagree with our holding will likely mark it as the product of an activist judge. If so, they will have erred as this is manifestly not an activist Court. Rather, this case came to us as the result of the activism of an ill-informed faction on a school board, aided by a national public interest law firm eager to find a constitutional test case on ID, who in combination drove the Board to adopt an imprudent and ultimately unconstitutional policy. The breathtaking inanity of the Board's decision is evident when considered against the factual backdrop which has now been fully revealed through this trial. The students, parents, and teachers of the Dover Area School District deserved better than to be dragged into this legal maelstrom, with its resulting utter waste of monetary and personal resources.

To preserve the separation of church and state mandated by the Establishment Clause of the First Amendment to the United States Constitution, and Art. I, § 3 of the Pennsylvania Constitution, we will enter an order permanently enjoining Defendants from maintaining the ID Policy in any school within the Dover Area School District, from requiring teachers to denigrate or disparage the scientific theory of evolution, and from requiring teachers to refer to a religious, alternative theory known as ID. We will also issue a declaratory judgment that Plaintiffs' rights under the Constitutions of the United States and the Commonwealth of Pennsylvania have been violated by Defendants' actions. Defendants' actions in violation of Plaintiffs' civil rights as guaranteed to them by the Constitution of the United States and 42 U.S.C. § 1983 subject Defendants to liability

---

DID YOU KNOW?

Pat Robertson's Warning to the Citizens of Dover, Pennsylvania

In November 2005, shortly after the citizens of Dover, Pennsylvania, had voted out of office the members of the Dover area school board, Christian Broadcasting Network founder Pat Robertson stated on his daily television show, *The 700 Club*, that if a disaster struck the area, the residents of Dover, who had just "rejected [God] from your city," should not ask God for help because "He might not be there." By removing the school board members, Robertson claimed, residents had "voted God out of your city." The school board members had instituted a policy requiring area schools to read to students a brief statement in biology classes announcing that the theory of evolution is not factually confirmed and that gaps exist in the theory. The statement also suggested that students read a book that explained Intelligent Design as an alternative to the theory of evolution. A federal court ultimately ruled against the school board.

with respect to injunctive and declaratory relief, but also for nominal damages and the reasonable value of Plaintiffs' attorneys' services and costs incurred in vindicating Plaintiffs' constitutional rights.

SOURCE: U.S. District Court for the Middle District of Pennsylvania, Judge John E. Jones, *Kitzmiller, et al. v. Dover Area School District, et al.* Case No. 04CV2688.

ANALYSIS

In 1859 British naturalist Charles Darwin published *Origin of Species*, in which he set out a completely materialistic explanation for the existence of biological species, including human beings. The scientific theory left no room for purpose or direction in creation. Although some Christians attempted to reconcile their religious beliefs to the new theory, others resolved to resist the new ideas about human origins, including supporting laws prohibiting the teaching of evolution.

When Tennessee state legislators passed a law in 1925 prohibiting the teaching of evolution in the state's public schools, the American Civil Liberties Union supported a young teacher, John T. Scopes, who was willing to violate the new law in a test case. Thus a symbolic contest was orchestrated between traditional religious belief and modernism, with William Jennings Bryan, three-time Democratic presidential candidate, representing the former, and Clarence Darrow, noted defense attorney, defending the views of the latter. As part of the prosecution team, Bryan, who strongly believed that the theory of evolution threatened the moral foundations of society, faced the shrewd defense lawyer Darrow. The trial gained national attention and resembled high theater, as Darrow called Bryan to the stand in an attempt to ridicule Bryan's fundamentalist religious beliefs. The jury found Scopes guilty and the judge fined him $100, a conviction that the Tennessee Supreme Court overturned on a technicality. Although the trial was an embarrassment to fundamentalist religious forces, subsequently science textbook publishers dealt cautiously with the topic of evolution.

Opponents of the theory of evolution have tried various strategies to limit its use in education, including requiring the teaching of creationism as an alternative scientific explanation, and having evolution labeled a religious belief. The actions of the Dover, Pennsylvania, school board represent a recent effort, requiring a statement to be read in biology classes. The plaintiffs in the case argued that the school board members took this action for religious reasons. The defendants, represented by the Thomas More Law Center, responded that they were expressing legitimate concern about the claimed inadequacies of the theory of evolution.

Relying on U.S. Supreme Court precedent and examining the background of the school board's actions, Judge John E. Jones decided in favor of the plaintiffs, ruling that the school board action violated the Establishment Clause of the First Amendment to the U.S. Constitution. Supporters of the theory of evolution applauded the decision as a vindication of their claim that Intelligent Design theory is simply

William Jennings Bryan (seated, with fan) and Clarence Darrow (standing, arms folded) represented the prosecution and defense, respectively, at the July 1925 trial of science teacher John Scopes in Dayton, Tennessee. A circus-like atmosphere often prevailed in the outdoor courtroom, and the trial was the first to be broadcast by radio nationwide. (Library of Congress, Prints & Photographs Division, New York *World-Telegram* and the *Sun Newspaper* Photograph Collection, LC-USZ62–114986)

creationism in new clothing, while evolution opponents attacked the decision for contributing to a government mandate of materialism. Given the view of many Christians that evolution theory has major flaws, the struggle over the content of science education—particularly biology—very likely will continue.

"Objection: Responding to the Top Ten Objections Against Intelligent Design"

- **Document:** Statement by William A. Dembski and Sean McDowell in defense of Intelligent Design as a scientific alternative to the theory of evolution.
- **Date:** 2008.
- **Where:** *Christian Research Journal.*
- **Significance:** Despite the decision in the *Kitzmiller* case and criticisms of Intelligent Design by scientists, supporters continue to express confidence in ID as a scientifically valid alternative to evolution theory. The stakes are high in this conflict, which involves what will be taught to students in public school science classes.

DOCUMENT

"Evolution wars!" proclaimed the cover story of *Time* magazine, August 15, 2005. The following year *Time* ran another cover story titled, "God vs. Science," featuring a debate between human-genome researcher Francis Collins and evolutionary biologist Richard Dawkins. The controversy surrounding intelligent design (ID) continues to appear in major newspapers, magazines, popular television shows, and various forums on the Internet. In the major motion picture documentary, *Expelled: No Intelligence Allowed*, [1] actor Ben Stein examines how dogmatic Darwinists suppress the academic freedom of anyone who dissents from their theory, especially proponents of ID. The debate surrounding ID therefore continues to heat up and shows no signs of dying down.

Despite incessant proclamations by the media and the academic establishment regarding the demise of ID, interest in ID is exploding, [2] and philosopher J. P. Moreland contends that the ID movement cannot be stopped. [3] Despite ID's growing success, however, objections against it regularly appear in both scholarly and popular literature. In this article, we respond to ten of the most common criticisms raised against ID. Given the widespread misinformation in our culture about ID, it has become increasingly important for Christians to respond effectively to challenges posed against it.

Objection #1: Imperfection in Living Things Counts Against ID

In his book *Why Darwin Matters*, skeptic Michael Shermer claims that the imperfect anatomy of the human eye disconfirms design. He asks, "For optimal vision, why would an intelligent designer have built an eye upside down and backwards?" [4] According to Shermer, such imperfections are evidence for evolution and evidence against design.

Shermer has overlooked a basic point, however; *design does not have to be perfect—it just has to be good enough*. Imperfection speaks to the quality of design, not its reality. Consider successive versions of the iPod. The various versions have minor imperfections, but each clearly was designed; none evolved without guidance from programmers. Our ability to envision a better design hardly means the object in question lacks design.

What is true for the iPod is also true in biology. Living systems bear unmistakable marks of design, even if such design is, or appears to be, imperfect. In the real world, perfect design does not exist. Real designers aim for the best overall compromise among constraints needed to accomplish a function. Design is a give-and-take process. For instance, a larger computer screen may be preferable to a smaller one, but designers must also consider cost, weight, size, and transportability. Given competing factors, designers choose the best overall compromise—and this is precisely what we see in nature.

For instance, all life forms are part of a larger ecology that recycles its life forms. Most life forms survive by consuming other life forms, either living or dead. In due time, all life forms must die.

Suppose we object to design because foxes catch rabbits and eat them. If rabbits had perfect defenses, however, foxes would starve. Then rabbits, by reproducing without limit and eating all the vegetation, also would starve. The uncatchable rabbit, ironically, then, would upset its ecosystem and create far more difficulties for design than it would resolve. Given this larger perspective, it seems that the "imperfections" of individual organisms in nature are actually part of a larger design plan for life.

What about the human eye? Is the eye built upside down and backwards, as many critics of design argue? Despite common claims that the eye is poorly designed, there actually are good reasons for its construction, [5] and no one has demonstrated how the eye's function might be improved without diminishing its visual speed, sensitivity, and resolution.

Objection #2: ID Must Explain Who Designed the Designer

Richard Dawkins has raised this criticism against design arguments for years now, most recently in his book *The God Delusion*. According to Dawkins, ID fails because it doesn't explain the origin of the designer. If the universe bears the marks of design, as ID proponents claim, does the designer bear such marks of design in turn? We are led to ask, "Who designed the designer?" If we can't answer this question, says Dawkins, then ID is fruitless.

Is this, however, how science works? Can scientists only accept explanations that themselves have been explained? The problem with this objection is that it is *always* possible to ask for further explanation. There comes a point, however, when scientists must deny the request for further explanation and accept the progress they have made. As apologist Greg Koukl has observed, "An explanation can be a good one even if you do not have an explanation for the explanation." [6]

For example, if an archaeologist discovers an ancient object that looks like an arrowhead or digging tool, she would be fully justified in drawing a design inference. In fact, after a few clear instances she would be irrational *not* to infer design. She may have no clue as to the origin or identity of the designer, but certain patterns that the artifacts exhibit would point beyond natural forces to the work of an intelligent designer.

If every explanation needed a further explanation, then nothing could ever be explained! For example, if designer B was responsible for having designed designer A, then the question inevitably would arise, "Who designed B?" The answer, of course, is designer C. And so on without end. Given such an infinite regress of explanations, nothing could ever be explained, since every explanation would require still further explanation. Science itself would come to a standstill!

Objection # 3: ID Is Not Testable

This criticism is meant to disqualify ID as a science. For ID to be considered untestable, however (and hence, unscientific), there has to be a clear definition of what it means for something to be testable and a clear failure of ID to meet that definition. As it stands, no such definition exists.

If by "testable" we mean that a theory should be open to confirming or disconfirming evidence, then ID most certainly passes the test. Darwin presented what he regarded as strong evidence against design. Claiming that ID has been tested by such evidence and shown to be false, however, creates a catch-22 for the critic: If evidence can count *against* a theory, evidence must also be able to count in *favor* of a theory. The knife cuts both ways.

One cannot say, "Design is not testable," and then turn around and say, "Design has been tested and shown to be false!" For evidence to show that something is false implies that evidence also might show it to be true, even if one thinks the particular evidence in question fails to establish a claim.

Researchers have confirmed the evidence for ID across a wide range of disciplines including molecular biology, physics, and chemistry. [7] Even if critics reject the evidence for ID, in the very act of rejecting the evidence, they put design to the test (which is exactly what they do when no one is looking!).

A simple way to see that ID is testable is to consider the following "thought experiment." Imagine what would happen if microscopic investigation revealed the words, "Made by Yahweh" inscribed in the nucleus of every cell. Of course, cells are not inscribed with the actual words, "Made by Yahweh," but that's not the point.

The point is that we wouldn't know this unless we actually "tested" cells for this sign of intelligence, which we couldn't do if ID were not testable. If ID fails, it won't be for lack of testability.

Objection #4: ID Violates the Scientific Consensus

In 2003, Nobel Prize-winning physicist Steven Weinberg testified before the Texas State Board of Education about the methods of science. He explained, "By the same standards that are used in the courts, I think it is your responsibility to judge that it is the theory of evolution through natural selection that has won general scientific acceptance. And therefore, it should be presented to students as the consensus view of science, without any alternatives being presented." [8] Judge John Jones made a similar declaration in *Kitzmiller v. Dover* (2005). [9]

Darwinian evolution undeniably is accepted by the majority of practicing biologists. Appealing to the majority view as a way to exclude alternative explanations, however, is highly problematic. Here's why: scientific consensus in the past has been notoriously unreliable. In 1960, for instance, the geosynclinal theory was the consensus explanation for mountain formation. The authors of *Geological Evolution of North America* considered geosynclinal theory "one of the great unifying principles of geology." [10]

Whatever happened to geosynclinal theory? Within ten years of this declaration it had been utterly abandoned and decisively replaced with plate tectonics, which explains mountain formation through continental drift and sea-floor spreading.

This is not an isolated example in the history of science. In 1500, the scientific consensus was that the Earth was at the center of the universe, but Copernicus and Newton shattered that misconception by showing that astronomical data were better explained by the Earth circling the Sun. The scientific consensus in the mid-1700s was that a substance called phlogiston caused heat, but Lavoisier shattered that misconception by showing that combustion was due to oxygen. At the end of the nineteenth century—forty years after the publication of *The Origin of Species*—the scientific consensus was to reject Darwinian evolution!

Today, when Darwinism is touted so widely as fact, it surprises many to learn that most biologists at the start of the twentieth century rejected Darwin's theory of evolution. In the 1930s Darwinism revived when a handful of scientists merged Darwin's theory with Mendelian genetics, which is now known as neo-Darwinism. Within neo-Darwinism, natural selection acted on genes that were randomly mutating.

DID YOU KNOW?

An Islamic Response to the Theory of Evolution

Criticisms of Darwin's theory of evolution come from religious traditions other than Christianity. Muslim Adnan Oktar (pen name Harum Yahya) has published a lavishly illustrated book (*Atlas of Creation*, Istanbul, Turkey: Global Publishing) which was translated into English in 2006. In the first three-fourths of the 800-page book, Oktar provides color photographs of fossils from various regions of the world, including North and South America, Europe, Africa, the Middle East, and Australia and New Zealand. Oktar claims that the fossil evidence demonstrates that evolution has not occurred. In the appendix, which composes the last one-fourth of the volume, Oktar presents evidence he claims refutes the theory of evolution and discredits its proponents, who are charged with propagandizing, forging evidence, and intimidating critics. Oktar asserts that fundamental to evolution is the notion of conflict, which he associates with racism, fascism, and communism. In contrast to the assumption of conflict and competition in the theory of evolution, Oktar claims that Islam is a religion of peace and justice and offers a solution to worldwide discord, including terrorism.

The history of science is filled with such turnabouts. As ID develops, we can expect Darwinism's fortunes to change again, this time for the worse.

Darwinism remains the scientific consensus, but that consensus is shrinking. Dissent from Darwinism continues to grow in the scientific population. In 2001, Seattle's Discovery Institute launched the Web site www.dissentfromdarwin.org to encourage scientists who are skeptical of Darwinism to make their dissension public. Since its inception, more than seven-hundred scientists from top universities worldwide have stepped forward and signed their names in dissent. Moreover, for every signatory of this list, there are tens if not hundreds who would sign it if their research and livelihoods would not be threatened by challenging Darwinism. (The documentary *Expelled* makes this perfectly clear.)

The very idea of "consensus science," ironically, is bogus. In a speech at the California Institute of Technology, medical doctor, author, and public intellectual Michael Crichton said it best:

I regard consensus science as an extremely pernicious development that ought to be stopped cold in its tracks. Historically, the claim of consensus has been the first refuge of scoundrels; it is a way to avoid debate by claiming that the matter is already settled. Whenever you hear the consensus of scientists agrees on something or other, reach for your wallet, because you're being had.

Let's be clear: the work of science has nothing whatever to do with consensus. Consensus is the business of politics. Science, on the contrary, requires only one investigator who happens to be right, which means that he or she has results that are verifiable by reference to the real world. In science consensus is irrelevant. What is relevant is reproducible results. The greatest scientists in history are great precisely because they broke with the consensus.

There is no such thing as consensus science. If it's consensus, it isn't science. If it's science, it isn't consensus. Period. [11]

Objection #5: ID Doesn't Go Far Enough/Isn't Honest Enough to Admit That Its Designer Is the Christian God

ID does not identify the designer. Why not? Is it for lack of honesty, as this objection suggests? No. The *identity* of the designer goes beyond the scientific evidence for design. Most advocates of ID are in fact Christians, but many Jews, Buddhists, Muslims, Hindus, and agnostics also see evidence for design in nature. (David Berlinski's recent book *The Devil's Delusion* [12] is a case in point.) The evidence of science can identify a designer consistent with the God of the Bible (one that is powerful, creative, skilled, and so forth), but science *alone* cannot prove that this designer is the Christian God or, for that matter, the God of any other religious faith.

In the foreword for our book *Understanding Intelligent Design*, apologist Josh McDowell offers a helpful comparison between ID and archaeology. To make the strongest case possible for the historical resurrection of Jesus, the deity of Christ, and the reliability of the Scriptures, for example, McDowell often uses recent findings from the field of archaeology. Regardless of the religious conviction of the archaeologist, the findings still can be used to support the biblical accounts of history—we owe some of the most significant archaeological finds that support the Bible to non-Christians.

As McDowell suggests, we ought to think of ID scientists in the same way as these archeologists. Should we dismiss an archaeological find because it happens also to be consistent with Judaism, Islam, Mormonism, or some other religion? Of course not. Regardless of their religious beliefs, ID theorists are finding evidence for design in the natural world that is consistent with the biblical view of creation. If they don't identify the designer in their academic work, it is because such claims go beyond the scientific data.

Objection #6: ID Is Creationism in a Cheap Tuxedo

Darwinists and the media regularly confuse ID with traditional creationism. Why? To discredit it. In their minds, creationism has no intellectual credibility. To refer to ID as creationism is thus meant to ensure that ID likewise will be denied intellectual credibility. This is why Leonard Krishtalka, professor at the University of Kansas, famously referred to ID as "creationism in a cheap tuxedo." [13] Creationism and ID, however, are distinct.

Creationism holds that a Supreme Being created the universe. Creationists come in two varieties: *young-earth* and *old-earth creationists*.[14] Young-earth creationists interpret Genesis as teaching that creation took place in six twenty-four-hour days, that the universe is between six- and ten-thousand years old, and that most fossils were deposited during Noah's global flood.

Old-earth creationists, on the other hand, allow a wider range of interpretations of Genesis. They accept contemporary scientific dating, which places the age of the Earth at roughly 4.5 billion years old and the universe at 13.7 billion years old. They accept microevolution as God's method of adapting existing species to their changing environments, but they reject macroevolution (the large-scale transformation of one species into a completely different species).

ID, though often confused with creation science, is in fact quite different from it. Rather than beginning with some particular interpretation of Genesis (as young-earth and old-earth creationists typically do), ID begins with investigating the natural world. ID looks for patterns in nature that are best explained as the product of intelligence. Given what the world reveals about itself, ID proponents reason that a designing intelligence best explains certain patterns in nature.

The great difference between ID and creation science, then, is that ID relies *not* on prior assumptions about divine activity in the world, but on methods developed within the scientific population for recognizing intelligence. [15] Even Judge Jones in the *Kitzmiller v. Dover* trial mentioned earlier recognized that ID proponents do *not* base their theory on "the Book of Genesis," "a young earth," of "a catastrophic Noachic flood." Despite incessant comparisons in the media with creation science, ID is actually quite different from it (although the majority of ID proponents believe in some form of creation, and, indeed, many of them are Christians).

Objection #7: ID Is Religiously Motivated

According to many critics of ID, design proponents oppose evolution not because they have fairly assessed the evidence for it, but because they are religiously motivated. In particular, critics suppose that design theorists worry that Darwinism undermines traditional morality. Now, it *is* true historically that Darwinism has been used to undercut traditional morality. History professor Richard Weikart, for instance, details how Darwinism has been used to justify eugenics, abortion, and racism in his must-read book *From Darwin to Hitler.* [16]

Although the tension between Darwinism and traditional morality is undoubtedly fascinating and noteworthy, design theorists reject Darwinism for a more basic reason: its lack of scientific support. Design theorists oppose Darwinian evolution because natural selection acting on random variation gives no evidence of being able to account for the diversity and complexity of life as found in nature.

Biochemist Michael Behe, who is a Roman Catholic and perhaps the best-known design theorist, has repeatedly declared that his opposition to Darwinian evolution stems *not* from religious reasons, but on account of the scientific data. Behe had no theological problem wedding Darwinian evolution with his Catholic faith. The issue for Behe was the lack of evidence for evolution and the positive case for design.

Even if design proponents were religiously motivated, how would that render their findings unscientific? Why is motivation even relevant? The motivation of scientists is immaterial to the status of their research. Cambridge physicist Stephen Hawking hopes his work in physics will help us understand the mind of God. Nobel laureate Steven Weinberg hopes his work in physics will help destroy religion: "I hope that this [i.e., the destruction of religion] is something to which science can contribute and if it is, then I think it may be the most important contribution that we can make." [17] Weinberg is not less of a scientist than Hawking because of his atheistic motivations, and Hawking is not less of a scientist than Weinberg because of his theistic motivations. Likewise, ID is not less of a science because its proponents happen to be motivated one way or another.

The real question for ID is not motivation, but evidence. Philosopher Francis Beckwith explains that "labeling a point of view, or the motives of its proponents, 'religious' or 'nonreligious' contributes nothing to one's assessment of the quality of the arguments for that point of view. Either the arguments work or they don't work or, more modestly, they are either reasonable or unreasonable, plausible or implausible." [18]

Objection #8: ID Is a Science-Stopper

Design critics regularly warn the public that allowing ID into science will either destroy science or significantly deter its progress. According to science writer Michael Shermer, for example, "The point of the [ID] movement is not to expand scientific understanding—it is to shut it down." [19]

The truth, however, is just the opposite—by rigidly excluding ID from science, Darwinists themselves impede scientific progress. Consider "junk DNA." The word "junk" suggests that useless portions of DNA have arisen together through a blind, unguided process of evolution. Evolutionary theorists thus have come to regard only a small portion of DNA as functional. By contrast, if DNA is the product of design, we would expect much of it to be functional.

Current research indicates that much of what was previously termed "junk DNA" is now known to have a function. This finding has become so well known in the scientific community that the popular press has picked up on it. In a recent *Newsweek* article, Mary Carmichael describes the transformation in how DNA is understood: "Researchers have realized that this forgotten part of the genome is, in fact, profoundly important. It contains the machinery that flips the switches, manipulating much of the rest of the genome. . . . Genes make up only 1.2 percent of our DNA. The rest of the DNA, once called 'junk DNA' was thought to be filler. Recent finds prove otherwise." [20]

Design thus encourages scientists to look for deeper insight into nature, whereas Darwinian evolution discourages it. The criticism that design stifles scientific progress is therefore mistaken. The criticism applies more readily to Darwinism than to design.

Objection #9: ID Is Inherently Religious, Not Scientific

One of the most common tactics that critics of design employ is to label ID as religious rather than scientific. According to philosopher of biology David Hull, Darwin rejected design not just because he thought the evidence was against it, but because he thought it wasn't even scientific: "He [Darwin] dismissed it [design] not because it was an incorrect scientific explanation, but because it was not a proper scientific explanation at all." [21] Critics, accordingly, suppose design to be an inherently religious idea.

How can this be? As noted earlier, ID studies patterns in nature that are best explained as the result of intelligence. Many special or specific sciences already study such patterns and draw agency or design inferences. Examples include forensic science (agency—did that person die of natural causes, or was there foul play?) and archaeology (design—is that an arrowhead or a naturally formed rock?). It is scientifically legitimate to recognize the work of an intelligent agent, even if the identity of that agent is unknown, as is often the case in archaeology.

Critics counter that we cannot apply design to biology because we only have experience with human designers (and any designer in biology would be nonhuman). The sciences of design, however, do not apply merely to human designers. We have evidence of animals that design things. Beavers, for instance, build dams that we recognize as designed. Design also need not be restricted to Earth. The Search for Extraterrestial Intelligence (SETI, as seen in the movie *Contact*) is a well-established scientific program that attempts to identify radio signals sent from outer space by intelligent aliens. The working assumption of SETI is that we can distinguish an intelligently produced signal from random radio noise.

Some critics discount ID because its designer is supposed to be unobservable. These same critics, however, often will turn around and postulate the "many-worlds hypothesis" (i.e., that multiple universes exist) to discount how finely tuned the laws of physics are to allow for the emergence and sustenance of life. If we are only one of many universes, critics surmise, then it shouldn't surprise us that we find ourselves in a universe uniquely crafted for our existence. The existence of multiple universes has never been observed. In fact, they are such that they can never be observed! Does this mean the many-worlds hypothesis is rendered unscientific? Of course not. Science often progresses by proposing theoretical entities that have yet to be observed and even may be unobservable, because of their explanatory power. Observability is therefore not a necessary condition for an explanation to be scientific; macroevolution has never been observed, yet it is still considered scientific.

Another common way of excluding ID from science is to charge that science only deals with what is repeatable, and nature's designs are unrepeatable. The problem is that scientists study many things that are unrepeatable, such as the Big Bang and the origin of life. Scientists have no clue how to repeat either of these events in a laboratory; yet they are clearly within the realm of science. If repeatability is considered a necessary condition for science, then disciplines such as archaeology, anthropology, cosmology, and paleontology must be excluded from science as soon as they discover some unique artifact or feature of nature. Since those disciplines are included within the realm of science despite their unrepeatability, ID also must be included. The repeatability objection therefore fails to exclude ID.

Other objections to ID's status as a science are also readily answerable. [22] The answers presented here, however, suffice to demonstrate that ID does not have to prove that it is a science—it already is. Popular atheist Richard Dawkins, surprisingly, agrees. Dawkins says, "the presence or absence of a creative super-intelligence is unequivocally a scientific question." [23]

Objection #10: ID Is an Argument from Ignorance

Sometimes also called the "God-of-the-gaps" objection, the argument-from-ignorance objection is perhaps the most common criticism leveled against ID. In an argument from ignorance, the lack of evidence against a proposition is used to argue for its truth. For instance, a typical argument-from-ignorance might be: "Ghosts and goblins exist because it hasn't been shown that they don't exist." The proponent of this view believes the lack of evidence against ghosts and goblins is positive evidence for their existence, which, of course, is logically absurd. According to critics, design theorists argue for the truth of ID simply because design has not been shown to be false.

On closer inspection, however, it is the Darwinists who are arguing from ignorance. Darwinists frequently charge that just because it is not known how complex biological systems evolved doesn't mean that Darwinism is false. If Darwinists can't explain *how* complex biological systems evolved, however, what right do they have to claim *that* such systems evolved in the first place? Lacking an evidentially based model for how certain biological structures evolved means that Darwinists are arguing from ignorance.

In these encounters, Darwinists will often attempt to turn the tables, suggesting the ID reasons from, "Gee, I can't see how evolution could have done it," to the conclusion, "Shucks, I guess God must have done it." This misrepresents ID, however. When we examine complex biological systems, we do not infer design merely because naturalistic approaches to evolution fail. We infer design not from what we *don't* know, but from what we *do* know.

We have empirical evidence for the capacity of intelligent agents to design irreducibly complex systems such as the bacterial flagellum (the bacterial flagellum is a bidirectional motor-driven propeller on the backs of certain bacteria). Human engineers invented motors like this long before the flagellum was even discovered. If we apply the same reasoning to the flagellum as we do to human technology, it is obvious that the flagellum bears the marks of intelligence. ID is a positive argument from what we do know, not from ignorance.

Many evolutionary biologists pretend that the "house of evolution" is in good order, but occasionally a few come clean about its disarray. University of Chicago biologist James Shapiro, for instance, admits that "there are no detailed Darwinian accounts for the evolution of any fundamental biochemical or cellular system, only a variety of wishful speculations." [24] University of Iowa rhetorician David Depew likewise concedes, "I could not agree more with the claim that contemporary Darwinism lacks models that can explain the evolution of cellular pathways and the problem of the origin of life." [25]

There currently are no naturalistic explanations for the origin of life, the information content of DNA, the fine-tuning of the laws of physics, the privileged status of Earth, irreducibly complex biological structures, human consciousness, and morality. Given the lack of scientific evidence for these basic elements of life, it is more than fair to ask, "Who is ignorant here?" Naturalistic causes give no evidence of adequately accounting for *any* of these features of the universe. Intelligent causes, by contrast, have demonstrated this ability time and again.

It is high time not only to give ID the credit it deserves, but also to give Darwinism the discredit it deserves. Intelligent design is a young research program that still has a long way to go. Darwinism, by contrast, has become an outdated dogma ready to be consigned to the trash heap of history, and evolutionary theory, as developed by Darwin and prolonged by contemporary devotees, is essentially a relic of failed nineteenth-century economic theories about competition for scarce resources. We, on the other hand, live in the twenty-first century, an age of information where information is limitless. ID theory is the study of intelligently produced information. Despite all the protestations by Darwinists that ID is unscientific, ID is the cutting-edge of science. Get on board!

NOTES

[1] Kevin Miller and Ben Stein, *Expelled: No Intelligence Allowed*, directed by Nathan Frankowski (Dallas: Premise Media, 2008).

[2] See William Dembski and Sean McDowell, *Understanding Intelligent Design: Everything You Need to Know in Plain Language* (Eugene, OR: Harvest House, 2008); William Dembski and Jonathan Wells, *The Design of Life: Discovering Signs of Intelligence in Biological Systems* (Dallas: Foundations for Thought and Ethics, 2008); Michael Behe, *The Edge of Evolution: The Search for the Limits of Darwinism* (New York: Free Press, 2007); Benjamin Wiker and Jonathan Witt, *A Meaningful World: How the Arts and Sciences Reveal the Genius of Nature* (Downers Grove, IL: InterVarsity Press, 2006); Guillermo Gonzalez and Jay W. Richards, *The Privileged Planet: How Our Place in the Cosmos Is Designed for Discovery* (Washington, DC: Regnery, 2004).

[3] J. P. Moreland, *Kingdom Triangle* (Grand Rapids: Zondervan, 2007), 13.

[4] Michael Shermer, *Why Darwin Matters: The Case against Intelligent Design* (New York: Time Books, 2006), 17.

[5] See Dembski and McDowell.

[6] Gregory Koukl, "Answering the New Atheists, Part 1," *Solid Ground* (May/June, 2008), 4, available at –http://www.str.org/site/DocServer/5–6_SG_2008.pdf?docID=3021.

[7] See Dembski and Wells; Gonzalez and Richards.

[8] Inside Science News Service, "Physics Nobelist Takes Stand on Evolution," Story Archive (2003), American Institute of Physics, http://www.aip.org/isns/reports/2003/081.html.

[9] The case of *Kitzmiller v. Dover* evaluated whether teachers were required to read a four-paragraph statement to students, informing them that ID is an alternative theory to Darwinian evolution.

[10] Thomas Clark and Colin Stearn, *Geological Evolution of North America: A Regional Approach to Historical Geology* (New York: The Ronald Press Company, 1960).

[11] Michael Crichton, "Aliens Cause Global Warming" (Caltech Michelin Lecture, California Institute of Technology, Pasadena, CA, January 17, 2003), available at http://www.crichton-official.com/speech-alienscauseglobalwarming.html (last accessed July 23, 2008).

[12] David Berlinski, *The Devil's Delusion: Atheism and Its Scientific Pretensions* (New York: Crown Forum, 2008).

[13] See this link: https://tv.ku.edu/news/2005/11/08/evolution-and-faith-a-peaceful-coexistence/.

[14] Ken Ham and Hugh Ross are well-known defenders of young-earth and old-earth creationism, respectively. For a good discussion on the different interpretations of Genesis see, *The Genesis Debate: Three Views on the Days of Creation*, ed. David Hagopian (Mission Viejo, CA: Crux Press, 2001).

[15] William Dembski, *The Design Inference* (Cambridge, England: Cambridge University Press, 1998), chaps. 2, 7.

[16] Richard Weikart, *From Darwin to Hitler* (New York: Palgrave Macmillan, 2004).

[17] "Nobel Laureate Steven Weinberg: Free People from Superstition," *Free Thought Today* (April 2000), Freedom From Religion Foundation, available at http://ffrf.org/fttoday/2000/april2000/weinberg.html (last accessed July 23, 2008).

[18] Francis J. Beckwith, "Intelligent Design, Religious Motives, and the Constitution's Religion Clauses" in *Intelligent Design: William Dembski and Michael Ruse in Dialogue*, ed. Robert B. Stewart (Minneapolis: Fortress Press, 2007).

[19] Shermer, 99.

[20] Mary Carmichael, "A Changing Portrait of DNA," *Newsweek*, December 10, 2007: 64.

[21] David Hull, *Darwin and His Critics: The Reception of Darwin's Theory of Evolution by the Scientific Community* (Cambridge, MA: Harvard University Press, 1973), 26.

[22] See Dembski and McDowell, chap. 5.

[23] Richard Dawkins, *The God Delusion* (London: Bantam Books, 2006), 58–59.

[24] James Shapiro, "In the Details . . . What?" (Review of Michael Behe's *Darwin's Black Box*), *National Review*, September 16, 1996, 62–65.

[25] David Depew, "Intelligent Design and Irreducible Complexity: A Rejoinder," in *Darwinism, Design, and Public Education*, ed. Stephen C. Meyer (East Lansing, MI: Michigan State University, 2003), 447.

SOURCE: William A. Dembski and Sean McDowell, "Objection: Responding to the Top Ten Objections Against Intelligent Design," *Christian Research Journal* 31, no. 5 (2008): 20–29. Reprinted courtesy of William A. Dembski and Sean McDowell.

ANALYSIS

The arguments for, and defenses of, Intelligent Design, as well as criticisms of the Darwinian theory of evolution, appear to be based on the approach to the history of science provided by such writers as Thomas Kuhn, who began a major discussion about the nature of science in his 1970 book *The Structure of Scientific Revolutions*. According to Kuhn, science is characterized by long periods in which scientists involve themselves in puzzle solving, arriving at solutions to questions within a larger scientific perspective called a "paradigm." These periods he referred to as "normal science." As more and more of these puzzles remain unresolved, a condition of crisis arises within a scientific community, which is resolved only when an especially gifted scientist presents an alternative paradigm to replace the existing approach. This briefer period Kuhn refers to as a "scientific revolution." Following this revolution, which resembles to some extent a political revolution, or a culture war, scientists are converted to the new approach, or younger scientists ultimately take control from the older ones, who remain committed to the previous paradigm. The rise of modern physics with Galileo and Isaac Newton and the rise of relativity theory and quantum mechanics in the twentieth century are examples of such revolutions, which, as Kuhn claimed, represent a choice between "incompatible modes of community life" (Kuhn 1970, 93–94).

William Dembski and Sean McDowell's defense of Intelligent Design appears to follow fairly closely Kuhn's outline of a scientific revolution, claiming that a crisis situation has arisen in the theory of evolution and that Intelligent Design theory promises to provide a more satisfying resolution to many of the observations in biology. A distinction between Kuhn's model of scientific revolutions and the Dembski-McDowell discussion is that the latter appear to provide a much more extended understanding of "community" than does the former. While Kuhn speaks of a revolution within science among scientists, Dembski and McDowell appeal to the opinions of non-scientists—particularly Christians—within the larger society. Scientists generally deny the label of science to Intelligent Design, which raises questions about what distinguishes science from what is referred to as pseudoscience and how clearly that distinction can be drawn. Dembski and other proponents of Intelligent Design argue that their approach merits being classified as science and claim that although many of their supporters are Christians, the ID theory itself can be separated from religious belief. Nonetheless, religious belief about a creator appears to be a major dividing line between ID supporters and those who adhere to the evolution paradigm explanation for the present state of human beings. Due to its connection with religious belief, any proposal to include ID in the public school curriculum will continue as a significant element in the culture wars.

"Debate Over Evolution Not Going Away"

- *Document:* An opinion piece by John G. West about the differing positions that conservatives have taken on the theory of evolution.
- *Date:* November 13, 2006.
- *Where:* Human Events.
- *Significance:* West presents the major arguments that opponents of the theory of evolution have raised, associating supporters of Charles Darwin's theory of evolution with radical social reform proposals such as eugenics, and with a rejection of traditional conceptions of morality. The author criticizes the claimed intolerance of evolutionists toward anyone who challenges the scientific validity of the theory of evolution.

DOCUMENT

The debate over Darwinian evolution is typically framed by the news media as a clash between "right" and "left." Conservatives are presumed to be critical of Darwin's theory, while liberals are presumed to support it.

As in most cases, reality is more complicated.

There always have been liberal critics of Darwin. In the early 20th Century, progressive reformer William Jennings Bryan fought for women's suffrage, world peace—and against Darwinism. More recently, left-wing novelist Kurt Vonnegut, a self-described "secular humanist," has called our human bodies "miracles of design" and faulted scientists for "pretending they have the answer as to how we got this way when natural selection couldn't possibly have produced such machines."

Evolution to the Rescue?

Just as there have been critics of Darwin on the left, there continue to be champions of Darwinism on the right. In the last few years, pundits such as George Will, Charles Krauthammer and John Derbyshire, along with social scientist James Q. Wilson and political theorist Larry Arnhart, have stoutly defended Darwin's theory and denounced Darwin's critics.

Some of Darwin's conservatives are even promoting Darwinian biology as a way to save conservatism. In his book, *The Moral Sense*, James Q. Wilson draws on Darwinian biology to support traditional morality. Law professor John O. McGinnis opines that the future success of conservatism depends on evolutionary biology: "Any political movement that hopes to be successful must come to terms with the second rise of Darwinism."

No one has been more articulate in championing evolution on the right than political theorist Larry Arnhart at Northern Illinois University, who in his recent book, *Darwinian Conservatism*, argues that "[c]onservatives need Charles Darwin . . . because a Darwinian science of human nature supports conservatives in their realist view of human imperfectibility and their commitment to ordered liberty. . . . "

Darwin's Allure

The allure of Darwinian conservatism is not hard to understand. While 19th-Century giants such as Karl Marx and Sigmund Freud have been debunked, Darwin retains his prestige among the elites as a secular saint. Moreover, Darwinists have clothed themselves in the mantle of modern science, successfully stigmatizing those who criticize them as bigoted Bible-thumpers who are "anti-science."

No wonder a number of conservative intellectuals either refrain from becoming involved in the debate over Darwinism or take the side of Darwin as a matter of course. In some quarters, it is regarded as unfashionable or even embarrassing to be on the other side of Darwin's critics. And who wants to be unfashionable and embarrassed?

One suspects that this concern for being fashionable has something to do with the dismissive attitude taken by conservative columnists such as George Will and Charles Krauthammer, neither of whom, however, shows evidence of having read or considered the arguments made by intelligent-design proponents. If they had, they would not assert tritely that intelligent design is merely "warmed-over creationism" (Krauthammer) or an attempt "to compel public education to infuse theism into scientific education" (Will). Nor would Krauthammer have denounced the Kansas Board of Education for "forcing intelligent design into the statewide biology curriculum" when the board made clear it had done the exact opposite: "We also emphasize that the Science Curriculum Standards do not include Intelligent Design. . . . " Which part of the phrase "do not include Intelligent Design" did Krauthammer fail to understand? Sadly, he probably never bothered to look at the Kansas science standards he so excoriates.

It is ironic that such conservatives, who would not trust left-wing reporting about, say, the war in Iraq, apparently will accept wholesale anything the mainstream report about evolution.

'Random' Redefined

Other more careful conservatives remain troubled by what they regard as the excesses of Darwinian ideologues, but they seem to think they can tame or neutralize Darwinian evolution by redefining it. For example, physicist Stephen Barr has argued in [the conservative publication] *First Things* that neo-Darwinism, properly understood, need not require a process that is "unguided" or "unplanned." "The word 'random' as used in science does not mean uncaused, unplanned, or inexplicable; it means uncorrelated," he writes.

The problem is not that Barr is wrong about the appropriate meaning of "random" but that mainstream Darwinists do not accept his point and never have. Darwinism from the start has been defined as an undirected process. That is its core, and that is why Darwin himself emphasized that "no shadow of reason can be assigned for the belief that variations . . . were intentionally specially guided."

In the Darwinian view, biological structures such as the vertebrate eye, or the wings of butterflies, or the bacterial flagellum, "must have" developed through the interplay of chance (random mutations, according to modern Darwinists) and necessity (natural selection or "survival of the fittest"). The same holds true for the higher animals, including human beings. In the words of Harvard paleontologist George Gaylord Simpson, "Man is the result of a purposeless and natural process that did not have him in mind."

Barr may be correct that a more modest Darwinism that does not insist on evolution's being undirected would be harmless, but then it also no longer would be Darwinism. Conservatives cannot resolve the problems with Darwinian evolution merely by offering their own idiosyncratic definition of the term.

Still other conservatives such as Arnhart and Wilson believe that, properly understood, Darwin's theory can be used to support moral universals and temper utopian schemes. But their argument flies in the face of both Darwinism's internal logic and an historical record that demonstrates the opposite.

Promoting Eugenics

For the past hundred years, mainstream Darwinists have drawn on Darwin's theory to promote relativism and utopian social reforms such as eugenics. Of course, these Darwinists could have been wrong, but a strong case can be made that their efforts were logically connected to Darwin's theory.

If one believes that all human behaviors are equally the products of natural selection and that ultimately they all exist because they promote biological survival, it is hard to see an objective ground for condemning any particular behavior. The maternal instinct is natural, according to Darwinism, but so is infanticide. Monogamy is natural, but so are polygamy and adultery. If a certain man prefers five wives to one, who are we to judge? Obviously, natural selection has preserved the desire for multiple wives in that male, so polygamy must be "right" for him.

I am not quarreling here with the attempt by Darwinian conservatives to enlist biology to support traditional morality. I actually agree with them that showing a biological basis for certain moral desires conceivably reinforce traditional morality

—but only if we have reason to assume that those biological desires are somehow normative.

If one believes that natural desires have been implanted in human beings by intelligent design, or even that they represent irreducible and unchanging truths inherent in the universe, it is rational to accept those desires as grounding for a universal code of morality. But Darwinism explicitly denies that natural desires are either the result of intelligent design or an unchanging nature.

Darwinian Moral Relativism

According to the Darwinian view, nature may—on occasion—sanction traditional virtues because, at the moment, they happen to promote biological survival. But even Darwin would acknowledge, if pressed, that given a different set of circumstances, a radically different conception of morality would be required.

At one point, he said as much: "If, for instance ... men were reared under precisely the same conditions as hive-bees, there can hardly be a doubt that our unmarried females would, like worker-bees, think it a sacred duty to kill their brothers, and mothers would strive to kill their fertile daughters; and no one would think of interfering."

Although this startling passage refers to the behavior of hive bees, it is making a point about *human* morality and how it is ultimately a function of the conditions of survival. Whenever those conditions change, Darwin seems to say, so, too, will the maxims of human morality. Hence, relativism is perfectly rational within the Darwinian universe.

Similarly, if one believes that human progress is dependent on a vigorous struggle for existence, then any diminishment of natural selection in human society will raise legitimate concerns, and efforts to reinstate selection through eugenics may well appear rational. In addition, once one understands the evolving nature of "human nature," it is difficult to see any "in principle" objection to efforts to transform human nature through bioengineering.

Natural selection is a messy, hit-or-miss process of dead ends and false starts. Why shouldn't human beings use their reason to direct their evolution in order to produce a new kind of human being? What is so sacrosanct about existing human dispositions and capacities, since they were produced by such an imperfect and purposeless process?

Conservatives who would rather sit out the evolution controversy need to understand that the current debate is not primarily about religious fundamentalism, nor is it simply an irrelevant rehashing of certain esoteric points of biology and philosophy. Darwinian reductionism has become culturally pervasive and inextricably intertwined with contemporary conflicts over traditional morality, personal responsibility, sex and family, and bioethics.

Darwinism is also central to an important debate about the role of scientific expertise in American society that dates back to the Progressive era. Darwin's defenders have been at the forefront of promoting technocracy—the claim that scientific experts ultimately have the right to rule free from the normal restraints of democratic accountability. Disparaging the wisdom of ordinary citizens and their elected representatives, dogmatic Darwinists essentially argue that public policy should be dictated by the majority of scientific experts without input from anyone else. Today, this bold assertion is made not just with regard to evolution, but concerning a host of other controversial issues such as sex education, euthanasia, embryonic stem-cell research, cloning, and global warming. Those on the left declare that any dissent from liberal orthodoxy on these issues represents a "war on science."

Demonizing Dissent

The effort to demonize normal democratic dissent in the area of science and public policy has been fomented by Fenton communications, the far-left public relations firm for such groups as MoveOn.org, Planned Parenthood, the American Trial Lawyers Association, Greenpeace and the National Abortion Rights Action League (NARAL). With funding from the Tides Center, Fenton has set up a group bearing the Orwellian name of the "Campaign to Defend the Constitution" ("DefCon"). According to DefCon, good science just happens to equal the political agenda to the left, and anyone who says otherwise is a "theocrat" who opposes "scientific progress."

Of course, there is much that can be said in favor of the authority of scientific expertise in modern life. In an increasingly complex and technologically-driven world, the need for scientific input on public policy would seem obvious.

While this line of reasoning exhibits a surface persuasiveness, it ignores the natural limits of scientific expertise. As C. S. Lewis pointed out in the 1950's, "government involves questions about the good for man, and justice, and what things are worth having at what price, and on these a scientific training gives a man's opinion no added value."

Technocracy poses a further difficulty: Experts can be wrong, sometimes egregiously. If the history of "Social Darwinism" in politics shows anything, it is that scientific experts can be as fallible as anyone else. What is true of individual scientists is often true of the scientific community as a whole. For example, eugenics was embraced for decades by America's leading evolutionary biologists and scientific organizations such as the American Association for the Advancement of Science. Critics of eugenics, meanwhile, were roundly stigmatized as anti-science and religious zealots. Yet the critics were the ones who turned out to be right, while the "consensus" was wrong.

As equal citizens before the law, scientists have every right to inform policymakers of the

---

DID YOU KNOW?

Scientists Dissenting from Darwin's Theory of Evolution

The Center for Science and Culture of the Discovery Institute maintains a list of scientists worldwide who have signed a statement questioning the validity of the theory of evolution. More than 700 scientists have signed the statement. One signer, Michael Egnor, professor of neurosurgery and pediatrics at the State University of New York at Stony Brook, commented in 2007 that the theory is a "trivial idea" that has been raised to the position of the prevailing scientific theory in biology. The statement declares that "We are skeptical of claims for the ability of random mutation and natural selection to account for the complexity of life. Careful examination of the evidence for Darwinian theory should be encouraged." John West, associate director of the Center, has claimed that new scientific data point to the inadequacy of the theory of evolution and evidence in support of the theory is crumbling. The statement and its signatories indicate that, unlike scientific investigation generally, debate is being carried out in the public realm.

scientific implications of their actions. But they have no special right to demand that policymakers listen to them alone or to ignore dissidents in their own ranks.

Atmosphere of Intolerance

Even conservatives who accept Darwinian theory, therefore, should think twice before embracing the dogmatic claims to authority made by Darwinists. Such claims have resulted in a concerted effort to shut down honest debate through caricatures and intimidation. While evolutionists continue to portray themselves as the victims of fundamentalist intolerance, in most places today it is the evolutionists who have turned inquisitors.

At George Mason University in Virginia, biology professor Caroline Crocker made the mistake of favorably discussing intelligent design in her cell biology class. She was suspended from teaching the class, and then her contract was not renewed.

At the Smithsonian Institution, evolutionary biologist Richard Sternberg, the editor of a respected biology journal, faced retaliation by Smithsonian executives in 2005 after accepting for publication a peer-viewed article favoring intelligent design. Investigators for the U.S. Office of Special Counsel later concluded that "it is . . . clear that hostile work environment was created with the ultimate goal of forcing [Dr. Sternberg] . . . out of the [Smithsonian]."

These efforts to purge the scientific community of any critics of Darwin are fueled by increasingly vehement rhetoric on the part of some evolutionists. In many states, it has become routine to apply the label of "Taliban" to anyone who supports teaching students about scientific criticisms of Darwinian theory.

Biology professor P. Z. Myers at the University of Minnesota, Morris, has demanded "the public firing and humiliation of some teachers" who express their doubts about Darwin. He further says, "It's time for scientists to break out the steel-toed boots and brass knuckles, and get out there and hammer on the lunatics and idiots."

Whatever one's personal view of Darwinism, the current atmosphere of intolerance is unhealthy for science, and it's unhealthy for a free society.

Conservatives who are discomfited by the continuing debate over Darwin's theory need to understand that it is not about to go away. It is not going away, because the accumulating discoveries of science undercut rather than confirm the claim of neo-Darwinism. It is not going away, because Darwinism fundamentally challenges the traditional Western understanding of human nature and the universe. Finally, it is not going away, because free people do not like to be told that there are some questions they are not allowed to ask and some answers they are not allowed to question.

If conservatives want to address root causes rather than just symptoms, they need to join the debate over Darwinism, not scorn it or ignore it.

SOURCE: John G. West, "Debate Over Evolution Not Going Away," *Human Events*, November 13, 2006: 15–16. Reprinted courtesy of *Human Events*.

ANALYSIS

Since the publication of Charles Darwins's *Origin of Species*, conservative thinkers and supporters of traditional religious belief have raised objections to the theory of evolution. One major argument, championed by William Jennings Bryan, involves the consequences of the theory. If the general population accepts the theory of evolution, then traditional moral standards will be rejected. Darwin's theory appears to threaten the notions of "irreducible and unchanging truths" and "a universal code of morality" that are considered crucial to the continuation of ordered societies and their dependence on maintaining personal responsibility and the basic family unit. Conservative critics also associate the theory of evolution with direct applications of scientific knowledge to human and social conditions, such as attempts, through eugenics, to produce a biologically superior human being. Scientists supposedly claim an ability to govern and improve society that others do not possess, and consequently scientists should be granted special authority. Such proposals West associates with groups that advocate left-liberal positions on such other issues as stem-cell research, global warming, and cloning. Contrary to the claims of supporters of the theory of evolution, and the mainstream scientific community as a whole, who look upon those opposed to the theory of evolution as attempting to squelch objective scientific research (the so-called "war on science"), those who question the theory of evolution brand mainstream scientists with the same charge, arguing that any attempt to raise objections to the theory are not allowed to participate in academic institutions. The Scopes trial of 1925, challenging a Tennessee law prohibiting the teaching of the theory of evolution in the public schools, continues to stand out for proponents of evolution as the representative example of attempts to thwart objective scientific investigation and education. In addition to criticizing certain conservatives who disparage Intelligent Design theory, West mentions liberals such as Kurt Vonnegut who have questioned the theory of evolution. In Vonnegut's case, this is not surprising, given the preference of literary people for the symbolic and their suspicion of science as the destroyer of mystery, and Vonnegut's questioning of science and technology through his fictional works, including *Cat's Cradle*, a novel in which a discovery resulting from a scientist's idle curiosity leads to the destruction of the world. However, critics of creationism and Intelligent Design theory continue to assert that these approaches to biology ultimately rely on religious belief, and therefore have no role to play in scientific research.

"Ben Stein's Trojan Horse: Mobilizing the State House and Local News Agenda"

- **Document:** Matthew C. Nisbet's review of the film documentary *Expelled: No Intelligence Allowed* with actor and conservative activist Ben Stein.
- **Date:** September/October 2008.
- **Where:** *Skeptical Inquirer* magazine.
- **Significance:** Nisbet's review emphasizes what he considers the misleading claims that Ben Stein makes in this documentary criticizing the theory of evolution.

DOCUMENT

Back in April 2008, as the documentary *Expelled: No Intelligence Allowed* premiered in more than 1,000 theaters across the country, I gathered with friends for a Friday-evening screening in downtown Washington, D.C. The medium-sized Regal Cinemas theater was about 80 percent full, with an audience that appeared to be the typical urban professional crowd for the surrounding arts and entertainment district, a demographic that is more likely to read the *New York Times* at a coffee house on Sunday than to attend church.

As I watched the film and monitored audience reaction, I grew convinced that although *Expelled's* claims have been thoroughly debunked (NCSE [National Center for Science Education] 2008; *Scientific American* 2008; see also the critique in SI [*Skeptical Inquirer*], May/June 2008 by Dan Whipple and Nathan Bupp's piece in SI, July/August 2008), the documentary's long-term impact remains dangerously underestimated.

In the film, the comedic actor Ben Stein plays the role of a conservative Michael Moore, taking viewers on an investigative journey into the realm of "Big Science," an institution in which, Stein concludes, "scientists are not allowed to even think thoughts that involve an intelligent creator." *Expelled* outrageously suggests that Darwinism, as Stein calls evolution, led to the Holocaust. He also suggests that scientists have been denied tenure and that research has been suppressed, all in the service of hiding the supposedly fatal flaws in evolutionary theory.

Expelled employs several techniques common to political advertising. First, Stein's narrative relies heavily on the use of metaphor. For example, his version of the "3 A.M. phone call" is to bookend the film with historic footage of the Berlin Wall and a repetitive emphasis on freedom as a central American value. The sinister implication is that "Darwinism" has led to atheism, fascism, and communism. As a corollary, if Americans can join Stein in tearing down the wall of censorship in science, it would open the way to religious freedom and cultural renewal.

Expelled also strategically manipulates emotions while playing to ignorance among movie-going audiences. For example, as a way of triggering anger, Stein misleadingly defines celebrity atheists such as Richard Dawkins, P. Z. Myers, Daniel Dennett, and Christopher Hitchens as representatives of "establishment science." In interviews, as these scientists compare religion to fairies, hobgoblins, and knitting, the implication for viewers is that in order to leave room for God in society, intelligent design (ID) needs to be taken seriously.

In the screening I attended, somewhat predictably there were chuckles and positive laughter in reaction to Stein and audibly negative emotion directed toward the comments of Dawkins and the other scientists. As the film credits rolled to the end, there was even a strong round of *approving applause*.

Expelled's misleading emphasis on atheist punditry as representative of science even had film critics bristling. In reviews otherwise harshly dismissive of the documentary, Jeffrey Kluger of *Time* magazine described Dawkins and Myers's performances as "sneering, finger in the eye atheism," while Justin Chang of *Variety* referred to Dawkins' commentary as "atheism taken to hateful extremes."

There is no way of telling how representative the Washington, D.C., audience might be of the nation at large, although I have observed similar emotional reactions among university students with whom I have tested *Expelled*'s YouTube clips. At various other locations across the country, several bloggers reported that they were the only person in the theater for a Sunday matinee or a weekly evening show. One thing, however, is certain: by documentary box-office standards, *Expelled* has made its mark.

With more than $7.5 million in ticket sales according to the Web site Box Office Mojo, Stein's propaganda film ranks as either the sixth or seventh top grossing public affairs documentary of all time. Only Al Gore's *An Inconvenient Truth*, Morgan Spurlock's *Supersize Me*, and Michael Moore's *Fahrenheit 9/11*, *Sicko*, and *Bowling for Columbine* have grossed more than *Expelled*. (After adjusting for inflation, add Moore's 1989 *Roger and Me*.)

Premise Media, Inc., the production company that marketed *Expelled*, targeted two key demographics for the film. Predictably, a main segment included evangelicals and social conservatives, with the production company advertising heavily on political talk-radio stations and by way of Christian media and church networks. But in running advertising spots during *The Daily Show* and on *CNN*, the company

Al Gore's *An Inconvenient Truth* (2006), a documentary film recreating his climate change presentation, exponentially increased public awareness about this issue. Here, Gore speaks on climate change at the United Nations. (UN Photo/Mark Garten)

also hoped to appeal to less religious twenty- and thirty-somethings, an audience more familiar with Ben Stein as a comedic actor and satirist than with the recent political skirmishes over evolution.

Despite these savvy marketing efforts, *Expelled* was unlikely to break the forces of ideological selectivity that have snared even the most successful documentaries. For example, polling data [show] that the theater audience for *Fahrenheit 9/11*, which earned $120 million at the box office, skewed heavily liberal and was more likely to live in "blue" rather than "red" counties of the country (Pew 2004). Moreover, a recent study finds that rather than converting movie-goers to support John Kerry during the 2004 election, the effects of the film were most likely to reinforce and intensify already strong anti-Bush sentiment (Stroud 2007). In short, *Fahrenheit 9/11* helped activate and mobilize the existing anti-Bush segment rather than persuade new converts.

Survey data specific to *Inconvenient Truth* and *Sicko* reveal similar selectivity bias and ideological reinforcement (Nisbet 2008; Kaiser 2007). Although similar data is not yet available for *Expelled*, according to news reports, Premise Media's own exit survey data from theaters in six states showed that 80 percent of the film's viewers during opening weekend considered themselves "born again" Christians (Hall 2008).

Yet, *Expelled*'s influence stretches well beyond the theater and any ideological impact on viewers. As I reviewed in a recent report to the Ford Foundation, these indirect influences can be tracked across several different dimensions, with the most important impacts related to the general news and policy agenda (Nisbet 2007).

For example, although many mainstream film critics have savaged the documentary, Stein's arguments have received either uncritical or positive coverage in reviews at Christian or conservative Web sites, in appearances on *CNN with Wolf Blitzer*, ABC's *Jimmy Kimmel Live*, and by way of strong endorsements on conservative talk radio and cable news programs such as Rush Limbaugh, *Headline News'* Glenn Beck, and Fox News' *Hannity and Colmes*.

Since the 2005 Dover court decision, intelligent design had been off the national news radar, yet *Expelled* helped restart the media conversation, at least temporarily. Perhaps most importantly, by way of columns, op-eds, uncritical features, and letters to the editor at local newspapers across the country, the film offered an opening and a new "authoritative" reference point of ID proponents to once again misleadingly argue that there are holes in evolutionary theory and censorship in schools.

Perhaps most troubling has been the advanced screenings for policymakers, interest groups, and other influentials. *Expelled*'s producers have previewed the film for the Missouri and Florida state legislatures, connecting the film's message to a proposed "Academic Freedom Act" in each state that would encourage teachers to discuss the alleged flaws in evolutionary science. As Stein strategically framed the matter at the screening in Florida: "This bill is not about teaching intelligent design. It's about free speech" (Julian 2008).

With each of these dozens of screenings there has likely been a strong intensification of commitment and emotion among the conservative activist base in attendance along with advocacy training, the raising of money, and the distribution of other resources, such as DVDs and literature. In particular, *Expelled* provides these activists with an increased repertoire of arguments, talking points, and examples to use with neighbors and friends.

There is even the possibility that the screening helped anti-evolution groups link up with the new conservative coalition partners not previously involved in the issue. For example, Stein has shown *Expelled* at several meetings and venues here in Washington, D.C., including a special screening for Congressional staffers.

When the film moves to DVD distribution, expect more of these types of *Expelled* screenings, house parties, and church gatherings across the country, all aimed at mobilizing a political movement in favor of anti-evolution bills. As *Reason* magazine's Ronald Bailey (2008) reports, at an April 15 press conference at the conservative Heritage Foundation, *Expelled*'s financial backer Walt Ruloff said that as many as twenty-six states had been targeted this year [2008] with so-called "freedom bills." So far, bills introduced in Florida, Alabama, and Missouri have been voted down while similar bills are still up for full legislative vote in South Carolina and Louisiana (NCSE 2008b).

Over the next few years, *Expelled*'s enduring impact will be to serve as a vehicle for recruiting and mobilizing anti-evolution activists at the state and local level across the country. The targeted audience will include school-board members, church leaders, legislators, journalists, and other opinion leaders. Shown in its entirety or perhaps more effectively repackaged in 10–15 minute outtakes, these screenings will combine emotionally powerful metaphors with the commentary of various outspoken atheists to manipulate viewers' understanding of the important differences between science, religion, and atheism.

REFERENCES

Bailey, Ronald. 2008. April 16. Flunk this movie. *Reason*. Available online at www
   .reason.com/news/show/125988.html.

Box Office Mojo. Gross earnings for documentary genre since 1982. Available online at
   www.boxofficemojo.com/genres/chart/?id=documentary.htm.

Chang, Justin. 2008. April 11. Review: Expelled: No intelligence allowed. *Variety*. Available
   online at www.variety.com/review/VE1117936783.html?categoryid=31&cs=1.

Hall, Cheryl. 2008. April 28. Intelligent design documentary creates stir. *Dallas Morning
   News*. Available for purchase at www.dallasnews.com.

Julian, Liam. 2008. March 28. Academic anarchy. *Tampa Bay Tribune*. Available online at www2.tbo.com/content/2008/mar/28/na-academic-anarchy.

Kaiser Family Foundation. 2007. Awareness and perceptions of *Sicko*. Available online at www.kff.org/kaiserpolls/pomr082707pkg.cfm.

Kluger, Jeffrey. 2008. April 10. Ben Stein dukes it out with Darwin. *Time*. Available online at www.time.com/time/magazine/article/0,9171,1729703,00.html.

National Center for Science Education. 2008a. Expelled exposed. Available online at www.expelledexposed.com/.

National Center for Science Education. 2008b. Louisiana's latest creationism bill moves to House floor. Available online at http://ncseweb.org/news/2008/05/louisianas-latest-creationism-bill-moves-to-house-floor-00152.

Nisbet, Matthew C. 2007. Understanding the social impact of documentary film. In K. Hirsch's Documentaries on a mission: How non-profits are making movies for public engagement. A Future of Public Media Project, funded by the Ford Foundation. Center for Social Media, American University. Available online at www.centerforsocial media.org/files/pdf/docs_on_a_mission.pdf.

———. 2008. Moving beyond Gore's message: A look back (and ahead) at climate change communications. Committee for Skeptical Inquiry. Available online at www.csicop.org/scienceandmedia/beyond-gores-message.

Pew Internet and American Life Project. 2004. Data memo. Available online at http://www.pewinternet.org/Reports/2005/Political-documentaries-in-2004/Data-Memo.aspx?r=1.

Scientific American. 2008. Expelled: No intelligence allowed: *Scientific American*'s take. Available online at www.sciam.com/article.cfm?id=sciam-reviews-expelled.

Stroud, Natalie Jomini. 2007. Media effects, selective exposure, and Fahrenheit 9/11. *Political Communication*, 24 (4): 415–432.

Whipple, Dan. 2008. Expelling all reason. *Skeptical Inquirer* May/June, 32 (3): 52–53.

SOURCE: Matthew C. Nisbet, "Ben Stein's Trojan Horse: Mobilizing the State House and Local News Agenda," *Skeptical Inquirer* 32 (September/October 2008), 16–18. Reprinted courtesy of *Skeptical Inquirer*.

ANALYSIS

Expelled: No Intelligence Allowed, with Ben Stein, has elicited negative responses from many, including Matthew C. Nisbet, who consider challenges to the theory of evolution to be nothing more than warmed-over biblical creationism. Labeled the "conservative Michael Moore," Stein lodges allegations against evolution theory, associating it with the Nazi Holocaust, eugenics, and a decline in moral values generally. In addition, Stein claims that supporters of the theory dominate institutions of higher learning and do not allow any of their colleagues to question the theory, which amounts to asserting that scientists have abandoned any pretense to objective investigation, opting instead for liberal ideological purity. What is claimed to be at stake is free speech and academic freedom. Those responding to this charge present a very different perspective. Rather than silencing scientific dissent, scientists view themselves as being attacked from outside the scientific community and judged by popular opinion, to which media productions such as *Expelled* appeal. As commentators such as Chris Mooney assert, the public attacks by those supporting Intelligent Design and other claimed alternatives to the theory of evolution not only attempt to introduce religious belief into scientific investigation, but also divert science away from its normal activities. Hence, scientists who accept evolution as a well-established theory resist taking seriously claims they consider to be non-scientific, and when they do respond, they tend to be dismissive.

"Creationist Perspectives"

- **Document:** Excerpt from the National Academy of Sciences Institute of Medicine, *Science, Evolution, and Creationism.*
- **Date:** 2008.
- **Where:** Published in Washington, DC.
- **Significance:** Scientists responding to the Intelligent Design movement argue that the very nature of science must involve the development of hypotheses and theories that are testable. Evolution theory meets these criteria and evidence continues to mount in favor of the theory. In contrast, they assert that Intelligent Design and creationism fail to meet the standards of science.

DOCUMENT

Advocates of the ideas collectively known as "creationism" and, recently, "intelligent design creationism" hold a wide variety of views. Most broadly, a "creationist" is someone who rejects natural scientific explanations of the known universe in favor of special creation by a supernatural entity. Creationism in its various forms is not the same thing as belief in God because . . . many believers as well as many mainstream religious groups accept the findings of science, including evolution. Nor is creationism necessarily tied to Christians who interpret the Bible literally. Some non-Christian religious believers also want to replace scientific explanations with their own religion's supernatural accounts of physical phenomena.

In the United States, various views of creationism typically have been promoted by small groups of politically active religious fundamentalists who believe that only a supernatural entity could account for the physical changes in the universe and for the biological diversity of life on Earth. But even these creationists hold very different views. Some, known as "young Earth" creationists, believe the biblical account that the universe and the Earth were created just a few thousand years ago.

Proponents of this form of creationism also believe that all living things, including humans, were created in a very short period of time in essentially the forms in which they exist today. Other creationists, known as "old Earth" creationists, accept that the Earth may be very old but reject other scientific findings regarding the evolution of living things.

No scientific evidence supports these viewpoints. On the contrary . . . several independent lines of evidence indicate that the Earth is about 4.5 billion years old and that the universe is about 14 billion years old. Rejecting the evidence for these age estimates would mean rejecting not just biological evolution but also fundamental discoveries of modern physics, chemistry, astrophysics, and geology.

Some creationists believe that Earth's present form and the distribution of fossils can be explained by a worldwide flood. But this claim also is at odds with observations and evidence understood scientifically. The belief that Earth's sediments, with their fossils, were deposited in a short period does not accord either with the known processes of sedimentation or with the estimated volume of water needed to deposit sediments on the top of some of Earth's highest mountains.

Creationists sometimes cite what they claim to be an incomplete fossil record as evidence that living things were created in their modern forms. But this argument ignores the rich and extremely detailed record of evolutionary history that paleontologists and other biologists have constructed over the past two centuries and are continuing to construct. Paleontological research has filled in many of the parts of the fossil record that were incomplete in Charles Darwin's time. The claim that the fossil record is "full of gaps" that undermine evolution is simply false. Indeed, paleontologists now know enough about the ages of sediments to predict where they will be able to find particularly significant transitional fossils, as happened with *Tiktaalik* and the ancestors of modern humans. Researchers also are using new techniques, such as computed axial tomography (CT), to learn even more about the internal structures and composition of delicate bones of fossils. Exciting new discoveries of fossils continue to be reported in both the scientific literature and popular media.

Another compelling feature of the fossil record is its consistency. Nowhere on Earth are fossils from dinosaurs, which went extinct 65 million years ago, found together with fossils from humans, who evolved in just the last few million years. Nowhere are the fossils of mammals found in sediments that are more than about 220 million years old. Whenever creationists point to sediments where these relationships appear to be altered or even reversed, scientists have clearly demonstrated that this reversal has resulted from the folding of geological strata over or under others. Sediments containing the fossils of only unicellular organisms appear earlier in the fossil record than do sediments containing the remains of both unicellular and multicellular organisms. The consequence of fossils across Earth's sediments points unambiguously toward the occurrence of evolution.

Creationists sometimes argue that the idea of evolution must remain hypothetical because "no one has ever seen evolution occur." This kind of statement also reveals that some creationists misunderstand an important characteristic of scientific reasoning. Scientific conclusions are not limited to direct observation but often depend on inferences that are made by applying reason to observations. Even with the launch of Earth-orbiting spacecraft, scientists could not directly see the Earth going around the Sun. But they inferred from a wealth of independent measurements that the Sun is at the center of the solar system. Until the recent development of extremely powerful microscopes, scientists could not observe atoms, but the behavior of physical objects left no doubt about the atomic nature of matter. Scientists hypothesized the existence of viruses for many years before microscopes became powerful enough to see them.

Thus, for many areas of science, scientists have not directly observed the objects (such as genes and atoms) or the phenomena (such as the Earth going around the Sun) that are now well-established facts. Instead, they have confirmed them indirectly by observational and experimental evidence. Evolution is no different. Indeed . . . evolutionary science provides one of the best examples of a deep understanding based on scientific reasoning.

This contention that nobody has seen evolution occurring further ignores the overwhelming evidence that evolution has taken place and is continuing to occur. The annual changes in influenza viruses and the emergence of bacteria resistant to antibiotics are both products of evolutionary forces. Another example of ongoing evolution is the appearance of mosquitoes resistant to various insecticides, which has contributed to a resurgence of malaria in Africa and elsewhere. The transitional fossils that have been found in abundance since Darwin's time reveal how species continually give rise to successor species that, over time, produce radically changed body forms and functions. It also is possible to directly observe many of the specific processes by which evolution occurs. Scientists regularly do experiments using microbes and other model systems that directly test evolutionary hypotheses.

Creationists reject such scientific facts in part because they do not accept evidence drawn from natural processes that they consider to be at odds with the Bible. But science cannot test supernatural possibilities. To young Earth creationists, no amount of empirical evidence that the Earth is billions of years old is likely to refute their claim that the world is actually young but that God simply made it *appear* to be old. Because such appeals to the supernatural are not testable using the rules and processes of scientific inquiry, they cannot be a part of science.

Some members of the newer school of creationists have temporarily set aside the question of whether the solar system, the galaxy, and the universe are billions or just thousands of years old. But these creationists unite in contending that the physical universe and living things show evidence of "intelligent design." They argue that certain biological structures are so complex that they could not have evolved through processes

---

DID YOU KNOW?

Texas Changes Policy on Science Education

As in other states, Texas has experienced conflict over science education—specifically the teaching of the theory of evolution—in the public schools. For twenty years the Texas State Board of Education maintained a provision in education policy permitting public schools to teach "both the strengths and weaknesses" of the theory of evolution, a phrase that created controversy between science educators and those supporting some version of creationism or Intelligent Design. However, in January 2008, a seven-member conservative group on the board failed in their efforts to keep the provision. Hence, the new policy, which was expected to become effective in the 2010–2011 school year, would eliminate the previous wording, and students would be encouraged to "analyze and evaluate scientific explanation using empirical evidence, logical reasoning, and experimental and observational testing." Opponents of the new standard argued that freedom of speech and freedom of religion were at stake, while supporters claimed that the revised policy allowed for discussion and ultimately proper science education.

of undirected mutation and natural selection, a condition they call "irreducible complexity." Echoing theological arguments that predate the theory of evolution, they contend that biological organisms must be designed in the same way that a mousetrap or a clock is designed—that in order for the device to work properly, all of its components must be available simultaneously. If one component is missing or changed, the device will fail to operate properly. Because even such "simple" biological structures as the flagellum of a bacterium are so complex, proponents of intelligent design creationism argue that the probability of all of their components being produced and simultaneously available through random processes of mutation are infinitesimally small. The appearance of more complex biological structures (such as the vertebrate eye) or functions (such as the immune system) is impossible through natural processes, according to this view, and so must be attributed to a transcendent intelligent designer.

However, the claims of intelligent design creationists are disproven by the findings of modern biology. Biologists have examined each of the molecular systems claimed to be the products of design and have shown how they could have arisen through natural processes. For example, in the case of the bacterial flagellum, there is no single, uniform structure that is found in all flagellar bacteria. There are many types of flagella, some simpler than others, and many species of bacteria do not have flagella to aid in their movement. Thus, other components of bacterial cell membranes are likely the precursors of the proteins found in various flagella. In addition, some bacteria inject toxins into other cells through proteins that are secreted from the bacterium and that are very similar in their molecular structure to the proteins in parts of flagella. This similarity indicates a common evolutionary origin, where small changes in the structure and organization of secretory proteins could serve as the basis for flagellar proteins. Thus, flagellar proteins are not irreducibly complex.

Evolutionary biologists also have demonstrated how complex biochemical mechanisms, such as the clotting of blood or the mammalian immune system, could have evolved from simpler precursor systems. With the clotting of blood, some of the components of the mammalian system were present in earlier organisms, as demonstrated by the organisms living today (such as fish, reptiles, and birds) that are descended from these mammalian precursors. Mammalian clotting systems have built on these earlier components.

Existing systems also can acquire new functions. For example, a particular system might have one task in a cell and then become adapted through evolutionary processes for different use. The *Hox* genes . . . are a prime example of evolution finding new uses for existing systems. Molecular biologists have discovered that a particularly important mechanism through which biological systems acquire additional functions is gene duplication. Segments of DNA are frequently duplicated when cells divide, so that a cell has multiple copies of one or more genes. If these multiple copies are passed on to offspring, one copy of a gene can serve the original function in a cell while the other copy is able to accumulate changes that ultimately result in a new function. The biochemical mechanisms responsible for many cellular processes show clear evidence for historical duplications of DNA regions.

In addition to its scientific failings, this and other standard creationist arguments are fallacious in that they are based on a false dichotomy. Even if their negative arguments against evolution were correct, that would not establish the creationists' claims. There may be alternative explanations. For example, it would be incorrect to conclude that because there is no evidence that it is raining outside, it must be sunny. Other explanations also might be possible. Science requires testable evidence for a hypothesis, not just challenges against one's opponent. Intelligent design is not a scientific concept because it cannot be empirically tested.

Creationists sometimes claim that scientists have a vested interest in the concept of biological evolution and are unwilling to consider other possibilities. But this claim, too, misrepresents science. Scientists continually test their ideas against observations and submit their work to their colleagues for critical peer review of ideas, evidence, and conclusions before a scientific paper is published in any respected scientific journal. Unexplained observations are eagerly pursued because they can be signs of important new science or problems with an existing hypothesis or theory. History is replete with scientists challenging accepted theory by offering new evidence and more comprehensive explanations to account for natural phenomena. Also, science has a competitive element as well as a cooperative one. If one scientist clings to particular ideas despite evidence to the contrary, another scientist will attempt to replicate relevant experiments and will not hesitate to publish conflicting evidence. If there were serious problems in evolutionary science, many scientists would be eager to win fame by being the first to provide a better testable alternative. That there are no viable alternatives to evolution in the scientific literature is not because of vested interests or censorship but because evolution has been and continues to be solidly supported by evidence.

The potential utility of science also demands openness to new ideas. If petroleum geologists could find more oil and gas by interpreting the record of sedimentary rocks (where deposits of oil and natural gas are found) as having resulted from a single flood, they would certainly favor the idea of such a flood, but they do not. Instead, petroleum geologists agree with other geologists that sedimentary rocks are the products of billions of years of Earth's history. Indeed, petroleum geologists have been pioneers in the recognition of fossil deposits that were formed over millions of years in such environments as meandering rivers, deltas, sandy barrier beaches, and coral reefs.

The arguments of creationists reverse the scientific process. They begin with an explanation that they are unwilling to alter—that supernatural forces have shaped biological or Earth systems—rejecting the basic requirements of science that hypotheses must be restricted to testable natural explanations. Their beliefs cannot be tested, modified, or rejected by scientific means and thus cannot be a part of the processes of science.

Despite the lack of scientific evidence for creationist positions, some advocates continue to demand that various forms of creationism be taught together with or in place of evolution in science classes. Many teachers are under considerable pressure from policy makers, school administrators, parents, and students to downplay or eliminate the teaching of evolution. As a result, many U.S. students lack access to information and ideas that are both integral to modern science and essential for making informed, evidence-based decisions about their own lives and our collective future.

Regardless of the careers that they ultimately select, to succeed in today's scientifi-cally and technologically sophisticated world, *all* students need a sound education in science. Many of today's fast-growing and high-paying jobs require a familiarity with the core concepts, applications, and implications of science. To make informed deci-sions about public policies, people need to know how scientific evidence supports those policies and whether that evidence was gathered using well-established scien-tific practice and principles. Learning about evolution is an excellent way to help students understand the nature, processes, and limits of science in addition to con-cepts about this fundamentally important contribution to scientific knowledge.

Given the importance of science in all aspects of modern life, the science curricu-lum should not be undermined with nonscientific material. Teaching creationist ideas in science classes confuses what constitutes science and what does not. It com-promises the objectives of public education and the goal of a high-quality science education.

SOURCE: Reprinted with permission from *Science, Evolution, and Creationism,* © 2008 by the National Academy of Sciences, Courtesy of the National Academies Press, Washington, D.C.

ANALYSIS

Supporters of Intelligent Design contend that so-called scientific materialism presents a threat to western culture's moral, social, and political traditions, and to a theistic perspective that human beings and the natural world were created by God —in effect, that an intelligence *intended* that human beings be present on Earth. However, in order to challenge the theory of evolution from more than a moral or religious standpoint, opponents of evolution must confront evolutionary biologists on their own turf by arguing that the theory contains various weaknesses as science and that a credible scientific alternative exists. To some extent this challenge presents scientists with a dilemma: do they try to ignore Intelligent Design, regarding its proponents as nonscientific, thus leaving the claims unanswered; or do they engage in discussion with proponents of ID, thus possibly granting a level of legiti-macy to what they consider pseudo-science? In fact, some ID supporters state that their objective is to "teach the controversy," thus purportedly raising scientific objections to evolution theory.

Advocates of evolution theory emphasize five points in their critique of ID and other varieties of creationism. First, contrary to the views of "young Earth" creation-ists, they point to scientific evidence that the earth is estimated to be 4.5 billion years old rather than just a few thousand years old. Second, responding to the crea-tionist emphasis on the incompleteness of the fossil record, evolutionary biologists note that research since Darwin's time has completed much of the fossil record. Third, lack of direct observation does not necessarily limit scientific conclusions; indirect examination often is sufficient to provide evidence supporting a theory. Fourth, in response to Intelligent Design's "irreducible complexity" argument, biologists have explained how molecular systems could have resulted from natural processes. Finally, contrary to creationist charges, scientific investigation is self-correcting in that scientists, as a basic part of their enterprise, engage in challenging accepted theory. According to supporters of evolution theory, Intelligent Design theory is based upon unalterable assumptions.

Occasionally scientists have been willing to engage in discussions with advocates of Intelligent Design, especially when they perceive that the quality of science education may be threatened. The *Dover* case represents such an instance in which supporters of the theory of evolution confronted Intelligent Design advocates, challenging their claim to scientific status. What they want to avoid is carrying on the "controversy" in the classroom, where they insist Intelligent Design, which they consider simply a version of creationism, has no place. However, the "middle ground" for many Americans in this case appears to be that evolution theory and Intelligent Design both should be taught in the public schools. Scott Keeter (2005), director of survey research at the Pew Research Center, reported survey findings indicating that as much as two-thirds of those interviewed during a twenty-year period "has supported teaching *both* accounts of the origins of life," a "compromise" alternative that Intelligent Design advocates would welcome, but the bulk of scientists would strongly oppose.

Commenting on scientific research more generally, Chris Mooney (2006) argues that those on the left as well as the right of the political spectrum have politicized various areas of scientific investigation—including embryonic stem cell research, evolutionary biology, and environmental pollution and global warming. Mooney acknowledges that liberals as well as conservatives have engaged in the abuse of scientific findings to further ideological causes, and considers ideological intervention into the scientific enterprise to have deleterious consequences for science and education as well as for society in general, which depends on objective scientific investigation.

The ideological origins of the notion that science, along with all other human activities, is based on subjective foundations and that scientific facts are "socially constructed" can be traced in part, according to mathematical physicist Alan Sokal (2008), to the postmodernist left. The arguments that left intellectuals such as sociologists of science Bruno Latour and Harry Collins expressed are used now by conservatives to attack scientific findings. Sokal, in agreement with Mooney's analysis, states that "The assault on reason and science now clearly comes from

DID YOU KNOW?

Galileo Then and Now

Galileo Galilei (1564–1642), an Italian astronomer, constructed a telescope to view the heavens and was tried as a heretic in 1633 for his scientific efforts. Although the Catholic Church held that the Earth resided at the center of the universe, Galileo concluded from evidence he collected that the Earth revolved around the sun, thus setting off a culture war in the seventeenth century between religious belief and scientific discoveries. The astronomer was convicted of the heresy charges, was forced to recant the heliocentric view, and spent the remainder of his life under house arrest. More than 350 years later, in 1992, Pope John Paul II announced that the judgment against Galileo was in error due to "tragic mutual incomprehension." In December 2008, as the 400th anniversary of Galileo's invention of the telescope approached, Pope Benedict XVI honored Galileo, stating that he was among those scientists who helped believers to "contemplate with gratitude the Lord's works." A month earlier, Cardinal Tarcisio Bertone proclaimed at a Vatican conference that Galileo "lovingly cultivated his faith and his profound religious conviction." Once branded a heretic, the Catholic Church has begun to rehabilitate Galileo into a defender of the faith. Could Charles Darwin experience a similar reassessment once the current culture wars fade from memory?

the right, led by an unholy (and uneasy) alliance of big corporations seeking to escape environmental and safety regulations and religious fundamentalists seeking to impose their dogmas on education and health policy" (2008, xv). Some of these left intellectuals now admit that their proclamations of subjectivity in science have supplied to conservatives the intellectual resources to question scientific consensus on such issues as global warming and biological evolution, thus creating the foundations for an interesting cultural alliance of left and right against the mainline scientific community.

FURTHER READING

Baird, Robert M., and Stuart E. Rosenbaum, editors. *Intelligent Design: Science or Religion? Critical Perspectives*. Amherst, NY: Prometheus Books, 2007.

Behe, Michael. *The Edge of Evolution: The Search for the Limits of Darwinism*. New York: Simon & Schuster, 2007.

Brockman, John, editor. *Intelligent Thought: Science Versus the Intelligent Design Movement*. New York: Vintage Books, 2006.

Brush, Stephen G. "Should the History of Science Be Rated X?" *Science* 183 (March 1974), 1164–72.

Keeter, Scott. "What's Not Evolving Is Public Opinion." *The Washington Post* (October 2, 2005). www.washingtonpost.com/wp-dyn/content/article/2005/09/30/AR2005093002083_pf.html.

Koertge, Noretta, ed. *A House Built on Sand: Exposing Postmodernist Myths about Science*. New York: Oxford University Press, 1998.

Kuhn, Thomas S. *The Structure of Scientific Revolutions*. Third edition. Chicago: University of Chicago Press, 1996.

Mooney, Chris. *The Republican War on Science*. Jackson, TN: Perseus Books, 2006.

Pennock, Robert T., and Michael Ruse, eds. *But Is It Science? The Philosophical Question in the Creation/Evolution Controversy*. Amherst, NY: Prometheus Books, 2008.

Ruse, Michael. *Can a Darwinian Be a Christian? The Relationship Between Science and Religion*. New York: Cambridge University Press, 2001.

Sokal, Alan. *Beyond the Hoax: Science, Philosophy and Culture*. New York: Oxford University Press, 2008.

Sokal, Alan, and Jean Bricmont. *Fashionable Nonsense: Postmodern Intellectuals' Abuse of Science*. New York: St. Martin's Press, 1997.

8

THE U.S. ROLE IN THE WORLD AND THE GLOBAL CULTURE WAR

Document: Robert de Mattei, "A Clash of Civilizations," in *Holy War, Just War: Islam and Christendom at War* (2007)

Document: Juan Cole, "Combating Muslim Extremism: America Should Give Diplomacy a Chance" (2007)

Document: Roger Scruton, "The Political Problem of Islam" (2002)

Document: Barack Obama, "Remarks by the President on a New Beginning" (2009)

"A Clash of Civilizations"

- *Document:* Excerpt from Robert de Mattei, *Holy War, Just War: Islam and Christendom at War* (Rockford, IL: Chronicles Press).
- *Date:* 2007.
- *Where:* Published by the Rockford Institute, Rockford, Illinois.
- *Significance:* Conservative Christians assert that Islam and Christianity were historically conflicting religions; that Western civilization developed distinct cultural artifacts, including a superior legal system; and that Islam currently remains hostile to Christianity.

DOCUMENT

Islam may appear as a complex and protean reality lacking an institutionalized core, but beyond the ancient religious divisions (such as those between Sunnis and Shiites) and the new ones (more often than not political and strategic in nature), the Koran remains the one single reference point just as the goal remains one: namely, the conquest of the world, according to the words of the Prophet that state that "the whole earth is a mosque." Irrespective of its several doctrines, movements, organizations or peoples, Islam is in fact one single community of believers, the *Umma*, subject to one single law, the *sharia*.

"The *Umma* of the Muslims is the final stage of humanity since it is the authentic community of the elect people," remarks Guolo. [1] "The pan-Islamism of the *Umma*, in its radical version, closes the circle of the jihad's offensive vision." [2]

There are countries that accept Western secularization and others, such as Saudi Arabia, that seek to separate the West's technology from its culture. However, as Bernard Lewis notes, "in most Muslim countries Islam still remains the supreme yardstick of group identity and allegiance. It's Islam which makes for one's ego to be distinguished from the other." [3]

The "other" *par excellence* is nowadays represented by the West, which means Europe and the United States. For Muslims, the West is not only a theological mistake but a corrupt and degrading reality, responsible for the moral degeneration of the whole world.

The incompatibility of Islam and the West, this clash of civilizations, is rooted, even more than in the obvious religious differences, in the fact that Islam lacks any distinction between the political and religious spheres.

The propelling force behind this clash, as rightly pointed out by Samuel Huntington, does not lie in "fundamentalism" but in the very nature of Islam. [4] Islam, which does not forget and whose justice is an eye for eye and a tooth for a tooth, regrets the loss of [the Spanish provinces of] Cordoba, Granada, and [the Sicilian city of] Palermo and does not forgive Europe for having dominated Islamic nations for centuries. [5]

The core doctrine of both traditional and contemporary Islam is that of *jihad*, [6] which, says Guolo, "manifests itself as a pure form of the new religious civil world war, which holds in radical Islam its warring party." [7]

The terrorist attacks on New York's City's World Trade Center (above), the Pentagon, and United Airlines Flight 93, which evidently was intended by the attackers to be redirected to a target in Washington, DC, ushered in a defensive new era in American history. E24 (http://www.bigfoto.com)

While the West debates modern *versus* postmodern, Muslims do not plan to "modernize" Islam but to overcome the West and "Islamicize" modernity. [8] By the same token, the West must not be confused with its modernization, nor with consumer society, which is saturated with neopaganism. The peculiar features of the West, remarks Huntington, already existed considerably before its modernization: "The West was the West long before it was modern. The central characteristics of the West, those which distinguish it from other civilizations, outdate the modernization of the West." [9]

We must face the fact that the Islamic vision of the world is not only opposed to our secularized and modern world, but even more so to the traditional Christian society of the West. Islam is antimodern also in its most Westernized variety, such as Saudi Arabia's, and even in its most secularized variety, such as Iraq's, but, above all, is always and utterly radically anti-Christian. Before it was anti-Western and antimodern, Islam was anti-Christian. In the clash of civilizations that is ushering in the 21st century, the challenge of Islam is first of all a cultural and moral one. The West, which, in the course of its history, defined itself in part by defending itself against Islam, is today doomed to defeat if it deludes itself into opposing Muslims with the ideology of secularization. The only form of civilization that can prevail over Islam is unquestionably the Christian one.

NOTES

[1] Renzo Guolo, *Il partito di Dio. L'Islam radicale contro l'Occidente* (Milan: Guerini e Associati, 1994), pp. 58–59.

[2] *Ibid.*, p. 75.

[3] Bernard Lewis, *La rinascita islamica* (Bologna: Il Mulino, 1991), pp. 14–15.

[4] Samuel P. Huntington, *The Clash of Civilizations and the Remaking of World Order* (New York: Simon and Schuster, 2003), pp. 286–87.

[5] Alexandre Del Valle, *L'Islamisme et les Etats-Unis. Une alliance contre L'Europe* (Lausanne: L'Age d'Homme, 1997), pp. 14–15.

[6] Valeria Fiorani Piacentini, "Il pensiero militare nel mondo islamico," vol. I, "Credenti e non credenti: il pensiero militare e la dottrina del jihad," *Rivista Militare* (1991), p. 233.

[7] Renzo Guolo, *Avanguardia della fede. L'Islamismo tra ideologia e politica* (Milan: Guerini e Associati, 1999), p. 28.

[8] Olivier Roy, *Généalogie de l'Islamisme* (Paris: Hachette, 1995), pp. 53, 62.

[9] Huntington, *op. cit.*, p. 69.

SOURCE: Robert de Mattei, *Holy War, Just War: Islam and Christendom at War* (Rockford, IL: Chronicles Press, 2007), 52–53. Reprinted courtesy of the Rockford Institute—Chronicles Press.

ANALYSIS

With terrorist assaults against Western nations, including the September 11, 2001, attacks on the World Trade Center in New York and the Pentagon, the March 2004 train bombing in Madrid, Spain, and the July 2005 subway bombing in London, England, many conservative Christians responded with assertions that such attacks were not the work of isolated groups within the worldwide Muslim community that have perverted the religion's message of peace, but instead represent the basic nature of Islam as an aggressive religion ultimately bent on vanquishing Christianity and other religions. Conservative commentators such as Diana West emphasize the historical relationship between Islam and the dhimmi—non-Muslims who have lived in Islamic-dominated countries. West concludes that this relationship is "at best, a master-servant relationship, pitting an identifiable authority figure against an identifiable supplicant" (West 2007, 182). While the mainline press and Western leaders are accused of "dhimmitude"—attitudes and behavior that express inferiority and subservience to Islamic law (sharia), conservative Christians such as Roberto de Mattei, a professor of modern history at the University of Casino and a professor of the history of Christianity at the European University of Rome, highlight what they consider a long and continuing conflict between Islamic countries and the West that only can be won if those in the West acknowledge their Christian heritage.

Roger Scruton (2002), in the wake of the 2001 terrorist attacks, analyzed the distinctions between Western culture and the rest of the world. Tolerance, Scruton asserts, developed as a distinctly Western product and would have been an unlikely development of an Islamic regime (41–42). Contrary to Western tradition—which began perhaps with Thomas Hobbes in the seventeenth century and continued with the development of the liberal tradition—that differing conceptions of the good can be tolerated by the political authority, Muslims hold that the Islamic conception of the good exclusively "gives legitimacy to the political order: a thought which has the disturbing corollary that the political order is almost everywhere illegitimate, and nowhere more so than in the states where Islam is the official faith" (15).

Native Europeans often are more concerned than the United States about the clash of cultures between their traditional Christian, but increasingly secularized, societies and Muslim immigrants. Peter H. Schuck (2008, 371–72) notes that the approximately 2.5 million Muslims who reside in the United States are far less alienated from society than Muslims residing in European countries. A significant factor leading to the difference may be that although many Muslim families have been in the United States for at least three generations, Muslim migration

DID YOU KNOW?

Oriana Fallaci on Islam in Europe

When Italian author and journalist Oriana Fallaci died at the age of 77 in September 2006, obituaries noted her strong criticisms of Islam. Following the September 11, 2001, terrorist attacks, Fallaci began a verbal attack of Islam, asserting that radical Islam constituted a version of Nazi fascism. In *La rabbia e l'orgoglio* (2001; Eng. tr., *The Rage and the Pride*, 2002), she spoke out against Islamic terrorists and fundamentalism, and criticized European officials for making concessions to Muslim immigrants who refused to accept Western values and customs. Fallaci advocated Western resistance to jihad, which she saw as a war on Western civilization and freedom, including religious freedom. As a consequence of her expressed opinions, a court in Bergamo indicted Fallaci for allegedly "defaming Islam."

into European countries began in the 1950s and only more recently reached higher levels (372). In addition, Schuck suggests that the higher level of religious belief among Americans provides a more welcoming climate than the more secularized European countries. De Mattei, as a conservative Christian, would agree with Schuck's analysis about the significance of religious belief, but contends that a secular society fails to provide the cultural resources to resist what he considers the onslaught of the adherents of an aggressive religion into a traditionally Western culture.

"Combating Muslim Extremism: America Should Give Diplomacy a Chance"

- *Document:* An article by Juan Cole.
- *Date:* November 19, 2007.
- *Where:* *The Nation* magazine.
- *Significance:* Juan Cole presents a liberal view of the difficulties facing the United States and other Western democracies due to Muslim extremists and the terrorist attacks they foment. Cole critiques present government policy and makes recommendations for alternative strategies to limit the activities of extremist Muslim groups.

DOCUMENT

All the major Republican presidential candidates have bought into George W. Bush's rhetoric of a central struggle against Muslim extremism and have thus committed themselves to a generational, often self-generating war. By foregrounding this issue, they have ensured that it will be pivotal to the 2008 presidential race. The Democratic candidates have mostly been timid in critiquing Bush's "war on terror" or pointing out its dangers to the Republic, a failing that they must redress if they are to blunt their rivals' fearmongering.

Republican front-runner [in late 2007] Rudy Giuliani in his recent *Foreign Affairs* article complains that the United States has been on the "defensive" in the war on "radical Islamic fascism" and says with maddening vagueness that it must find ways of going "on the offensive." He promises that "this war will be long." Giuliani is being advised on such matters by Representative Peter King, who has complained that "unfortunately we have too many mosques in this country"; by Daniel Pipes, who has questioned the wisdom of allowing American Muslims to vote; and by Norman Podhoretz, author of *World War IV: The Long Struggle Against Islamofascism*. Combining the word "Islam" with a European term like "fascism" is profoundly offensive; a subtext of anti-Muslim bigotry pervades Giuliani's campaign, a sop to the Christian and Zionist right.

John McCain depicts withdrawal from Iraq as "defeat," saying in Michigan on September 21 that it "would strengthen Al Qaeda, empower Iran and other hostile powers in the Middle East, unleash a full-scale civil war in Iraq that could quite possibly provoke genocide there and destabilize the entire region." But continued occupation of Iraq, a major Muslim country, is just as likely to lead to the consequences McCain fears. Some front-runners, like Mitt Romney, argue for a big expansion in US military forces, without explaining how that would help with counterterrorism.

The Republican candidates have taken their cues from Bush and his Administration. They have continued to vastly exaggerate the threat from terror attacks (far more Americans have died for lack of healthcare or from hard drugs) and have demonized Muslims. India's Hindu-extremist RSS, the Tamil Tigers of

In January 2007, hundreds of protesters gathered outside the American Embassy in London to demand the closure of the U.S. prison camp at Guantanamo Bay, Cuba. Reported abuses at "Gitmo" inflamed public opinion in Muslim countries as well as in Western Europe and the United States itself. (Shutterstock)

Sri Lanka, the Lord's Resistance Army of Uganda, and Colombia's FARC (a hard-drug smuggler) are seldom referred to by Republican politicians worried about terrorists, even though all these movements have been extremely violent and have threatened US interests.

Advocates of the "war on terror" fantasize about the Muslim world as a Soviet Union-type challenge to the United States. In fact, the dozens of countries with majority Muslim populations are mostly strong allies of the United States. One, Turkey, is a NATO ally, and six (Morocco, Egypt, Jordan, Bahrain, Kuwait and Pakistan) are non-NATO allies. Only fourteen countries have this status, so Muslim states make up nearly half. The United States counts many other friends in the region, having significant frictions only with Sudan, Syria and Iran, and those are mixed pictures (Syria and Sudan helped against Al Qaeda, and Iran sought a strategic alliance with the United States against Saddam Hussein in early 2003).

The Republicans are playing Russian roulette with America's future with their bigoted anti-Muslim rhetoric. Muslims may constitute as much as a third of humankind by 2050, forming a vast market and a crucial labor pool. They will be sitting on the lion's share of the world's energy resources. The United States will increasingly have to compete with emerging rivals such as China and India for access to those Muslim resources and markets, and if its elites go on denigrating Muslims, America will be at a profound disadvantage during the next century.

Some Muslim extremist groups are indeed a threat, but they have not been dealt with appropriately. [President George W.] Bush has argued that terrorist groups have state backing, a principle that authorizes conventional war against their sponsor. In fact, asymmetrical terrorist groups can thrive in the interstices of states, and September 11 was solely an Al Qaeda operation. In his speech about the conquest of Iraq on the USS *Abraham Lincoln* on May 1, 2003, George W. Bush announced, "We have removed an ally of Al Qaeda, and cut off a source of terrorist funding." It was a bald-faced lie.

Imperial occupations under the pretext of fighting terrorism suck up scarce resources and multiply terrorism, and so are self-defeating. They benefit only the military-industrial complex and political elites pursuing American hegemony. The backlash is growing. Sympathy bombings deriving from Muslim distress at brutal US military actions against Iraqis have been undertaken in Madrid, London and Glasgow, and a handful of formerly secular Iraqi Sunnis have suddenly expressed interest in Al Qaeda.

Worse, the hypocritical Bush Administration has ties to Muslim terror groups. The US military, beholden to Iraqi Kurds for support, permits several thousand fighters of the PKK terrorist organization, which bombs people in Turkey, to make safe harbor in Iraqi Kurdistan. The Bush Administration has used against Tehran the expatriate Iranian Mujahedeen-e-Khalq terror network, on which Saddam Hussein bestowed a base in Iraq. Democrats have mysteriously declined to denounce these unsavory alliances.

The Administration clearly is not very interested in doing the hard work of dealing effectively with small fringe terrorist networks. That is why Osama bin Laden is at large and the CIA unit tracking him disbanded. Successful counterterrorism involves good diplomacy and good police work. A case in point is the plot last summer [2006] by young Muslim men in London to bomb several airliners simultaneously using liquid explosives in innocent-looking bottles and detonators hidden in disposable cameras. Contrary to the allegations of skeptics, the techniques they envisaged were perfectly workable. The plotters were determined enough to make chilling martyrdom videos.

The plot was broken up in part because some of the conspirators were turned in to Scotland Yard by British Muslim acquaintances disturbed by their behavior. They had been alerted to the seriousness of radical views by the bombing of London's public transport system in July 2005. British police infiltrated an undercover operative into the group. The Pakistani security forces helped monitor a radical in that country, Rashid Rauf, who was in contact with the London group. That is, the foiling of this operation depended very largely on the good will of other Muslims. Such police and community awareness work has had proven results. In contrast, invading and occupying Muslim states risks reducing the fund of good will on which successful terror prevention depends.

Since resources are scarce, it is important that the magnitude of the threat not be exaggerated. Al Qaeda has at most a few thousand members. It holds no territory and its constituent organizations have been roundly defeated in Egypt, Algeria and other Muslim nations. Its command and control networks have been effectively disrupted. Most threats now come from amateur copycats. Al Qaeda has no prospect whatsoever of taking over any state in the Muslim world. It probably would be dead altogether if Bush had not poured gasoline on the flames with his large-scale invasions and occupations. For [Senator] John McCain to proclaim that Al Qaeda is a bigger threat to US security than was the Soviet Union, which had thousands of nuclear warheads aimed at this country, is to enter Alice's Wonderland.

Very few Muslims are either violent or fundamentalist; most are traditionalist, mystic, modernist or secularist. Murder rates in the Muslim world are remarkably low. About 10 to 15 percent of Muslims throughout the world, or 130 million to 215 million, generally support a fundamentalist point of view, including the implementation of Islamic law as the law of the state. But they are not typically violent, and the United States has managed to ally with some of them, as with the Shiite fundamentalist Dawa Party of Iraqi Prime Minister Nuri al-Maliki. The fundamentalists are atypical. In a 2006 Pew poll, majorities in Egypt, Jordan and Indonesia were optimistic that democracy would work in their countries.

Because of its support for or acquiescence to Israel's creeping erasure of the Palestinian nation and for Israel's attack on Lebanon in 2006, and because of Washington's own brutal war in Iraq, the United States is poorly positioned to win hearts and minds in the Muslim world. In the last year of Bill Clinton's presidency, some 75 percent of the population of Indonesia (the world's largest Muslim country) had a favorable view of the United States. By the time Bush had invaded two Muslim countries, in 2003, America's favorability rating there had fallen to 15 percent. It recovered a bit after US magnanimity during the tsunami but then fell back to less than half the pre-Bush level. In Turkey, the favorability rating has fallen from 52 to 12 percent in the same period (all polling figures from the Global Attitudes Project of the Pew Charitable Trust).

America does itself no favors by neglecting to promote knowledge of the United States, or its political philosophies and social and political system, in the Muslim world. The United States Information Service was gutted and folded into the State Department in the late 1990s. There are very few American Studies programs at Arabophone universities, and very little US political philosophy or history has been translated. Likewise, Congress funds the study of the Middle East at American Universities at shockingly low levels, given the need for Americans who understand the region and its languages.

Extremist Muslim networks have a specific history, almost entirely rooted in reaction to many decades of European colonial domination or in the Reagan jihad against the Soviet Union, during which the United States gave extremists $5 billion, pressured Saudi Arabia to do the same and trained the extremists at CIA facilities in Afghanistan. Much of their subsequent violence can properly be seen as a form of blowback—black operations that go bad and boomerang on the initiating country.

Marc Sageman, a CIA case officer in Afghanistan in the late 1980s who is now at the Foreign Policy Research Institute in Philadelphia, has estimated the number of extremists who could and would do violence to the United States at less than a thousand. There is a larger group that supports the creation of Taliban-style rigid theocracies in their countries and who are willing to deploy violence to achieve that goal. While their ideology may be unpleasant, they do not necessarily pose a security threat to the United States.

American politicians should cease implying that Muslim nations and individuals are different from, or somehow more dangerous than, any other group of human beings, a racist idea promoted by the Christian and Zionist right. They should acknowledge that most Muslim nations are US friends and allies. A wise American policy toward the small networks of Muslim extremists would reduce their recruitment pool by the quick establishment of a Palestinian state and by a large-scale military drawdown from Iraq, thus removing widespread and major grievances. An increase in visible humanitarian and development aid to Muslim countries has a demonstrable effect on improving the US image.

The reconstitution of the United States Information Service as an independent body would allow better public diplomacy. Promoting American studies in the Muslim world, in its major languages rather than just in English, would help remove widespread misconceptions about the United States among educated Muslim observers. Increasing federal funding for Middle East studies at home would better equip this country to deal with this key region. More adept diplomacy with the Muslim states, most of which are as afraid of terrorism as we are, could lead to further cooperation in the security field. Better police work and cooperation with the police of Middle Eastern states would be much more effective than launching invasions. It would also help if we stopped insulting Muslims by calling their religion "fascist."

SOURCE: Juan Cole, "Combating Muslim Extremism: America Should Give Diplomacy a Chance," *The Nation* 285 (November 19, 2007): 26–28. Reprinted courtesy of *The Nation*.

ANALYSIS

Juan Cole, writing during the early months of the competition for two major parties' presidential nominations, attacks Republican candidates for their strong rhetoric about fighting extremist Muslim groups. Liberals generally criticize any approach to Muslim extremism that labels Islam as a fundamentally aggressive religion that presents a challenge to the United States similar to that of the Soviet Union during the Cold War years. Interestingly, both liberal commentators and conservatives such as Patrick Buchanan have expressed opposition to the U.S. invasion of Iraq, claiming that the military action drew attention and resources away from the real threat. Both sides place the blame on so-called neo-conservatives, those former liberals who advocate a strong military and a foreign policy that actively pursues the democratization of countries around the world. The consensus between liberals and conservatives ends at this point, for while conservatives tend to view Muslim societies as essentially hostile to the Christian (or, for them, the regrettably post-Christian) West, liberals search for ways to bridge the cultural gaps between the United States and non-Western societies. They assert that ideological and religious emphases on the differences with Muslim countries is self-defeating, creating potential enemies where opportunities for productive alliances exist. Although many liberals supported action against terrorists following the September 11, 2001, terrorist attacks, many criticized the Iraq invasion as an unhelpful adventure that diverted resources away from what should have been the focus of the U.S. response. They view the Iraq enterprise as the instigator of further attacks on Western targets, such as the Madrid and London train bombings. If such activities are to be defended against, the cooperation of Muslims must—and can—be nurtured.

Cole concludes that although the United States does face a threat from terrorist groups, decision makers must not exaggerate the danger. Al Qaeda reportedly has no more than a few thousand members, and the vast majority of Muslims are neither fundamentalist in their religious beliefs nor prone to acts of violence. However, the military actions of the Bush administration may well have alienated large segments of the Muslim world.

Unlike the conservative Christian view, which focuses on the traditional conflict between Western societies and Muslim culture, the liberal perspective emphasizes the potential benefit to the United States of greater interchange across cultures, with more Americans studying non-Western cultures and with greater emphasis on disseminating to the populations of other nations knowledge of the United States and its social and political institutions. Cole advocates the establishment of American Studies programs in other countries—taught in the language of those countries—and translating writings in U.S. history and political philosophy into other languages. In turn, greater funding should be dedicated to the study of the Middle East in U.S. universities in order to meet the need for Americans to understand the culture and languages of that region of the world.

"The Political Problem of Islam"

- **Document:** Excerpt from an article by Roger Scruton detailing the origins and objectives of Islamic extremism.
- **Date:** 2002.
- **Where:** *The Intercollegiate Review.*
- **Significance:** Scruton presents a deeper analysis of Islam, its contrast to modern Western societies, and the development of Islamic extremism that generally is not known in the United States. The author tends to support the more conservative perspective on Islam.

DOCUMENT

Those who see religion simply as a set of doctrines concerning the origin of the world, the laws that govern it, and the destiny of mankind will think of faith merely as a substitute for rational argument, destined to crumble before the advance of science or to persist, if at all, as a jumble of tattered superstitions in the midst of a world that refutes them. But doctrine is the least important part of religion, as Muhammad came quickly to see. Communities are not formed by doctrine, but by obedience, and the two great instruments for securing obedience are ritual and law. The Muslim faith involves constant rehearsal of the believer's submission to God. The repetition of sacred words and formulae, the exact performance of gestures whose only explanation is that they have been commanded, the obligatory times of prayer, the annual fast and all the duties required by it, the dietary laws, the pilgrimage to Mecca with its myriad obligatory actions—all this, which is meaningless to the skeptical outsider, is the stuff of consolation. [1] Ritual places individuals on a plane of absolute equality; it overcomes distance, extinguishes the self in the flow of collective emotion, and refreshes the worshipper with a sense that he has regained favor in God's sight and hence his place in the community of believers. Ritual is a discipline of the body that conveys and reinforces a discipline of the soul. It is the outward manifestation of the collective act of submission (*islam*) that unites the community of believers. And it is one undeniable source of the peace and gentleness of the old Muslim city.

In short, Islam offers an unparalleled form of *membership*, and one whose appeal is all the greater in that it transcends time and place, joining the believer to a universal *umma* whose only sovereign is God. Even if it may appear, to the skeptical modernist, as a medieval fossil, Islam has an unrivalled ability to compensate for what is lacking in modern experience. It rationalizes and validates the condition of exile: the condition in which we all find ourselves, severed by the hectic motion of mechanized life from the archaic need for membership. Nothing evokes this more clearly than the collective rite in which the faithful turn to Mecca with their prayers—projecting their submission and their longing away from the place where they are to that other and holy place where they are not, and whose contours are defined not by geography but by religious need.

Islam, in other words, is less a theological doctrine than a system of *piety*. To submit to it is to discover the rules for an untroubled life and an easy conscience. Moreover, rooted in the ritual and taking constant nourishment from it is a system of morality that clarifies those matters which must be clarified if people are to live with each other in peace. It is a system that safeguards the family as the primary object of loyalty and trust; that clarifies and disciplines sexual conduct; that sanctifies ordinary obligations of friendship and kinship; and that lays down rules for business which have a power to exonerate as well as to blame. Even if this morality, like the rituals that feed it, threatens those freedoms which Westerners take for granted and which the rising generation of Muslim immigrants wish to exploit, it has the singular advantage of clarity. It tells the faithful what they must do in order to be on good terms with God; and what they must do is entirely a matter of private life, ritual, and worship. The public sphere can be left to look after itself. [2]

In the context of Western *anomie* and self-indulgence, therefore, Muslim immigrants cling to their faith, seeing it as something superior to the surrounding moral chaos, and therefore more worthy of obedience than the secular law which permits so much sin. Their children may rebel for a while against the strict sexual codes and patriarchal absolutes of the Muslim family; but they too, in any crisis, are drawn to their ancestral faith, which offers a vision of moral security they find nowhere in the public space that Western political systems have devoted themselves to generating.

DID YOU KNOW?

The United States, the United Nations, and Homosexuality

In December 2008 the United States declined to support a non-binding resolution presented at the United Nations that called for the worldwide decriminalization of homosexuality. The resolution, co-sponsored by France and the Netherlands, was signed by all 27 European Union members, Japan, Australia, Mexico, and 36 other countries. U.S. officials reportedly expressed concern that portions of the declaration could raise difficulties by charging the federal government with responsibilities normally under the jurisdiction of state governments. Gay rights organizations, including the International Gay and Lesbian Human Rights Commission, criticized the U.S. decision not to sign the resolution. Carolyn Vadino, a spokeswoman for the United States mission to the United Nations, stated that despite its refusal to sign the resolution, the United States condemns human rights violations based on sexual orientation. More than 70 U.N. member countries legally restrict homosexuality, and 50 countries, including members of the Organization of the Islamic Conference, issued a statement criticizing the resolution.

The writ of holy law runs through all things, but this does not mean that Islamic societies have been governed solely by *shari'a*. On the contrary, in almost all respects relevant to the government of a large society, the *shari'a* is radically deficient. It has therefore been necessary in every epoch for the ruler to lay down laws of his own which will guarantee his power, facilitate administration, and permit the collection of taxes. But these laws have no independent legitimacy in the eyes of those compelled to obey them. They do not create a space outside religion in which freedom is the norm. On the contrary, they merely add to the constraints of the holy law the rules of a political order which is backed by no *de jure* authority, only by *de facto* power. In any upheaval they are rejected entirely as the arbitrary edicts of a usurper. Hence, there is no scope in a traditional Islamic society for the kinds of purely political development, through the patient building of institutions and secular laws, that we know in the West. Change, when it comes, takes the form of a crisis, as power is challenged from below in the name of the one true Power above.

If the only way in which a law can be legitimated is by deriving it from a command of God, then clearly all secular laws are seen as mere expedients adopted by the ruler. In such circumstances it is unlikely that any kind of constitutional, representative, or democratic government will emerge. Although the Ottoman Empire attempted reforms that would give legitimacy to its centralized administration, these reforms—which led first to the destruction of the Empire, and then to the emergence of the modern Turkish state under Mustafah Kemal Atatürk—were explicitly "Westernizing," involving both a deliberate move away from Islamic ideas of legitimacy, and a ruthless secularization of society, with the *'ulama'* losing whatever power they had once possessed in the education, legal, and administrative process.

The Westernizing of Turkey was made possible by its imperial history, which had imposed the obligation to govern distant provinces and recalcitrant tribes by a system of law which could only here and there be justified by some divine genealogy, and which was therefore constantly seeking legitimacy of another kind. By remaking Turkey as a territorial rather than an imperial power, and by simultaneously secularizing and Turkifying the Ottoman culture, Atatürk created a national loyalty, a territorial jurisdiction, and a from of constitutional government. As a consequence, Turkey has been the only durable democracy in the Muslim world—although a democracy maintained as such by frequent interventions by an army loyal to the Kemalist project. This transition has not been without cost, however. Modern Turkey has been effectively severed from its past. In the ensuing search for a modern identity, young people are repeatedly attracted to radical and destabilizing ideologies, both Islamist and utopian.

This search for identity takes another but related form in the Arabic-speaking countries, and the al-Qa'eda organization should be understood as one significant result of it. [3] Of course, terrorism of the al-Qa'eda kind is an abnormality, repudiated by the majority of Muslims. It would be the greatest injustice to confuse Islam, as a pious way of life, with contemporary Islamism, which is an example of what [Edmund] Burke, writing of the French Revolutionaries, called an "armed doctrine"—a belligerent ideology bent on eradicating all opposition to its claims. Nevertheless, Islamism is not an accidental product of the crisis that Islam is currently undergoing, and the fundamental tenets of the faith must be borne in mind by those who wish to understand the terrorist movements. [4]

Al-Qa'eda is the personal creation of Osama bin Laden, but it derives from three pre-existing sociopolitical forces: the Wahhabite movement in Saudi Arabia; the Muslim Brotherhood that emerged in modern Egypt; and, finally, the technological education now available to disaffected Muslims throughout the Middle East.

The Wahhabite movement has its roots in the sect (*madhhab*) founded by Ahmad ibn Hanbal (780–855), whose collection of 30,000 hadiths formed the basis of the Hanbali *fiqh*. The leading principle of Hanbali jurisprudence is that law should not be formalized in rules or maxims but constantly derived afresh from the original sources by an effort of *ijtihad* that renews both the faith and the understanding of the judge. Hence, Muslims must be constantly returned to the Koran and the words of the Prophet, the authority of which cannot be overridden by political decrees or formal legal systems. Although Hanbalism has always been recognized as a legitimate school of *fiqh*, its uncompromising emphasis on the origins of the Muslim faith has made it a permanent source of opposition to the established powers in Muslim countries.

Hence, when Muhammad ibn 'Abd al-Wahhab (1691–1765), a native of central Arabia, sought to restore the true faith to the Prophet's sacred territory, he expressed himself in Hanbali terms. The aim was to return from the corrupt practices that flourished under the Ottoman Empire and its [factitious] rules and offices to the original teachings of the Prophet and his Companions. Compelled to seek asylum in Deraiah, al-Wahhab attracted the local chieftain, Muhammad ibn Sa'ud, to his cause. And it was Ibn Sa'ud's grandson who, with a fanatical and puritanical following, "liberated" Mecca from the idolatrous practices that had rooted themselves there, establishing at the same time a short-lived kingdom in Arabia, and thereafter paying for his presumption with his life.

Despite this political failure, Wahhabism took root in the Arabian peninsula. The Wahhabis preached purity of lifestyle and absolute obedience to the Koran, free from all compromise with the *dar al-harb*. They rejected the official schools of *fiqh*, including the Hanbali *madhhab* that had inspired their founder, and argued that whoever can read the Koran can judge for himself in matters of doctrine. After the death of the Companions, therefore, no new consensus (*ijma'*) could be admitted.

In the early twentieth century a group of Wahhabis gathered around a descendent of the original Ibn Sa'ud to form a brotherhood (*ikhwan*) dedicated to the re-establishment of a purified faith by *jihad*. Starting out with a handful of followers in 1902, ibn Sa'ud, as the world now knows him, gradually drove the Turkish clients from their paper thrones in the Arabian peninsula. By the time that the Ottoman Empire collapsed, ibn Sa'ud was able to declare a kingdom of Saudi Arabia in the peninsula, and for a brief while the *ikhwan* exerted their influence over the holy places, causing widespread alarm in the region. However Ibn Sa'ud, now a player on the stage of international politics, came to see that he must negotiate with the British for the secure possession of his kingdom, and that the suppression of his following would be a necessary price.

Although the *ikhwan* were brought to heel, many of them through absorption into the Saudi National Guard, they did not forget their original intention, which was to engage in a *jihad* against the infidel. Nor did they forget that this aim had been diverted in the interests of a secular power. Instead of returning the sacred places to God, they had handed them over to an earthly sovereign, and one who had the impertinence, moreover, to name this holy territory for himself. It has never been forgotten by the puritan *'ulama'* of Saudi Arabia, therefore, that the spiritual legacy of Wahhabism has been betrayed by the family that purported to fight for it.

The other important Islamic movement in the formation of al-Qa'eda was also an *ikhwan*. The Muslim Brotherhood was founded in Egypt in 1928 by Hassan al-Banna, then a twenty-two-year-old elementary school teacher in Ismailia, a featureless new town controlled by the Franco-British Suez Canal Company. Surrounded on all sides by the signs and symbols of the infidel way of life, living under a jurisdiction that had lost authority in Muslim eyes and which stood idly by as the Muslim way of life decayed, al-Banna, who had received a rigorous Islamic education and had already acquired a reputation for piety, responded to the appeals of his contemporaries to found a movement that would bring faith, hope, and charity to the rural migrants who were crowding into the shanty towns around the cities. For al-Banna, however, charity was an insufficient proof of faith: a *jihad* was also needed, which would expel the infidel from Muslim soil. Islamic clubs and discussion groups abounded in the Egypt of the time, but the Brotherhood was to be different—a return to the militant Islam of the Prophet, the goal of which would be to re-establish the reign of purity and piety that the Prophet had created in Medina.

Hassan al-Banna was profoundly influenced by the Wahhabite movement. The conquest of the Holy Places was a triumphant proof of what could be achieved by faith, '*asabiya*,' and violence. Within a decade the Brotherhood had become the best organized indigenous political force in Egypt. Its anti-British sentiment caused it to look to the Axis powers in World War II, hoping for the liberation of Egypt and its own seizure of power thereafter. After the Allied victory, it confined itself to a campaign of terrorism, through which to "bear witness" to Islamic truth against the infidel.

This campaign was to provide the model for future Islamist movements in Iran and Lebanon. Cinemas were blown up, along with the haunts of the "infidels and heretics," while women wearing "inadequate dress" were attacked with knives. Prominent public figures were tried by the Brotherhood *in absentia* and found guilty of "causing corruption on earth": their deaths followed as a matter of course. Two prime ministers and many other officials were murdered in this way. Young Muslims from elsewhere in the Middle East were recruited to the Brotherhood, which operated in secret, al-Banna denying all involvement in terrorism until his arrest and execution in 1949. By this time the Brotherhood had trained over a hundred terrorists from other Islamic countries, who traveled to their homelands to initiate the same kind of destabilizing mayhem that had brought chaos to Egypt. This unrest facilitated the army coup which led to the destruction of Egypt's fragile monarchy and the assumption of power by Gamal Abdul-Nasir (or Nasser, as he is generally known in the West).

The Muslim Brotherhood was outlawed and savagely repressed by Nasser. But it lived on as a secret society, proliferating through cells formed to study the letters sent from prison by its new leading personality, Sayyed Qutb (1906–66), who had lived in the United States from 1949 until 1951, and who preached the impossibility of compromise between Islam and the world of ignorance (*jahiliyya*). Qutb was a self-conscious intellectual in the Western sense, who attempted to give Islam a decidedly modernist, even "existentialist" character. The faith of the true Muslim was, for Qutb, an expression of his innermost being against the inauthentic otherness of the surrounding world. [5] Islam was therefore the answer to the rootlessness and comfortlessness of modernity, and Qutb did not stop short of endorsing both suicide and terrorism as instruments in the self-affirmation of the believer against the *jahiliyya*. In place of the *credo quia absurdum* of Tertullian he preached the *facio quia absurdum* (I do it because it is absurd) of the existentialist, believing that this absurdity would also be a triumph of the spirit over the surrounding pagan culture.

Qutb and hundreds of his followers were executed by Nasser in 1966, but not before their message had spread through a younger generation that was enjoying for the first time a Western-style university education and the excitement of global communications. Although [Anwar] Sadat [president of Egypt from 1970 until his assassination in 1981] and his successor, [Muhammad] Hosni-Mubarak, have tried to accommodate the Brotherhood by permitting it to reorganize as a political party, with a share in power accorded to its official leaders, the real movement continued independently, not as a form of politics, but as a form of *membership*, whose "brothers" would one day be martyrs.

Many of the ideological leaders of the Egyptian Islamist movement have been, like [September 11 highjacker] Mohammed Atta, graduates in technical or scientific subjects. Some have had the benefit of postgraduate study in the West. Their scientific training opens to them the secrets of Western technology while at the same time revealing the emptiness of a civilization in which only technology seems to matter. Although Osama bin Laden is a Saudi by birth, his most active followers are Egyptians, shaped by Western technology and Qutbist Islamism to become weapons in the fight to the death against technology. Al-Qa'eda offers them a new way of life which is also a way of death—an Islamist equivalent of the "being-towards-death" extolled by [German philosopher Martin] Heidegger, in which all external loyalties are dissolved in an act of self-sacrificial commitment.

Al-Qa'eda appeals to North African Muslims partly because it is an Arabist organization, expressing itself in the language and imagery of the Koran and pursuing a conflict that has its roots in the land of the Prophet. It has given to the Sunni and Arab branch of Islamism the same sense of identity that the Shi'ite and Persian branch received from the Islamic Republic of Ayatollah Khomeini. Indeed, its vision is virtually indistinguishable from that of Khomeini, who once described the killing of Western corrupters as a "surgical operation" commanded by God himself.

Khomeini's sentiments do not merely reflect his reading of the Koran. They are the fruit of a long exile in the West, where he was protected by the infidels whose destruction he conjures. They are a vivid testimony to the fact that the virtues of Western political systems are, to a certain kind of Islamic mind, imperceptible—or perceptible, as they were to Qutb and Atta, only as hideous moral failings. Even while enjoying the peace and freedom that issue from a secular rule of law, a person who regards the *shari'a* as the unique path to salvation may see these things as the signs of a spiritual emptiness or corruption. For someone like Khomeini—a figure of great historic importance—human rights and secular government display the decadence of Western civilization, which has failed to arm itself against those who intend to destroy it. The message is that there can be no compromise, and systems that make compromise and conciliation into their ruling principles are merely aspects of the Devil's work.

Islam originally spread through the world on the wings of military success. Conquest, victory, and triumph over enemies are a continual refrain of the Koran, offered as proof that God is on the side of the believers. The Shi'ites are remarkable among Muslims, however, in commemorating, as the central episode in their cult, a military defeat. To some extent they share the Christian vision of divinity as proved not through worldly triumph but through the willing acceptance of failure. Like Christians, Shi'ites take comfort in an eschatology of redemption, looking forward to the return of the Hidden Imam in the way that many Christians anticipate the Second Coming of Christ.

Hussein Ibn 'Ali, whom the Shi'ites recognize as their third Imam, was killed, together with his followers, by the armies of the Umayyad Caliph Yazid at the battle of Karbala in 680. Hussein was, for his followers, a symbol of all that is pure, innocent, and good in the Islamic way of life, and Yazid a proof that the community formed by the Prophet had fallen into the hands of corrupt and evil usurpers. By each year lamenting the defeat of Hussein, in rituals that may extend to excesses of self-inflicted injury, the Shi'ites rehearse their conviction that Islam must be constantly returned to its original purity, and that the powers that prevail in the world will always seek to corrupt it. At the same time Shi'ites internalize the goal of self-sacrificial death as the final proof of merit. This last feature became immensely important in the war against Iraq, which succeeded the Islamic Revolution in Iran. Following in the tradition of the assassins, Khomeini issued a new call to martyrdom, which was taken up by children and teenagers who expended their lives in clearing minefields.

The example set by the followers of Khomeini was soon projected around the world. Sunni Muslims, who believe on the authority of the Koran that suicide is categorically forbidden, have nevertheless been sucked into the Shi'ite maelstrom to become martyrs in the war against Satan. The cult of death seems to make sense of a world in which evil prevails; moreover it gives unprecedented power to the martyr, who no longer has anything to fear. The cult is both a protest against modern nihilism and a form of it—a last-ditch attempt to rescue Islam from the abyss of nothingness by showing that it can still demand the ultimate proof of devotion.

And the attempt seems to have succeeded. It is not too great an exaggeration to say that this new confluence of Sunni orthodoxy and Shi'ite extremism has laid the foundation for a worldwide Islamic revival. For the first time in centuries Islam appears, both in the eyes of its followers and in the eyes of the infidel, to be a single religious movement united around a single goal. Nor is it an exaggeration to suggest that one major factor in producing this unwonted unity is Western civilization and the process of globalization which it has set in motion. In the days when East was East and West was West it was possible for Muslims to devote their lives to pious observances and to ignore the evil that prevailed in the *dar al-harb*. But when that evil spreads around the globe, cheerfully offering freedoms and permissions in place of the austere requirements of a religious code, so that the *dar al-islam* is invaded by it, old antagonisms are awakened. This is what the West now faces.

NOTES

[1] On the rituals and the prayers of orthodox Sunni Islam, see Maurice Gaudefroy-Demombeynes's classic account in *Muslim Institutions*, tr. John P. MacGregor (London, 1950).

[2] Since law derives from God and not the ruler, there is in any case a complex problem, for the Muslim, posed by enforcement. See Michael Cook's exemplary work of scholarship, *Commanding Right and Forbidding Wrong in Islamic Thought* (Cambridge, 2001).

[3] See the thorough account by Peter L. Berger, *Holy War Inc: Inside the Secret World of Osama bin Laden* (London, 2001).

[4] See Daniel Pipes, "Islam and Islamism: Faith and Ideology," *The National Interest* No. 59, Spring 2000.

[5] See Leonard Binder, *Islamic Liberalism: A Critique of Development Ideologies* (Chicago, 1988).

SOURCE: Roger Scruton, "The Political Problem of Islam," *The Intercollegiate Review* 38, no. 1 (2002). Reprinted courtesy of the Intercollegiate Studies Institute.

ANALYSIS

Roger Scruton, writing soon after the terrorist attacks of September 11, 2001, distinguishes between the minority of Islamists, who are committed to terrorist acts of violence against Western targets, and the majority of Muslims living in peace. He calls Osama bin Ladin's al-Qa'eda organization an "abnormality." However, Scruton does not view Islamism as an "accidental product of the crisis that Islam is currently undergoing" due to the confrontation with the secularism and technological superiority of the West, and he asserts that the basic Islamic beliefs help us to understand the rise of terrorist organizations.

Of more immediate relevance to the development of Islamist movements, Scruton identifies the education of young Muslims in Western science and technology. While being inundated with Western technical education, such Muslims rejected the Western secular culture that made possible the scientific and technological advances, thus providing extremist groups with a source of potential members.

Ultimately, Scruton holds that the differences in understanding between Western and Islamic culture, with their unique understandings of the legitimate role of secular authority, present a fundamental problem for both societies. The potential exists within Islamic societies for the outright rejection of the global influences of Western science and technology because they are viewed as dangerous threats to traditional culture.

"Remarks by the President on a New Beginning"

- **Document:** Speech by President Barack Obama on U.S. relations with Muslim nations.
- **Date:** June 4, 2009.
- **Where:** Cairo University, Cairo, Egypt.
- **Significance:** President Barack Obama's much-anticipated speech during his visit to the Middle East gained a great deal of praise for the president's attempt to find common ground between two cultures that traditionally have been antagonistic toward each other.

DOCUMENT

Thank you very much. Good afternoon. I am honored to be in the timeless city of Cairo, and to be hosted by two remarkable institutions. For over a thousand years, Al-Azhar has stood as a beacon of Islamic learning; and for over a century, Cairo University has been a source of Egypt's advancement. And together, you represent the harmony between tradition and progress. I'm grateful for your hospitality, and the hospitality of the people of Egypt. And I'm also proud to carry with me the good-will of the American people, and a greeting of peace from Muslim communities in my country: Assalaamu alaykum [peace be upon you].

We meet at a time of great tension between the United States and Muslims around the world—tension rooted in historical forces that go beyond any current policy debate. The relationship between Islam and the West includes centuries of coexistence and cooperation, but also conflict and religious wars. More recently, tension has been fed by colonialism that denied rights and opportunities to many Muslims, and a Cold War in which Muslim-majority countries were too often treated as proxies without regard to their own aspiration. Moreover, the sweeping change brought by modernity and globalization led many Muslims to view the West as hostile to the traditions of Islam.

Violent extremists have exploited these tensions in a small but potent minority of Muslims. The attacks of September 11, 2001, and the continued efforts of these extremists to engage in violence against civilians has led some in my country to view Islam as inevitably hostile not only to America and Western countries, but also to human rights. All this has bred more fear and more mistrust.

So long as our relationship is defined by our differences, we will empower those who sow hatred rather than peace, those who promote conflict rather than the cooperation that can help all of our people achieve justice and prosperity. And this cycle of suspicion and discord must end. I've come here to Cairo to seek a new beginning between the United States and Muslims around the world, one based on mutual interest and mutual respect, and one based upon the truth that America and Islam are not exclusive and need not be in competition. Instead, they overlap, and share common principles—principles of justice and progress; tolerance and the dignity of all human beings.

I do so recognizing that change cannot happen overnight. I know there's been a lot of publicity about this speech, but no single speech can eradicate years of mistrust, nor can I answer in the time that I have this afternoon all the complex questions that brought us to this point. But I am convinced that in order to move forward, we must say openly to each other the things we hold in our hearts and that too often are said only behind closed doors. There must be a sustained effort to listen to each other; to learn from each other; to respect one another; and to seek common ground. As the Holy Koran tells us, "Be conscious of God and speak always the truth." That is what I will try to do today—to speak the truth as best I can, humbled by the task before us, and firm in my belief that the interests we share as human beings are far more powerful than the forces that drive us apart.

Now part of this conviction is rooted in my own experience. I'm a Christian, but my father came from a Kenyan family that includes generations of Muslims. As a boy, I spent several years in Indonesia and heard the call of the azaan [call to worship] at the break of dawn and at the fall of dusk. As a young man, I worked in Chicago communities where many found dignity and peace in their Muslim faith.

As a student of history, I also know civilization's debt to Islam. It was Islam—at places like Al-Azhar—that carried the light of learning through so many centuries, paving the way for Europe's Renaissance and Enlightenment. It was innovation in Muslim communities that developed the order of algebra; our magnetic compass and tools of navigation; our mastery of pens and printing; our understanding of how disease spreads and how it can be healed. Islamic culture has given us majestic arches and soaring spires; timeless poetry and cherished music; elegant calligraphy and places of peaceful contemplation. And throughout history, Islam has demonstrated through words and deeds the possibilities of religious tolerance and racial equality.

I also know that Islam has always been a part of America's story. The first nation to recognize my country was Morocco. In signing the Treaty of Tripoli in 1796, our second President, John Adams, wrote, "The United States has in itself no character of enmity against the laws, religion or tranquility of Muslims." And since our founding, American Muslims have enriched the United States. They have fought in our wars, they have served in our government, they have stood for civil rights, they have started businesses, they have taught at our universities, they've excelled in our sports arenas, they've won Nobel Prizes, built our tallest building, and lit the Olympic Torch. And when the first Muslim American was recently elected to Congress, he took the oath to defend our Constitution using the same Holy Koran that one of our Founding Fathers—Thomas Jefferson—kept in his personal library.

So I have known Islam on three continents before coming to the region where it was first revealed. That experience guides my conviction that partnership between America and Islam must be based on what Islam is, not what it isn't. And I consider it part of my responsibility as President of the United States to fight against negative stereotypes of Islam wherever they appear.

But that same principle must apply to Muslim perceptions of America. Just as Muslims do not fit a crude stereotype, America is not the crude stereotype of a self-interested empire. The United States has been one of the greatest sources of progress that the world has ever known. We were born out of a revolution against an empire. We were founded upon the ideal that all are created equal, and we have shed blood and struggled for centuries to give meaning to those words—within our borders, and around the world. We are shaped by every culture, drawn from every end of the Earth, and dedicated to a simple concept: E pluribus unum—"Out of many, one."

Now, much has been made of the fact that an African American with the name Barack Hussein Obama could be elected President. But my personal story is not so unique. The dream of opportunity for all people has not come true for everyone in America, but its promise exists for all who come to our shores—and that includes nearly 7 million American Muslims in our country today who, by the way, enjoy incomes and educational levels that are higher than the American average.

Moreover, freedom in America is indivisible from the freedom to practice one's religion. That is why there is a mosque in every state in our union, and over 1,200 mosques within our borders. That's why the United States government has gone to court to protect the right of women and girls to wear the hijab [head cover] and to punish those who would deny it.

So let there be no doubt: Islam is a part of America. And I believe that America holds within her the truth that regardless of race, religion, or station in life, all of us share common aspirations—to live in peace and security; to get an education and to work with dignity; to love our families, our communities, and our God. These things we share. This is the hope of all humanity.

Of course, recognizing our common humanity is only the beginning of our task. Words alone cannot meet the needs of our people. These needs will be met only if we act boldly in the years ahead; and if we understand that the challenges we face are shared, and our failure to meet them will hurt us all.

For we have learned from recent experience that when a financial system weakens in one country, prosperity is hurt everywhere. When a new flu infects one human being, all are at risk. When one nation pursues a nuclear weapon, the risk of nuclear attack rises for all nations. When violent extremists operate in one stretch of mountains, people are endangered across an ocean. When innocents in Bosnia and Darfur are slaughtered, that is a strain on our collective conscience. That is what it means to share this world in the 21st century. That is the responsibility we have to one another as human beings.

And this is a difficult responsibility to embrace. For human history has often been a record of nations and tribes—and, yes, religions—subjugating one another in pursuit of their own interests. Yet in this new age, such attitudes are self-defeating. Given our interdependence, any world order that elevates one nation or group of people over another will inevitably fail. So whatever we think of the past, we must not be prisoners to it. Our problems must be dealt with through partnership; our progress must be shared.

Now, that does not mean we should ignore sources of tension. Indeed, it suggests the opposite: We must face these tensions squarely. And so in that spirit, let me speak as clearly and as plainly as I can about some specific issues that I believe we must finally confront together.

The first issue that we have to confront is violent extremism in all of its forms.

In Ankara, I made clear that America is not—and never will be—at war with Islam. We will, however, relentlessly confront violent extremists who pose a grave threat to our security—because we reject the same thing that people of all faiths reject: the killing of innocent men, women, and children. And it is my first duty as President to protect the American people.

The situation in Afghanistan demonstrates America's goals, and our need to work together. Over seven years ago, the United States pursued al Qaeda and the Taliban with broad international support. We did not go by choice; we went because of necessity. I'm aware that there's still some who would question or even justify the events of 9/11. But let us be clear: Al Qaeda killed nearly 3,000 people on that day. The victims were innocent men, women and children from America and many other nations who had done nothing to harm anybody. And yet al Qaeda chose to ruthlessly murder these people, claimed credit for the attack, and even now states their determination to kill on a massive scale. They have affiliates in many countries and are trying to expand their reach. These are not opinions to be debated; these are facts to be dealt with.

Now, make no mistake: We do not want to keep our troops in Afghanistan. We seek no military bases there. It is agonizing for America to lose our young men and women. It is costly and politically difficult to continue this conflict. We would gladly bring every single one of our troops home if we could be confident that there were not violent extremists in Afghanistan and now Pakistan determined to kill as many Americans as they possibly can. But that is not yet the case.

And that's why we're partnering with a coalition of 46 countries. And despite the costs involved, America's commitment will not weaken. Indeed, none of us should tolerate these extremists. They have killed in many countries. They have killed people of different faiths—but more than any other, they have killed Muslims. Their actions are irreconcilable with the rights of human beings, the progress of nations, and with Islam. The Holy Koran teaches that whoever kills an innocent is as—it is as if he has killed all mankind. And the Holy Koran also says whoever saves a person, it is as if he has saved all mankind. The enduring faith of over a billion people is so much bigger than the narrow hatred of a few. Islam is not part of the problem in combating violent extremism—it is an important part of promoting peace.

Now, we also know that military power alone is not going to solve the problems in Afghanistan and Pakistan. That's why we plan to invest $1.5 billion each year over the next five years to partner with Pakistanis to build schools and hospitals, roads and businesses, and hundreds of millions to help those who've been displaced. That's why we are providing more than $2.8 billion to help Afghans develop their economy and deliver services that people depend on.

Let me also address the issue of Iraq. Unlike Afghanistan, Iraq was a war of choice that provoked strong differences in my country and around the world. Although I believe that the Iraqi people are ultimately better off without the tyranny of Saddam Hussein, I also believe that events in Iraq have reminded America of the need to use diplomacy and build international consensus to resolve our problems whenever possible. Indeed, we can recall the words of Thomas Jefferson, who said: "I hope that our wisdom will grow with our power, and teach us that the less we use our power the greater it will be."

Today, America has a dual responsibility: to help Iraq forge a better future—and to leave Iraq to Iraqis. And I have made it clear to the Iraqi people that we pursue no bases, and no claim on their territory or resources. Iraq's sovereignty is its own. And that's why I ordered the removal of our combat brigades by next August. That is why we will honor our agreement with Iraq's democratically elected government to remove combat troops from Iraqi cities by July, and to remove all of our troops from Iraq by 2012. We will help Iraq train its security forces and develop its economy. But we will support a secure and united Iraq as a partner, and never as a patron.

And finally, just as America can never tolerate violence by extremists, we must never alter or forget our principles. Nine-eleven was an enormous trauma to our country. The fear and anger that it provoked was understandable, but in some cases, it led us to act contrary to our traditions and our ideals. We are taking concrete actions to change course. I have unequivocally prohibited the use of torture by the United States, and I have ordered the prison at Guantanamo Bay closed by early next year.

So America will defend itself, respectful of the sovereignty of nations and the rule of law. And we will do so in partnership with Muslim communities which are also threatened. The sooner the extremists are isolated and unwelcome in Muslim communities, the sooner we will be safer.

The second major source of tension that we need to discuss is the situation between Israelis, Palestinians and the Arab world.

America's strong bonds with Israel are well known. This bond is unbreakable. It is based upon cultural and historical ties, and the recognition that the aspiration for a Jewish homeland is rooted in a tragic history that cannot be denied.

Around the world, the Jewish people were persecuted for centuries, and anti-Semitism in Europe culminated in an unprecedented Holocaust. Tomorrow, I will visit Buchenwald, which was part of a network of camps where Jews were enslaved, tortured, shot and gassed to death by the Third Reich. Six million Jews were killed —more than the entire Jewish population of Israel today. Denying that fact is baseless, it is ignorant, and it is hateful. Threatening Israel with destruction—or repeating vile stereotypes about Jews—is deeply wrong, and only serves to evoke in the minds of Israelis this most painful of memories while preventing the peace that the people of this region deserve.

On the other hand, it is also undeniable that the Palestinian people—Muslims and Christians—have suffered in pursuit of a homeland. For more than 60 years they've endured the pain of dislocation. Many wait in refugee camps in the West Bank, Gaza, and neighboring lands for a life of peace and security that they have never been able to lead. They endure the daily humiliations—large and small—that come with occupation. So let there be no doubt: The situation for the Palestinian people is intolerable. And America will not turn our backs on the legitimate Palestinian aspiration for dignity, opportunity, and a state of their own.

For decades, then, there has been a stalemate: two peoples with legitimate aspirations, each with a painful history that makes compromise elusive. It's easy to point fingers—for Palestinians to point to the displacement brought about by Israel's founding, and for Israelis to point to the constant hostility and attacks throughout its history from within its borders as well as beyond. But if we see this conflict only from one side or the other, then we will be blind to the truth: The only resolution is for the aspirations of both sides to be met through two states, where Israelis and Palestinians each live in peace and security.

That is in Israel's interest, Palestine's interest, America's interest, and the world's interest. And that is why I intend to personally pursue this outcome with all the patience and dedication that the task requires. The obligations—the obligations that the parties have agreed to under the road map are clear. For peace to come, it is time for them—and all of us—to live up to our responsibilities.

Palestinians must abandon violence. Resistance through violence and killing is wrong and it does not succeed. For centuries, black people in America suffered the lash of the whip as slaves and the humiliation of segregation. But it was not violence that won full and equal rights. It was a peaceful and determined insistence upon the ideals at the center of America's founding. This same story can be told by people from South Africa to South Asia; from Eastern Europe to Indonesia. It's a story with a simple truth: that violence is a dead end. It is a sign neither of courage nor power to shoot rockets at sleeping children, or to blow up old women on a bus. That's not how moral authority is claimed; that's how it is surrendered.

Now is the time for Palestinians to focus on what they can build. The Palestinian Authority must develop its capacity to govern, with institutions that serve the needs of its people. Hamas does have support among some Palestinians, but they also have to recognize they have responsibilities. To play a role in fulfilling Palestinian aspirations, to unify the Palestinian people, Hamas must put an end to violence, recognize past agreements, recognize Israel's right to exist.

At the same time, Israelis must acknowledge that just as Israel's right to exist cannot be denied, neither can Palestine's. The United States does not accept the legitimacy of continued Israeli settlements. This construction violates previous agreements and undermines efforts to achieve peace. It is time for these settlements to stop.

And Israel must also live up to its obligation to ensure that Palestinians can live and work and develop their society. Just as it devastates Palestinian families, the continuing humanitarian crisis in Gaza does not serve Israel's security; neither does the continuing lack of opportunity in the West Bank. Progress in the daily lives of the Palestinian people must be a critical part of a road to peace, and Israel must take concrete steps to enable such progress.

And finally, the Arab states must recognize that the Arab Peace Initiative was an important beginning, but not the end of their responsibilities. The Arab-Israeli conflict should no longer be used to distract the people of Arab nations from other problems. Instead, it must be a cause for action to help the Palestinian people develop the institutions that will sustain their state, to recognize Israel's legitimacy, and to choose progress over a self-defeating focus on the past.

America will align our policies with those who pursue peace, and we will say in public what we say in private to Israelis and Palestinians and Arabs. We cannot impose peace. But privately, many Muslims recognize that Israel will not go away. Likewise, many Israelis recognize the need for a Palestinian state. It is time for us to act on what everyone knows to be true.

Too many tears have been shed. Too much blood has been shed. All of us have a responsibility to work for the day when the mothers of Israelis and Palestinians can see their children grow up without fear; when the Holy Land of the three great faiths is the place of peace that God intended it to be; when Jerusalem is a secure and lasting home for Jews and Christians and Muslims, and a place for all of the children of Abraham to mingle peacefully together as in the story of Isra, when Moses, Jesus, and Mohammed, peace be upon them, joined in prayer.

The third source of tension is our shared interest in the rights and responsibilities of nations on nuclear weapons.

This issue has been a source of tension between the United States and the Islamic Republic of Iran. For many years, Iran has defined itself in part by its opposition to my country, and there is in fact a tumultuous history between us. In the middle of the Cold War, the United States played a role in the overthrow of a democratically elected Iranian government. Since the Islamic Revolution, Iran has played a role in acts of hostage-taking and violence against U.S. troops and civilians. This history is well known. Rather than remain trapped in the past, I've made it clear to Iran's leaders and people that my country is prepared to move forward. The question now is not what Iran is against, but what future it wants to build.

I recognize it will be hard to overcome decades of mistrust, but we will proceed with courage, rectitude, and resolve. There will be many issues to discuss between our two countries, and we are willing to move forward without preconditions on the basis of mutual respect. But it is clear to all concerned that when it comes to nuclear weapons, we have reached a decisive point. This is not simply about America's interests. It's about preventing a nuclear arms race in the Middle East that could lead this region and the world down a hugely dangerous path.

I understand those who protest that some countries have weapons that others do not. No single nation should pick and choose which nation holds nuclear weapons. And that's why I strongly reaffirmed America's commitment to seek a world in which no nations hold nuclear weapons. And any nation—including Iran—should have the right to access peaceful nuclear power if it complies with its responsibilities under the nuclear Non-Proliferation Treaty. That commitment is at the core of the treaty, and it must be kept for all who fully abide by it. And I'm hopeful that all countries in the region can share in this goal.

The fourth issue that I will address is democracy.

I know there has been controversy about the promotion of democracy in recent years, and much of this controversy is connected to the war in Iraq. So let me be clear: No system of government can or should be imposed by one nation [on] any other.

That does not lessen my commitment, however, to governments that reflect the will of the people. Each nation gives life to this principle in its own way, grounded in the traditions of its own people. America does not presume to know what is best for everyone, just as we would not presume to pick the outcome of a peaceful election. But I do have an unyielding belief that all people yearn for certain things: the ability to speak your mind and have a say in how you are governed; confidence in the rule of law and the equal administration of justice; government that is transparent and doesn't steal from the people; the freedom to live as you choose. These are not just American ideas; they are human rights. And that is why we will support them everywhere.

Now, there is no straight line to realize this promise. But this much is clear: Governments that protect these rights are ultimately more stable, successful and secure. Suppressing ideas never succeeds in making them go away. America respects the rights of all peaceful and law-abiding voices to be heard around the world, even if we disagree with them. And we will welcome all elected, peaceful governments—provided they govern with respect for all their people.

This last point is important because there are some who advocate for democracy only when they're out of power; once in power, they are ruthless in suppressing the rights of others. So no matter where it takes hold, government of the people and by the people sets a single standard for all who would hold power: You must maintain your power through consent, not coercion; you must respect the rights of minorities, and participate with a spirit of tolerance and compromise; you must place the interests of your people and the legitimate workings of the political process above your party. Without these ingredients, elections alone do not make true democracy....

The fifth issue that we must address is religious freedom.

Islam has a proud tradition of tolerance. We see it in the history of Andalusia and Cordoba during the inquisition. I saw it firsthand as a child in Indonesia, where devout Christians worshiped freely in an overwhelmingly Muslim country. That is the spirit we need today. People in every country should be free to choose and live their faith based upon the persuasion of the mind and the heart and the soul. This tolerance is essential for religion to thrive, but it's being challenged in many different ways.

Among some Muslims, there's a disturbing tendency to measure one's own faith by the rejection of somebody else's faith. The richness of religious diversity must be upheld—whether it is for Maronites in Lebanon or the Copts in Egypt. And if we are being honest, fault lines must be closed among Muslims, as well, as the divisions between Sunni and Shia have led to tragic violence in Iraq.

Freedom of religion is central to the ability of peoples to live together. We must always examine the ways in which we protect it. For instance, in the United States, rules on charitable giving have made it harder for Muslims to fulfill their religious obligation. That's why I'm committed to working with American Muslims to ensure that they can fulfill zakat [alms giving].

Likewise, it is important for Western countries to avoid impeding Muslim citizens from practicing religion as they see fit—for instance, by dictating what clothes a Muslim woman should wear. We can't disguise hostility towards any religion behind the pretence of liberalism.

In fact, faith should bring us together. And that's why we're forging service projects in America to bring together Christians, Muslims, and Jews. That's why we welcome efforts like Saudi Arabian King Abdullah's interfaith dialogue and Turkey's leadership in the Alliance of Civilizations. Around the world, we can turn dialogue into interfaith service, so bridges between peoples lead to action—whether it is combating malaria in Africa, or providing relief after a natural disaster.

The sixth issue that I want to address is women's rights. I know, and you can tell from this audience, that there is a healthy debate about this issue. I reject the view of some in the West that a woman who chooses to cover her hair is somehow less equal, but I do believe that a woman who is denied an education is denied equality. And it is no coincidence that countries where women are well educated are far more likely to be prosperous.

Now, let me be clear: Issues of women's equality are by no means simply an issue for Islam. In Turkey, Pakistan, Bangladesh, Indonesia, we've seen Muslim–majority countries elect a woman to lead. Meanwhile, the struggle for women's equality continues in many aspects of American life, and in countries around the world.

I am convinced that our daughters can contribute just as much to society as our sons. Our common prosperity will be advanced by allowing all humanity—men and women—to reach their full potential. I do not believe that women must make the same choices as men in order to be equal, and I respect those women who choose to live their lives in traditional roles. But it should be their choice. And that is why the United States will partner with any Muslim-majority country to support expanded literacy for girls, and to help young women pursue employment through micro-financing that helps people live their dreams.

Finally, I want to discuss economic development and opportunity.

I know that for many, the face of globalization is contradictory. The Internet and television can bring knowledge and information, but also offensive sexuality and mindless violence into the home. Trade can bring new wealth and opportunities, but also huge disruptions and change in communities. In all nations—including America—this change can bring fear. Fear that because of modernity we lose control over our economic choices, our politics, and most importantly our identities—those things we most cherish about our communities, our families, our traditions, and our faith.

But I also know that human progress cannot be denied. There need not be contradictions between development and tradition. Countries like Japan and South Korea grew their economies enormously while maintaining distinct cultures. The same is true for the astonishing progress within Muslim–majority countries from Kuala Lumpur to Dubai. In ancient times and in our times, Muslim communities have been at the forefront of innovation and education.

And this is important because no development strategy can be based only upon what comes out of the ground, nor can it be sustained while young people are out of work. Many Gulf states have enjoyed great wealth as a consequence of oil, and some are beginning to focus it on broader development. But all of us must recognize that education and innovation will be the currency of the 21st century, and in too many Muslim communities, there remains underinvestment in these areas. I'm emphasizing such investment within my own country. And while America in the past has focused on oil and gas when it come to this part of the world, we now seek a broader engagement.

On education, we will expand exchange programs, and increase scholarships, like the one that brought my father to America. At the same time, we will encourage more Americans to study in Muslim communities. And we will match promising Muslim students with internships in America; invest in online learning for teachers and children around the world; and create a new online network, so a young person in Kansas can communicate instantly with a young person in Cairo.

On economic development, we will create a new corps of business volunteers to partner with counterparts in Muslim-majority countries. And I will host a Summit on Entrepreneurship this year to identify how we can deepen ties between business leaders, foundations and social entrepreneurs in the United States and Muslim communities around the world.

On science and technology, we will launch a new fund to support technological development in Muslim-majority countries, and to help transfer ideas to the marketplace so they can create more jobs. We'll open centers of scientific excellence in Africa, the Middle East and Southeast Asia, and appoint new science envoys to collaborate on programs that develop new sources of energy, create green jobs, digitize records, clean water, grow new crops. Today I'm announcing a new global effort with the Organization of the Islamic Conference to eradicate polio. And we will also expand partnerships with Muslim communities to promote child and maternal health.

All these things must be done in partnership. Americans are ready to join with citizens and governments; community organizations, religious leaders, and businesses in Muslim communities around the world to help our people pursue a better life.

The issues that I have described will not be easy to address. But we have a responsibility to join together on behalf of the world that we seek—a world where extremists no longer threaten our people, and American troops have come home; a world where Israelis and Palestinians are each secure in a state of their own, and nuclear energy is used for peaceful purposes; a world where governments serve their citizens, and the rights of all God's children are respected. Those are mutual interests. That is the world we seek. But we can only achieve it together.

I know there are many—Muslim and non-Muslim—who question whether we can forge this new beginning. Some are eager to stoke the flames of division, and to stand in the way of progress. Some suggest that it isn't worth the effort—that we are fated to disagree, and civilizations are doomed to clash. Many more are simply skeptical that real change can occur. There's so much fear, so much mistrust that has built up over the years. But if we choose to be bound by the past, we will never move forward. And I want to particularly say this to young people of every faith, in every country—you, more than anyone, have the ability to reimagine the world, to remake this world.

All of us share this world for but a brief moment in time. The question is whether we spend that time focused on what pushes us apart, or whether we commit ourselves to an effort—a sustained effort—to find common ground, to focus on the future we seek for our children, and to respect the dignity of all human beings.

It's easier to start wars than to end them. It's easier to blame others than to look inward. It's easier to see what is different about someone than to find the things we share. But we should choose the right path, not just the easy path. There's one rule that lies at the heart of every religion—that we do unto others as we would have them do unto us. This truth transcends nations and peoples—a belief that isn't new; that isn't black or white or brown; that isn't Christian or Muslim or Jew. It's a belief that pulsed in the cradle of civilization, and that still beats in the hearts of billions around the world. It's a faith in other people, and it's what brought me here today.

We have the power to make the world we seek, but only if we have the courage to make a new beginning, keeping in mind what has been written.

The Holy Koran tells us: "O mankind! We have created you male and female; and we have made you into nations and tribes so that you may know one another."

The Talmud tells us: "The whole of the Torah is for the purpose of promoting peace."

The Holy Bible tells us: "Blessed are the peacemakers, for they shall be called sons of God."

The people of the world can live in peace. We know that is God's vision. Now that must be our work here on Earth.

Thank you. And may God's peace be upon you. Thank you very much. Thank you.

SOURCE: Barack Obama, "Remarks by the President at Cairo University," www .whitehouse.gov/the_press_office/Remarks-by-the-President-at-Cairo-University-6-04-09.

ANALYSIS

President Barack Obama, during his June 2009 trip to the Middle East and Europe, delivered a much-anticipated speech at Cairo University, in which he expressed the hope of initiating greater cooperation between Muslim-majority countries and the United States. While reaching out to Muslim-majority nations and pointing to common values and interests, President Obama also highlighted the daunting problems involved in America's relations with these countries. The president began his speech by referring to the September 11, 2009, terrorist attacks—which he attributed to a minority of Muslims—and then quickly moved on to the common concerns of Muslims and the United States. The president focused on seven issues. First, he assured the Muslim audience that the United States is not at war with Islam, a faith that claims the allegiance of more than one billion people. Instead, the United States wishes to find common ground in the struggle against extremists. Second, President Obama discussed the tense situation involving Israel, the Palestinians, and the rest of the Arab world, calling for each side to be willing to recognize the right of both Israelis and Palestinians to have an independent state and to live in peace. Third, the president referred to the dangers of introducing nuclear weapons into the Middle East, focusing on the claimed intention of Iran to become a nuclear power. Fourth, President Obama pledged his commitment to supporting democratic governments that protect the rights of the people. Fifth, the president also advocated freedom of religion and encouraged efforts to bring people of different faiths together to reach common humanitarian goals. Sixth, President Obama addressed the issue of women's rights and urged that women be offered the same educational and employment opportunities as men. Finally, the president emphasized the importance of economic development based on improved education and innovation.

Although many praised President Obama for reaching out to Muslim-majority nations, some conservative American commentators continue to view Islam with suspicion as a traditional foe of Christianity and the West. For instance, Diana West (2007, 166), a columnist for the Washington *Times*, asserts that the conflict between western nations and the rest of the world is the "real" culture war, and emphasizes what she considers a major contrast between "civilizations that enshrine human rights" and those that do not, noting that those in the West unfortunately no longer confidently make that distinction. West refers to the differing understandings of fundamental concepts between Western culture and Islam (168), presenting as examples incompatible understandings of freedom and human rights. Many in the West, she asserts, assume a universal set of values held by all cultures. For instance, West quotes from President George W. Bush's 2004 State of the Union Address: "It is mistaken and condescending to assume that whole cultures and great religions are incompatible with liberty and self-government" (17). However, West and other conservative critics assert that history demonstrates otherwise. For instance, many conservatives consider sharia (Islamic law) to stand in fundamental opposition to secular human rights. More traditional conservatives tended to object to the claimed dominance of so-called neo-conservatives in President Bush's administration who apparently wished to disseminate an American conception of democracy worldwide, and especially in the Middle East. In his speech, President Obama, referring specifically to Iraq, assured his audience that the United States should not attempt to impose a particular type of regime on another nation.

Subsequent to President Obama's speech, Iran failed to respond to U.S. overtures for increased communication between the two nations, and the Iranian government security forces suppressed public protests following the announcement that Mahmoud Ahmadinejad had been reelected president. Such events may indicate that although the United States has expressed a willingness to cooperate in bridging many of the cultural differences with Muslim-majority nations, the international culture war may continue into the future.

FURTHER READING

Bawer, Bruce. *While Europe Slept: How Radical Islam Is Destroying the West from Within.* New York: Random House, 2007.

Carlson, Allan. "The Long Culture War: The Christian Democratic Response to Modernity and Materialism." *Touchstone* (November 2006): 36–42.

Carosa, Alberto. "Holding a New Line: Pope Benedict, Islam, and the Media." *Chronicles* (December 2006): 20–21.

Gottschalk, Peter, and Gabriel Greenberg. *Islamophobia: Making Muslims the Enemy.* Lanham, MD: Rowman and Littlefield, 2007.

Jansen, Hans. "An Irreverent Look at Religion in the Netherlands." *Free Inquiry*, February/March 2007: 45–47.

Jordan, Stuart. "How We Can Win the Global Culture War." *Free Inquiry*, February/March 2006: 35–37.

Mead, Walter Russel. *God and Gold: Britain, America, and the Making of the Modern World.* New York: Knopf, 2007.

Murchison, William. "Vanishing Sea of Faith: European Islam and the Doubtful Future of Christian Europe." *Touchstone*, October 2005: 36–40.

Murphy, John F., Jr., *Sword of Islam: Muslim Extremism from the Arab Conquests to the Attack on America.* Amherst, NY: Prometheus Books, 2002.

Omstead, Thomas. "Culture Clash in Denmark." *U.S. News and World Report*, January 8, 2007: 40–45.

Roy, Olivier. *Secularism Confronts Islam.* Translated by George Holoch. New York: Columbia University Press, 2007.

Schuck, Peter H. "Immigration." In *Understanding America: The Anatomy of an Exceptional Nation*, edited by Peter H. Schuck and James Q. Wilson. New York: Public Affairs Press, 2008.

Scruton, Roger. *The West and the Rest: Globalization and the Terrorist Threat.* Wilmington, DE: Intercollegiate Studies Institute, 2002.

Scruton, Roger. *Culture Counts: Faith and Feeling in a World Besieged.* New York: Encounter Books, 2007.

Spencer, Robert. *The Politically Incorrect Guide to Islam (and the Crusades).* Washington, DC: Regnery, 2005.

Swaine, Lucas. *The Liberal Conscience: Politics and Principle in a World of Religious Pluralism.* New York: Columbia University Press, 2006.

Webb, Adam K. *Beyond the Global Culture War.* New York: Routledge, 2006.

Weigel, George. "The War Against Jihadism: Why Can't We Call the Enemy by Its Name? We're Going to Have to in Order to Win." *Newsweek*, February 4, 2008:, 49.

West, Dianna. *The Death of the Grown-Up: How America's Arrested Development Is Bringing Down Western Civilization.* New York: St. Martin's Press, 2007.

9

THE CULTURE WARS:
RETROSPECT AND PROSPECT

Document: George Packer, "The Fall of Conservatism: Have the Republicans Run Out of Ideas?" (2008)

Document: Gertrude Himmelfarb, "The Other Culture War," in *Is There a Culture War? A Dialogue on Values and Public Life*, edited by James Davison Hunter and Alan Wolfe (2006)

Document: Richard Kim, "The Culture War Disarmed" (2008)

Document: Inaugural Address by President Barack Hussein Obama (2009)

"The Fall of Conservatism: Have the Republicans Run Out of Ideas?"

- *Document:* Excerpts from an article by George Packer tracing the modern history of the Republican Party and its leaders as they patterned electoral victories on conservative economic and social principles.
- *Date:* May 2008.
- *Where:* The New Yorker
- *Significance:* George Packer traces a liberal interpretation of the ascendence of the Republican Party out of the "cultural chaos of the 1960s" largely through the strategy developed by Richard Nixon and ultimately Ronald Reagan. Packer argues that this strategy has become bankrupt, due to the lack of Republican emphasis on governing and too great a desire to bring about a smaller government, something Americans actually do not want, even though generally they prefer lower taxes.

DOCUMENT

The era of American politics that has been dying before our eyes was born in 1966. That January, a twenty-seven-year-old editorial writer for the St. Louis *Globe-Democrat* named Patrick Buchanan went to work for Richard Nixon, who was just beginning the most improbable political comeback in American history. Having served as Vice-President in the [Dwight D.] Eisenhower Administration, Nixon had lost the Presidency by a whisker to John F. Kennedy, in 1960, and had been humiliated in a 1962 bid for the California governorship. But he saw that he could propel himself back to power on the strength of a new feeling among Americans who, appalled by the chaos of the cities, the moral heedlessness of the young, and the insults to national pride in Vietnam, were ready to blame it all on the liberalism of President Lyndon B. Johnson. Right-wing populism was bubbling up from below; it needed to be guided by a leader who understood its resentments because he felt them, too.

"From Day One, Nixon and I talked about creating a new majority," Buchanan told me recently, sitting in the library of his Greek-revival house in McLean, Virginia, on a secluded lane bordering the fenced grounds of the Central Intelligence Agency. "What we talked about, basically, was shearing off huge segments of F. D. R.'s New Deal coalition, which L. B. J. had held together: Northern Catholic ethnics and Southern Protestant conservatives—what we called the Daley-Rizzo Democrats in the North and, frankly, the Wallace Democrats in the South." Buchanan grew up in Washington, D.C., among the first group—men like his father, an accountant and a father of nine, who had supported Roosevelt but also revered Joseph McCarthy. The Southerners were the kind of men whom Nixon whipped into a frenzy one night in the fall of 1966, at the Wade Hampton Hotel, in Columbia, South Carolina. Nixon, who was then a partner in a New York law firm, had travelled there with Buchanan on behalf of Republican congressional candidates. Buchanan recalls that the room was full of sweat, cigar smoke, and rage; the rhetoric, which was about patriotism and law and order, "burned the paint off the walls." As they left the hotel, Nixon said, "This is the future of the Party, right here in the South."

Nixon and Buchanan visited thirty-five states that fall, and in November the Republicans won a [1966] midterm landslide. It was the end of Lyndon Johnson's Great Society, the beginning of his fall from power. But his Administration adopted an undercover strategy for building a Republican majority, working to create the impression that there were two Americas: the quiet, ordinary, patriotic, religious, law-abiding Many, and the noisy, élitist, amoral, disorderly, condescending Few.

This strategy was put into action near the end of Nixon's first year in office, when antiwar demonstrators were becoming a disruptive presence in Washington. Buchanan recalls urging Nixon, "We've got to use the siege gun of the Presidency, and go right *after* these guys." On November 3, 1969, Nixon went on national television to speak about the need to avoid a shameful defeat in Vietnam. Looking benignly into the camera, he concluded, "And so tonight—to you, the great silent majority of Americans—I ask for your support." It was the most successful speech of his Presidency. Newscasters criticized him for being divisive and for offering no new vision on Vietnam, but tens of thousands of telegrams and letters expressing approval poured into the White House. It was Nixon's particular political genius to rouse simultaneously the contempt of the *bien-pensants* and the admiration of those who felt the sting of that contempt in their own lives.

Buchanan urged Nixon to enlist his Vice-President, Spiro Agnew, in a battle against the press. In November, Nixon sent Agnew—despised as dull-witted by the media—on the road, where he denounced "this small and unelected élite" of editors, anchormen, and analysts. Buchanan recalls watching a broadcast of one such speech —which he had written for Agnew—on television in his White House office. Joining him was his colleague Kevin Phillips, who had just published "The Emerging Republican Majority," which marshalled electoral data to support a prophecy that Sun Belt conservatism—like Jacksonian Democracy, Republican industrialism, and

New Deal liberalism—would dominate American politics for the next thirty-two years. (As it turns out, Phillips was slightly too modest.) When Agnew finished his diatribe, Phillips said two words: "Positive polarization."

Polarization is the theme of Rick Perlstein's new narrative history *Nixonland* (Scribner), which covers the years between two electoral landslides: [Republican] Barry Goldwater's defeat in 1964 and [Democrat] George McGovern's in 1972. During that time, Nixon figured out that he could succeed politically "by *using* the angers, anxieties, and resentments produced by the cultural chaos of the 1960s," which were also his own. . . . The sixties, which began in liberal consensus over the Cold War and civil rights, became a struggle between two apocalyptic politics that each saw the other as hell-bent on the country's annihilation. The result was violence like nothing the country had seen since the Civil War, and Perlstein emphasizes that bombings, assaults, and murders committed by segregationists, hardhats, and vigilantes on the right were at least as numerous as those by radical students and black militants on the left. . . .

Perlstein argues that the politics of "Nixonland" will endure for at least another generation. On his final page, he writes, "Do Americans not hate each other enough to fantasize about killing one another, in cold blood, over political and cultural disagreements? It would be hard to argue they do not." Yet the polarization of America, which we now call the "culture wars," has been dissipating for a long time. Because we can't anticipate what ideas and language will dominate the next cycle of American politics, the previous era's key words—"élite," "mainstream," "real," "values," "patriotic," "snob," "liberal"—seem as potent as ever. Indeed, they have shown up in the current [2008] campaign: North Carolina and Mississippi Republicans have produced ads linking local Democrats to Jeremiah Wright, Barack Obama's controversial former pastor. The right-wing group Citizens United has said that it will run ads portraying Obama as yet another "limousine liberal." But these are the spasms of nerve endings in an organism that's brain-dead. Among Republicans, there is no energy, no fresh thinking, no ability to capture the concerns and feelings of millions of people. In the past two months, Democratic targets of polarization attacks have won three special congressional elections, in solidly Republican districts in Illinois, Louisiana, and Mississippi. Political tactics have a way of outliving their ability to respond to the felt needs and aspirations of the electorate: Democrats continued to accuse Republicans of being like Herbert Hoover well into the nineteen-seventies; Republicans will no doubt accuse Democrats of being

---

DID YOU KNOW?

Ideological Implications of the 2008 Election

With Democrat Barack Obama winning the presidential election and Democrats gaining representation in both houses of Congress, much speculation occurred regarding the consequences for conservatives. Sean Wilentz, a professor of history at Princeton University, and Grover G. Norquist, president of Americans for Tax Reform, presented differing understandings of the prospects for conservative politics in the December 8, 2008, issue of *U.S. News and World Report*. Wilentz argued that the voters had rejected the ideology of the Ronald Reagan era, including unwise deregulation and advocacy of "small government," thus ushering in a new epoch in American politics. Norquist, on the other hand, largely blamed the Republican defeat on that party and its president's continued expansion of federal government programs, including Medicare, education, and the war in Iraq. Norquist predicted that conservative principles and Republicans will emerge victorious in the 2010 elections after voters observe that the Democrats will have brought higher taxes, more regulation, and lower employment. Which analyst has provided the more accurate prognosis will indicate what direction cultural conflict will take in the next decade.

out of touch with real Americans long after George W. Bush retires to Crawford, Texas. But the 2006 and 2008 elections are the hinge on which America is entering a new political era. . . .

Only a few years ago, on the night of Bush's victory in 2004, the conservative movement seemed indomitable. In fact, it was rapidly falling apart. Conservatives knew how to win elections; however, they turned out not to be very interested in governing. Throughout the decades since Nixon, conservatism has retained the essentially negative character of an insurgent movement.

Nixon himself was more interested in global grand strategy and partisan politics than in any conservative policy agenda. By today's standards, his achievements in office look like those of a moderate liberal: he eased the tensions of the Cold War, expanded the welfare state, and supported affirmative action (albeit in ways calculated to split Democrats). "L. B. J. built the foundation and the first floor of the Great Society," Buchanan said. "We built the skyscraper. Nixon was *not* a Reaganite conservative."

Even Reagan, the Moses of the conservative movement, was more ideological in his rhetoric than in his governance. Conservatives have canonized him for cutting taxes and regulation, moving the courts to the right, and helping to vanquish the Soviet empire. But he proved less dogmatic than most of his opponents and some of his followers expected, especially on ending the Cold War. Reagan emphasized the first word in "positive polarization," turning the Nixon playbook into a kind of national celebration. Like F. D. R., he dominated an era by reconciling opposites through force of personality: just as Roosevelt the patrician became the tribune of the people, Reagan turned conservatism into a forward-looking, optimistic ideology. "We started in 1980 and played addition," Ed Rollins, Reagan's political director, recalls. " 'Let's go out and get Democrats.' We attracted a great many young people to the Party. Reagan made them feel good about the country again. After the '84 election, we did polling—Why did you vote for Reagan? They said, 'He's a winner.' "

The Princeton historian Sean Wilentz, in his book, "The Age of Reagan: A History, 1974–2008" (Harper), argues that Reagan "learned how to seize and keep control of the terms of public debate." On taxes, race, government spending, national security, crime, welfare, and "traditional values," he made mainstream what had been the positions of the right-wing fringe, and he kept Democrats on the defensive. He also brought a generation of doctrinaire conservatives into the bureaucracy and the courts, making appointments based on ideological tests that only a genuine movement leader would impose. The rightward turn of the judiciary will probably be the most lasting achievement of Reagan and his movement.

In retrospect, the Reagan Presidency was the high-water mark of conservatism. "In some respects, the conservative movement was a victim of success," Wilentz concludes. "With the Soviet Union dissolved, inflation reduced to virtually negligible levels, and the top tax rate cut to nearly half of what it was in 1980, all of Ronald Reagan's major stated goals when he took office had been achieved, leaving perplexed and fractious conservatives to fight over where they might now lead the country." Wilentz omits one important failure. According to Buchanan, who was the White House communications director in Reagan's second term, the President once told his barber, Milton Pitts, "You know, Milt, I came here to do five things, and four out of five ain't bad." He had succeeded in lowering taxes, raising morale, increasing defense spending, and facing down the Soviet Union; but he had failed to limit the size of government, which, besides anti-Communism, was the abiding passion of Reagan's political career and of the conservative movement. He didn't come close to achieving it and didn't try very hard, recognizing early that the public would be happy to have its taxes cut as long as its programs weren't touched. And Reagan was a poor steward of the unglamourous but necessary operations of the state. Wilentz notes that he presided over a period of corruption and favoritism, encouraging hostility toward government agencies and "a general disregard for oversight safeguards as among the evils of 'big government.'" In this, and in a notorious attempt to expand executive power outside the Constitution—the Iran-Contra affair—Reagan's Presidency presaged that of George W. Bush.

After Reagan and the end of the Cold War, conservatism lost the ties that had bound together its disparate factions—libertarians, evangelicals, neoconservatives, Wall Street, working-class traditionalists. Without the Gipper and the Evil Empire, what was the organizing principle? In 1994, the conservative journalist David Frum surveyed the landscape and published a book called "Dead Right." Reagan, he wrote, had offered his "Morning in America" vision, and the public had rewarded him enormously, but in failing to reduce government he had allowed the welfare state to continue infantilizing the public, weakening its moral fibre. That November, Republicans swept to power in Congress and imagined that they had been deputized by the voters to distill conservatism into its purest essence. Newt Gingrich declared, "On those things which are at the core of our philosophy and on those things where we believe we represent the vast majority of Americans, there will be no compromise." Instead of just limiting government, the Gingrich revolutionaries set out to disable it. Although the legislative reins were in their hands, these Republicans could find no governmental project to organize their energy around. David Brooks said, "The only thing that held the coalition together was hostility to government." When the *Times Magazine* [columnist] asked William Kristol what ideas he was *for*— in early 1995, high noon of the Gingrich Revolution—Kristol could think to mention only school choice and "shaping the culture."

At the end of that year, when the radical conservatives in the Gingrich Congress shut down the federal government, they learned that the American public was genuinely attached to the modern state. "An anti-government philosophy turned out to be politically unpopular and fundamentally un-American," Brooks said. "People want something melioristic, they want government to do things." . . .

Though conservatives were not much interested in governing, they understood the art of politics. They hadn't made much of a dent in the bureaucracy, and they had done nothing to provide universal health-care coverage or arrest growing economic inequality, but they had created a political culture that was inhospitable to welfare, to an indulgent view of criminals, to high rates of taxation. They had controlled the language and moved the political parameters to the right. Back in November, 1967, [William F.] Buckley wrote in an essay on Ronald Reagan, "They say that his accomplishments are few, that it is only the rhetoric that is conservative. But the rhetoric is the principal thing. It precedes all action. All thoughtful action."

In 2000, George W. Bush presented himself as Reagan's heir, but he didn't come into office with Reagan's ideological commitments or his public-policy goals. According to Frum, who worked as a White House speechwriter during Bush's first two years, Bush couldn't have won if he'd run as a real conservative, because the country was already moving in a new direction. Bush's goals, like Nixon's, were political. Nixon had set out to expand the Republican vote; Bush wanted to keep it from contracting. At his first meeting with Frum and other speechwriters, Bush declared, "I want to change the Party"—to soften its hard edge, and make the Party more hospitable to Hispanics. "It was all about positioning," Frum said, "not about confronting a new generation of problems." Frum wasn't happy; although he suspected that Bush might be right, he wanted him to govern along hard-line conservative principles.

The phrase that signalled Bush's approach was "compassionate conservatism," but it never amounted to a policy program. Within hours of the Supreme Court decision that ended the disputed Florida recount, Dick Cheney met with a group of moderate Republican senators, including Lincoln Chafee, of Rhode Island. According to Chafee's book, "Against the Tide: How a Compliant Congress Empowered a Reckless President" (Thomas Dunne), the Vice President-elect gave the new order of battle: "We would seek confrontation on every front. . . . The new Administration would divide Americans into red and blue, and divide nations into those who stand with us or against us." Cheney's combative instincts and belief in an unfettered and secretive executive proved far more influential at the White House than Bush's campaign promise to be "a uniter, not a divider." Cheney behaved as if, notwithstanding the loss of the popular vote, conservative Republican domination could continue by sheer force of will. On domestic policy, the Administration made tax cuts and privatization its highest priority; and its conduct of the war on terror broke with sixty years of relatively bipartisan and multilateralist foreign policy. . . .

In its final year, the Bush Administration is seen by many conservatives (along with seventy percent of Americans) to be a failure. Among true believers, there are two explanations of why this happened and what it portends. One is the purist version: Bush expanded the size of government and created huge deficits; allowed Republicans in Congress to fatten lobbyists and stuff budgets full of earmarks; tried to foist democracy on a Muslim country; failed to secure the border; and thus won the justified wrath of the American people. This account—shared by Pat Buchanan, the columnist George F. Will, and many Republicans in Congress—has the appeal of asking relatively little of conservatives. They need only to repent of their sins, rid themselves of the neoconservatives who had agitated for the Iraq invasion, and return to first principles. Buchanan said, "The conservatives need to, in Maoist terms, go back to Yenan."

The second version—call it reformist—is more painful, because it's based on the recognition that, though Bush's fatal incompetence and Rove's shortsighted tactics hastened the conservative movement's demise, they didn't cause it. In this view, conservatism has a more serious problem than self-betrayal: a doctrinaire failure to adapt to new circumstances, new problems. Instead of heading back to Yenan to regroup, conservatives will have to spend some years or even decades wandering across a bleak political landscape of losing campaigns and rebranding efforts and earnest policy retreats, much as liberals did after 1968, before they can hope to reëstablish dominance.

Recently, I spoke with a number of conservatives about their movement. The younger ones—say, those under fifty—uniformly subscribe to the reformist version. They are in a state of glowing revulsion at the condition of their political party. . . .

Polls reveal that Americans favor the Democratic side on nearly every domestic issue, from Social Security and health care to education and the environment. The all-purpose Republican solution of cutting taxes has run its course. Frum writes, "There are things only government can do, and if we conservatives wish to be entrusted with the management of government, we must prove that we care enough about government to manage it well."

This is a candid change of heart from a writer who, in "Dead Right," called Republican efforts to compete with [President Bill] Clinton's universal-health-care-coverage plan "cowardly." In the new book, Frum asks, "Who agreed that conservatives should defend the dysfunctional American health system from all criticism?" Well—he did! Frum now identifies health care as the chief anxiety of the middle class. But governing well, in conservative terms, doesn't mean spending more money. It means doing what neither Reagan nor Bush did: mastering details, knowing the options, using caution—that is, taking government seriously. . . .

When I met David Brooks in Washington, he was even more scathing than Frum. Brooks had moved through every important conservative publication—*National Review*, the *Wall Street Journal* editorial page, the Washington *Times*, the *Weekly Standard*—"and now I feel estranged," he said. "I just don't feel it's true, fundamentally *true*." In the eighties, when he was a young movement journalist, the attacks on regulation and the Soviet Union seemed "true." Now most conservatives seem incapable of even acknowledging the central issues of our moment: wage stagnation, inequality, health care, global warming. They are stuck in the past, in the dogma of limited government. Perhaps for that reason, Brooks left movement journalism and, in 2003, became a moderately conservative columnist for the [New York] *Times*. "American conservatives had one defeat, in 2006, but it wasn't a big one," he said. "The big defeat is probably coming, and then the thinking will happen. I have not yet seen the major think tanks reorient themselves, and I don't know if they can." . . .

It's probably not an accident that the most compelling account of the crisis [for conservative Republicans] was written by two conservatives who are still in their twenties and have made their careers outside movement institutions. Ross Douthat and Reihan Salam, editors at the *Atlantic Monthly*, are eager to cut loose the dead weight of the Gingrich and Bush years. In their forthcoming book, "Grand New Party: How Republicans Can Win the Working Class and Save the American Dream" (Doubleday), Douthat and Salam are writing about, if not for, what they call "Sam's Club Republicans"—members of the white working class, who are the descendants of Nixon's "northern ethnics and southern Protestants" and the Reagan Democrats of the eighties. In their analysis, America is divided between the working class (defined as those without a college education) and a "mass upper class" of the college educated, who are culturally liberal and increasingly Democratic. The New Deal, the authors acknowledge, provided a sense of security to working-class families; the upheavals of the sixties and afterward broke it down. Their emphasis is on the disintegration of working-class cohesion, which they blame on "crime, contraception, and growing economic inequality." Douthat and Salam are cultural conservatives—Douthat became a Pentecostal and then a Catholic in his teens—but they readily acknowledge the economic forces that contribute to the breakdown of families lacking the "social capital" of a college degree. Their policy proposals are an unorthodox mixture of government interventions (wage subsidies for lower-income workers) and tax reforms ([Ramesh] Ponnuru's increased child-credit idea, along with a revision of the tax code in favor of lower-income families). Their ultimate purpose is political: to turn as much of the working class into Sam's Club Republicans as possible. They don't acknowledge the corporate interests that are at least as Republican as Sam's Club shoppers, and that will put up a fight on many counts, potentially tearing the Party apart. Nor are they prepared to accept as large a role for government as required by the deep structural problems they identify. Douthat and Salam are as personally remote from working-class America as any élite liberal; Douthat described their work to me as "a data-driven attempt at political imagination." Still, any Republican politician worried about his party's eroding base and grim prospects should make a careful study of this book.

Frum's call for national-unity conservatism and Douthat and Salam's program for "Sam's Club Republicans" are efforts to shorten the lean years for conservatives, but political ideas don't materialize on command to solve the electoral problems of one party or another. They are generated over time by huge social transformations, on the scale of what took place in the sixties and seventies. "They're not real, they're ideological constructs," Buchanan said, "and you can write columns and things like that, but they don't engage the heart. The heart was engaged by law and order. You reached into people—there was feeling."

SOURCE: George Packer, "The Fall of Conservatism: Have the Republicans Run Out of Ideas?" *The New Yorker*, May 26, 2008: 47–54. Reprinted courtesy of George Packer.

ANALYSIS

George Packer, focusing on the conservative side of the culture war, argues that the reasons for the ascendency of the Republican Party in the 1980s also help to explain the more recent decline of the party's electoral fortunes. To the extent that the Republican Party has supported the agenda of the Religious Right and corporate interests, its decline would deprive those groups of a major vehicle for furthering their cause, and thus would signal a lessening of the intensity of the culture war. According to Packer, the unwillingness or inability of Republicans in government to deliver on their promise to restrict government growth contributed to dissatisfaction among conservative voters. However, although citizens called for reduced taxes, they had come to enjoy the benefits that government could provide. When a movement that had offered itself as an antagonist of "big government"—attributed to Democratic presidents and a Democratic-controlled Congress—finally gained

DID YOU KNOW?

President Obama and International Aid for Family Planning

Three days after Barack Obama's inauguration, and one day following the 37th anniversary of the U.S. Supreme Court decision in *Roe v. Wade* permitting legal abortion, the new president reversed a ban on U.S. assistance to international aid organizations that offer abortion services in other countries. President Ronald Reagan originally established the ban in 1984, which critics called a "global gag rule" because aid organizations that received U.S. financial assistance could not refer to the abortion procedure when conducting family planning education programs. President Bill Clinton revoked the rule soon after taking office in 1993, but President George W. Bush reestablished the ban in 2001. Although President Obama announced that his action was intended to remove family planning assistance as a "political wedge issue," conservatives viewed the decision as politically divisive. Thus abortion likely would remain a key issue in any continuation of the culture wars.

control of both branches of government but could not deliver on the promise of reducing the size of government and instead engaged in the same use of government to deliver political favors in the form of pork barrel legislation and earmarks, the general population and members of the party themselves became disillusioned with the ability of Republicans to fulfill their pledges. The ability of the Republican Party to regroup may depend on Republican strategists to appeal once again to the groups that helped elect Ronald Reagan and brought about the election of a Republican majority in Congress. The use once more of "wedge" issues such as abortion and gay marriage could contribute to a political resurgence; but if so, the culture war would undoubtedly gain momentum. However, if issues such as economic well being, environmental pollution, and alternative energy sources remain salient for voters, such socially conservative wedge issues may not contribute to Republican electoral renewal, at least in the near future.

"The Other Culture War"

- **Document:** Gertrude Himmelfarb's analysis of the present state of the culture war.
- **Date:** 2006.
- **Where:** Included in *Is There a Culture War? A Dialogue on Values and American Public Life*, edited by James Davison Hunter and Alan Wolfe. Washington, DC: Brookings Institution Press, pp. 74–82.
- **Significance:** Gertrude Himmelfarb largely rejects the declaration of victory by many on both sides of the culture war. Himmelfarb argues instead that declines in such measures as rates of crime, violence, and illegitimacy notwithstanding, evidence indicates that worsening cultural conditions provide a reason for conservatives to continue the struggle.

DOCUMENT

The culture war has taken an interesting turn. Combatants on both sides are declaring victory and, in doing so, pronouncing the culture war over and done with. This is especially odd at a time when the [Terri] Schiavo case, the Supreme Court nominations, abortion, and gay marriage have inflamed tempers and exacerbated the divisions between liberals and conservatives, Democrats and Republicans. Before that there was the election of 2004 that produced the map demarcating "red" and "blue" America as cultural as well as political entities. And before that there were the evangelicals who brought the religious-secular divide into the public arena and made it a major subject of contention. Yet it is now, in this overheated climate, that liberals and conservatives seem to be agreeing on one thing and one thing only: that the culture war is over.

Indeed, for some—for Alan Wolfe, most notably—there never was a war, at least not among the "suburban middle class Americans" who were the subject of his *One Nation, After All*; it was primarily "intellectuals" who were fighting that war. [1] ... Most Americans, ordinary Americans, he then argued, are not involved in a culture war because, unlike these intellectuals, they are "nonjudgmental," share much the same moral values, and conduct their lives in very similar ways. This is still his view of the American public, although he now modifies his conclusion slightly, perhaps in view of all the controversies that have had such high political visibility. He no longer claims that there is no culture war, rather that it is "on its last legs." Those who persist in fighting it, he predicts, "are likely to find themselves on the sideline in America's political future."

Some conservatives, who were once on the front lines in the culture war and do not welcome being shunted to the sideline, are now pleased to report that the war is over (or almost over) because they are winning. It is in this spirit that administration spokesmen took the overwhelmingly patriotic response to September 11 as evidence of the "soundness," of the moral and social health of the American people. Others have come to the same conclusion for different reasons. They cite the social indicators showing a decline in the incidence of crime, violence, abortion, drug use, divorce, and out-of-wedlock births among adults and, more important, among young people. Andrew Sullivan, in the London *Times*, takes these as a refutation of American "cultural declinists" and as an object lesson for the British, who are urged to learn from American experiences—from American conservatives in particular, who sponsored policies that reduced crime and domestic violence, discouraged welfare dependency, deterred abortions and teenage pregnancy, and removed the incentives for "anti-social behavior." [2]

These "cultural triumphalists" (as one might call them in contrast to the "cultural declinists" Sullivan criticizes) have found their voice in such conservative organs as the *City Journal*, which has reported upon the considerable improvements in New York City in particular and in America as a whole. "Yessiree," Kay Hymowitz exults in an article entitled "It's Morning After in America," "family values are hot! Capitalism is cool! Seven-grain bread is so yesterday, and red meat is back!" Citing some of the now familiar statistics about crime, violence, abortions, and the like, she concludes that we are witnessing the emergence of "a vital, optimistic, family-centered, entrepreneurial, and yes, morally thoughtful, citizenry." This is a new kind of "bourgeois normality," she says, albeit one very different from the old. "The 1950s, this ain't." [3] But it is the 2000s, and a very good thing, too.

An earlier article in the same journal introduced still other evidence to explain why "We're Not Losing the Culture Wars Anymore." Brian Anderson cites three "seismic events": cable TV, the Internet, and book publishing, all of which provide conservative alternatives to what were once almost exclusively liberal domains. Cable TV, for example, gives us not only the Fox News channel but also Comedy Central's highest-rated program, the cartoon series *South Park*, featuring (this is Anderson's description) "four crudely animated and impossibly foul-mouthed fourth graders." The latter are Anderson's heroes, their "exuberant vulgarity" exposing the liberal pieties and PC mentality of the dominant culture. He quotes Andrew Sullivan who praised the show for being "the best antidote to PC culture we have," and who labeled its fans "South Park Republicans." [4] Anderson himself prefers "South Park Conservatives," the title of his recent book expanding upon his article. [5]

But it is more than the antiliberal, anti-PC thrust of the show that endears it to Anderson and qualifies it as "conservative." It is its vulgarity and raunchiness as well. He quotes one college student: "The label [South Park Republican] is really about rejecting the image of conservatives as uptight squares—crusty old men or nerdy kids in blue blazers. We might have long hair, smoke cigarettes, get drunk on weekends, have sex before marriage, watch R-rated movies, cuss like sailors—and also happen to be conservative, or at least libertarian." [6] One is reminded of the group of young, or not so young, conservative women some years ago who, in a similar effort to *épater les bourgeois*, flaunted their defiance of the conventional image of conservative womanhood by boasting that they could drink, cuss, smoke (cigars, not cigarettes), tell dirty jokes, and be as raunchy as the best of them.

To an old culture warrior like myself, South Park conservatism is an oxymoron, being not only antiliberal but anticonservative as well (and unfunny, to boot, its humor and pranks being more appropriate to fourth-grade louts than to sophomoric college students). It is disturbing, therefore, to find it being touted by serious conservatives. Conservatives, so astute about politics and economics, have always had difficulty doping with the culture. They were slow in coming to terms with the counterculture of the 1960s, in appreciating how much of a threat it was to the values and sensibilities, the social structures and institutions that had long been taken for granted. It was not until the counterculture had become the dominant culture that they began to take it seriously. And even then they were goaded to do so by religious groups who had taken its measure and had resisted it from the beginning, and who helped create, in effect, a counter-counterculture.

It is this counter-counterculture that is reflected in the statistics now cited by conservatives as evidence that they are winning the culture war. The statistics are encouraging and very welcome—but not, unhappily, altogether conclusive. If the divorce rate is stable (or very slightly falling), it is because fewer people are getting married, and the separation rate among couples living together without benefit of marriage is higher than the divorce rate among married couples. If the proportion of children in married-parent families rose by a single percent, that still leaves a third of the children with unmarried parents. If high school teenagers are drinking less and being less sexually active, college students are drinking more and being more active; binge-drinking and hooking up are major problems on many campuses. Young people may be less "alienated" from their parents than they used to be and more inclined to "believe in the values" of their parents. [7] But that is perhaps because their parents are more inclined to believe in the values of their children—not necessarily a sign of cultural maturity. (It would not be the first time that a generation of adults decided to surrender and call it victory.)

And so it goes for most of the other statistics. In any case, none of these indicators bring[s] the family in particular, or the culture in general, back to the precounterculture situation. It has often been observed that in pre-counterculture 1965, when Senator Daniel Patrick Moynihan wrote his percipient report on the breakdown of the black family, the figure for black illegitimacy was lower than that for whites today and a fraction of that for blacks today. The conservative columnist David Brooks, who has been a staunch defender of the "culture war is dead" thesis, wrote one column presenting evidence that we are in the midst of a "moral revival," only to follow it with another piece three days later, based on other evidence, that concluded, "We are replacing marriage, one of our most successful institutions, with hooking up. This is a deep structural problem, and very worrying." [8]

There is another "structural problem" that does not lend itself to quantification but is no less troubling. Wolfe quotes my *One Nation, Two Cultures*, describing the situation as I saw it in 1999: "the collapse of ethical principles and habits, the loss of respect for authorities and institutions, the breakdown of the family, the decline of civility, the vulgarization of high culture, and the degradation of popular culture." [9] Vulgarization and degradation—one can hardly use those words today, any more than one can comfortably speak of indecency, incivility, or impropriety. They sound hopelessly prudish, old-fogyish, and—horrors!—judgmental; one is almost inclined to put quotation marks around them. Yet how can one take account of the coarsening (another no-no word) of the culture—the South Park culture—without such words. Moynihan once coined the phrase "defining deviancy down" to describe the situation: what was once stigmatized as deviant behavior is now tolerated; what was once regarded as abnormal has been normalized. Today, the very word "deviancy" is taboo.

Wolfe protests that the lives of "ordinary Americans" are not affected by the issues that have loomed so large in the culture war: the Schiavo case, abortion, gay marriage. But their lives are enormously affected, every day in every way, by the kind of culture symbolized by those South Park brats. That culture, the "popular culture"—the term is very apt—is most dramatically reflected in (and in part created by) television, movies, the Internet, and video games. In my book I quoted accounts of TV shows that were "pushing the envelope" with ever more egregious displays of violence, profanity, prurience, and promiscuity. "Like a child," the *New York Times* reported, "acting outrageously naughty to see how far he can push his parents, mainstream television this season [spring 1998] is flaunting the most vulgar and explicit sex, language, and behavior that it has ever sent into American homes." [10] One now rarely hears talk of "pushing the envelope" because the envelope has been pushed so far that reporters no longer think such language and behavior exceptionable or newsworthy.

"Where is the outrage?" Bill Bennett once asked, deploring the insufficient public reaction to President Clinton's sexual misconduct. When one event did elicit expressions of outrage—the breast-baring on the 2004 Super Bowl intermission (the [Janet Jackson's] "wardrobe malfunction," as it was delicately put)—journalists were taken aback by the reaction to what seemed to them to be a rather amusing episode. It was the outrage, more than the event itself, that was newsworthy. And it took something like an intermission, that now-hallowed family occasion, to arouse dormant sensibilities and instincts. The public, almost as much as the press, has become inured to the escalating assaults upon traditional values.

Even Bennett could not have envisaged the slew of reality shows that flaunt, even celebrate—and as "reality," not fiction—a degree of moral and esthetic nihilism (vulgarity, grossness, exhibitionism, and egregious materialism) that was once, if not quite unthinkable, certainly unviewable. And viewable now not only on cable channels that are unregulated but on the networks that presumably pass the test of regulators. The kind of casual, amiable promiscuity we got used to on *Friends* was replaced by the cold, calculating promiscuity of *Hooking Up*. (The titles themselves are suggestive, the one innocent and benign, the other unashamed and provocative.) Commenting on the last episode of the *Friends* series, the *New York Times* noted that the cast had "paired off in nearly every conceivable geometric combination over the years." [11] But at least that "pairing off" was among friends. *Hooking Up* (a documentary, not fiction) took place among strangers who meet on the Internet and coolly appraise each other; one participant cheerfully explains that she gives her dates twenty minutes to prove themselves worthy of her interest (that is, her bed).

Another pseudodocumentary, *The Aristocrats*, was hailed by the reviewer in the *New York Times* as "a work of painstaking and original scholarship, and, as such, one of the most original and rigorous pieces of criticism in any medium I have encountered in quite some time." This "essay film," the reviewer hastened to add, is "possibly the filthiest, vilest, most extravagantly obscene documentary ever made. … There is scarcely a minute of screen time that does not contain a reference to scatology, incest, bestiality, and practices for which no euphemisms or Latinate names have been invented." [12] The subject of the film is a single dirty joke, repeated 60 or 70 times (95 to 100 times, according to other counts)—a joke so dirty that it could not be printed in the *Times* or, so far as I know, any other respectable newspaper. My first thought on reading this review was that, of course, it was meant ironically. Not at all. The reviewer was quite serious in her admiration, as were the other reviewers cited in the ads for this "obscene, disgusting, vulgar and vile" film, the "funniest movie you'll ever see" (and a great commercial success).

As movies have been trumped by television and television by the Internet, so video games trump them all in being more accessible, more aggressive ("transgressive," in academese), and more addictive. The Internet prides itself on being interactive, but that is nothing compared with the interactive nature of video games— "virtual" (not merely passive) violence, sex, profanity, and wanton rage. One used to hear complaints about the time children spent watching TV. But that is nothing compared to the much more time-consuming and addictive nature of the Internet and video games, which can be indulged in private, without adult scrutiny. And not only by children but (as the evidence now suggests) by young and not so young adults, for whom these media have become so much the reality of their lives. [13]

Nor has the old medium, the written word, been laggard. A few years ago I wrote an article deploring what I took to be egregious examples of familial disloyalty and disrespect: a memoir by a well-known literary critic about his more distinguished wife, describing in excruciating detail her physical and mental degeneration as a result of Alzheimer's disease; another by a daughter about her prolonged (and voluntary) sexual relationship with her father (a minister); still another by a son about his father's (one of America's foremost intellectuals) putative (and entirely unproved) mental and moral debility. [14] Today, these demeaning and salacious memoirs are so common as to constitute an accepted literary genre. Not only celebrities but ordinary mothers and fathers, wives and lovers are fair game. "Mom died of Alzheimer yesterday," a piece in the *New York Times Magazine* opened. [15] "Yesterday"!—the only son could not wait to rush into print. (Indeed, he must have prepared his piece, and it must have been accepted for publication, even printed, some time before her death.) Such revelations are by now so familiar that the reader is more inclined to be bored than shocked by them. And self-revelations as well. Confessions of marital infidelities or sexual perversities have at least some redeeming titillating quality. But what can be the appeal of an article by a respectable syndicated columnist in a respectable newspaper reporting, in graphic detail, on the frequency, texture, and quality of her bowel movements over the course of her lifetime? [16]

"Culture war" and "culture wars": the terms are used interchangeably. But perhaps the plural form is the more accurate. Conservatives (or, as James Hunter puts it, "traditionalists") may be winning the war over one sense of culture, that measured by the indices of crime, violence, illegitimacy, and the like. But they are losing the other war, the war over the popular culture—losing it by default, by sheer, willful inattention.

There are, to be sure, countervailing forces, people waging not war but a kind of passive resistance, opting out, so to speak, from the popular culture and founding a dissident culture of their own. Thus parents, displeased with the public school system (for moral as well as educational reasons), may choose, at considerable financial sacrifice, to send their children to private or religious schools, or (at even greater personal sacrifice) to teach them at home; more than a million children are now homeschooled. Professors, dissatisfied with the curriculum or mode of instruction in their colleges but knowing that it would be futile to try to transform or even reform them, may create (with the help of friendly foundations) oases in those institutions —centers, institutes, programs—that reflect their interests and values. And students, seeking something other than an aggressively secular education, may avail themselves of an ever expanding number of religious colleges. So, too, parents, despairing of the increasingly offensive fare on television and the Internet, no longer agitate for governmental regulation (or even self-regulation) of those media. Instead they act as their own regulators and censors. Some families adhere to what is called "TV abstinence." [17]

These groups represent something like a dissident culture—a valuable alternative to the dominant culture but hardly a victory over it. In this sense the culture wars are not over; they are only in abeyance. If conservatives are winning the body count, as measured by statistics of crime, violence, abortion, and illegitimacy, they are losing the soul—the minds and hearts, the sensibilities and spirits of all too many people who are in thrall to the popular culture. The other war will have to be fought by other means and by other people. Not all has been won, by either side. But neither has all been lost.

NOTES

[1] Alan Wolfe, *One Nation, After All: What Middle Class Americans Really Think about God, Country, Family, Racism, Welfare, Immigration, Homosexuality, Work, the Right, the Left, and Each Other* (New York: Viking Penguin, 1998), p. 276.

[2] Andrew Sullivan, "It's a Wonderful Life," *Times* (London), August 14, 2005.

[3] Kay S. Hymowitz, "It's Morning After in America," *City Journal* 14 (Spring 2004): 56–57.

[4] Brian C. Anderson, "We're Not Losing the Culture Wars Anymore," *City Journal* 13 (Autumn 2003): 15–21.

[5] Brian C. Anderson, *South Park Conservatives: The Revolt against Liberal Media Bias* (Washington: Regnery, 2005).

[6] Anderson, "Culture Wars," p. 22; *South Park Conservatives*, p. 99.

[7] Hymowitz, "It's Morning After," p. 60.

[8] David Brooks, "The Virtue of Virtues," *New York Times*, August 7, 2005, p. WK 12; "Sex and the Cities," *New York Times*, August 10, 2005, p. A27.

[9] Gertrude Himmelfarb, *One Nation, Two Cultures* (New York: Knopf, 1999), p. 20.

[10] Lawrie Mifflin, "TV Stretches Limits of Taste, to Little Outcry," *New York Times*, April 6, 1998, p. A1.

[11] Tom Shales, "A Big Hug Goodbye to 'Friends' and Maybe to the Sitcom," *New York Times*, May 7, 2004, p. C1.

[12] A. O. Scott, "A Filthy Theme and Variations," *New York Times*, July 29, 2005, p. B1. If I quote the *New York Times* so often, it is not only because I happen to read it but also because it is representative of respectable, mainstream journalistic opinion.

[13] See Christine Rosen, "Playgrounds of the Self," *New Atlantis* (Summer 2005): 3–27.

[14] Gertrude Himmelfarb, "A Man's Own Household His Enemies," *Commentary* 108, no. 1 (July 1999).

[15] Steve Gettinger, "The Zen of Alzheimer's," *New York Times Magazine*, August 15, 1999, p. 68.

[16] Jane E. Brody, "Looking Beyond Fiber to Stay 'Regular,'" *New York Times*, August 2, 2005.

[17] These TV abstainers have been called "a band of internal exiles," recalling the "inner emigration" of dissidents in Nazi Germany who sought to retreat to a private haven uncontaminated by the regime. See Himmelfarb, *One Nation*, pp. 133–34.

SOURCE: Gertrude Himmelfarb, "The Other Culture War," in *Is There a Culture War? A Dialogue on Values and American Public Life*, edited by James Davison Hunter and Alan Wolfe, reprinted courtesy of the Permissions Department, Brookings Institution Press, Washington, D.C. © 2006.

ANALYSIS

Gertrude Himmelfarb's evaluation of the culture war, from the conservative side of the conflict, presents some victories for her preferred side. However, many signs of cultural drift toward vulgarity and materialism lead to serious doubts about the conclusion of the culture war. As others have noted, at least until 2006, conservatives succeeded in winning more political battles than liberals, but at the same time the overall social milieu, particularly popular culture, continued to shift away from the traditional values that conservatives hold dear. Himmelfarb notes that some conservatives appear to have surrendered to the vulgar characteristics of popular culture at the same time they think they are defending the conservative cause. Her solution to what she describes as an all-pervasive decline in traditional values brings to

DID YOU KNOW?

Continuing Evangelical Christian Support for Conservative Positions

In December 2008 Reverend Richard Cizik, vice president for government relations of the National Association of Evangelicals, was forced to resign his office after an interview on National Public Radio's *Fresh Air* program in which Cizik stated that he supports same-gender civil unions. Cizik already had angered conservatives, including Donald Wildmon, chairman of the American Family Association, Tony Perkins, president of the Family Research Council, and Gary Bauer, president of Coalitions for America, for advocating that evangelicals should take a stand on the issue of global warming. Cizik's removal indicated that conservative groups would likely continue to emphasize such social issues as abortion, traditional marriage, and sexual abstinence before marriage. Nonetheless, other evangelicals undoubtedly will focus on a broader set of issues, including global warming, poverty, and medical care.

mind the biblical admonition to "come out from among them and be separate" (2 Corinthians 6:17), recommending that parents send children to private or religious schools, or home-school them. College and university professors dissatisfied with the mandated curriculum can establish special programs that reflect conservative values, and students can opt for religious colleges to avoid the secularizing influences of the general culture. Parents can limit, or eliminate, television viewing, and encourage their children to practice sexual abstinence. While seeing promising signs for the future, Himmelfarb does not accept the conclusion that the culture war is subsiding. Instead, she expects its continuation, which apparently includes an increasing separation of the United States into two distinct cultures, with conservatives inoculating themselves and their families against the larger culture that Himmelfarb believes shows definite signs of continuing deterioration.

"The Culture War Disarmed"

- **Document:** An opinion piece by Richard Kim announcing a de-escalation in the culture war.
- **Date:** June 9, 2008.
- **Where:** *The Nation*
- **Significance:** Richard Kim examines recent trends, particularly with regard to the issue of gay marriage, and concludes that a reduction in public concern for such divisive issues raises expectations that the culture war is subsiding.

DOCUMENT

In mid-May [2008] Democrats were finally riding high again. Their contentious primary appeared to be drawing to a close, they had routed Republicans for a third time in a Congressional special election and Americans were looking to them to address a failed war and a failing economy. Then on May 15 the California Supreme Court voted four to three to legalize same-sex marriages. As if on cue, gays and lesbians took to the streets of The Castro, Mayor Gavin Newsom vowed to turn San Francisco's City Hall into a hot pink wedding chapel and right-wing demagogues announced that they would place a constitutional amendment banning same-sex marriage on California's fall ballot. Suddenly, conservatives like William Kristol were crowing about how resentment over "judicial activism" would help deliver John McCain the White House, and Democrats were seeing shades of 2004—when anti-gay marriage initiatives supposedly contributed to [Democratic presidential candidate] John Kerry's defeat.

But in fact, California's marital fireworks represent a more comforting reality for Democrats—the beginning of the end of the culture war. Nowhere is this sea change more evident than in the Golden State, where gay marriage has become a thoroughly mainstream proposition. In 2005 and 2007 the California State Legislature passed bills granting gays and lesbians the right to marry; on both occasions, Governor Arnold Schwarzenegger vetoed the bills. But by directly expressing their support for gay marriage through the democratic process, the State Legislature undercut the right-wing claim that gay marriage is something "activist judges" foist onto an unwilling public. Indeed, the majority on the state's Supreme Court, comprising three Republicans and one Democrat, weren't "legislating from the bench"; they were reaffirming legislative will. And despite his vetoes, Schwarzenegger has said that he respects the court's opinion and opposes an amendment to the California Constitution, something he calls "a waste of time."

None of this will deter conservatives from pouring money, ground troops and vitriol into their campaign to get a marriage amendment passed, and they may well succeed this fall. But even that short-term victory won't change two fundamentals: in the presidential race, California will go to the Democratic candidate, and the idea of gay marriage—endorsed by the State Legislature, accepted by the Republican governor and supported by growing numbers of gay-friendly voters—has become for Californians as banal as a Hollywood divorce.

Indeed, for all the hoopla, the number of new rights California's gay couples picked up from the decision was this: zero. That's because California already had a same-sex domestic partnership statute on the books. Passed by the legislature in 1999 and expanded on several occasions to include more rights, California's domestic partnership laws are the most comprehensive in the nation, granting every right of coupledom a state can give absent federally recognized marriage. All the court did was give queers the m-word. This decision may have legal repercussions down the line, but in terms of actual economic and legal rights like access to spousal health insurance, hospital visitation and inheritance, Californians had already arrived at the conclusion that these should be available to all regardless of sexual orientation. To be sure, the symbol of marriage may matter a lot to some, mainly marriage-minded gays and Christian conservatives, but few voters are willing to hang a national election on it. According to a May [2008] Gallup poll, just 16 percent of Americans think that a presidential candidate must share their view on gay marriage.

The California gay marriage debate illustrates important national trends for Democrats. Growing numbers of Americans favor gay rights,

DID YOU KNOW?

Gay Marriage in Connecticut

In October 2008 Connecticut became the third state to legalize gay marriage when the state supreme court, in a 4-to-3 decision, ruled that same-gender couples had the right to marry in the state. In 2005 the Connecticut legislature had passed a civil union statute that granted to those in a civil union the same legal benefits, protections, and responsibilities that couples in a marriage enjoyed. Republican Governor M. Jodi Rell insisted that the statute include a provision defining marriage as "the union of one man and one woman." Eight gay and lesbian couples filed suit, claiming that the legislation established an unequal condition for gays and lesbians relative to a man and a woman who enter into marriage. The court majority ruled that civil unions and marriage could not be considered "separate but equal" institutions and therefore homosexual couples must be granted the same legal status as heterosexual couples. In all three states—Massachusetts, California, and Connecticut—gay marriage was established through judicial rulings. Seven states and the District of Columbia have approved civil unions or domestic partnerships, but 27 states have approved constitutional amendments to define marriage as a union between one man and one woman. The rulings added to the conjecture that the gay marriage issue would continue to contribute to the disagreements referred to as the culture war.

including some form of partnership recognition for same-sex couples, especially when framed as economic and legal rights. This is particularly true of young voters; in California 55 percent of voters under 30 support gay marriage, and nationwide 63 percent of voters under 40 support civil unions or domestic partnerships. But this trend also holds true for voters of all ages; a 2007 Field poll reported that Californians young and old were four times more likely to say they are becoming more accepting of gay relationships than less accepting. Moreover, when the symbolic weight of marriage is removed from the equation, support for gay rights becomes overwhelming. Nationwide, a whopping 89 percent of voters favor protecting gays and lesbians from employment discrimination.

Instead of fearing an anti-gay backlash, then, Democrats should take this moment to reconsider their longstanding assumption that cultural antagonism can only hurt their national electoral prospects. Fearing the worst, for decades the Democrats caved to or triangulated around cultural conservatives, making ill-fated examples out of every Sister Souljah in the house and offering insulting sops to "family values," like video-game ratings. Indeed, the premise that Democrats are still on the losing side of the culture war defined the last weeks of Hillary Clinton's campaign, which, aided by the mainstream media, dredged up nearly every assumed liberal Achilles' heel of the past forty years—race, religion, guns, elitism, patriotism and '60s radicalism—in order to paint Barack Obama as a general election loser. But, like Christian conservative attempts to portray same-sex marriage as a "threat to civilization," the culture war against Obama—waged around flag pins, Reverend [Jeremiah] Wright [Obama's controversial former pastor], Bill Ayers and bowling scores—was a whole lot of sound and fury signifying nothing. Thankfully, the majority of Democratic voters refused to be manipulated by these symbols sheared of substance, and now it is time to retire the paradigm altogether. An overdetermined catchphrase, "The culture war," was always an insult—most of all to the concept of culture itself, which the right wing reduced from a good or an aspiration to a series of cheap slurs aimed at liberals who drank too many lattes or hailed from the wrong places, like Massachusetts and San Francisco. But demography was always trending the other way, and now Starbucks lattes can be found in every small town, hip-hop is everywhere and homosexuals are here, queer and on the bridal registry—all of which elicits a collective yawn from the under-40 set.

SOURCE: Reprinted with permission from the June 9, 2008, issue of *The Nation*. Richard Kim, "The Culture War Disarmed," 4, 6. For subscription information, call 1-800-333-8536. Portions of each week's *Nation* magazine can be accessed at http://www.thenation.com.

ANALYSIS

Although the fate of gay marriage in California remained to be decided in the November 2008 election (California voters ultimately approved the proposition to amend the state constitution to define marriage as a union between one man and

DID YOU KNOW?

The Culture War in the 2008 Election Campaigns

The 2008 elections gave indications that the intensity of the U.S. culture wars was subsiding. The reaction to Senator Elizabeth Dole's campaign ads represents one of those indications. Senator Dole of North Carolina, facing a strong challenge in her reelection bid from state senator Kay Hagan, in the last week of the campaign launched a television ad that accused Hagan of being "godless." The Dole ad called attention to a September 2008 fund-raiser in Boston organized by author Wendy Kaminer and her husband, Woody Kaplan, that Hagan planned to attend. Kaplan had been a member of the advisory board for the Godless Americans political action committee and supported a more secular society. The ad ended with a photograph of Hagan and a voice—not Hagan's—saying "There is no God." Hagan, a former Sunday school teacher and a member and elder in a Presbyterian church, threatened to bring legal action against Dole if the ad was not withdrawn. Dan McLagan, a spokesman for Dole, defended the ad, stating that by supposedly accepting contributions from Godless Americans, Hagan had undertaken an obligation to support the organization's agenda, including removing reference to God from the public arena. What in past elections might have been considered an effective strategy failed to bring about the desired result. Hagan ultimately won the election, indicating that other issues were more salient and perhaps that voters reacted negatively to the ad.

one woman), Richard Kim viewed the decision of that state's supreme court as indicative of a nationwide trend in the so-called culture war that the public was becoming more accepting of such controversial subjects as same-gender marriage, or at least legally recognized gay unions. Such issues appeared to play a smaller role in state and national politics and elections, as symbolized by the Democratic Party's nomination of Barack Obama as its 2008 presidential candidate.

Attempts to employ the tactics more closely associated with the culture war—including religious commitment, gun control and gun rights, and patriotism—appeared less virulent than in past election cycles, thus suggesting that the culture war that many considered so important to past elections was losing its relevance to voters. Kim urged liberal Democrats not to shy away from confronting conservatives now that the general population tended to support more liberal positions on such issues as gay rights. Some of the same trends that trouble Gertrude Himmelfarb, and that she finds 'vulgar" and "gross," Kim celebrates as welcome cultural change. If parents are accepting the cultural trends of their children, that is all to the good. Any upsurge in the culture war may depend on whether conservative apprehension about the social trends that Himmelfarb has labeled "gross" and "materialistic" is able to energize the general electorate despite the growing concern for the economic health of the nation.

Inaugural Address

- *Document:* President Barack Hussein Obama's inaugural address.
- *Date:* January 20, 2009.
- *Where:* On the steps of the Capitol Building, Washington, DC.
- *Significance:* An estimated two million people came to the nation's capital to celebrate the inauguration of Barack Obama as president of the United States, and millions more, including news analysts, listened carefully to the new president's inaugural address, anticipating that President Obama would signal a direction for the country very different than that followed by the more conservative George W. Bush administration and would take stands on issues associated with the culture wars at odds with the previous administration.

DOCUMENT

My fellow citizens, I stand here today humbled by the task before us, grateful for the trust you've bestowed, mindful of the sacrifices borne by our ancestors.

I thank President Bush for his service to our nation as well as the generosity and cooperation he has shown throughout this transition.

Forty-four Americans have now taken the presidential oath. The words have been spoken during rising tides of prosperity and the still waters of peace. Yet, every so often, the oath is taken amidst gathering clouds and raging storms. At these moments, America has carried on not simply because of the skill or vision of those in high office, but because we, the people, have remained faithful to the ideals of our forebears and true to our founding documents.

So it has been; so it must be with this generation of Americans.

That we are in the midst of crisis is now well understood. Our nation is at war against a far-reaching network of violence and hatred. Our economy is badly weakened, a consequence of greed and irresponsibility on the part of some, but also our collective failure to make hard choices and prepare the nation for a new age. Homes have been lost, jobs shed, businesses shuttered. Our health care is too costly, our schools fail too many—and each day brings further evidence that the ways we use energy strengthen our adversaries and threaten our planet.

These are the indicators of crisis, subject to data and statistics. Less measurable, but no less profound, is a sapping of confidence across our land; a nagging fear that America's decline is inevitable, that the next generation must lower its sights.

Today I say to you that the challenges we face are real. They are serious and they are many. They will not be met easily or in a short span of time. But know this America: They will be met.

On this day, we gather because we have chosen hope over fear, unity of purpose over conflict and discord. On this day, we come to proclaim an end to the petty grievances and false promises, the recriminations and worn-out dogmas that for far too long have strangled our politics. We remain a young nation. But in the words

Barack Obama takes the oath of office as 44th president of the United States, January 20, 2009. (Department of Defense)

of Scripture, the time has come to set aside childish things. The time has come to reaffirm our enduring spirit; to choose our better history; to carry forward that precious gift, that noble idea passed on from generation to generation: the God-given promise that all are equal, all are free, and all deserve a chance to pursue their full measure of happiness.

In reaffirming the greatness of our nation we understand that greatness is never a given. It must be earned. Our journey has never been one of short-cuts or settling for less. It has not been the path for the faint-hearted, for those that prefer leisure over work, or seek only the pleasures of riches and fame. Rather, it has been the risk-takers, the doers, the makers of things—some celebrated, but more often men and women obscure in their labor—who have carried us up the long rugged path towards prosperity and freedom.

For us, they packed up their few worldly possessions and traveled across oceans in search of a new life. For us, they toiled in sweatshops, and settled the West, endured the lash of the whip, and plowed the hard earth. For us, they fought and died in places like Concord and Gettysburg; Normandy and Khe Sahn.

Time and again these men and women struggled and sacrificed and worked till their hands were raw so that we might live a better life. They saw America as bigger than the sum of our individual ambitions, greater than all the differences of birth or wealth or faction.

This is the journey we continue today. We remain the most prosperous, powerful nation on Earth. Our workers are no less productive than when this crisis began. Our minds are no less inventive, our goods and services no less needed than they were last week, or last month, or last year. Our capacity remains undiminished. But our time of standing pat, of protecting narrow interests and putting off unpleasant decisions—that time has surely passed. Starting today, we must pick ourselves up, dust ourselves off, and begin again the work of remaking America.

For everywhere we look, there is work to be done. The state of our economy calls for action, bold and swift. And we will act, not only to create new jobs, but to lay a new foundation for growth. We will build the roads and bridges, the electric grids and digital lines that feed our commerce and bind us together. We will restore science to its rightful place, and wield technology's wonders to raise health care's quality and lower its cost. We will harness the sun and the winds and the soil to fuel our cars and run our factories. And we will transform our schools and colleges and universities to meet the demands of a new age. All this we can do. All this we will do.

Now, there are some who question the scale of our ambitions, who suggest that our system cannot tolerate too many big plans. Their memories are short, for they have forgotten what this country has already done, what free men and women can achieve when imagination is joined to common purpose, and necessity to courage. What the cynics fail to understand is that the ground has shifted beneath them, that the stale political arguments that have consumed us for so long no longer apply.

The question we ask today is not whether our government is too big or too small, but whether it works—whether it helps families find jobs at a decent wage, care they can afford, a retirement that is dignified. Where the answer is yes, we intend to move forward. Where the answer is no, programs will end. And those of us who manage the public's dollars will be held to account, to spend wisely, reform bad habits, and do our business in the light of day, because only then can we restore the vital trust between a people and their government.

Nor is the question before us whether the market is a force for good or ill. Its power to generate wealth and expand freedom is unmatched. But this crisis has reminded us that without a watchful eye, the market can spin out of control. The nation cannot prosper long when it favors only the prosperous. The success of our economy has always depended not just on the size of our gross national product, but on the reach of our prosperity, on the ability to extend opportunity to every willing heart—not out of charity, but because it is the surest route to our common good.

As for our common defense, we reject as false the choice between our safety and our ideals. Our Founding Fathers . . . our Founding Fathers, faced with perils that we can scarcely imagine, drafted a charter to assure the rule of law and the rights of man—a charter expanded by the blood of generations. Those ideals still light the world, and we will not give them up for expedience sake.

And so, to all the other peoples and governments who are watching today, from the grandest capitals to the small village where my father was born, know that America is a friend of each nation, and every man, woman and child who seeks a future of peace and dignity. And we are ready to lead once more.

Recall that earlier generations faced down fascism and communism not just with missiles and tanks, but with sturdy alliances and enduring convictions. They understood that our power alone cannot protect us, nor does it entitle us to do as we please. Instead they knew that our power grows through its prudent use: our security emanates from the justness of our cause, the force of our example, the tempering qualities of humility and restraint.

We are the keepers of this legacy. Guided by these principles once more we can meet those new threats that demand even greater effort, even greater cooperation and understanding between nations. We will begin to responsibly leave Iraq to its people and forge a hard-earned peace in Afghanistan. With old friends and former foes, we'll work tirelessly to lessen the nuclear threat, and roll back the specter of a warming planet.

We will not apologize for our way of life, nor will we waver in its defense. And for those who seek to advance their aims by inducing terror and slaughtering innocents, we say to you now that our spirit is stronger and cannot be broken—you cannot outlast us, and we will defeat you.

For we know that our patchwork heritage is a strength, not a weakness. We are a nation of Christians and Muslims, Jews and Hindus, and non-believers. We are shaped by every language and culture, drawn from every end of this Earth; and because we have tasted the bitter swill of civil war and segregation, and emerged from that dark chapter stronger and more united, we cannot help but believe that the old hatreds shall someday pass; that the lines of tribe shall soon dissolve; that as the world grows smaller, our common humanity shall reveal itself; and that America must play its role in ushering in a new era of peace.

To the Muslim world, we seek a new way forward, based on mutual interest and mutual respect. To those leaders around the globe who seek to sow conflict, or blame their society's ills on the West, know that your people will judge you on what you can build, not what you destroy.

To those who cling to power through corruption and deceit and the silencing of dissent, know that you are on the wrong side of history, but that we will extend a hand if you are willing to unclench your fist.

To the people of poor nations, we pledge to work alongside you to make your farms flourish and let clean waters flow; to nourish starved bodies and feed hungry minds. And to those nations like ours that enjoy relative plenty, we say we can no longer afford indifference to the suffering outside our borders, nor can we consume the world's resources without regard to effect. For the world has changed, and we must change with it.

As we consider the role that unfolds before us, we remember with humble gratitude those brave Americans who at this very hour patrol far-off deserts and distant mountains. They have something to tell us, just as the fallen heroes who lie in Arlington whisper through the ages.

We honor them not only because they are the guardians of our liberty, but because they embody the spirit of service—a willingness to find meaning in something greater than themselves.

And yet at this moment, a moment that will define a generation, it is precisely this spirit that must inhabit us all. For as much as government can do, and must do, it is ultimately the faith and determination of the American people upon which this nation relies. It is the kindness to take in a stranger when the levees break, the self-lessness of workers who would rather cut their hours than see a friend lose their job which sees us through our darkest hours. It is the firefighter's courage to storm a stair-way filled with smoke, but also a parent's willingness to nurture a child that finally decides our fate.

Our challenges may be new. The instruments with which we meet them may be new. But those values upon which our success depends—honesty and hard work, courage and fair play, tolerance and curiosity, loyalty and patriotism—these things are old. These things are true. They have been the quiet force of progress throughout our history.

What is demanded, then, is a return to these truths. What is required of us now is a new era of responsibility—a recognition on the part of every American that we have duties to ourselves, our nation and the world; duties that we do not grudgingly accept, but rather seize gladly, firm in the knowledge that there is nothing so satisfying to the spirit, so defining of our character than giving our all to a difficult task.

This is the price and the promise of citizenship. This is the source of our confidence—the knowledge that God calls on us to shape an uncertain destiny. This is the meaning of our liberty and our creed, why men and women and children of every race and every faith can join in celebration across this magnificent mall; and why a man whose father less than 60 years ago might not have been served in a local restaurant can now stand before you to take a most sacred oath.

So let us mark this day with remembrance of who we are and how far we have traveled. In the year of America's birth, in the coldest of months, a small band of patriots huddled by dying campfires on the shores of any icy river. The capital was abandoned. The enemy was advancing. The snow was stained with blood. At the moment when the outcome of our revolution was most in doubt, the father of our nation ordered these words to be read to the people:

"Let it be told to the future world . . . that in the depth of winter, when nothing but hope and virtue could survive . . . that the city and the country, alarmed at one common danger, came forth to meet [it]."

America: In the face of our common dangers, in this winter of our hardship, let us remember these timeless words. With hope and virtue, let us brave once more the icy currents, and endure what storms may come. Let it be said by our children's children that when we were tested we refused to let this journey end, that we did not turn back nor did we falter; and with eyes fixed on the horizon and God's grace upon us, we carried forth that great gift of freedom and delivered it safely to future generations.

Thank you. God bless you. And God bless the United States of America. (Applause.)

SOURCE: Inaugural Address by President Barack Hussein Obama, January 20, 2009, www.whitehouse.gov/blog/inaugural-address.

DID YOU KNOW?

Pastor Rick Warren and Barack Obama's Inauguration

President-elect Barack Obama's choice of Rick Warren, pastor of the Saddleback Church in Lake Forest, California, and author of the best-selling book *The Purpose Driven Life*, to give the invocation at the presidential inauguration on January 20, 2009, resulted in a strong reaction from liberals who expressed concern over Warren's opposition to same-gender marriage. Warren had supported California Proposition 8, which amended the state constitution, defining marriage as only a union between one man and one woman. Joe Solmonese, president of Human Rights Campaign, a homosexual rights organization, wrote to Obama that inviting Warren to the inauguration "tarnished the view that gay, lesbian, bisexual and transgender Americans have a place at your table." Congressman Barney Frank (D-MA), the first openly gay member of Congress, declared that president-elect Obama had made a mistake by selecting Warren to deliver the invocation. The Sunday before the inauguration, a small number of individuals demonstrated outside Warren's church in Lake Forest. However, Warren delivered the invocation at the inauguration without incident. He made references in his prayer that suggested religious inclusiveness. Despite Obama's plea to focus on the things that Americans hold in common, this controversy gave the indication that the culture wars might continue into the next presidential administration.

ANALYSIS

President Barack Obama in his inaugural address understandably focused primarily on the economic difficulties the United States was facing. However, the general tenor of the address as well as various specific references indicated a definite shift to a more liberal policy-making emphasis in the coming years. Although often stating his positions in general terms, the new president's statements could be interpreted as both a repudiation of the previous administration as well as an expression of an intention to disarm the culture wars. For instance, early in the speech Obama stated that "the time has come to set aside childish things" (I Corinthians 13:11). Among the "childish things" undoubtedly were the ideological conflicts that appeared much less important given the monumental economic and foreign policy questions facing the nation.

Obama's election fueled speculation that the culture wars had run their course, and, as far as liberals were concerned, their side had triumphed. Lou Dubose (2008) commented that Republican leaders, who continued to cultivate an intimate relationship with religious conservatives, had lost the presidency and several seats in the U.S. House of Representatives and Senate. Dubose also noted that younger voters, for whom the traditional values issues appear to be less salient tend to support the Democratic Party. Such a shift in party support does not necessarily signal a subsiding of the culture wars because both conservatives and liberals continue to attract significant support in the political process. However, to the extent that economic issues remain salient, those subjects upon which the culture war is built may become less significant in the political realm. Conservative columnist David Brooks (2008) concludes that if the culture wars are subsiding, the reason lies with conservatives who have failed to maintain their appeal among middle America and have not succeeded in developing an intellectual base from which to maintain an identifiable ideology with which to challenge the liberal perspective. Certainly the future of U.S. politics involves many uncertainties, and the nature of cultural battles, if any, will depend on the uncertainties of the national and worldwide economies and the possible reactions of public officials, public opinion leaders, and the general public to a more liberal administration.

FURTHER READING

Brooks, David. "Why Modern Conservatism Is a Thing of the Past." *Houston Chronicle*, October 11, 2008.

Dionne, E. J., Jr. "Liberals, Conservatives Find Solace in Obama's Speech." *Houston Chronicle*, January 23, 2009.

Dubose, Lou. "Evangelicals and the Republican Party." *The Washington Spectator* 34, no. 22 (December 1, 2008): 1–3.

Gushee, David P. *The Future of Faith in American Politics: The Public Witness of the Evangelical Center*. Waco, TX: Baylor University Press, 2008.

Hunter, James Davison. "The Enduring Culture War." In *Is There a Culture War? A Dialogue on Values and American Public Life*, edited by James Davison Hunter and Alan Wolfe. Washington, DC: Brookings Institution Press, 2006.

Norquist, Grover G. "Conservatives Will Rise Again." *U.S. News and World Report*, December 1/December 8, 2008: 17.

Poniewozik, James. "Pop Goes Washington: The New President Embodies a Changing Culture. But Can He Change the Culture's Tone Too?" *Time*, February 2, 2009: 30.

Thomas, Cal, and Bob Beckel. "A Cultural Disconnect: The NRA. The Brady Bill. Pro-life. Pro-choice. Big Oil. The Sierra Club. Cal and Bob Wonder, Do We Really Want to Go Down This Road Again?" *USA Today*, September 18, 2008.

Wilentz, Sean. "The Reagan Coalition Is Kaput." *U.S. News and World Report*, December 1/December 8, 2008: 16.

Wolfe, Alan. "The Culture War That Never Came." In *Is There a Culture War? A Dialogue on Values and American Public Life*, edited by James Davison Hunter and Alan Wolfe. Washington, DC: Brookings Institution Press, 2006.

SELECTED RESOURCES

WEB SITES

The Web sites are categorized according to the major areas of contention within the U.S. culture wars.

General Web Sites on the Culture Wars

Conservative Politics and Perspectives

http://usconservatives.about.com

> This site provides links to various topics relevant to the culture wars from a conservative perspective, including abortion, embryonic stem cell research, the environment, and church-state issues.

Culture Wars 101

http://sep.stanford.edu/sep/jon/family/jos/culture/index.html

> This Web site, no longer updated, includes information on such issues as abortion, homosexuality, and the separation of church and state.

Heritage Foundation

www.heritage.org

> The Heritage Foundation states that its mission is "to formulate and promote conservative public policies based on the principles of free enterprise, limited government, individual freedom, traditional American values, and a strong national defense. The Web site contains information about the organization's many activities.

Liberal and Progressive Politics and Perspectives

http://usliberals.about.com

This site contains links to many topics relevant to the culture wars from a liberal perspective, including immigration reform, the environment, abortion, embryonic stem cell research, the death penalty, and the military.

Rockford Institute

www.rockfordinstitute.org

The Rockford Institute, founded in 1976, works "to preserve the institutions of the Christian West: the family, the Church, and the rule of law; private property, free enterprise, and moral discipline; high standards of learning, art, and literature."

Third Way

www.thirdway.org

This site of the Third Way nonpartisan organization, founded in 2005, presents alternative approaches to national security, economic, and cultural issues. Attempting to defuse the culture wars, the organization presents progressive approaches to such cultural topics as immigration, abortion, and pornography.

Religion-Related Issues and the Culture Wars

American Atheists

www.atheists.org

American Atheists, a group that noted atheist activist Madalyn Murray O'Hair established in 1963, defends the separation of religion and government, supports the civil rights of atheists, and provides information about atheism.

Americans United for Separation of Church and State

www.au.org

Founded in 1947, Americans United strives to maintain a strict separation between religious institutions and the public realm, including government and the public schools.

Christian Coalition

www.cc.org

The Christian Coalition states that its mission is to represent the pro-family viewpoint in the mass media, train leaders for social and political action, inform and educate pro-family voters about issues and legislation, and confront anti-Christian discrimination.

Government Is Not God Political Action Committee

http://govnotgod.org

This conservative political action committee, established by William J. Murray in 1992, supports political candidates who share the organization's social conservative agenda.

GlobalWarming.org

www.globalwarming.org

This Web site provides information and data critical of the position that global warming caused by human activity is a serious threat to the Earth.

Internet Infidels

www.infidels.org

This Web site, founded in 1995, promotes and defends a naturalistic worldview, holding that nothing not a part of the natural world has any effect on it.

The Nature Conservancy

www.nature.org

This environmental organization, claiming a membership of one million, works to protect lands considered ecologically significant. The Web site provides information relevant to the disagreement among evangelicals over the issue of global warming.

Secular Coalition of America

http://secular.org

This coalition of member organizations provides information about atheism, humanism, free thought, and non-theism in government institutions.

Vision America

www.visionamerica.us

The Web site of Vision America, an organization established by Rick Scarborough, encourages pastors and congregations to take action in "restoring Judeo-Christian values to the moral and civic framework in their communities, states, and our nation."

WWF-World Wide Fund For Nature (formerly World Wildlife Fund)

www.panda.org

This Web site of WWF, although not a religious organization, provides a viewpoint relevant to the division among evangelicals regarding environmentalism and the seriousness and causes of global warming.

Abortion, Stem Cells, and the Right to Die

Abortion Facts

www.abortionfacts.com

This anti-abortion Web site provides a wide variety of information about abortion from a religious perspective. The site also includes a discussion of euthanasia.

Abortion Information

www.fwhc.org

This Web site contains information about surgical abortion, options other than surgery, including the abortion pill and adoption, and ways of finding an abortion clinic.

Abortion Is Prolife

www.abortionisprolife.com

The Web site includes essays on abortion, abortion statistics, and a frequently asked questions section.

American Association for the Advancement of Science

www.aaas.org/spp/cstc/briefs/stemcells

The American Association for the Advancement of Science Web site presents extensive material on stems cell research, including the ethical dispute, President George W. Bush's position and actions on the issue, and scientific advances.

American Life League

www.all.org

This Web site of the American Life League contains information and news stories in opposition to abortion and the birth control pill.

Americans for Cures Foundation

www.americansforcures.org

The Americans for Cures Foundation states that its mission is to support those advocating stem cell research as a means of discovering cures for diseases.

Bedford Stem Cell Research Foundation

www.bedfordresearch.org

Founded in 1996, this foundation advocates human stem cell research as an avenue for treating presently incurable diseases.

Center for Reproductive Rights

www.reproductiverights.org

The Center for Reproductive Rights, which advocates reproductive freedom for women, provides information about political decisions in Congress, the state legislatures, and the courts regarding right of abortion.

Compassion and Choices

http://www.compassionandchoices.org/

The Web site supports the right to make end-of-life choices and provides information about legislative and court decisions.

Death with Dignity National Center

www.deathwithdignity.org

This Web site provides information about the effort to pass death with dignity laws in the states.

Do No Harm: The Coalition of Americans for Research Ethics

www.stemcellresearch.org

This organization holds that deriving stem cells from human embryos is unethical because the process necessarily results in the destruction of those embryos.

ERGO (Euthanasia Research and Guidance Organization)

www.finalexit.org

The Web site provides sources in support of euthanasia, including films, books, and legal information.

Euthanasia

www.euthanasia.com

The Web site provides many articles about euthanasia, including those from medical professionals, and from groups concerned about the issue. Several sources on Oregon and the Netherlands are also available.

Feminist Majority Foundation

http://feminist.org

The Feminist Majority Foundation provides information about abortion clinic availability, accessibility to the abortion pill RU 486, and the political struggle to maintain the legal right of abortion.

International Society for Stem Cell Research

www.isscr.org

Representing more than 2,500 stem cell researchers worldwide, the International Society for Stem Cell Research encourages the dissemination of information about stem cells and the conduct of research using all types of stem cells.

NARAL Pro-Choice America

www.prochoiceamerica.org

This pro-choice organization offers information regarding women's freedom of reproductive choice and advocates the election of pro-choice candidates.

National Abortion Federation

www.prochoice.org

This association of abortion providers in the United States and Canada provides training and other services to abortion providers and information and referral services to women.

National Organization for Women

www.now.org

The National Organization for Women supports the availability of safe and legal abortion and emergency contraception and provides information about the continuing political and legal struggle with anti-abortion groups.

National Right to Life Committee

www.nrlc.org

In addition to conducting lobbying efforts at the federal level to limit abortions, the NRLC provides information for affiliated organizations at the state level, the mass media, and the general public.

Planned Parenthood

www.plannedparenthood.org

Planned Parenthood's Web site provides information on such topics as medication abortion, in-clinic abortions, birth control, and emergency contraception.

Priests for Life

www.priestsforlife.org

This Web site has available graphic photographs of aborted babies at various stages of development, descriptions of abortion procedures, and information about so-called partial birth abortions.

ProLife.com

www.prolife.com

This anti-abortion Web site invites people to email their stories and questions, and offers anti-abortion DVDs, books, CDs, and literature.

Research!America

www.researchamerica.org

This organization, supported by universities, research foundations, and pharmaceutical companies, supports additional federal government funding for medical research, including embryonic stem cell research.

The Right to Die

www.law.umkc.edu/faculty/projects/ftrials/conlaw/righttodie.htm

This Web site, maintained by the University of Missouri-Kansas City Law School, provides information for law school students about selected U.S. Supreme Court decisions regarding the right to die.

Stem Cell Research Facts

www.stemcellresearchfacts.com

This Web site publicizes what are considered the dangers of embryonic stem cell research, focuses on the bioethical problems of such research, and advocates adult stem cell research.

Theology Library: Euthanasia

http://shc.edu/theolibrary/euthan.htm

This Web site of Spring Hill College, a Jesuit school, provides resources in opposition to euthanasia.

Gun Control and Gun Rights

Armed Females of America

www.armedfemalesofamerica.com/

This pro-gun rights women's organization attempts to oppose pro-gun control groups. Considering itself a no-compromise organization, Armed Females of America calls for the repeal of all gun laws going back to the National Firearms Act of 1934.

Brady Center to Prevent Gun Violence

www.bradycenter.org

Established by Jim and Sarah Brady, the Brady Center strives to strengthen enforcement of existing firearms laws and to extend background checks for gun purchases.

CCRKBA—Citizens Committee for the Right to Keep and Bear Arms

www.ccrkba.org

The Citizens Committee, headquartered in Bellevue, Washington, encourages people to defend the right—as found in the U.S. and various state constitutions—to keep and bear arms.

Coalition to Stop Gun Violence

www.csgv.org

This coalition of 45 national religious, child advocate, public health, and social justice organizations works to reduce firearm violence.

Doctors for Sensible Gun Laws

http://dsgl.org

This organization advise doctors and patients to question those medical researchers and organizations who have advocated further gun control policies.

Firearms Coalition

www.firearmscoalition.org

Composed of more than 3,000 individual members and nearly 1,000 member organizations, the Firearms Coalition supports an unrestricted right to self-defense and the right to possess firearms.

GOA—Gun Owners of America

http://gunowners.org

Established in 1975 by Senator H. L. (Bill) Richardson, Gun Owners of America works to reinstate gun rights the organization claims have been lost.

iansa—International Action Network on Small Arms

www.iansa.org

This organization works internationally to stop the spread and misuse of small arms and light weapons through establishing more effective regulation of guns in societies and improved controls on arms exports.

Jews for the Preservation of Firearms Ownership

www.jpfo.org

This Wisconsin-based organization supports a right to keep and bear arms, emphasizes what it considers the racist roots of gun control, and opposes the alleged United Nations attack on the U.S. Bill of Rights, especially the Second Amendment.

Liberty Belles

http://libertybelles.org

This organization supports an individual right to keep and bear arms for self-defense, claiming that guns "save lives 2.5 million times per year."

Mothers Arms

www.mothersarms.org/

Advocating self-defense strategies, Mothers Arms provides information and resources to assist women in learning how to defend themselves and their children.

National Association of Firearms Retailers

www.nafr.org

A division of the National Shooting Sports Foundation, the NAFR represents firearms retailers before government regarding the regulation of firearms.

National Rifle Association

www.nra.org

The National Rifle Association, often considered the most influential gun rights organization, has been at the forefront of lobbying efforts to oppose gun control proposals.

National Shooting Sports Foundation

www.nssf.org

Established in 1961, the NSSF represents the interests of more than 4,000 firearms manufacturers, distributors, retailers, and sports organizations.

Paul Revere Network

www.paulrevere.org

Leroy Pyle established the Paul Revere Network in 1995 as a communications network for activists interested in defending a right to keep and bear arms.

Project Safe Neighborhoods

http://psn.gov

Announced in May 2001, this federal government initiative focuses on deterring and punishing crimes committed with firearms.

Second Amendment Committee

www.libertygunrights.com

Bernadine Smith established the Second Amendment Committee in 1984 to provide information to those concerned about defending gun rights.

Second Amendment Foundation

www.saf.org

The Second Amendment Foundation is involved in educational programs to inform the public about the right of private individuals to possess firearms.

SAS—Second Amendment Sisters

www.2asisters.org

Five women established Second Amendment Sisters in 1999 in support of gun rights and in response to demonstrations such as the Million Mom March in favor of more stringent gun control.

Stop Handgun Violence

www.stophandgunviolence.com

Founded in 1995, Stop Handgun Violence seeks to reduce handgun violence through public awareness and "sensible" state and federal legislation.

Student Pledge Against Gun Violence

www.pledge.org

This organization strives, primarily through a yearly Day of National Concern about Young People and Gun Violence, to reduce gun violence by encouraging young people to pledge not to engage in firearm violence.

Students for Concealed Carry on Campus

www.concealedcarry.org

With a claimed membership of 35,000, this organization advocates the right of state-issued handgun licensees to carry concealed handguns for self-protection on college and university campuses.

Violence Policy Center

www.vpc.org

> The Violence Policy Center works aggressively to publicize gun violence as a public health issue and calls for policies to keep the workplace and the home safe from gun violence.

Women Against Gun Control

www.wagc.com

> Claiming that guns are "the great equalizer" in defense against criminal attack, WAGC supports enactment by state legislatures of laws to allow individuals to carry concealed weapons.

Immigration

About.com: Immigration Issues

http://immigration.about.com

> This Web site contains information about various immigration issues, including immigration law, the policy positions of public officials, visas, green cards, U.S. citizenship, and the history of immigration.

AILA (American Immigration Lawyers Association) InfoNet

www.aila.org

> The Web site of the American Immigration Lawyers Association, an organization of more than 11,000 attorneys and law professors, provides information for attorneys who provide legal assistance to individuals and families seeking permanent residence in the United States and to businesses who wish to hire foreign workers.

Center for Immigration Studies

www.cis.org

> The Center for Immigration Studies, which advocates a "pro-immigrant, low-immigration vision," provides information on several topics, including immigration history; national, state and local government policy; refugees; and national security.

Eagle Forum

www.eagleforum.org

> The Eagle Forum calls for increased border security to prevent the entry of illegal aliens and illegal drugs into the United States and opposes the notion of U.S. economic integration into a North American Community.

U.S. Census Bureau

www.census.gov/population/www/socdemo/immigration.html

> The U.S. Census Bureau maintains data on the foreign-born population of the United States, including demographic, social, economic, geographic, and housing information.

Sex Education, Homosexuality, and Gay Marriage

American Civil Liberties Union

www.aclu.org

> Among its various activities, the 500,000-member American Civil Liberties Union works to gain equal rights for homosexuals.

American Family Association

www.afa.net

> Among its activities, the American Family Association supports traditional family values and campaigns against the entertainment industry's frequent portrayal of premarital sex.

American Values

www.ouramericanvalues.org/

> This organization, headed by Gary L. Bauer, former Republican presidential hopeful, defends the notion of traditional marriage and family values.

CWA—Concerned Women for America

www.cwfa.org

> Concerned Women for America, founded by Beverly LaHaye, seeks to reverse what the organization considers a decline in moral values and supports the traditional family structure.

Family Research Council

www.frc.org/

> The Family Research Council and organization president Tony Perkins advocate the ideal of the traditional family and opposes legalized abortion.

Focus on the Family

www.focusonthefamily.com

> This organization, headed by religious right leader James Dobson, holds that God has established the institutions of the family and that the church and government should serve God's purposes for humankind.

Gay and Lesbian Alliance Against Defamation

www.glaad.org

> This Web site reports on efforts to promote the rights of gays and lesbians by monitoring the mass media and advocating a more positive public image for gays and lesbians.

Human Rights Campaign

www.hrc.org

> This Web site provides information about the Human Rights Campaign, which claims to be the largest organization advocating the civil rights of lesbian, gay, bisexual, and transgender people.

Lambda Legal

www.lambdalegal.org

> The Web site of Lambda Legal provides reports via online newsletters about the organization's legal efforts to defend the civil rights of gays, lesbians, and those with HIV and offers information about such issues as employment rights, marriage and family law, and HIV.

Log Cabin Republicans

http://online.logcabin.org

> Log Cabin Republicans strives to gain an equal footing for gays and lesbians in the Republican Party. The Web site contains the organization's positions on current political events.

National Gay and Lesbian Task Force

http://thetaskforce.org

> This Web site reports on efforts to represent the interests of gays and lesbians in Washington, D.C. to gain equal rights and full participation in the democratic system.

Promise Keepers

www.promisekeepers.org

> Founded in 1990 and based in Denver, Colorado, this organization supports the crucial role of men in the traditional family.

Stonewall Democrats

www.stonewalldemocrats.org

> Composed of gays and lesbians who identify with the Democratic Party, the organization mobilizes members to engage in electoral politics to help elect Democratic candidates with the ultimate objective of furthering the rights of gay and lesbian people.

Traditional Values Coalition

www.traditionalvalues.org

> Founded in 1980 by Louis P. Sheldon, the Traditional Values Coalition strives to maintain "strong, unified families" and opposes the so-called homosexual agenda.

Science and Education

AAAS—American Association for the Advancement of Science

www.aaas.org

> The American Association for the Advancement of Science Web site contains information about various science topics, including explanations for various aspects of the theory of evolution. The site claims that there ultimately is no evidence against contemporary evolution theory.

Center for Scientific Creation

www.creationscience.com

> This Web site provides arguments in favor of a creation theory of the world. The site advertises Walt Brown's online book, *In the Beginning: Compelling Evidence for Creation and the Flood.*

Creation/Evolution Reference Database

www.baz.com/litm/CERD/

> The Web site can be used to find references for many of the topics related to the theory of evolution and creationism.

Creation Research Society

www.creationresearch.org

> The Web site of the Creation Research Society, an organization "firmly committed to scientific special creation," offers free publications, an archive of the popular publication *Creation Matters*, and selected articles from the journal *CRS Quarterly.*

Creation Science

http://emporium.turnpike.net/C/cs/

> The Creation Science home page offers information in support of science from a creationist perspective. Among the topics covered are the beliefs of creation scientists, evidence against the theory of evolution, and the influence of the theory of evolution.

Evolution at NYU

www.nyu.edu/projects/fitch/courses/evolution/index.html

> David H. A. Fitch, professor of biology at New York University, developed this Web site as part of a course on the theory of evolution. Included are notes about the evidence that Charles Darwin collected to support the theory and the mechanism of natural selection.

IDEA—Intelligent Design and Evolution Awareness Center

www.ideacenter.org

> This Web site declares that its mission is to promote the scientific validity of intelligent design theory and to expose the weaknesses of naturalistic explanations for the presence of life.

Live Science

www.livescience.com

> This Web site contains essays on a variety of scientific subjects, including several postings explaining the theory of evolution, which is contrasted with Intelligent Design.

NCSE—National Center for Science Education

http://ncseweb.org

> The National Center for Science Education offers information and assistance to local citizens who are attempting to resist challenges from those wishing to introduce creationism and Intelligent Design into the public school curriculum. The Web site contains information about the evolution/creation controversy.

The Panda's Thumb

http://pandasthumb.org

> This Web site presents the views of those critical of the Intelligent Design movement.

Pathlights

www.pathlights.com

> The Pathlights Web site contains several documents—including creationist-related explanations of the stars and the solar system, and the origin and age of the earth —that attempt to debunk the theory of evolution.

Reasons to Believe

www.reasons.org

> Reasons to Believe is an organization founded by Hugh Ross that holds that science and religious faith are compatible; the Web site offers many sources holding that science confirms a belief in a creator.

Talk Reason

http://talkreason.org

> The Web site posts articles that argue against creationism, intelligent design, and defenses of religion.

Union of Concerned Scientists

www.ucsua.org

> The Union of Concerned Scientists, an organization that strives to maintain a healthy environment and scientific integrity in public policy making, takes a position on the organization's Web site that is critical of Intelligent Design as an alternative to evolution theory.

UCMP—University of California Museum of Paleontology

http://ucmp.berkeley.edu/history/evolution.html

This site provides an explanation of the theory of evolution, including the mechanisms of evolution and its impact on everyday lives and a history of evolutionary thought.

PRINT

AbuKhalil, As'ad. *Bin Laden, Islam, and America's New "War on Terrorism."* New York: Seven Stories Press, 2002.

Al-Sulami, Mishal Fahm. *The West and Islam: Western Liberal Democracy Versus the System of Shura.* New York: Routledge, 2007.

Baldwin, John D. *Ending the Science Wars.* Boulder, CO: Paradigm Publishers, 2009.

Balmer, Randall. *Thy Kingdom Come: How the Religious Right Distorts the Faith and Threatens America.* New York: Basic Books, 2007.

Bar, Shmuel. *Warrant for Terror: The Fatwas of Radical Islam and the Duty to Jihad.* Lanham, MD: Rowman and Littlefield, 2008.

Behe, Michael. *The Edge of Evolution: The Search for the Limits of Darwinism.* New York: Simon & Schuster, 2007.

Berry, Roberta M. *The Ethics of Genetic Engineering.* New York: Routledge, 2007.

Bickel, Bruce, and Stan Jantz. *Creation and Evolution 101: A Guide to Science and the Bible in Plain Language.* Irvine, CA: Harvest House, 2003.

Bork, Robert H. *Slouching Towards Gomorrah: Modern Liberalism and American Decline.* New York: Harper Collins, 2003.

Brewer, Paul R. *Value War: Public Opinion and the Politics of Gay Rights.* Lanham, MD: Rowman and Littlefield, 2008.

Burns, Eric. *The Spirits of America: A Social History of Alcohol.* Philadelphia, PA: Temple University Press, 2004.

Corey, Michael A. *The God Hypothesis: Discovering Divine Design in Our "Just Right" Goldilocks Universe.* Lanham, MD: Rowman and Littlefield, 2007.

Coulter, Ann. *Guilty: Liberal "Victims" and Their Assault on America.* New York: Crown Publishing Group, 2009.

————. *How to Talk to a Liberal (If You Must): The World According to Ann Coulter.* New York: Random House, 2005.

Coyne, Jerry. *Why Evolution is True.* New York: Viking Penguin, 2009.

Crowley, Sharon. *Toward a Civil Discourse: Rhetoric and Fundamentalism.* Pittsburgh, PA: University of Pittsburgh Press, 2007.

Davis, Percival, and Dean H. Kenyon. *Of Pandas and People: The Central Question of Biological Origins.* Second edition. Richardson, TX: Foundation for Thought and Ethics, 1993.

Dawkins, Richard. *The God Delusion.* Boston, MA: Houghton Mifflin, 2008.

De Marco, Donald, and Benjamin Wiker. *Architects of the Culture of Death.* Ft. Collins, CO: Ignatius Press, 2004.

Diaz, Tom. *Making a Killing: The Business of Guns in America.* New York: New Press, 1999.

Dionne, E. J. *Souled Out: Reclaiming Faith and Politics after the Religious Right.* Princeton, NJ: Princeton University Press, 2008.

Dowbiggin, Ian. *A Concise History of Euthanasia: Life, Death, God, and Medicine.* Lanham, MD: Rowman and Littlefield, 2007.

D'Souza, Dinesh. *The Enemy at Home: The Cultural Left and Its Responsibility for 9/11.* New York: Bantam Books, 2008.

Espinosa, Gastón. *Religion, Race, and the American Presidency.* Lanham, MD: Rowman and Littlefield, 2008.

Estrich, Susan. *Soulless: Ann Coulter and the Right-Wing Church of Hate.* New York: Harper Collins, 2006.

Fernandes, Deepa. *Targeted: Homeland Security and the Business of Immigration.* New York: Seven Stories Press, 2007.

Fleming, Bruce. *Why Liberals and Conservatives Clash: A View from Annapolis.* New York: Routledge, 2006.

Formicola, Jo Renee. *The Politics of Values: Games Political Strategists Play.* Lanham, MD: Rowman and Littlefield, 2008.

Fowler, Robert Booth. *Enduring Liberalism: American Political Thought Since the 1960s.* Lawrence, KS: University Press of Kansas, 1999.

Gabriel, Brigitte. *They Must Be Stopped: Why We Must Defeat Radical Islam and How We Can Do It.* New York: St. Martin's Press, 2008.

Geaves, Ron. *Aspects of Islam.* Washington, DC: Georgetown University Press, 2005.

Gelman, Andrew. *Red State, Blue State, Rich State, Poor State: Why Americans Vote the Way They Do.* Princeton, NJ: Princeton University Press, 2008.

Giberson, Karl W. *Saving Darwin: How to Be a Christian and Believe in Evolution.* New York: Harper One, 2008.

Gilgoff, Dan. *The Jesus Machine: How James Dobson, Focus on the Family, and Evangelical America Are Winning the Culture War.* New York: St. Martin's Griffin, 2008.

Gingrich, Newt. *Rediscovering God in America: Reflections on the Role of Faith in Our Nation's History.* Nashville, TN: Thomas Nelson, 2006.

Goldberg, Bernard. *Crazies to the Left of Me, Wimps to the Right.* New York: Harper Collins, 2007.

Gottlieb, Sanford. *Red to Blue: Congressman Chris Van Hollen and Grassroots Politics.* Boulder, CO: Paradigm Publishers, 2009.

Gottschalk, Peter, and Gabriel Greenberg. *Islamophobia: Making Muslims the Enemy.* Lanham, MD: Rowman and Littlefield, 2007.

Griffith, R. Marie, and Melani McAlister, eds. *Religion and Politics in the Contemporary United States.* Washington, DC: Johns Hopkins University Press, 2008.

Hahn, Scott, and Benjamin Wiker. *Answering the New Atheism: Dismantling Dawkins' Case Against God.* Charlotte, NC: Emmaus Road Publishing, 2008.

Hamel, Ronald P., and James J. Walter, eds. *Artificial Nutrition and Hydration and the Permanently Unconscious Patient.* Washington, DC: Georgetown University Press, 2007.

Hankins, Barry. *American Evangelicals: A Contemporary History of a Mainstream Religious Movement.* Lanham, MD: Rowman and Littlefield, 2008.

Harris, Lee. *The Suicide of Reason: Radical Islam's Threat to the West.* New York: Basic Books, 2008.

Hedges, Chris. *American Fascists: The Christian Right and the War on America.* Washington, DC: Free Press, 2007.

Heyer, Kristin E., J. Rozell, and Michael A. Genovese, eds. *Catholics and Politics: The Dynamic Tension between Faith and Power.* Washington, DC: Georgetown University Press, 2008.

Hillygus, D. Sunshine, and Todd G. Shields. *The Persuadable Voter: Wedge Issues in Presidential Campaigns.* Princeton, NJ: Princeton University Press, 2008.

Hitchens, Christopher, ed. *The Portable Atheist: Essential Readings for the Nonbeliever.* Cambridge, MA: Da Capo Press, 2007.

Humphry, Derek. *Final Exit: The Practicalities of Self-Deliverance and Assisted Suicide for the Dying.* Third edition. New York: Bantam Books, 2002.

Hunter, James Davison, and Alan Wolfe. *Is There a Culture War? A Dialogue on Values and American Public Life.* Washington, DC: Brookings Institution Press, 2006.

Johns, A. H., ed. *Islam in World Politics.* New York: Routledge, 2005.

Jones, Robert P. *Progressive and Religious: How Christian, Jewish, Muslim, and Buddhist Leaders Are Moving Beyond the Culture Wars and Transforming American Public Life.* Lanham, MD: Rowman and Littlefield, 2008.

Kellner, Douglas. *Guys and Guns Amok: Domestic Terrorism and School Shootings from the Oklahoma City Bombing to the Virginia Tech Massacre.* Boulder, CO: Paradigm Publishers, 2008.

Kelly, David F. *Medical Care at the End of Life: A Catholic Perspective.* Washington, DC: Georgetown University Press, 2006.

Khosrokhavar, Farhad. *Inside Jihadism: Understanding Jihadi Movements Worldwide.* Boulder, CO: Paradigm Publishers, 2009.

Kleck, Gary. *Targeting Guns: Firearms and Their Control.* New York: Aldine de Gruyter, 1997.

Kohut, Andrew, and Bruce Stokes. *America Against the World: How We Are Different and Why We Are Disliked.* New York: Henry Holt, 2007.

Lambert, Frank. *Religion in American Politics: A Short History.* Princeton, NJ: Princeton University Press, 2008.

Laycock, Douglas, Anthony R. Picarello Jr., and Robin Fretwell Wilson, eds. *Same-Sex Marriage and Religious Liberty: Emerging Conflicts.* Lanham, MD: Rowman and Littlefield, 2008.

Lewis-Beck, Michael S., William G. Jacoby, Hemut Horpoth, and Herbert F. Weisberg. *The American Voter Revisited.* Ann Arbor: University of Michigan Press, 2008.

Lindsey, Brink. *The Age of Abundance: How Prosperity Transformed America's Politics and Culture.* New York: Harper Collins, 2007.

Lott, John R. *More Guns, Less Crime: Understanding Crime and Gun Control Laws.* Chicago: University of Chicago Press, 1998.

Marsden, Lee. *For God's Sake: The Christian Right and US Foreign Policy.* New York: Palgrave Macmillan, 2008.

McCarthy, Nolan, Keith T. Poole, and Howard Rosenthal. *Polarized America: The Dance of Ideology and Unequal Riches.* Cambridge, MA: MIT Press, 2008.

McLean, Edward B. *The Most Dangerous Branch: The Judicial Assault on American Culture.* Lanham, MD: University Press of America, 2008.

Medved, Michael. *Hollywood vs. America.* New York: Harper Collins, 1992.

Meisel, Alan, and Kathy L. Cerminara. *The Right to Die: The Law of End-of-Life Decisionmaking.* Third edition. New York: Wolters Kluwer Law and Business, 2004.

Mellow, Nicole. *The State of Disunion: Regional Sources of Modern American Partisanship.* Washington, DC: Johns Hopkins University Press, 2008.

Melzer, Scott. *Gun Crusaders: The NRA's Culture War.* New York: NYU Press, 2009.

Mooney, Chris. *The Republican War on Science.* New York: Basic Books, 2006.

Mucciaroni, Gary. *Same Sex, Different Politics: Success and Failure in the Struggles over Gay Rights.* Chicago, IL: University of Chicago Press, 2008.

Navarro, Armando. *The Immigration Crisis: Nativism, Armed Vigilantism, and the Rise of a Countervailing Movement.* Lanham, MD: Alta Mira Press, 2009.

Noll, Mark A. *God and Race in American Politics: A Short History.* Princeton, NJ: Princeton University Press, 2008.

Onfray, Michel. *Atheist Manifesto: The Case Against Christianity, Judaism, and Islam.* New York: Little, Brown, 2007.

Orchowski, Margaret Sands. *Immigration and the American Dream: Battling the Political Hype and Hysteria.* Lanham, MD: Rowman and Littlefield, 2008.

O'Reilly, Bill. *Culture Warrior.* New York: Broadway, 2007.

Palmer, Monte, and Princess Palmer. *Islamic Extremism: Causes, Diversity, and Challenges.* Lanham, MD: Rowman and Littlefield, 2007.

Parenti, Michael. *The Culture Struggle.* New York: Seven Stories Press, 2006.

———. *Superpatriotism.* San Francisco: City Lights Books, 2004.

Perry, Marvin, and Howard E. Negrin, eds. *The Theory and Practice of Islamic Terrorism: An Anthology.* New York: Palgrave Macmillan, 2008.

Peters, Ted, Karen Lebacqz, and Gaymon Bennet. *Sacred Cells? Why Christians Should Support Stem Cell Research.* Lanham, MD: Rowman and Littlefield, 2008.

Phares, Walid. *The Confrontation: Winning the War against Future Jihad.* New York: Palgrave Macmillan, 2008.

———. *The War of Ideas: Jihadism Against Democracy.* New York: Palgrave Macmillan, 2008.

Pollard, Tom. *Sex and Violence: The Hollywood Censorship Wars.* Boulder, CO: Paradigm Publishers, 2009.

Putnam, Robert D. *Democracies in Flux: The Evolution of Social Capital in Contemporary Society.* New York: Oxford University Press, 2002.

Rana, Fazale. *The Cell's Design: How Chemistry Reveals the Creator's Artistry.* Ada, MI: Baker Publishing Group, 2008.

Rana, Fazale, and Hugh Ross. *Origins of Life: Biblical and Evolutionary Models Face Off.* Colorado Springs, CO: Nav Press, 2004.

———. *Who Was Adam? A Creation Model Approach to the Origin of Man.* Colorado Springs, CO: Nav Press, 2005.

Richards, Jay W., and Guillermo Gonzalez. *The Privileged Planet: How Our Place in the Cosmos Is Designed for Discovery.* Washington, DC: Regnery Publishing, 2004.

Rimmerman, Craig A. *The Lesbian and Gay Movements: Assimilation or Liberation?* Boulder, CO: Westview Press, 2007.

Roded, Ruth. *Women in Islam and the Middle East.* New York: Palgrave Macmillan, 2008.

Romero, Victor C. *Everyday Law for Immigrants.* Boulder, CO: Paradigm Publishers, 2009.

Ross, Hugh. *Creation as Science: A Testable Model Approach to End the Creation/Evolution Wars.* Menasha, WI: Nav Press, 2006.

———. *The Creator and the Cosmos: How the Latest Scientific Discoveries Reveal God.* Menasha, WI: Nav Press, 2001.

Roy, Olivier. *Secularism Confronts Islam.* New York: Columbia University Press, 2007.

Ruse, Michael. *Can a Darwinian Be a Christian?* New York: Cambridge University Press, 2001.

Salaita, Steven. *The Uncultured Wars: Arabs, Muslims and the Poverty of Liberal Thought—New Essays.* New York: Palgrave, Macmillan, 2009.

Schaefer, Jame. *Theological Foundations for Environmental Ethics: Reconstructing Patristic and Medieval Concepts.* Washington, DC: Georgetown University Press, 2009.

Schneider, Gregory. *The Conservative Century: From Reaction to Revolution.* Lanham, MD: Rowman and Littlefield, 2008.

Scruton, Roger. *Culture Counts: Faith and Feeling in a World Besieged.* New York: Encounter Books, 2007.

Shaffer, Brenda, ed. *The Limits of Culture: Islam and Foreign Policy.* Cambridge, MA: MIT Press, 2006.

Shahram, Akbarzadeh, and Abdullah Saeed, eds. *Islam and Political Legitimacy.* New York: Routledge, 2007.

Shannon, Thomas A., and Charles N. Faso. *Let Them Go Free: A Guide to Withdrawing Life Support.* Washington, DC: Georgetown University Press,

Silk, Mark, and Andrew Walsh. *One Nation, Divisible: How Regional Religious Differences Shape American Politics*. Lanham, MD: Rowman and Littlefield, 2008.

Simon, James F. *Lincoln and Chief Justice Taney: Slavery, Secession, and the President's War Powers*. New York: Simon & Schuster, 2006.

Sokal, Alan. *Beyond the Hoax: Science, Philosophy and Culture*. New York: Oxford University Press, 2008.

Sokal, Alan, and Jean Bricmont. *Fashionable Nonsense: Postmodern Intellectuals' Abuse of Science*. New York: Picador USA, 1998.

Solo, Pam, and Gail Pressberg. *The Promise and Politics of Stem Cell Research*. Westport, CT: Praeger, 2006.

Sowell, Thomas. *A Conflict of Visions: Ideological Origins of Political Struggles*. New York: Basic Books, 2007.

Spencer, Robert. *The Politically Incorrect Guide to Islam (and the Crusades)*. Washington, DC: Regnery Publishing, 2005.

Spickard, Paul. *Almost All Aliens: Race, Colonialism, and Immigration in American History and Identity*. New York: Routledge, 2007.

Springer, Devin R., James L. Regens, and David N. Edger. *Islamic Radicalism and Global Jihad*. Washington, DC: Georgetown University Press, 2009.

Stroup. John M., and Glenn W. Shuck. *Escape into the Future: Cultural Pessimism and its Religious Dimension in Contemporary American Popular Culture*. Waco, TX: Baylor University Press, 2007.

Thomas, R. Murray. *God in the Classroom: Religion and America's Public Schools*. Lanham, MD: Rowman and Littlefield, 2008.

Tyler, Aaron. *Islam, the West, and Tolerance: Conceiving Coexistence*. New York: Palgrave Macmillan, 2008.

Urban, Hugh B. *The Secrets of the Kingdom: Religion and Concealment in the Bush Administration*. Lanham, MD: Rowman and Littlefield, 2007.

Wald, Kenneth, and Allison Calhoun-Brown. *Religion and Politics in the United States*. Fifth edition. Lanham, MD: Rowman and Littlefield, 2006.

Webb, Adam K. *Beyond the Global Culture War*. New York: Routledge, 2006.

Wells, Johathan. *The Politically Incorrect Guide to Darwinism and Intelligent Design*. Washington, DC: Regnery, 2006.

West, Diana. *The Death of the Grown-Up: How America's Arrested Development Is Bringing Down Western Civilization*. New York: St. Martin's Press, 2007.

Wiker, Benjamin. *Darwin: The Life and Poisonous Legacy of Charles Darwin*. Washington, DC: Regnery Publishing, 2009.

Wiker, Benjamin, and Jonathan Witt. *A Meaningful World: How the Arts and Science Reveal the Genius of Nature*. Westmont, IL: InterVarsity Press, 2006.

Wood, Ralph C. *Contending for the Faith: The Church's Engagement with Culture*. Waco, TX: Baylor University Press, 2003.

Wucker, Michele. *Lockout: Why America Keeps Getting Immigration Wrong When Our Prosperity Depends on Getting It Right*. New York: Public Affairs, 2007.

Young, Mitchell. *Culture Wars: Opposing Viewpoints*. Chicago, IL: Greenhaven Press, 2007.

FILMS, VIDEOS AND COMPACT DISKS

The Abortion War: Thirty Years after Roe v. Wade. 22 min. Hamilton, NJ: Films for the Humanities and Sciences, 2003.

America's Leading Dissenter: Noam Chomsky. 52 min. Hamilton, NJ: Films for the Humanities and Sciences, 1988.

Battle for the Minds: A Shocking Tale of Politics, Fundamentalism and Women. 74 min. Harriman, NY: New Day Films, 1998.

Bill Moyers Journal: Christian Zionism and the Quest for Mid-East Peace. 54 min. Hamilton, NJ: Films for the Humanities and Sciences, 2007.

Bill Moyers Journal: Christian Zionism and the Rhetoric of Preemptive War. 58 min. Hamilton, NJ: Films for the Humanities and Sciences, 2007.

Bill Moyers Journal: Conservative Movement Woes. 56 min. Hamilton, NJ: Films for the Humanities and Sciences, 2008.

Bill Moyers Journal: Race and Politics in America's Cities. 58 min. Hamilton, NJ: Films for the Humanities and Sciences, 2008.

Bill Moyers Journal: Reconciling History in Black and White. 50 min. Hamilton, NJ: Films for the Humanities and Sciences, 2007.

Bill Moyers Journal: The Reverend Jeremiah Wright Speaks Out. 57 min. Hamilton, NJ: Films for the Humanities and Sciences, 2008.

Bill Moyers Journal: Slavery, Race, and Inequality in America. 57 min. Hamilton, NJ: Films for the Humanities and Sciences, 2008.

Breaking the Silence Surrounding Gay and Lesbian Teens. 68 min. Harriman, NY: New Day Films, 2006.

Broken Border: America's Immigration Dilemma. 45 min. Hamilton, NJ: Films for the Humanities and Sciences, 2004.

The Case for a Creator. 90 min. Peabody, MA: Christian Book Distributors, 2006.

A Christian Worldview. 12 presentations by R. C. Sproul, 23 min./presentation. Lake Mary, FL: Ligonier Ministries, n.d.

Christianity and Postmodernism. 83 min. Manitou Spring, CO: Summit Ministries, 2008.

The Conservatives. 88 min. Hamilton, NJ: Films for the Humanities and Sciences, n.d.

Cosmic Fingerprints. Pasadena, CA: Reasons to Believe, 2005.

The Darwinian Revolution. 24 lectures by Frederick Gregory, 30 min./lecture. Chantilly, VA: The Teaching Company, 2008.

A Death of One's Own. 87 min. Hamilton, NJ: Films for the Humanities and Sciences, 2000.

Ends of the Spectrum: The Left and the Right in the 1960s. 2 parts, 54 min. each. Hamilton, NJ: Films for the Humanities and Sciences, 1963–1967.

Essentials of Faith: Islam. 24 min. Hamilton, NJ: Films for the Humanities and Sciences, 2006.

Examining Islam. 72 min. Hamilton, NJ: Films for the Humanities and Sciences, 2006.

Expelled: No Intelligence Allowed. 90 min. Peabody, MA: Christian Book Distributors, 2007.

Faith and Politics: The Christian Right. 49 min. Hamilton, NJ: Films for the Humanities and Sciences, 1995.

Friends of God: A Road Trip with Alexandra Pelosi. 56 min. New York: Home Box Office, 2007.

Gay Marriage and the Constitution. 22 min. Hamilton, NJ: Films for the Humanities and Sciences, 2004.

Global Jihad. 22 min. Hamilton, NJ: Films for the Humanities and Sciences, 2004.

The Great Debate on Science and the Bible: How and When Did God Create? Pasadena, CA: Reasons to Believe, 2006.

Image Crisis: How Is the U.S. Viewed in the Middle East? 23 min. Hamilton, NJ: Films for the Humanities and Sciences, 2004.

Intelligent Design vs. Evolution. 22 min. Hamilton, NJ: Films for the Humanities and Sciences, 2005.

Interview with R. C. Sproul and Ben Stein—Intelligent Design and Expelled (the Movie). Compact disk. Orlando, FL: Ligonier Ministries, 2008.

Islam. 27 min. Hamilton, NJ: Films for the Humanities and Sciences, 2007.

It's Still Elementary: Talking about Gay Issues in School. 78 min. Harriman, NY: New Day Films, 1996.

Journey Toward Creation: A Breathtaking Guided Tour through Space and Time Back to the Beginning of the Universe. Pasadena, CA: Reasons to Believe, 2003.

Kansas vs. Darwin. 82 min. Harriman, NY: New Day Films, 2008.

Leona's Sister Gerri: A Provocative Film about Abortion. 57 min. Harriman, NY: New Day Films, 2007.

Letters from the Other Side: A Post-FAFTA Immigration Story Told by the Mexican Women Left Behind. 74 min. Harriman, NY: Side Street Films, 2006.

Letter to America: How Arabs View the United States. 45 min. Hamilton, NJ: Films for the Humanities and Sciences, 2001.

Majesty of the Maker: Evidence for Design. Pasadena, CA: Reasons to Believe, 2007.

Mapping Stem Cell Research: Terra Incognita. New York: Cinema Guild, 2006.

Miles from the Border: A Mexican-American Family Caught Between Cultures. 15 min. Harriman, NY: Frankenstein Productions, 1987.

Moyers on America: Is God Green? 57 min. Hamilton, NJ: Films for the Humanities and Sciences, 2006.

The New Americans. 411 min. (3 DVDs.) New York: Cinema Guild, 2004.

NOW with Bill Moyers: Benjamin Barber on Globalization. 27 min. Hamilton, NJ: Films for the Humanities and Sciences, 2003.

NOW with Bill Moyers: Katie Roiphe on Pornography, Censorship, and Feminism. 22 min. Hamilton, NJ: Films for the Humanities and Sciences, 2003.

NOW with Bill Moyers: Richard Rodriguez on Being American. 40 min. Hamilton, NJ: Films for the Humanities and Sciences, 2002.

One Wedding and a Revolution: The Frantic Planning Inside City Hall for the First Gay Marriage. 19 min. Harriman, NY: New Day Films, 2004.

Physician-Assisted Suicide. 26 min. New York: Insight Media, 2002.

The Politics of Gay Marriage and Abortion Rights. 22 min. Hamilton, NJ: Films for the Humanities and Sciences, 2004.

The Privileged Planet/Unlocking the Mystery of Life. 120 min. (2 DVDs.) Peabody, MA: Christian Book Distributors,

A Question of Age: Conference on Creation, the Bible, and Science. Pasadena, CA: Reasons to Believe, 2006.

Religion, Politics, and Law. 35 min. New York: Insight Media, 2008.

Religulous. 101 min. Santa Monica, CA: Lions Gate, 2008.

The Right to Die: Terri Schiavo. 23 min. New York: Insight Media, 2003.

Scout's Honor: Gays in the Boy Scouts of America. 60 min. Harriman, NY: New Day Films, 2001.

Sex, Censorship, and the Silver Screen. 243 min. (4 DVDs.) Hamilton, NJ: Films for the Humanities and Sciences, 2007.

Silent Choices: African Americans and Abortion. 60 min. Harriman, NY: New Day Films, 2008.

State of the Union: Politics in Red and Blue. 43 min. Hamilton, NJ: Films for the Humanities and Sciences, 2006.

The Terri Schiavo Case. 30 min. New York: Insight Media, 2005.

The Theory of Evolution: A History of Controversy. 12 lectures by Edward J. Larson, 30 min./lecture. Chantilly, VA: The Teaching Company, 2002.

Thomas L. Friedman Reporting: Does Europe Hate Us? 45 min. Hamilton, NJ: Films for the Humanities and Sciences, 2005.

A War on Science: Intelligent Design in the Classroom. 50 min. Hamilton, NJ: Films for the Humanities and Sciences, 2006.

INDEX

Index

About the Author

GLENN H. UTTER, professor and chair of the Political Science Department at Lamar University, was educated at Binghamton University, the University of Buffalo, and the University of London. Utter specializes in modern political theory and American political thought. He wrote *Encyclopedia of Gun Control and Gun Rights* (2000) and *Mainline Christians and U.S. Public Policy* (2007), coedited *American Political Scientists: A Dictionary* (1993, 2002), and cowrote *Religion and Politics* (2002), *Conservative Christians and Political Participation* (2004), *The Religious Right* (1995, 2001, 2007), and *Campaign and Election Reform* (1997, 2008).